LOGICAL INVESTIGATIONS

International Library of Philosophy and Scientific Method

EDITOR: TED HONDERICH
ADVISORY EDITOR: BERNARD WILLIAMS

A Catalogue of books already published in the
International Library of Philosophy and Scientific Method
will be found at the end of this volume

LOGICAL
INVESTIGATIONS

EDMUND HUSSERL

Translated by
J. N. FINDLAY
From the Second German Edition
of *Logische Untersuchungen*

VOLUME TWO

ON THE THEORY OF WHOLES AND PARTS
(Investigation III, Volume II of the German Edition)

THE DISTINCTION BETWEEN INDEPENDENT AND
NON-INDEPENDENT MEANINGS
(Investigation IV, Volume II of the German Edition)

ON INTENTIONAL EXPERIENCES AND
THEIR 'CONTENTS'
(Investigation V, Volume II of the German Edition)

ELEMENTS OF A PHENOMENOLOGICAL ELUCIDATION
OF KNOWLEDGE
(Investigation VI, Volume II, Part II, of the Second
German Edition)

NEW YORK
HUMANITIES PRESS

'Logische Untersuchungen' first published
by M. Niemeyer, Halle, 1900

Second German edition Vol. II, Part I
published 1913

Second German edition Vol. II, Part II
published 1921

This edition first published in the United States
of America 1970
by Humanities Press Inc., 303 Park Avenue South
New York, N.Y. 10010

SBN 391 00053 5

Printed in Great Britain

CONTENTS

INVESTIGATION III
ON THE THEORY OF WHOLES AND PARTS

CHAPTER TWO

Thoughts Towards a Theory of the Pure Forms of Wholes and Parts

INVESTIGATION IV
THE DISTINCTION BETWEEN INDEPENDENT AND NON-INDEPENDENT MEANINGS AND THE IDEA OF PURE GRAMMAR

INVESTIGATION V
ON INTENTIONAL EXPERIENCES AND
THEIR 'CONTENTS'

CHAPTER ONE
Consciousness as the Phenomenological Subsistence of the Ego and Consciousness as Inner Perception

CHAPTER TWO
Consciousness as Intentional Experience

viii

CHAPTER THREE

The Matter of the Act and its Underlying Presentation

CHAPTER FOUR

*Study of Underlying Presentations with Special Regard to the
Theory of Judgement*

CHAPTER FIVE

*Further Contributions to the Theory of Judgement.
'Presentation' as a Qualitatively Unitary Genus of Nominal
and Propositional Acts*

CHAPTER SIX

*Summing-Up of the Most Important Ambiguities in the
Terms 'Presentation' and 'Content'*

VOLUME II, PART II OF THE SECOND GERMAN EDITION

INVESTIGATION VI
ELEMENTS OF A PHENOMENOLOGICAL ELUCIDATION OF KNOWLEDGE

FIRST SECTION
OBJECTIFYING INTENTIONS AND THEIR FULFILMENTS: KNOWLEDGE AS A SYNTHESIS OF FULFILMENT AND ITS GRADATIONS

CHAPTER ONE
Meaning-Intention and Meaning-Fulfilment

CHAPTER TWO

Indirect Characterization of Objectifying Intentions and Their Essential Varieties, Through Differences in the Syntheses of Fulfilment

CHAPTER THREE

The Phenomenology of the Levels of Knowledge

CHAPTER FOUR

Consistency and Inconsistency

CHAPTER FIVE

The Ideal of Adequation: Self-Evidence and Truth

SECOND SECTION
SENSE AND UNDERSTANDING

CHAPTER SIX
Sensuous and Categorial Intuitions

CHAPTER SEVEN
A Study in Categorial Representation

CHAPTER EIGHT

The 'A Priori' Laws of Authentic and Inauthentic Thinking

THIRD SECTION
CLARIFICATION OF OUR
INTRODUCTORY PROBLEM

CHAPTER NINE
Non-Objectifying Acts as Apparent Fulfilments of Meaning

APPENDIX
External and Internal Perception:
Physical and Psychical Phenomena

INVESTIGATION III

On the Theory of Wholes and Parts

INTRODUCTION[1]

THE difference between 'abstract' and 'concrete' contents, which is plainly the same as Stumpf's distinction between *dependent* (non-independent) and *independent* contents, is most important for all phenomenological investigations; we must, it seems, therefore, first of all submit it to a thorough analysis. As said in my previous Investigation, this distinction, which first showed up in the field of the descriptive psychology of sense-data, could be looked on as a special case of a universal distinction. It extends beyond the sphere of conscious contents and plays an extremely important role in the field of *objects as such*. The systematic place for its discussion should therefore be in the *pure (a priori) theory of objects as such*, in which we deal with ideas pertinent to the *category of object*, ideas such as Whole and Part, Subject and Quality, Individual and Species, Genus and Species, Relation and Collection, Unity, Number, Series, Ordinal Number, Magnitude etc., as well as the *a priori* truths which relate to these. Here again we cannot allow our analytic investigation to wait on the systematic development of our subject-matter. Difficult notions employed by us in our clarificatory study of knowledge, and made to work rather in the manner of a lever, cannot be left unexamined, till they spontaneously emerge in the systematic fabric of the logical realm. For we are not here engaged on a systematic exposition of logic, but on an epistemological clarification, as well as on the prolegomena to any future exposition of logic.

To plumb the difference between dependent and non-independent contents, therefore, points so directly to the fundamental questions of the Pure Theory of Wholes and Parts (which is a part of formal ontology) that we cannot avoid going into these questions in some detail.

[1] As regards these 'formal ontological categories' and the formal ontological truths of essence pertaining to them, see the statements of the last chapter of the Prolegomena, (I §§67*f*).

I-2

CHAPTER ONE

The Difference Between Independent and Non-Independent Objects

---

§ 1 *Complex and simple, articulated and unarticulated objects*

SINCE the Investigation which follows mainly concerns relations of Parts, we start off with a wholly general discussion of such relations.

Objects can be related to one another as Wholes to Parts, they can also be related to one another as coordinated parts of a whole. These sorts of relations have an *a priori* foundation in the Idea of an object. Every object is either actually or possibly a part, i.e. there are actual or possible wholes that include it. Not every object, on the other hand, need perhaps have parts, and we have therefore the ideal division of objects into the *simple* and the *complex*.

The terms 'complex' and 'simple' are therefore defined by the qualification of having parts or not having parts. They may, however, be understood in a second, possibly more natural sense, in which complexity, as the word's etymology suggests, points to a plurality of disjoined parts in the whole, so that we have to call *simple* whatever cannot be 'cut up' into a plurality of parts, i.e. that in which not even two *disjoined* parts can be distinguished. In the unity of a sensory phenomenon we can perhaps discover a wholly determinate 'moment' of redness as well as the generic 'moment' of colour. Colour and determinate redness are not, however, disjoined 'moments'. Redness on the other hand, and the extension that it covers, are such disjoined moments, since they have no community of content. They have, we may say, a mutual association in the widest sense of the word; we have here a general relation of parts which is that of disjoined parts in a whole, an association of such parts. It now seems appropriate to call the associated parts *members* of the association: but to give so

436

wide a sense to talk about members of a whole, means to count colour and shape as the associated parts of a coloured expanse. That goes against linguistic usage. For in such wholes the parts have relative dependence as regards one another: we find them so closely united as to be called 'interpenetrating'. It is quite different in the case of wholes which are broken up, or could be broken up, into *pieces*: in their case talk of members or of articulated structure alone comes natural. The parts are here not merely disjoined from each other, but relatively independent, they have the character of mutually-put-together *pieces*.

Even at the start of our discussion, we see that the relations of parts fall under characteristically different *forms*: these forms, we suspect, depend on the cardinal difference between independent and non-independent objects, which is our theme in the present section.

§2 *Introduction of the distinction between independent and non-independent objects (contents)*

We interpret the word 'part' in the *widest* sense: we may call anything a 'part' that can be distinguished 'in' an object, or, objectively phrased, that is 'present' in it. Everything is a part that is an object's real possession, not only in the sense of being a real thing, but also in the sense of being something really in something, that truly helps to make it up:[1] an object in itself, considered in abstraction from all contexts to which it is tied, is likewise a part. Every non-relative 'real' (*reale*) predicate therefore points to a part of the object which is the predicate's subject: 'red' and 'round', e.g., do so, but not 'existent' or 'something'. Every 'real' (*reale*) mode of association, e.g. the moment of spatial configuration, likewise counts as a proper part of the whole.

The term 'part' is not used so widely in ordinary discourse. If we now try to pin down the limitations which mark off this ordinary, from *our* notion of part, we come up against the fundamental distinction called by us that of *independent* and *non-independent* parts. Where one talks of 'parts' without qualification, one

---

[1] The two Husserlian terms, *real* and *reell*, here occur in the same sentence, the former connoting what is actually there in the space-time world, and not abstract or ideal, the latter what is actually immanent in an experience, and not merely 'meant' by it.

generally has the *independent* parts (those referred to as 'pieces') in mind. Since each part can be made the specific object (or, as we also have frequently said, 'content') of a presentation directed upon it, and can therefore be called an object or 'content', the distinction of parts just mentioned points to a distinction in objects (or contents) as such. The term 'object' is in this context always taken in its widest sense.

In ordinary talk of objects or of parts, one of course involuntarily thinks of independent objects. The term 'content' is less restricted in this respect since 'abstract contents' are also commonly talked of. But talk of 'contents' tends to move in a purely psychological sphere, a limitation with which we may start investigating our distinction, but which must be dropped as we proceed.[1]

As a matter of history the distinction between independent and non-independent contents arose in the psychological realm, more specifically in the field of the phenomenology of inner experience. In a polemic against Locke, Berkeley said: We have the ability to recall individual things previously seen, or to put them together or break them down in imagination. We can imagine a man with two heads, the trunk of a man tied to the body of a horse, or isolated pieces such as a separated head, nose, ear etc. As opposed to this, it is impossible to form 'abstract ideas', to separate the idea, e.g., of a movement from that of a moving body. We can only abstract, in the Lockean separative sense, such parts of a presented whole as are in fact unified with other parts, but as could also exist without them. Since *esse* for Berkeley here always means the same as *percipi*, this inability to exist means no more than an inability to be perceived. We must note, further, that for Berkeley ideas are the things perceived, i.e. contents of consciousness in the sense of things we really (*reell*) live through.

We may now make a statement that brings out the essential point of Berkeley's distinctions, making use of a readily understandable verbal change.[2]

---

[1] In the present discussion, there is no danger of confusion between 'presented content', in the sense of any presented object (in the psychological sphere: any psychological datum), and 'presented content' in the sense of 'what' the presentation signifies.

[2] Almost exactly as formulated by C. Stumpf in *Über den psychologischen Ursprung der Raumvorstellung* (1873), p. 9.

Seen in their mutual interrelations, contents presented together on any occasion fall into two main classes: independent and non-independent contents.[1] We have independent contents wherever the elements of a presentational complex (complex of contents) by their very nature *permit their separated presentation*; we have dependent contents wherever this is not the case.

§3 *The inseparability of non-independent contents*

To be more precise in regard to this ability or inability-to-be-separately-presented, we make use of some of Stumpf's observations – quite insufficiently noticed – and assert the following:

It is self-evident, in regard to *certain* contents, that the modification or elimination of at least *one* of the contents given with them (but not contained in them), must modify or eliminate those contents themselves. In the case of *other* contents, this is not at all self-evident; it is not absurd to suppose them remaining unaffected despite the modification or elimination of all coexistent contents. Contents of the former sort can *only* be conceived as parts of more comprehensive wholes, whereas the latter appear possible, even if nothing whatever exists beside them, nothing therefore bound up with them to form a whole.

In the sense just laid down every phenomenal thing and piece of a thing is *separably presentable*. The head of a horse can be presented 'on its own' or 'cut off', i.e. we can hold it in our fancy, while we allow the other parts of the horse, and its whole intuited setting, to alter and vanish at will. Strictly speaking, the phenomenal thing or its piece, i.e. the sensuous phenomenon as such, the spatial shape filled with sensuous qualities, never stays just the same in descriptive content: but the content of such a 'phenomenon' does not at least involve anything entailing a self-evident, necessary, functional dependence of its changes on those of coexistent phenomena. This holds, we may say, of phenomenal objects as such, as well as of the 'appearances', in the sense of the *experiences*, in which these things appear, as also in respect of the sensational complexes which are given an objective 'interpretation' in such experiences. Good examples in this field

[1] Stumpf previously used the expression 'partial content', but now prefers to speak of an 'attributive moment'.

are the phenomena of tones and chords, of smells and other experiences, that we can readily think of apart from all relation to existent thinghood.

§4 *Analyses of examples following Stumpf*

Let us now consider some instances of inseparable contents, e.g. the relation of *visual quality* to *extension*, or the relation of both to the *figure* which bounds them. It is doubtless true in a certain sense that these moments can be *independently* varied. Extension can stay the same while colour varies indefinitely, colour stay the same while extent and figure vary indefinitely. But, strictly speaking, such independent variability affects only the *specific forms* of the 'moments' in their various genera. While the moment of colour remains constant in respect of its specific shade, extension and shape may vary indefinitely in their sub-species, and vice versa. Specifically the same quality, and nuance of quality, may be stretched or spread out over every extension, and, conversely, the same extension may be covered by every quality. Scope, however, remains for relations of functional dependence among the changes of such moments, which, be it noted, are not exhausted by the ideal content of their Species. The moment of colour, as immediate part-content of the intuited concrete thing, is not the same in the concrete intuition, even when the quality, the lowest differentiation of the genus colour, remains the same. Stumpf has made the powerful observation:

> Quality shares after a fashion in changes of extension. We express this verbally when we say that colour diminishes, becomes smaller, even to the vanishing point. Increase and diminution are names for quantitative changes.
>
> Quality is indeed affected in sympathy with changes in extent, although its own peculiar manner of change is independent of extent. It does not thereby become less green or less red: it has itself no degrees, only sub-species, and can in itself neither increase nor diminish, only alter. But none the less, when we leave quality quite unchanged as regards its peculiar manner of change, e.g. let it stay green, it still is affected by quantitative change. And that this is perhaps not an improper or misleading verbal transfer, is shown by the fact that a quality can *decrease to nothing*, that in the end *mere change of quantity can bring it to nought*.[1]

[1] Loc. cit. p. 112.

We accept Stumpf's observation, only adding that it is not really the quality that is affected, but the immediate intuitive 'moment' falling under it. Quality must be looked on as a second-order abstraction, just like the figure and magnitude of an extension. But just on account of the law here under discussion, the moment in question can only be named by way of concepts determined by the genera of Quality and Extension. Quality is differentiated to the qualitative 'moment' now under consideration, by something not contained in the Genus Colour, since we rightly treat the quality, e.g. the determinate shade of red, as the *Infima Species* within this genus. Just so, a determinate figure is the last difference of the Genus Figure, though the corresponding immediate, intuitive 'moment' is further differentiated. But the combinations among the various last differences of the Genera Figure and Colour fully determine the 'moments' in question, determine whatever else may be like or unlike them. The dependence of the immediate 'moments' therefore means a certain necessary relationship among them, which is determined purely by their abstracta at the level just above them.

Stumpf adds the following valuable remarks:

> From this (i.e. the above described functional dependence of the 'moments' of Quality and Extension), it follows that both are *in their nature inseparable*, that they in some manner *compose a total content*, of which they are merely part-contents. Were they merely items in a sum, one might possibly think that, absolutely treated, disappearance of Extension might mean the concomitant disappearance of Quality, that they did not exist apart; but that Quality should gradually diminish and vanish through the mere diminution and vanishing of Quantity, without changing in its own fashion *as* Quality, would be unintelligible . . . they can in any case not be independent contents. *Their nature forbids them to have an isolated and mutually independent existence in our ideas.*[1]

The same sort of thing could be said of the relation of Intensity to Quality. The intensity of a tone is not something indifferent or so-to-speak alien to its quality. We cannot keep the intensity just as it is, while the quality varies at will, or is allowed to vanish. Eliminate quality and you unavoidably eliminate intensity, and vice versa. Evidently this is no mere fact, but an *a priori* necessity, rooted in the pure essences in question. In the response to change

[1] Loc. cit. p. 113.

we have a further analogy to the previously mentioned case: if intensity steadily approaches the zero-limit, we feel our qualitative impression likewise reduced, even though the quality as such remains specifically unaltered.

Further examples fully illustrate the *'moments' of unity* in the intuitive contents, 'moments' built on the elements that we primarily distinguish, by which such elements are similarly or dissimilarly *associated into sensuous intuitive wholes*. The use of such examples gives us our first narrower concepts of a whole, of an association etc., and, further, our distinctive concepts of various kinds and sorts of wholes, whether present to outer or inner sense.

These 'moments of unity' are of course the same as the contents called 'form-qualities' by von Ehrenfels, 'figural' moments by myself, and 'founded contents' by Meinong.[1] But one needs here a supplementary distinction between the *phenomenological* moments of unity, which give unity to the experiences or parts of experiences (the real phenomenological data), and the *objective* moments of unity, which belong *to the intentional objects and parts of objects, which in general* transcend the experiential sphere. The expression 'moment of unity', incidentally recommended to me by Riehl, has such obvious advantages in virtue of its immediate intelligibility, that it might well be universally adopted.

§5 *The objective determination of the concept of Inseparability*

Stumpf uses considerations of this sort to *prove* the mutual inseparability of Extension and Quality, and hence their non-independence: we shall rather make use of them to *define* inseparability or non-independence, or contrariwise separability or independence. Stumpf himself gives us the means to do this at the end of the last quoted passage.[2] What does it mean to say we can form an idea of a content 'by itself' or 'in isolation'? Does this mean, as regards the actually *experienced* contents of the phenomenological sphere, that such a content can be freed from all blending with coexistent contents, can therefore ultimately be

[1] Cf. Ehrenfels, '*Uber Gestaltqualitäten*', *Vierteljahrsschrift fur Philosophie* (1890); my *Philosophie der Arithmetik* (1891), particularly the whole of ch. xi, Meinong, '*Beiträge Zur Theorie der psychischen Analyse*', *Zeitschrift f. Psychologie u. Physiologie d Sinnesorgane, XI* (1893).

[2] Cf. the words italicized by us.

torn out of the unity of consciousness? Obviously not. In *this* sense no contents are isolable, and the same holds of the phenomenal *thing*-contents in their relation to the total unity of the phenomenon as such. If we form an independent idea of the content *head of a horse*, we inescapably present it in a context, the content stands relieved from an objective background that appears with it, it is inescapably given with many other contents, and is also in a way united to them. How then can this content be isolable in idea? The only answer we can give is the following:

Isolability means only that we can keep some content constant in idea despite boundless variation – variation that is free, though not excluded by a law rooted in the content's essence – of the contents associated with it, and, in general, given with it. This means that it is unaffected by the elimination of any given arrangement of compresent contents whatsoever.

This self-evidently entails: that the existence of this content, to the extent that this depends on itself and its essence, is not at all conditioned by the existence of other contents, that it could exist as it is, through an *a priori* necessity of essence, even if nothing were there outside of it, even if all around were altered at will, i.e. without principle.

Or what plainly amounts to the same: *In the 'nature' of the content itself, in its ideal essence, no dependence on other contents is rooted*; the essence that makes it what it is, also leaves it unconcerned with all other contents. It may *as a matter of fact* be that, with the existence of this content, other contents are given, and in accordance with empirical rules. In its ideally graspable essence, however, the content is independent; this essence by itself, i.e. considered in *a priori* fashion, requires no other essence to be interwoven with it.

The sense of non-independence (*Unselbständigkeit*) lies likewise in the positive thought of *dependence* (*Abhängigkeit*). The content is by its nature bound to other contents, it cannot be, if other contents are not there together with it. We need not emphasize the fact that they form a unity with it, for can there be essential coexistence without connection or 'blending', however loose? Contents which lack self-sufficiency can accordingly only exist as *partial contents*.

We need only say 'object' and 'partial object', instead of 'content' and 'partial content' – the term 'content' we regard as the narrower term, the one restricted to the sphere of phenomenology – to achieve an *objective distinction* freed from all relation to interpretative acts and to any phenomenological content that might be interpreted. *No reference back to consciousness is therefore needed, no reference to differences in the 'mode of presentation',* to determine the difference between 'abstract' and 'concrete' which is here in question. All determinations which make use of such a relation, either represent an incorrect, misguided confusion with other notions of 'abstract', or are merely subjectively slanted expressions of a purely objective, ideal state of affairs, a sort of slanting that we also feel natural and useful in other cases.

§6 *Continuation. Tie-up with a criticism of a much-favoured notional determination*

Occasionally one hears the difference between independent and non-independent contents expressed in the attractive formula: Independent contents (part-contents) could be presented by themselves, non-independent contents only noticed by themselves, not presented by themselves. To this formula one may object that 'by themselves' functions vary differently in the two expressions to be distinguished: 'presented by themselves' and 'noticed by themselves'. A thing is 'noticed by itself' if it is an object of an act of notice specially directed upon it (a direct act of attending), a thing is 'presented by itself' if it is an object of a specially directed presentation – this at least if 'by itself' functions analogously in the two cases. On such a basis, however, we cannot sustain the opposition between what can only be noticed and what can only be presented by itself. Could emphatic notice perhaps conflict with presentation in a class of cases, and exclude it? But non-independent moments such as attributes and terms of relations are as much the objects of presentations (as stated above) as are independent contents like *window, head* etc. Otherwise we should not be able to talk of them. To attend to something by itself, and to represent it by itself (in the sense just presupposed) are so little mutually exclusive, that we find them together. In perceptual 'interpretation' the thing we attend to by itself is at the same time *eo ipso* presented; and the complete content presented by itself, e.g. *head*, is also attended to by itself.

'By itself' in fact means something quite different in the case of a presentation from what we thought it did. The equivalent expression 'present in isolation' points plainly to this fact. What it plainly means is that it is possible to present the object as something *existing by itself*, as *independently there* in the face of all other objects. A thing or piece of a thing can be presented by itself – this means it would be what it is even if everything outside it were annihilated. If we form a presentation of it, we are not necessarily referred to something else, included in which, or attached to which, or associated with which, it has being, or on whose mercy it depends, as it were, for its existence. We can imagine it as existing by itself alone, and beyond it nothing else. If it is intuitively presented, a context, a whole including it, may nonetheless be presented with it, must inevitably be so presented. The visual content *head* cannot be presented without a visual background from which it stands relieved. This impossibility is, however, quite different from the impossibility used to define non-independent contents. If we let the visual content *head* count as independent, we think that, despite its inescapable, accompanying background, it *could* be presented as existing by itself, and *could* therefore be intuitively envisaged in isolation. We, however, cannot effect this, whether because of powerful original or acquired associations, or other purely factual connections. The 'logical' possibility remains unshaken, our visual field, e.g., 'could' shrink down to this single content etc.

What we here express by the word 'present', could be better expressed by the word 'think'. An attribute, a form of association and the like, cannot be *thought of* as self-existent, as isolated from all else, as being all that exists: this only can happen with 'thinglike' contents. Wherever the word 'think' occurs in this peculiar sense, we detect one of those subjective slantings of an objective, nay of an *a priori* state of affairs, which we referred to above. Differences such as this, that one object – we again choose the wider term, which includes the contents of intuitive experience – can be 'in and for itself', while another can only have being in, or attached to some other object – are no mere contingencies of our subjective thinking. They are real differences, grounded in the pure essence of things, which, since they obtain, and since we know of them, prompt us to say that a thought which oversteps them is impossible, i.e. a judgement deviating from them is wrong. What cannot be thought, cannot be, what cannot be, cannot be thought – this equivalence fixes the differences between the pregnant notion of thinking and the ordinary subjective sense of presentation and thought.

§7 *Further pointing up of our notional determination by introducing the concepts of Pure Law and Pure Genus*

Wherever therefore the word 'can' occurs in conjunction with the pregnant use of 'think', there is a reference, not to a subjective necessity, i.e. to the subjective incapacity-to-represent-things-otherwise, but to the objectively-ideal necessity of an inability-to-be-otherwise.[1] This is by its essence such as to be given in our consciousness of *apodictic self-evidence*. If we remain within the expressions of this consciousness, we must assert it to be of the essence of such an objective necessity that it is correlated with a definite pure law in each case. It is in the first place obvious in general that objective necessity is as such tantamount to a *being that rests on an objective law*. An individual matter of fact, considered as such, is contingent in its being: that it is necessary means that it stands in a context of law. What prevents its being otherwise is the law which says that it is not merely so here and now, but universally so, and with a lawful universality. Here we must note that, just as the 'necessity' relevant to our discussion of non-independent 'moments' stands for an ideal or *a priori* necessity rooted in the essences of things, so, correspondingly, our 'lawfulness' stands for a lawfulness of essence, a non-empirical, universal and unconditionally valid lawfulness. No relation to empirical existence may restrict the extension of our legal concepts, no empirical assertion of existence be inwoven into our consciousness of law, as occurs in the case of empirically general rules and laws. 'Natural laws', laws in the sense of the empirical sciences, are not laws of essence (ideal or *a priori* laws): empirical necessity is no necessity of essence.

The inability-to-exist-by-itself of a non-independent part points therefore to a *law of essence, according to which the existence of a content belonging to the part's pure Species* (e.g. the Species of Colour, Form

---

[1] The ontological transformation of the notion of self-evidence into one of pure essential lawfulness – a transformation which starts at this point and which decisively influences the content of the rest of the Investigation – has already been clearly carried out in my 'Bericht uber deutsche Schriften zur Logik', (1891) *Archiv für Syst. Philos. III*, p. 225, n. 1.

etc.) *presupposes the existence of contents of certain pertinent pure Species*, i.e. contents to which – if such an addition is still needed – the content in question can pertain as a part or an adjunct, an associate. Put more simply we can say: *Non-independent objects are objects belonging to such pure Species as are governed by a law of essence to the effect that they only exist (if at all) as parts of more inclusive wholes of a certain appropriate Species.* This is what we mean by the terser expression that they are parts which only exist as parts, that cannot be thought of as existing by themselves. The colour of this paper is a non-independent 'moment' of the paper. It is not merely an actual part, but its essence, its pure Species, predestines it to partial being: a colour *in general and purely as such* can exist only as a 'moment' in a coloured thing. In the case of independent objects such a law is lacking: they may, but need not, enter into more comprehensive wholes.

In clarifying what must be meant by the phrase 'presented by itself' in the formulation just criticized, we have therefore brought the essence of the difference to be pinned down into the sharpest focus. It has shown itself to be an objective difference, one rooted in the pure essence of the objects (or the partial contents) in question. We may now ask how it stands with the rest of the formula; how far does the statement that non-independent objects or 'moments' could 'only' be noticed by themselves, or singled out from their associates for exclusive attention, not presented by themselves, help us to pin down such objects? We can only answer: Not at all. For if the word 'only' is tied exclusively to the phrase 'presented by itself', such an exclusive opposition achieves everything for it that can be achieved. Strictly speaking our approach is positive in the case of what is non-independent, negative in the case of what is independent: when we say that the former cannot be presented by itself, we merely return in double negation to our real starting-point. However this may be, we need not fall back on the high-lighting role of attention, and it is not clear how it can help us. A head can certainly be presented apart from the person that has it. A colour, form etc., is not presentable in this fashion, it needs a substrate, in which it can be exclusively noticed, but from which it cannot be taken out. But the head also, considered, e.g. visually, can only be noticed by itself, since it is unavoidably given as an element in a total visual field. If we do not treat it as such an element, if we abstract from the background as something really foreign and indifferent, this does not depend on the peculiarity of our content, but on the circumstances of our thing-directed thought.

§7a *Independent and non-independent Ideas*

Our distinctions have first of all related to the being of particular individuals thought of in 'ideal universality', i.e. of such individuals treated purely as instances of Ideas. But they obviously carry over to Ideas themselves, which can, in a corresponding, if somewhat modified sense, be spoken of as 'independent' and 'non-independent'. A lowest difference of some highest pure Genus may be called relatively independent in relation to the hierarchy of pure Species which lead up to the highest Genus, just as every lower Species counts as relatively independent as against higher Species. Genera, the existence of whose corresponding individualizations represents an *a priori* impossibility, unless they simultaneously belong to the individual, but purely conceived extensions of other Genera, are non-independent in regard to these latter, and so *mutatis mutandis* in the case of other fields of instances.

§8 *Demarcation of the distinction of independent and non-independent contents and the distinction between intuitively emphatic and intuitively blended contents*

We must be prepared for a further objection. Some may perhaps point to the manner in which an independent content puts itself forward as a unity valid in its own right, and cut off from all around, while a non-independent content is contrariwise characterized as something only grounded on other, independent contents, and insist that we here have a *phenomenological* contrast that our discussion has not taken full account of.

We might deal, in the first place, with the following descriptive situation. The non-independent moments of an intuition, are not mere parts, but in a certain (notionally immediate) manner they must also be regarded *as* parts: they cannot be separately noticed unless all the concrete contents, in which they are contained, have been stressed as wholes: this does not mean that they become *objects* in the pregnant sense of the word. A figure or colour cannot be separately noticed unless the whole object, which *has* the figure or the colour, stands out in relief. A 'striking' colour or form may seem at times to impress us in isolation, but if we bring such an event back to mind we see that the whole object is here phenomenally emphatic, though it is so in respect of the peculiarity that strikes us, and which alone is objective in the strict sense of the word. The same relation obtains between an emphasized sensuous 'moment' of unity – the 'moment', e.g., of spatial configuration, which, together with other 'moments' of unity, underlies the internal closure of a sensory manifold, which makes it impressively one – and the apprehension of the sensuously-unified whole itself.[1] In this manner the setting in relief of one content is at times the basis for noticing another that intimately belongs to it.[2]

If we explore the deeper grounds of the matter, we note that a second distinction is mixed up with and crosses the previously discussed difference of independent and non-independent contents in the phenomenological field, (or the field of intuitive data as such). This is the distinction between *intuitively 'separated'* contents, contents *relieved from* or *cut apart from* associated contents, on the one hand, and contents which *blend* with their associates, or which *flow undividedly over* into them, on the other. Our terms are of course ambiguous, but to put them together makes plain that we really do have a new distinction before us.

A content, accordingly, is intuitively separated in relation to other contents if it does not flow over into them without a point of difference: it can thus make itself count on its own, and stand forth independently. The intuitively unseparated content forms a whole with other coexistent contents, but is not cut off in this manner within the whole; it is not merely bound up with its associates, but blends with them. Independent contents in our previous sense, which are what they are no matter what goes on around them, need not have the quite different independence of separateness. The parts of an intuitive surface of a uniform or continuously shaded white are independent, but not separated.

If we ask what is involved in intuitive separation, the image of a

---

[1] See my *Philosophie der Arithmetik* (1891), ch. XI, p. 228 (an 'avenue' of trees, a 'flock' of birds, a 'flight' of duck etc.).

[2] From my 'Psychologische Studien zur elementaren Logik', *Philos. Monatshefte*, (1894), XXX, p. 162.

mutual overflow points to cases where contents are continuously graded. This holds mainly in the case of sensuous concreta (i.e. of independent contents in the sphere of outer sense). Here separation often rests on *discontinuity*. One may affirm that:

Two contemporaneous sensuous concreta necessarily form an 'undifferentiated whole' if all the immediately constitutive 'moments' of the one pass unbrokenly over into corresponding constitutive 'moments' of the other. The case of exact likeness of any such corresponding moments shall here count as a legitimate limiting case of continuity, i.e. as a continuous 'passing over into self'.

We can apply this in readily understandable fashion to a multiplicity of concreta. Here each single concretum lacks separation, if the aggregated concreta form a series, at each step of which the items are continuously conjoined, i.e. if what we have described holds of each neighbouring pair of items. *An individual item already lacks separation from all other items if there is a single item from which it does not stand forth in relief.*

§9 *Continuation. Reference to the wider sphere of the phenomena of fusion*

These propositions are in a certain sense idealized expressions of facts. Continuity and discontinuity must of course not be taken in a mathematically exact sense. Points of discontinuity are not mathematical limits, and distances must not be 'too small'.

One might draw a somewhat finer distinction between sharper and more confused separation or limitation, in the empirically vague sense in which, in ordinary life, one speaks of sharp points and corners as opposed to blunt or even rounded ones. Plainly the essential forms of all intuitive data are not in principle to be brought under 'exact' or 'ideal' notions, such as we have in mathematics. The spatial shape of the perceived tree as such, taken precisely as a 'moment' found in the relevant percept's intentional object, is no geometric shape, no ideal or exact shape in the sense of exact geometry. Just so a seen colour as such is no ideal colour, whose Species occupies an ideal point in the colour-pyramid. The essences which direct ideation elicits from intuitive data are 'inexact essences', they may not be confused with the 'exact' essences which are Ideas in the Kantian sense, and which (like an 'ideal point', an ideal surface or solid, or ideal Species of colour in the ideal colour-pyramid) arise through a peculiar 'idealization'. The descriptive concepts of all pure description, i.e of description adapted to intuition immediately and with truth and so of all phenomenological description, differ in principle from those which dominate objective science. To clear up these matters is a phenomenological task never yet seriously undertaken and not carried out in relation to our present distinction.

It is also clear that this separation through discontinuity (or this fusion through continuity) only covers a very restricted field.

I recall Stumpf's instructive investigations into the remarkable facts of fusion,[1] in whose sphere we are here plainly moving. The cases stressed by us would play a peculiar role in the field of the phenomena of fusion. Considering these cases more closely, we are led back from the concreta, the independent total sensa, to their immediate, non-independent 'moments', or to the Species under which these immediately fall. Discontinuity relates as such to the lowest specific differences within one and the same immediately superordinate pure Genus: to qualities of colour, e.g., as compared with qualities of colour. But we do not define discontinuity as the mere distance of coexistent contents in respect of such lowest differences. Simultaneous tones have distance, but they lack discontinuity in the pregnant sense of the word. This only relates to specifically differing moments in so far as they are 'spread out' with common boundaries over a continuously varying spatial or temporal 'moment'. It is 'at' a spatial or temporal boundary that one visual quality, e.g., leaps over into another. In our continuous progress from spatial part to part there is at the same time no continuous progress in the covering quality: in one place at least the neighbouring qualities are finitely (and not too minutely) distant. The same holds of a discontinuity in phenomenal order. Here not merely qualities, e.g., colours, achieve separation, but whole concreta set bounds to one another, the visual field is split up into parts. The colour-distance in such a context of 'covering' – without which there can be no talk of discontinuity – also wins separation for the 'moments' bound up with it, the covered spatial parts of our example. These could otherwise not be free

---

[1] Stumpf as is well known at first defines 'fusion' in a narrower sense, as a relation of simultaneous sense-*qualities*, as a result of which they appear as parts of a sensational whole. He does not however fail to point to the wider concept that we here find pivotal. Cf. *Tonpsychologie*, II § 17, pp. 61 *ff.*

from the fusion. Spatiality necessarily varies continuously. A piece of such variation can only become separately noticeable and primarily emphatic in consciousness, when a discontinuity is provided by the covering 'moment', and the whole concretum which corresponds to it has thus been separated.

The first meaning we give to 'spatiality', is here the sensational 'moment' which, when objectively referred, first yields phenomenal spatiality properly so called. But we *can* also mean by it the spatiality which a given intuition helps us to apprehend in the phenomenal thing as such, spatiality therefore as the intentional moment in which the objective, and objectively measurable, spatial shape of the physical 'thing itself' is intuitively revealed to us, and is differently revealed in different intuitions.

The concrete thing of sensuous intuition therefore owes its isolation to the qualitative gap between neighbouring 'moments', but the relief achieved by the *whole* concretum has priority over the relief of the mutually separated moments of its content. This depends on the peculiarly intimate fusion of the different 'moments' of the concretum, their mutual 'penetration', which reveals itself in a mutual dependence as regard change and destruction. This fusion is not a fading into one another in the manner of the continuous, nor does it remove all separateness, but it is nonetheless a sort of peculiarly intimate mutual interconnection which must at a stroke set the whole complex of interpenetrating moments in relief, if only once a single discontinuous moment has provided the right conditions.

A profounder and more penetrating analysis could here lay bare a wealth of interesting descriptive differences; for our purposes these fairly rough treatments are enough. We have gone far enough to see that, in thus distinguishing stressed from unstressed contents, as was done above, or to employ a few readily suggested expressions, in distinguishing between contents that can, and contents that cannot be presented 'by themselves', or that are independent and non-independent respectively, we are dealing with differences of 'subjective', intuitive materials, which have their own remarkable peculiarities of essence, but which will not help us to grasp the universal, *ontological* difference between abstract and concrete contents, or, as we deliberately called them above, independent and non-independent contents. Our former distinction between contents separately singled out and confused background contents, pivots on the facts of analysis and fusion; the contents thus separated off, might as well be independent as non-independent. The two distinctions should not therefore be confused, as is done, e.g., when the non-independence of the *separate parts* of a uniformly coloured surface is put on a level with the descriptively quite different non-independence of an *abstract 'moment'*. It is also done when attempts are made to base the essence of the ontological difference between *concrete* and *abstract* on phenomenological facts which concern the sphere of acts, the fact, e.g., that the act which presents a concrete object is immediate, and is independent in not needing to be based on other presentations, whereas the act which apprehends an abstract content is mediate and non-independent, in that it *must* be based on the presentation of a suitable concretum. Our analyses show, however, that anything that holds water in *this* descriptive situation is mixed up with other quite alien matters, and is in any case unfitted to illuminate our ontological distinction.

§ 10 *The multiplicity of laws governing the various sorts of non-independent contents*

Our discussions so far have shown that there is always an *a priori* law governing what is non-independent, having its conceptual roots in what is universal in the whole and part in question. But this law can be interpreted and expressed with more or less definiteness. To pin down the concept of non-independence, it is enough to say that a non-independent object can only be what it is (i.e. what it is in virtue of its essential properties) in a more comprehensive whole. At times, however, a non-independent object can vary in Species: this entails varying the kind of supplementation it requires for existence. If we say, for example, that the 'moment' of sensory quality, e.g. of sensory colour, is non-independent, and requires a whole in which it may be embodied, we have only laid down *one* side of our governing law, the side of a part which belongs to the Genus Sensory Quality. We have not, however, laid down the character of the whole, the manner in which such a 'quality' is its part, nor the sort of supplement it needs to achieve existence. It is different when we say that a sensory quality can only exist in a sense-field, and a sensory colour in a visual sense-field, or that it can only exist as qualifying an extension. Here the law lays down the other sides as well; the notion of a visual sense-field is given; and it means a particular, definite sort of whole among various possible sorts of whole. Just so, the notion of 'qualifying an extension' points to quite specific possibilities of law-governed inherence that a non-independent 'moment' may have to a whole. The specific character of this inherence is fixed in general fashion both by the essence of Sensory Quality and the essence of Extension, but each is contained in its *own* manner in the essential unity of visual sensation, or of the visual field in which all such unities find their place. This manner cannot be further described. If we ask what differentiates the generic feature of *being a sensory 'moment'*, so as to yield the specific feature of *being a sensory quality*, we can give no answer that helps us; we can point to no additional feature in which the concept of quality is not included. Just so, if we are asked what must be added to *Colour* to produce its Species Redness we can only answer 'Redness'.

The notion of what is non-independent, with its indirectly, generally characterized definitory lawfulness, points to many factually determined, variable laws of essence. It is not a peculiarity of certain sorts of parts that they should only be parts in general, while it remains quite indifferent what they are conglomerated with, and into what sorts of connection they are fitted. There are fixed, necessary connections, pure laws definite in content, which vary with the pure Species of non-independent contents, and accordingly prescribe one sort of completion to one of them, another sort of completion to another. The Species associated in these laws, which mark off the spheres of contingent individuality presupposed by these laws – are occasionally, but not always, lowest specific differences. A law, for instance, may prescribe to contents of the Species Colour a connection with contents of the Species Extension, but it does not prescribe a definite extension to a definite colour, or vice versa. The values of the lowest differences are accordingly not functionally interrelated. The law only refers to lowest Species, i.e. Species having the multiplicity of ultimate specific differences *immediately* beneath them. On the other hand, if we consider the dependence of qualitative remoteness on the qualities on which it rests, we find it unambiguously determined by the lowest specific differences of these qualities, and so again determined as a lowest difference.

The concept of non-independence accordingly amounts to that of ideal *lawfulness in unified combinations*. If a part stands in an ideally law-bound and not merely factual combination, it *must* lack independence; since such a law-bound combination merely means that a part whose pure essence is of one sort, can exist lawfully only in association with certain other parts of these or those suitable sorts. And even where a law tells us of the impossibility, rather than the necessity *of an association*, where it says, e.g., that the existence of a part A excludes the existence of a part B as incompatible with A, our case still reduces to one of non-independence. For an A can only exclude a B, if both exclusively require the same thing. A colour excludes another colour, but only if both aim to cover an identical piece of surface, and both cannot do so completely. To each essential, law-bound exclusion of a determinate characterization, there corresponds a positive law-bound requirement of a corresponding characterization and vice versa.

§ 11 *The difference between these 'material' laws and 'formal' or 'analytic' laws*

The necessities or laws which serve to define given types of non-independent contents rest, as we often have emphasized, on the specific essence of the contents, on their peculiar nature. More precisely, they rest on the pure Genera, Species, differentiae under which, as contingent singulars, non-independent contents as well as their supplementing contents, fall. If we conceive of the totality of such ideal objects, we have with them the totality of pure essences, the essences of all ideally possible individual objects (existences). To these essences correspond the concepts or propositions which have content, which we sharply distinguish from purely formal concepts and propositions, which lack all 'matter' or 'content'. To the latter belong the categories of formal logic and the formal ontological categories mentioned in the last chapter of the *Prolegomena*, which are essentially related to these, as well as to all syntactical formations they engender. Concepts like Something, One, Object, Quality, Relation, Association, Plurality, Number, Order, Ordinal Number, Whole, Part, Magnitude etc., have a basically different character from concepts like House, Tree, Colour, Tone, Space, Sensation, Feeling etc., which for their part express genuine content.

Whereas the former group themselves round the empty notion of Something or Object as such, and are associated with this through formal ontological axioms, the latter are disposed about various highest material Genera or Categories, in which *material ontologies* have their root. This cardinal division between the 'formal' and the 'material' spheres of Essence gives us the true distinction between the *analytically a priori* and the *synthetically a priori* disciplines (or laws and necessities). The next section will make systematic pronouncements on these matters.

It is now immediately plain, that all the laws or necessities governing different sorts of *non-independent* items fall into the spheres of the *synthetic a priori*: one grasps completely what divides them from merely formal, contentless items. Laws of the type of the causal principle, which lay down the non-independence of changes in what is thinglike and real, or the laws – generally imperfectly formulated – which assert the non-independence of mere qualities, intensities, extensions, boundaries, relational forms etc. – would not be put on a level with a purely 'analytic' generalization such as 'A whole cannot exist without parts' or with analytic necessities such as 'There cannot be a king (master, father) without subjects (servants, children) etc.'. We may say in general: correlatives mutually entail one another, they cannot be thought of, or cannot be, without each other. If we set beside these any definite propositions of the opposite sort, e.g., 'A colour cannot exist without something coloured' or 'A colour cannot exist without some space that it covers' etc. – the difference leaps into view. 'Colour' is not a relative expression, whose meaning includes the idea of a relation to something else. Though colour is 'unthinkable' without something coloured, the existence of the latter, and more definitely that of a space, is not 'analytically' founded on the notion of colour.

The following discussion clears up the essence of the difference.

A part *as such* cannot exist at all without a whole whose part it is. On the other hand we say, with an eye to *independent* parts: A part often *can* exist without a whole whose part it is. Obviously this involves no contradiction. What we mean is that, if the part is treated in respect of its *internal content*, its own essence, then a thing having this same content can exist without a whole *in* which it exists; it can exist by itself, not associated with anything else, and will not then be a part. Change in, or complete elimination of associations, does not here affect the part's own, peculiarly qualified content, and does not eliminate its existence: only its relations fall away, the fact that it *is* a part. The contrary holds of other sorts of parts: without any association, as non-parts, they are unthinkable, *in virtue of their very content*. These impossibilities or possibilities are rooted in the essential specificity of the contents. The case is quite different in regard to the analytic triviality that a part as such cannot exist without a whole whose part it is. It would be a 'contradiction', i.e. a 'formal', 'analytical' absurdity, to call X a part where there was no whole belonging to X. Here the inner content of the part is irrelevant, the underlying 'formal' lawfulness of our case has nothing in common with the material lawfulness of our above cases, and can accordingly not disturb them.

That correlatives as such mutually condition one another certainly points to certain mutually requiring 'moments', it points to the mutually 'belonging' relationships and relative properties which we find in the case of every relation. But it does so only with formal indefiniteness. The legality which here obtains is one and the same for all relations as such: it is in fact a merely formal legality, rooted in mere analytic essences, here in fact in the essence of relation as a formal category. It takes over none of the material specificity of relations and of their members, and discourses merely of 'certain' relations and members. It will perhaps say in the simple case of dyadic relations: If a *certain A* stands in a *certain* relation to a certain B, this same B stands in a certain *corresponding* (converse) relation to that A; A and B are here *quite freely variable*.

§ 12 *Basic determinations in regard to analytic and synthetic propositions*

We may give the following general definitions:

Analytic Laws are unconditionally universal propositions, which are accordingly free from all explicit or implicit assertions of individual existence; they include none but formal concepts, and if we go back to such as are primitive, they contain only formal categories. Analytic Laws stand opposed to their *specifications*, which arise when we introduce concepts *with content*, and thoughts perhaps positing individual existence, e.g. *this*, *the*

Kaiser. The specification of laws always yields necessary connections: specifications of analytic laws therefore yield *analytically necessary connections*. What are called 'analytic propositions' are in general analytically necessary connections. When they imply existential assertions (e.g. *If this house is red, then redness pertains to this house*) such analytic necessity relates to that content of the proposition in virtue of which it empirically specifies the analytic law, not to its empirical assertion of existence.

We may define *analytically necessary propositions* as propositions whose truth is completely independent of the peculiar content of their objects (whether thought of with definite or indefinite universality) and of any possible existential assertions. They are propositions which permit of a *complete 'formalization'* and can be regarded as special cases or empirical applications of the formal, analytic laws whose validity appears in such formalization. In an analytic proposition it must be possible, without altering the proposition's logical form, to replace all material which has content, with an empty formal *Something*, and to eliminate every assertion of existence by giving all one's judgements the form of universal, unconditional laws.

It is, e.g., an analytic proposition that *the existence of this house includes that of its roof, its walls and its other parts.* For the *analytic* formula holds that the existence of a whole W (A, B, C...) generally includes that of its parts A, B, C... This law contains no meaning which gives expression to a material Genus or Species. The assertion of individual existence, implied by the *this* of our illustration, is seen to fall away by our passage into the pure law. This is an analytic law: it is built up exclusively out of formal–logical categories and categorial forms.

Having formed the concept of an analytic law and of an analytic necessity, we also have *eo ipso* formed the concept of a *synthetic a priori* law, and of a *synthetic a priori* necessity. Each pure law, which includes material concepts, so as not to permit of a formalization of these concepts *salva veritate* – each such law, i.e., that is not analytically necessary – is a *synthetic a priori* law. Specifications of such laws are synthetic necessities: empirical specifications of course are so also, e.g. *This red is different from this green.*

What we have said should be enough to make plain the essential distinction between laws grounded in the specific nature of the contents to which non-independent factors belong, and analytic and formal laws, which, being founded purely on formal 'categories', are unaffected by all 'material of knowledge'.

Note 1 The points here made may be compared with those of Kant, which in our view do not deserve to be called 'classical'. It seems to us that these points satisfactorily dispose of one of the most important problems in the theory of knowledge, and make a first, decisive step in the division of *a priori* ontologies. Future publications will carry the enquiry further.

Note 2 It is readily seen that the main concepts dealt with by us in this section: *Whole and Part, Independence* and *Non-independence, Necessity* and *Law*, are essentially changed in sense when they are not understood in the sense of *purely conceptual matters of essence*, but are given an empirical interpretation. For the purpose of the investigations which follow, it is not, however, necessary fully to discuss these empirical concepts and their relation to the pure ones.

§13 *Relative independence and non-independence*

Independence we have so far conceived absolutely, as a lack of dependence on all associated contents: non-independence was its contradictory opposite, a corresponding dependence on at least one such content. It is, however, important to treat both concepts relatively also, in such a way, that is, that the absolute distinction then becomes a limiting case of the relative. *In the sphere of mere sense-data* (not that of the things represented or apparent in such sense-data) the 'moment' of visual extent,[1] with all its parts, counts as non-independent, but *within this extent conceived in abstracto* each of its *pieces* counts as *relatively independent* while each of its '*moments*', e.g. the 'moment' of 'form' as opposed to that of position and magnitude, counts as *relatively non-independent*. Here we therefore have a relative sort of 'independence', which taken absolutely, or in some other relation, could have been a case of non-independence, it is an independence, relatively to a whole, whose total range of parts, together with the whole itself, constitutes a sphere within which the distinctions previously drawn unrestrictedly now must move.[2] We can therefore define as follows:

[1] The moment which is presentative of the *spatial extension* of the apparent coloured figure in space.

[2] 'Position' and 'magnitude' here naturally stand for phenomena in the sensational sphere, presentative moment for the intentional (apparent) position and magnitude in the straightforward sense.

Non-independence in and relative to the whole W or to the total range of contents determined by W, characterizes each of W's partial contents which can only exist as parts, and as parts of a sort of whole represented in this range. Every partial content regarding which this is not true, is called *independent in, and relative to, the whole W*. We also speak briefly of *non-independent or dependent parts of* the Whole, and in a corresponding sense of *non-independent and independent parts of parts (i.e. of part-wholes) of the whole*.

Our determinations can plainly be further generalized. One can interpret our definition so that it does not merely relate a partial content to a more comprehensive whole, but, *quite generally, a content to another content*, even if both are separated off. We define accordingly:

A content A is relatively non-independent in regard to a content B (or in regard to the total range of contents determined by B and all its parts), if a pure law, rooted in the peculiar character of the kinds of content in question, ensures that a content of the pure Genus A has an *a priori* incapacity to exist except in, or as associated with, other contents from the total ranges of the pure Genera of contents determined by B.

If such a law is absent, we say that *A is relatively independent in regard to B*.

More simply we can say: A content A is non-independent relatively to a content B, if there is a law rooted in the Generic Essences A, B, which lays down *a priori* that a content of the pure Genus A can only exist in or associated with a content of the Genus B. We naturally leave open the possibility that the Genera A and B should be Genera of combinations, so that in the elements of such combinations several corresponding Genera should be woven together. Our definition entails that an A as such, taken in unconditional universality, requires to be accompanied by, and unified with some B or other: otherwise put, the pure Genus requires, in respect of the possible existence of individuals falling under it, the Genus B, or to be joined with connected instances from B's range. Briefly we may say that the being of an A is relatively independent or non-independent in regard to the Genus B.

The necessary coexistence mentioned in our definition is either a coexistence relating to any point in time, or a coexistence for a certain stretch of time. In the latter case B is a temporal whole, and temporal determinations then play their part (as temporal relations or stretches) in the range of contents determined by B. A content K, e.g., which includes the time-determination t_0, may thus require the existence of another content with the time-determination $t_1 = t_0 + \Delta$, and accordingly be non-independent. In the sphere of the phenomenological events of the 'stream of consciousness', a law of essence paradigmatically illustrates the non-independence just mentioned, the law, namely, that each actual, fulfilled conscious-present necessarily and continuously passes over into one that *has* just existed, so that our present conscious state makes continuous demands on our conscious future. The law further requires that our retentive awareness of what has just been, which itself has the immanent character of being actually present, demands that the phenomenon we are aware of as having just existed should in fact just have existed. The time we are talking of in this context is of course the immanent temporality which belongs to the phenomenological stream of consciousness itself.

In the sense of our definition, to take somewhat differently slanted examples, each bit of our visual field, each concretely filled section of it, is independent within, and relatively to, the concrete totality of a momentary visual intuition, whereas each colour of such a portion, the colour-pattern of the whole etc., is non-independent. And again in, and relatively to, the whole of our momentary sense-intuition, the visual field with its contents, the tactual field with its contents etc., are independent, whereas the qualities, forms etc., whether attaching to whole fields, or their individual members, are non-independent. We observe at the same time that all that counted as non-independent or independent in relation to the whole of our previous example will count as such in relation to our present standard of reference. It is in fact generally true that:

Whatever is independent or non-independent in relation to a B, also maintains this property in relation to every whole B' in relation to which B is independent or non-independent – a proposition, whose converse is of course invalid. Although therefore, relations (and with them relative conceptions) vary as boundaries are differently drawn, nonetheless our law entails a certain relation for the groups of contents in the context referred to. Such a relation obtains, e.g., when we compare a coexistent group belonging to each point of time with successive groups which include such coexistent groups, or perhaps even with the inclusive group of unending, fully occupied phenomenological time. What counts as an independent element in the latter group is what is the more comprehensive element, and so not everything that counts as independent in the order of coexistence must for that reason count as independent in the order of succession. The converse holds, however. An independent thing in the order of coexistence, e.g. a bounded portion of the visual sense-field in its concrete fulness, is non-independent relatively to the whole of occupied time, to the extent that its time-determination is treated as a mere instant. Following on what we have said, an instant of time is as such non-independent: it can be concretely occupied only as part of the concrete occupation of a time-stretch or duration. If we replace the instant by a duration, in which our concrete content is thought of as remaining quite constant, then such an enduring coexist nce could count as independent even in this wider sphere.

CHAPTER TWO

Thoughts Towards a Theory of the Pure Forms of Wholes and Parts

§ 14 *The concept of Foundation and some relevant theorems*

THE law stated and applied in the last paragraph of the previous section is not an empirical proposition, and yet not an immediate proposition of essence. Like many similar laws, it permits of *a priori* proof. Nothing can show up the worth of a strict statement more clearly than the possibility of giving a deductive proof of such propositions as are familiar to us in another guise. In view of the great scientific interest that the constitution of a deductive theoretical transformation claims in every field, we wish to linger here a little.

Definitions. If a law of essence means that an A cannot as such exist except in a more comprehensive unity which associates it with an M, we say that an A *as such requires foundation by an M* or also that *an A as such needs to be supplemented by an M*. If accordingly A_0, M_0 are determinate instances of the pure kinds A or M, actualized in a single whole, and standing in the relations mentioned, we say that A_0 *is founded upon* M_0, and that it is *exclusively* founded on M_0, if A_0's need for supplementation is satisfied by M_0 alone. This terminology can of course be carried over to the Species, by a quite harmless equivocation. We say further, more indefinitely, that the two contents or two pure Species, stand in a *foundational relationship* or in a relationship of *necessary association*. This indeed leaves it open which of the two possible but not mutually exclusive relationships is meant. The indefinite expression: A_0 *requires supplementation by, is founded upon a certain moment*, plainly means the same as the expression: 'A_0 *is non-independent*'.

Proposition 1 If an A as such requires to be founded on an M, every whole having an A, but not an M, as a part, requires a similar foundation.

463

This proposition is axiomatically self-evident. If an A cannot *be* except when completed by M, a whole including an A but no M cannot satisfy A's need for supplementation and must itself share it.

As a corollary we can assert the following, making use of the definition of our previous section.

Proposition 2 A whole which includes a non-independent 'moment', without including, as its part, the supplement which that 'moment' demands, is likewise non-independent, and is so relatively to every subordinate independent whole in which that non-independent 'moment' is contained.

Proposition 3 If W is an independent part of (and so[1] also relatively to) F, then every independent part w of W also is an independent part of F.

If w needed a supplement M relatively to W, and so had a foundation M_0 in the range of W, this foundation would necessarily be included in W. For, if this were not so, W would require supplementation in respect of M in conformity with Prop. 1, and since M_0 is a part of F, it would, on Prop. 2, be non-independent relatively to F, which contradicts the assumption. But in accordance with this assumption, w is an independent part of W, and so also independent relatively to W: there can therefore be nothing in the range of W which could serve as a foundation for w, and so also nothing in the whole range of F.

The proposition before us can also, with suitable changes in symbolization, be expressed as follows:

If A is an independent part of B, and B an independent part of C, A is also an independent part of C or more briefly: An independent part of an independent part is an independent part of a whole.

Proposition 4 If C is a non-independent part of a whole W, it is also a non-independent part of every other whole of which W is a part.

C is non-independent relatively to W, i.e. it possesses a foundation in an M_0 belonging to the range of W. This M_0 must naturally also appear in the range of every whole superordinate to W, i.e. every whole which includes W as a part. C must therefore also be non-independent relatively to each such whole. (On the other hand, we add, C may very well be independent relatively to a subordinate

---

[1] In the sense namely of the abbreviated mode of speech defined in the last section, which must everywhere be remembered here.

whole: we need only so draw its boundaries that the required supplement M is excluded therefrom. A 'piece' of an extended phenomenon *in abstracto*, but taken as a 'moment', is independent relatively to such extension; this, however, itself lacks independence relatively to the concrete wholes of the occupied extension.)

Our proposition permits an expression analogous to the previous one, i.e. if A is a non-independent part of B, and B a non-independent part of C, then A too is a non-independent part of C.

A non-independent part of a non-independent part is a non-independent part of a whole.

Proposition 5 A relatively non-independent object also is absolutely non-independent, whereas a relatively independent object may be non-independent in an absolute sense.

For a proof see the previous section.

Proposition 6 If A and B are independent parts of some whole W, they are also independent relatively to one another. For if A required supplementation by B, or any part of B, there would be, in the range of parts determined by W, certain parts (those of B) in which A would be founded. A would therefore not be independent relatively to its whole W.

§15 *Transition to the treatment of the more important part-relations*

We shall now deal with some of the most remarkable differences among the *a priori* relationships holding between Whole and Part, and among the Parts of one and the same whole. The generality of these relationships leaves plenty of room for the most manifold differences. Not every part is included in its whole in the same fashion, and not every part is woven together with every other, in the unity of a whole, in the same way. In comparing the relations among the parts of different wholes, or even among the parts of one and the same whole, we come upon striking differences, on which our common talk of different sorts of wholes and parts is founded. A hand, e.g., forms part of a person in quite a different way from the colour of his hand, from his body's total extent, from his mental acts, and from the internal 'moments' of such phenomena. The parts of the extension are otherwise united with each other than they each are united with their colours etc. We shall see at once that all these differences belong to the sphere of our present investigations.

§16 *Reciprocal and one-sided, mediate and immediate foundation*

If we consider any pair of parts of a whole, the following possibilities obtain:

1. There is a relation of foundedness between both parts.
2. There is no such relation. In case 1 the foundedness can be:

(*a*) reciprocal

(*b*) one-sided, according as the law in question is convertible or not. Colour and extension accordingly are mutually founded in a unified intuition,[1] since no colour is thinkable without a certain extension, and no extension without a certain colour. The character of being a judgement is, on the other hand, one-sidedly founded on underlying presentations, since these latter need not function as foundations of judgements. Brentano's distinctions of parts mutually isolable, and parts having one-sided isolability, agrees in extension, though not in definition, with the notion before us. Brentano's additional talk of 'mutual isolability' rules out every sort of foundational relation.

There is some interest in asking how matters here stand in regard to the relative independence or non-independence of the parts, relatively, of course, to the whole in which they are considered. If there is a reciprocal relation of foundedness among two parts, their relative lack of independence is unquestionable, as is the case, e.g., in the unity of Quality and Place. The case differs when the relation is one-sided: in that case the foundational (though naturally not the founded) content can be independent. Thus in every extension the shape of a portion is founded on the portion in question: something non-independent relatively to the whole extension is accordingly founded on something which is independent in relation to this whole.

The foundation of one part in another can further be:

(*a*) an immediate foundation or

[1] More precisely: in the unity of a visual *intuitum* as such.

(*b*) a mediate foundation, according as the two parts are immediately or mediately associated. This relationship, like the previous one, is naturally not bound to the individually present 'moments', but concerns the essential being of the foundational relationship. If A_0 is immediately founded on B_0, but mediately on C_0 (in so far as B_0 is immediately founded on C_0), it holds universally and purely in virtue of essence that an A is in general immediately founded on a B, and mediately upon a C. This results from the fact that if an A and a B are associated at all, they are so immediately, and again that, if an A and a C are associated, they are only mediately associated. *The order of mediacy and immediacy is based by law on the pure Genera involved.* The generic 'moment' of Colour, for instance, and in quite different fashion the 'moment' of Brightness, can only be realized in and with a 'moment' of lowest difference such as Red, Blue etc., and the latter again only in combination with a certain definite extension. These associations and foundations, which are always immediate, condition the mediate associations and foundations between the 'moment' of Colour or Brightness and that of Determinate Extension. Plainly the laws of combination which concern such mediate foundations, are analytic, indeed syllogistic consequences of those which pertain to the immediate foundations.

§17 *Exact determination of the concepts of Piece (Portion), 'Moment', Physical Part, Abstractum, Concretum*

We may now also reduce a further series of familiar, fundamental concepts to the above defined concepts, and so give them an exact definition. Some of these terms may, we note in advance, be open to objection; the concepts correlated with them in what follows are nonetheless very valuable.

We first perform a fundamental division of the concept Part into *Pieces*, or Parts in the narrowest sense, and into *Moments* or *Abstract Parts* of the Whole. *Each part that is independent relatively to a whole W we call a Piece (Portion), each part that is non-independent relatively to W we call a Moment (an abstract part) of this same whole W.* It makes no difference here whether the whole itself, considered absolutely, or in relation to a higher whole, is independent or not. *Abstract parts can in their turn accordingly have pieces, and pieces in their turn abstract parts.* We speak of the portions of a duration, although this is something abstract, just as we speak of the portions of an extension. The forms of these portions are their immanent, abstract parts.

Pieces that have no piece identically in common are called *exclusive* (disjoined) pieces. The division of a whole into a plurality of mutually exclusive pieces we call a *piecing (Zerstückung)* of the same. Two such pieces may still have a common identical 'moment': their common boundary, e.g., is an identical 'moment' of the adjoining pieces of a divided continuum. Pieces are said to be *isolated* when they are disjoined in the strict sense, when they therefore also have *no identical 'moments'*.

Since an abstract part also is abstract in relation to each more comprehensive whole and, in general, to any range of objects embracing this whole,[1] what is abstract, relatively considered, is *eo ipso* abstract when considered absolutely. The latter can be defined as the limiting case of relative treatment, where the relation is determined by the total range of objects in general. We therefore needed no preliminary definition of the abstract or non-independent in the absolute sense. An *abstractum simpliciter* is therefore an object, in relation to which there is some whole of which it is a non-independent part.

When a whole permits the sort of 'piecing' in which the pieces essentially belong to the same lowest Genus as is determined by the undivided whole, we speak of it as an *extended whole*, and of its pieces as *extended parts*. Here belongs, e.g., the division of an extent into extents, in particular of a spatial stretch into spatial stretches, of a temporal stretch into temporal stretches etc.

We may here further add the following definition:

An object in relation to its abstract 'moments' is called a 'relative concretum', and in relation to its proximate 'moments', their 'proximate concretum'. (The difference here presupposed between remoter and nearer 'moments' will be more precisely pinned down in the following sections.) A concretum that itself is abstract in *no* direction can be called an 'absolute concretum'. Since the proposition holds that each absolutely independent content possesses abstract parts, each such content can also be looked on and spoken of as an absolute concretum. The two notions are thus of equal extent. For a similar reason one can also speak of a piece as a *concrete* part, whose concreteness is either to be

---

[1] From Prop. 4, p. 464.

understood as absolute or relative, according as the whole itself only has abstract parts, or is itself abstract. Where the word 'concretum' is used simply, an absolute concretum is usually intended.

§18 *The difference between the mediate and immediate parts of a whole*

The distinction between pieces and abstract parts is intimately connected with the distinction between *mediate* and *immediate parts*, or, more clearly, the distinction between *proximate* and *remote* parts. For talk of immediacy and mediacy can be understood in *two ways*. We shall first discuss the most natural sense of such talk.

If $P(W)$ is a part of the whole W, then a part of this part, e.g. $P(P(W))$, is again a part of the whole, but a *mediate* part. $P(W)$ may then be called a *relatively immediate* part of the whole. The distinction is a relative one, since $P(W)$ may itself again be a mediate part, in relation to another part of the whole in which it is contained as a part. The relative distinction is transformed into an absolute one, if we understand by *absolutely mediate parts* such parts as themselves enter into other parts in the whole, whereas *absolutely immediate* parts will be such as may enter as parts into *any* part of the same whole. Every geometrical part of an extension is in this absolute sense mediate, for there are always other geometric parts that include it. It is harder to adduce suitable examples of absolutely immediate parts. Perhaps the following might do: if we emphasize in a visual intuition the unified combination formed by all such internal 'moments' as remain identical despite all change of place, we have a part of the whole that can have no superordinate part above it. The same would hold of the totality of their mere extension in regard to the geometric bodies congruent with them in all except position. If we limit our distinction to parts of one and the same sort, then the 'moment' of total coloration is an absolutely immediate part, since there is no like moment of the whole, of which such coloration could be reckoned a part. As opposed to this, the coloration of a piece of the whole can be treated as mediate, in so far as it contributes to the total coloration of the whole. The same holds, in relation to the Species Extension, of the total extension of an extended thing: this is an absolutely immediate part of that thing, whereas a portion of that extension is an absolutely mediate part of that thing.

§19 *A novel sense of the distinction between the proximate and remote parts of the whole*

Our talk of immediate and mediate parts acquires quite a different content if we attend to certain remarkable differences that force themselves on us when we compare the relations between wholes and mediate parts.[1] If we think of an extensive whole as 'pieced together', its pieces in their turn permit of further 'piecings', the pieces of the pieces in their turn etc. Here the parts of the parts are parts of the whole in exactly the same sense as the original parts were. We do not merely observe this likeness in respect of the sort of partial relation which condition talk of 'the same sort of parts' in regard to the whole – the pieces of the pieces are in their turn pieces of the whole[2] – but we also observe a likeness of such relations between the whole and its mediate parts, on the one hand, and its relatively immediate parts, on the other. There are diverse possible divisions in which the same part comes up, sometimes earlier, sometimes later, so that we have no temptation to accord any privilege to one part over another as regards the way in which it is contained in the whole. The descending order of divisions here corresponds to no fixed, factually determined gradation in the relation of parts to wholes. This does not mean that talk about mediate and immediate parts is entirely arbitrary, and without objective foundation. The physical whole genuinely has the parts first dealt with, and these in their turn no less genuinely have the parts distinguished in them, which are therefore mediate parts in relation to the whole, and the same is true of each stage of the serial division. But in themselves the remotest of these parts are no further from the whole than the nearest. The parts in any case also owe their serial order to the serial order of our divisions, and these latter have no objective foundation. In an extended whole there is no division which is intrinsically primary, and no definitely delimited group of divisions forming the first

---

[1] See Bolzano's, *Wissenschaftslehre*, I, §58, p. 251, and Twardowski, loc. cit. §9, pp. 49 *f.*

[2] A new expression of Prop. 3 in §14, above p. 464.

grade in division; from a given division there is also no progress determined by the thing's nature to a new division or grade in division. We could *begin* with each division without violating an intrinsic prerogative. Each mediate part can, according to one's chosen mode of division, likewise count as an immediate part, each immediate part as a mediate one.

The case is quite different if we bring in other examples. An intuitively unified tone-sequence, e.g. a melody, is a whole, in which we find individual tones as parts. Each of these tones has further parts, a 'moment' of quality, of intensity etc., which as parts of parts are also parts of the melody. But it is clear in this case that the mediacy with which the qualitative 'moment' of the individual tone enters the whole, cannot be attributed to our subjective series of divisions or to any other subjective ground. It is no doubt certain that if the individual tone's moment of quality is to be singly noticed, the tone itself must be 'stressed'. To single out the mediate part presupposes the singling out of the immediate one. But this phenomenological relationship must not be confused with the objective situation we are here concerned with. It is evident that the quality in itself only forms part of the melody in so far as it forms part of the single tone: it belongs immediately to the latter, and only mediately to the total tone-pattern. This mediacy is not therefore bound up with some arbitrary, or some psychologically compulsive preference for a certain order of division which first makes us hit on the tone, and then on its 'moment' of quality: the tone in itself is a prior part in the whole melody, and its quality a later, mediate part. The same holds of the tone's intensity: it would here seem even to take us a step further from the melodic whole, being as it were no immediate 'moment' of the tone, but one more directly of its quality, and so a secondary part in relation to this melody (no doubt a somewhat objectionable conception, which requires closer scrutiny). If we are right in holding that there is a part of the quality, e.g. the pitch C, of the tone in question, which represents its generic 'moment', what it has in common with all tones, then this 'moment' primarily inheres in the quality, secondarily in the tone, and at least tertiarily in the whole tone-pattern etc. Just so the moment of colour or shape that inheres in an extended part of what is visually intuited as such, is primarily attached to this part, only secondarily to the intuited whole. It is even more

471

mediately related to the whole voluminousness[1] of the patterned extension, the magnitude that it primarily possesses. (We can of course not talk of a genuine quantitative pinning down in the sphere of mere data of intuition as such.)

After these discussions, the novel and important sense of the distinction between mediate and immediate parts should be clear. The difference is, however, not merely relative: in every whole there are parts which belong directly to the whole, and not first to one of its parts. It is definite for the single part whether it is mediate or not in our sense, and, if it is mediate, whether it is so primarily, secondarily or more remotely. To make a terminological distinction one could here speak of *nearer* and *remoter* parts, or to fix things more exactly of *primary, secondary*...parts of a whole; the terms *mediate* and *immediate part* we retain in the more general sense applicable to any parts. Secondary parts are primary parts of primary parts, tertiary parts, primary parts of secondary parts etc. The notions comprised in this series are obviously mutually exclusive.

Primary parts may be, and in general also will be, absolutely mediate. But there are also primary parts that are absolutely immediate, i.e. that are not included as parts in any part of their whole. Each portion of an extension is primarily contained in it, although it can always be regarded as a mediate part of the same extension. Objectively there are always parts whose part it is. As against this, the form of an extension is not included as a part in any of that extension's parts.

§ 20 *Nearer and remoter parts relatively to one another*

We spoke above of mediate and immediate, of nearer and remoter parts, in relation to the whole to which they belong. But even when we are dealing with *parts in relation to one another* we usually employ these terms, though in quite a different sense: we talk of an immediate or mediate connection of the terms and, in the latter case, draw further distinctions. Some parts, we say, are closer to one another, other parts further. Here the following relations are relevant. It often happens that a mode of association peculiarly

---

[1] [Husserl here has 'volumness' which I take to be an unsuccessful venture into English. *Trans.*]

unites two parts A, B into a partial unity which excludes other parts, but in which, further, B and not A is associated in just this manner with C. In this situation A is also associated with C, in virtue, that is, of a complex form of unity constituted by the two associations AB and BC. The latter associations we then call immediate, while we say that the association of A and C, achieved in the form ABC, is mediate. If there are further peculiar associations CD, DE etc., we shall say that A is associated with their final terms D, E...with progressively increased mediacy, D is a remoter part than C, E still more remote than D etc. We have obviously only characterized a simple special case. Each symbol A, B, C...could have summed up a complex partial unity, a whole group of unified members; in this case also the concatenations tying the partial unities together into wholes, would make the members of the different groups appear in relations of nearer or remoter connection.

As to whether other associations, and in particular other direct associations, subsist among the mediately associated members – and associations perhaps of the same kind as those among the immediately associated members – we have so far said nothing. We are considering the members exclusively in respect of the forms of the complex relationships determined by their elementary associations. Naturally the treatment of these forms will be of particular significance in that special class of cases, so frequently dealt with in theory and practice, whose peculiarity can readily be shown up in the relations of points in a straight line. If we select any series of points from a straight line, we observe that the immediate associations of the mediately associated members belong, with the associations of immediately neighbouring points, to one and the same lowest Genus of associations: they are further only different in respect of their lowest specific difference, whereas this difference itself is unambiguously determined by the differences of the varied mediating associations. This holds of time-sequences, of spatial configurations, in short of every case where associations can be characterized by *directed stretches* of one and the same Genus. In every case, to put it briefly, *stretches are addible*. But in our quite formal treatment we can pass all such matters by.

The essence of the matter can be conceptually laid out in the following fashion. Two associations form a concatenation, when they have some but not all members in common (i.e. do not coincide as when, e.g., the same members are united by several associations). Each concatenation is on this showing a complex association. Associations now divide into those which include concatenations and those which do not: associations of the former are combinations of associations of the latter sort. The members of an association that is free from concatenations are said to be *immediately associated* or proximate. In every concatenation, and therefore in every whole containing concatenations, there must be immediately associated members, which belong to associations of parts which include no further concatenations. All other members of such a whole are said to be *mediately associated* with one another. The member common to a simple concatenation *ABC* (simple because it contains no concatenation as a part) is, in the sense of our rulings, immediately associated with its neighbours, while these are mediately associated with one another etc. Talk of nearer and remoter parts always relates to concatenations. The concepts next neighbour (=immediately associated member), next-neighbour of a next-neighbour etc., yield, by an easily determined formal completion, the requisite gradations of 'distance', and are then no different from ordinal numbers: first, second etc. The completion naturally tries to make these concepts unambiguous by fixing a 'direction of progress', e.g. by bringing in the *asymmetry* of a class of relations, in consequence of which we form conceptual structures like 'right next-neighbour of *A*' (first man right of *A*), 'right next-neighbour of right next-neighbour of *A*' ('second man right of *A*') etc. The essential purposes of the present investigation do not require us to go more deeply into this not intrinsically trivial point.

§21 *Exact pinning down of the pregnant notions of Whole and Part, and of their essential Species, by means of the notion of 'Foundation'*

Our interest in the foregoing treatments was directed to the most general relations of essence between wholes and parts, or between parts among one another (i.e. of contents that combine into a whole). In our definitions and descriptions on these matters the notion of Whole was presupposed. It is however possible to *dispense* with this notion *in all cases*: for it can be substituted the simple *coexistence* of the contents that were denominated parts. One could, e.g., define as follows:

A content of the species A is founded upon a content of the species B, if an *A* can by its essence (i.e. legally, in virtue of its specific nature) not exist, unless a *B* also exists: this leaves open whether the coexistence of a *C,* a *D* etc. is needed or not.

One can proceed similarly with the other definitions. If all is taken thus generally, one could then give the following noteworthy definition of the *pregnant concept of Whole* by way of the *notion of Foundation*:

By a Whole we understand a range of contents which are all covered *by a single foundation* without the help of further contents. The contents of such a range we call its parts. Talk of the *singleness of the foundation* implies that *every content is foundationally connected, whether directly or indirectly, with every content*. This can happen in that all these contents are immediately or mediately founded on each other without external assistance, or in that all together serve to found a new content, again without external assistance. In the latter case the possibility remains open that this unitary content is built up out of partial contents, which in their turn are founded on partial groups from the presupposed range of contents, just as the Whole content is founded on its total range. Intermediate cases are finally also possible, where the unity of foundation is so formed, e.g., that *A* founds a new content together with *B, B* one together with *C, C* one together with *D* etc. In such cases the formation of new unities is in short concatenated.

One sees at once how such differences determine *essential divisions of the whole*. In the cases first referred to, the 'parts' (defined as members of the range in question) 'interpenetrated', in the other cases they were 'mutually external', but, whether taken all together, or concatenated in pairs, they embodied real forms of association. Where one speaks of connections, associations etc. in the narrower sense, one means wholes of the second sort, i.e. wholes where contents relatively independent as regards one another – where the whole falls apart into its *pieces* – serve to found *new* contents as their 'combinatory forms'. Talk of wholes and parts tends in general to be oriented exclusively to such cases.

The same whole can be interpenetrative in relation to certain parts, and combinatory in relation to others: the sensuous, phenomenal thing, the intuitively given spatial shape clothed with sensuous quality, is (just as it appears) interpenetrative in respect of reciprocally founded 'moments' such as colour and extension, and combinatory in respect of its 'pieces'.

§22 Forms of sensuous unity and wholes

Before we go further, it is well to indicate expressly that, *in harmony with our definition, there need not be a peculiar form for every whole, in the sense of a specific 'moment' of unity which binds all the parts.* If unity arises, e.g., by concatenation, so that each pair of next members founds a new content, the demands of our definition are satisfied, without the presence of a peculiar moment (i.e. one of unity) founded on all parts *together*. That such a moment must always be presumed can scarcely be maintained *a priori*. On our concept of a whole, it is not even requisite that the parts should be associated in groups or pairs by peculiar 'moments' of unity. Only if the whole is an extended whole, and in general one that can be broken down into 'pieces', are such moments obvious and indispensable *a priori*.

It might, however, seem odd that we make do with this definition, and can even dare to think that *all wholes*, with the sole exception of these which break up into 'pieces', lack binding forms of unity. It is odd to hold that the unity, e.g., of extension and colour, of tone-quality and tone-intensity, or between the sensational stuff of our percept of a thing and the peculiar phenomenological 'moments' brought to it by our perceptual consciousness, and all other similar unities, rest merely on one-sided or two-sided relations of foundation, without the added foundation, by way of such coexistence, of a peculiar form-content or 'moment' of unity. It is nonetheless obvious that wherever associative forms can really be demonstrated as peculiar moments in intuition, the things associated are relatively independent parts, parts such as tones in the unity of a melody, colours picked out piecemeal in the unity of a colour-pattern, or partial shapes taken from the unity of a complete shape etc. Contrariwise, it is vain to look in the unity of the visual phenomenon for special form-contents in addition to those which unify its pieces, form-contents which will bring together non-independent 'moments' such as colour and extension, or which will bring together colour-tone and brightness in the former, and the 'moments' of form and size in the latter. We are of course far from wishing to turn the undiscovered into the non-existent without more ado. But it is in any case most important to discuss *the possibility* of there being sensuous unities *without* abstractible sensuous form, and if this proves feasible, to clarify the notion.

It may at first seem extraordinary in this respect that mere necessities of coexistence, demands for supplementation, consisting in no more than the fact that the existence of certain sorts of contents conditions the mere coexistence of contents of certain coordinated sorts, that requirements of this kind, I say, should serve to produce unity. One at once objects: could contents in such a situation be side by side in complete isolation, dependent on each other for their existence and yet entirely uncombined, without their 'foundation' amounting to a connected unity in the manner here supposed?

Our answer is plain. Talk of separation implies a thought of the relative independence of the separated, which is just what we have excluded. The picture of side-by-side existence is revealing: it plainly presupposes relatively independent contents, which, since they are such, can serve to found this *sensuous* form of side-by-side existence. What recommends such an unsuitable picture – unsuitable since it tries to illustrate sensuous formlessness by a case of sensuous form – is the mutual indifference of the contents merely given together in space. The thought insinuates itself: where there is not even the loosest, but simply *no* unifying form, contents could really not have anything to do with each other: they could never therefore come together but would remain eternally isolated. Is it not absurd to want to bind contents together without any bond? This is no doubt quite right for the contents the image presupposes, but the contents of which we speak have plenty to do with each other, they are in fact 'founded' on one another, and for this reason they require no chains and bonds to chain or knit them together, or to bring them to one another. In their case all these expressions have in fact no sense at all. Where it makes nonsense to speak of isolation, the problem of overcoming such isolation is likewise nonsensical.

This conception is naturally not limited in its application to the sphere of the intuitive objects (phenomenological contents in particular) which served as our illustrations, but applies to the sphere of objects in general. *The only true unifying factors, we may roundly say, are relations of 'foundation'.* The unity even of independent objects is in consequence brought about by 'foundation'. Since they are not, as independent objects, 'founded' on one another, it remains their lot to 'found' new contents themselves, and to 'found' them together; it is only in virtue of this situation that these latter are thought of as unifying contents in respect of their 'founding' members. But the contents 'founded' on one another (whether one-sidedly or reciprocally) likewise have unity, and a much more intimate unity since less mediated unity. Such 'intimacy' consists simply in the fact that unity is here not engendered by a novel content, which again only engenders unity since it is 'founded' on many members separate in themselves. If one calls such a content 'unity', then unity is indeed a 'real predicate', a 'positive' 'real' content, and other wholes have, in *this* sense, no unity, and we shall not even be able to say that their own moment of unity is unified with each of the united members. If we refuse however to adopt such a wrong-headed terminology, which necessitates double-talk in practice, we shall speak of unities and wholes wherever we have a unitary foundation. We shall be entitled to say of each range of contents united in this manner that it *has* unity, though the predicate thus attributed to it is no 'real' one, though there is no constituent called 'unity' anywhere in our whole which can be prised out. *Unity is in fact a categorial predicate.*

One should also take into account the by no means small theoretical advantage which our notion promises as removing a long-known and troublesome difficulty in the theory of wholes. This concerns the endlessly complicated part-relations which seem required by the endlessly complicated 'moments' of unity in every whole. The view against which our objections are directed is based on the apparently plain truth that, wherever two contents form a real unity, there must be a peculiar part, a 'moment of unity', that binds them together. If then U is the moment of unity of A and B, there must be a new 'moment' of unity U_1, for A and U (since these two are unified) and again a new U_2, for B and U; and just so new 'moments' U_1^1, and U_2^1 for U and U_1, and for U and U_2 respectively, and so on *in infinitum*. If no distinction is drawn between associations and relations, between differences of 'sense-material' and 'categorial form', and if one then takes the boundlessly varied conceptual differences that are possible *a priori*, and which ideal principles allow one to complicate indefinitely, and puts all such differences *into* objects as their real moments, one gets the analyses which Twardowski has offered us in his 'psychological' researches, and which are as subtle as they are queer.

Our conception avoids these endless regresses of parts which are always splitting into further series. Nothing *really* exists – in the sense of being a possible object of sense-perception – beyond the aggregate of a whole's 'pieces', together with the sensuous forms of unity, which rest on these pieces conjointly. Unity is conferred on the 'moments' in the 'pieces', as also on the 'moments' of unity *and* the 'pieces', by the foundational relations in the sense of our definition.

The notion of the *moments of unity*, which we still distinguish from that of the 'form' which gives unity to a whole, has, lastly, been defined above in passing. Expressly put, we mean by it *a content founded on a plurality of contents, and on all of them together*, and not on some of them simply. (All this naturally presupposes *our* notion of foundation.) If we keep within the phenomenal sphere, this content may as readily belong to outer as to inner sense, according to the nature of its foundational contents.

Note. 'Moments' of unity, like all other abstract contents, fall into pure Genera and Species.[1] The Genus Spatial Figure differentiates itself into Triangular Figure, the latter into the lower Species of Definite Triangular Figure, in the sense in which we speak of the 'same' triangle however much we may shift or turn it. Such examples make clear that the Genus of 'Moments' of unity is determined by the Genus of the contents which found them, and that the lowest difference of the former is unambiguously determined by the lowest difference of the latter. One notes, further, that 'moments of unity' must be distinguished into 'moments' or forms of the first, second, third...level, according as the form is immediately 'founded' upon absolute contents, or on forms of the first level, or on forms founded on forms of the first level, and so on. One sees further that the form-contents of higher level necessarily form a whole with the whole descending series of forms of lower level, and in such combination always represent *complex forms relatively to the ultimately foundational*

[1] See my *Philosophie der Arithmetik* (1891), p. 232.

elements. In the sphere of complex sensuous shapes, particularly visual and auditory ones, this can be readily illustrated, whereas the general fact can be seen *a priori* from concepts.

§23 *Forms of categorial unity and wholes*

In the sense in which we are here trying to pin down the notion of a whole, *a mere aggregate* or mere coexistence of any contents is not to be called a *whole,* as little as a likeness (the being of the same sort) or a difference (the being of *another sort, or, in another sense, the not being identical) are wholes.*[1] 'Aggregate' is an expression for a categorial unity corresponding to the mere form of thought, it stands for the correlate of a certain *unity of reference* relating to all relevant objects. The objects themselves, being only held together in thought, do not succeed in founding a new content, whether taken as a group or together; no material form of association develops among them through this unity of intuition, they are possibly 'quite disconnected and intrinsically unrelated'. This is shown in the fact that the form of the aggregate is quite indifferent to its matter, i.e. it can persist in spite of wholly arbitrary variation in its comprised contents. A 'founded' content, however, depends on the specific 'nature' of its 'founding' contents: there is a pure law which renders the Genus of the 'founded' content dependent on the definitely indicated Genera of the 'founding' contents. A whole in the full and proper sense is, in general, a combination determined by the lowest Genera of the parts. A law corresponds to each material unity. There are different sorts of whole corresponding to these different laws, or, otherwise put,

---

[1] One must certainly distinguish the *sensuous moment of likeness* from *likeness as a categorial unity*: the former is related to the latter as the sensuous characters of plurality, which serve us as direct indications of multiplicity and diversity, stand to multiplicity and diversity themselves. See my *Phil. der Arithmetik*, p. 233. This first work of mine (an elaboration of my *Habilitationsschrift*, never published and only partially printed, at the University of Halle, 1887) should be compared with all assertions of the present work on aggregates, moments of unity, combinations, wholes and objects of higher order. I am sorry that in many recent treatments of the doctrine of 'form-qualities', this work has mostly been ignored, though quite a lot of the thought-content of later treatments by Cornelius, Meinong etc., of questions of analysis, apprehension of plurality and combination, is already to be found, differently expressed, in my *Philos. der Arithm.* I think it would still be of use today to consult this work on the phenomenological and ontological issues in question, especially since it is the first work which attached importance to acts and objects of higher order and investigated them thoroughly.

to the different sorts of contents that are to serve as parts. We cannot at will make the same content at one time part of one sort of whole, at another time part of another sort. To be a part, and, more exactly, to be a part of some determinate sort (a metaphysical, physical or logical part or whatever) is rooted in the pure generic nature of the contents in question, and is governed by laws which in our sense are *a priori* laws or 'laws of essence'. This is a fundamental insight whose meaning must be respected in all our treatments and formulations. And with this insight we have the foundation for a systematic theory of the relations of wholes and parts as regards their pure forms, the categorially definable types which abstract from the 'sensuous' material of such wholes.

Before we pursue these thoughts, we must remove a further difficulty. The form of an aggregate is a purely categorial form, in opposition to which the form of a whole, of a unity due to foundation, appeared to be a material form. But did we not say in the previous section that unity (and we were talking specifically of a unity based on foundation) was a categorial predicate? Here we must note that, on our doctrine, the Idea of unity or the Idea of a whole is based on the idea of 'Founding', and the latter Idea upon the Idea of a Pure Law; the Form of a Law is further as such categorial – a law is not thinglike, not therefore perceptible – and that *to this extent* the notion of a Founded Whole is a categorial notion. But the *content* of the law governing each such whole is determined by the material specificity of the 'founding' contents and consequently of the 'founded' types of content, and it is this law, definite in its content, which gives the whole its unity. For this reason we rightly call each ideally possible specification of the Idea of such unity a material or also a real (*reale*) unity.

According to our previous assertions,[1] the laws constitutive of the various sorts of whole are *synthetically a priori*, as opposed to laws which are analytically *a priori*, such as those governing pure categorial forms, e.g. the Form-Idea of a whole as such, and all merely formal specifications of this Idea. We prefer to dwell in what follows, on such formal specifications.

[1] See § 11, pp. 455 *ff*.

§24 The pure formal types of wholes and parts. The postulate of an 'a priori' theory

The pure forms of *wholes and parts* are determined by the *pure forms of law*. Only what is *formally* universal in the foundational relation, as expressed in our definition, is then relevant, together with the *a priori* combinations that it permits. We rise, in the case of any type of whole, to its pure form, its categorial type, by abstracting from the specificity of the sorts of content in question. More clearly expressed, this *formalizing abstraction* is something quite different from what is usually aimed at under the title of 'abstraction': it is a quite different performance from the one which sets in relief the universal Redness in a concrete visual datum, or the generic 'moment' of Colour in the Redness previously abstracted. In formalization we replace the names standing for the sort of content in question by indefinite expressions such as *a certain sort of content, a certain other sort of content etc.* At the same time, on the semantic side, corresponding substitutions of purely categorial for material thoughts take place.[1]

The distinctions between abstract parts and 'pieces' are purely formal, being in this sense drawn in purely categorial fashion, as can be seen at once from our pronouncements above. These pronouncements had however to be suitably interpreted in accordance with our present leaning towards final formalization: the pure concept of the whole, in the sense of our last definition, had to be made their basis. The distinction likewise between nearer and remoter parts that we merely explained, in descriptive fashion,[2] by means of illustrations, can now be reduced to the mere form of certain foundational relations, and so formalized.

In our examples we saw above that, in the case of many intuitive wholes, a graded series of fragmentations of such wholes always results in fragments of these wholes themselves, fragments all equally close to the whole, and which could with equal justice count as results of a *first* fragmentation. The sequence of the 'piecings' was in these instances not prescribed by the essence of

---

[1] See Vol. I (§§67–72) on the role of formalization for constituting the idea of a pure logic as *mathesis universalis*. We must emphasize again that where we speak simply of 'abstraction', as we have done so far, we mean the emphasis on a non-independent 'moment' of content, or the corresponding ideation under the title of 'ideating abstraction', but *not* formalization.

[2] See §19, p. 470.

the wholes. What is here relevant is first the proposition that *pieces of pieces of a whole are themselves pieces of the whole* – a proposition that we formally proved above[1] (in different words). But we were there dealing with 'pieces', for which the sequence of fragmentations was meaningless, since it corresponded to no graded series of '*foundations*'. All pieces always stood to the whole in the same relation of 'foundation'. There were no differences in the *form* of the relation to the whole, all parts were 'contained in the whole' in the same fashion. The matter would be quite different were we to fragment aesthetic unities, e.g. a star-shape built out of star-shapes, which in their turn are composed of stretches and ultimately of points. The points serve to 'found' stretches, the stretches serve to 'found', as new aesthetic unities, the individual stars, and these in their turn serve to 'found' the star-pattern, as the highest unity in the given case. The points, stretches, stars and the final star-pattern are not now coordinated as are partial stretches in a stretch. There is, in their case, a fixed order of 'foundations', in which what is founded at one level serves to 'found' the level next above, and in such a manner that at each level new forms, only reachable at that level, are involved. We may here add the universal proposition:

'*Pieces' are essentially mediate or remote parts of a whole whose 'pieces' they are, if combinatory forms unite them with other 'pieces' into wholes which in their turn constitute wholes of higher order by way of novel forms.*

The difference between the parts nearer or further in regard to the whole has accordingly its essential ground in the formally expressible diversity of foundational relations.

The case is similar in regard to non-independent 'moments', if we take account of the essential formal distinction between such 'moments' as can only satisfy their need for supplementation in the *complete whole*, and such as can satisfy this need in *pieces* of this whole. This makes a difference to the mode of belonging, to the *form of foundation*: by it certain parts, e.g. the total extent of the intuited thing, belong exclusively to the thing as a whole, while other parts, e.g. the extent of a 'piece', belong specifically to this 'piece', and only more remotely to the whole. This mediacy is no longer inessential, as is that of second-level 'pieces' in the division of a stretch, but is an essential mediacy, to be characterized in terms of the formal nature of the relationship. Obviously similar

---

[1] Prop. 3, p. 464. (*Cf.* p. 470 above.)

483

reasons place *'pieces' of non-independent 'moments' which pertain directly to the whole, further from the whole than the 'moments' are*: this at least is the case if the rule holds that we found valid in the field of intuition, that such 'pieces' can have their immediate foundation only in a 'piece' of the whole. The wider proposition also can be formally expressed: *Abstract parts are further from the whole, are in essence mediate parts, if their need for supplement is satisfied in the sphere of a mere part.* This part can then well either be a 'piece' of the whole, or be in need of further completion. The mediacy in the latter case consists in the fact that the law of supplementation in which the form of foundation resides, points, in the case of the originally mentioned abstract part, to a whole which, in virtue of a new law of supplementation is, and must be, a part of a more comprehensive whole, i.e. of the complete whole, which accordingly only includes the first part mediately. This permits us also to say that *abstract parts of the whole that are not abstract parts of its 'pieces', are nearer to the whole than the abstract parts of the 'pieces'.*

These thoughts can only be meant, and are only meant, to count as mere indications of a future treatment of the theory of Wholes and Parts. A proper working out of the pure theory we here have in mind, would have to define all concepts with mathematical exactness and to deduce all theorems by *argumenta in forma*, i.e. mathematically. Thus would arise a complete law-determined survey of the *a priori* possibilities of complexity in the form of wholes and parts, and an exact knowledge of the relations possible in this sphere. That this end can be achieved, has been shown by the small beginnings of purely formal treatment in our present chapter. In any case the progress from vaguely formed, to mathematically exact, concepts and theories is, here as everywhere, the precondition for full insight into *a priori* connections and an inescapable demand of science.

§ 25 *Additions regarding the 'piecing' of wholes through the 'piecing' of their 'moments'*

We may end with an additional observation that is perhaps not without interest.

It is an analytic proposition that 'pieces' considered in relation to the whole whose 'pieces' they are, cannot be founded on each other, either one-sidedly or reciprocally, and whether as wholes or in respect of their parts. But, on the other hand, we cannot at all conclude from the content of our basic definition that it is impossible that 'pieces' should enter into foundational relationships in regard to a more comprehensive whole in which they all count as non-independent 'moments'. In fact, however, we find no such example in the field of pure intuition and self-evidence that is open to us, and remarkable relationships among parts depend on this circumstance in precisely this field. We can in fact enunciate a proposition which is in a wider sense phenomenological. To each 'piece' in a relative abstraction there corresponds a 'piece' in each of its relative concreta, so that the mutually exclusive 'pieces' of the former serve to ground mutually exclusive pieces in each of the latter. In other words: *the fragmentation of a non-independent 'moment' conditions a fragmentation of the concrete whole, in so far as the mutually exclusive 'pieces', without themselves entering into a foundational relation with one another, attract new 'moments' to themselves in virtue of which they are singly distributed to 'pieces' of the whole.*

A few examples will make this clear. The fragmentation of the quasi-spatial extensity of a visual content, which endures unchanged, but which is considered in abstraction from its temporality, also effects a 'piecing' of this visual content itself. The same holds of spatial data of intuition in respect of spatial 'piecing'. The separated spatial pieces serve to 'found' mutually independent complementary 'moments'. The colouring of one piece is not, e.g., 'founded' upon the colouring of any other. To this extent one may say, further, that the complementary moments are themselves fragmented by the fragmentation of the spatiality which serves to 'found' them, or that they divide themselves piecemeal over the spatial 'pieces'. The colourings of the 'pieces' stand in the same whole-part relations (exclusion, inclusion, intersection) as the 'pieces' themselves. This peculiar fact, that here the 'piecing' of a 'moment' simultaneously entails a 'piecing' of the whole, obviously rests on the fact that the *'pieces' of the 'moment' do not serve to 'found' one another even within the more inclusive whole*, but that they need new 'moments' to 'found' them in each case: it also depends on the further fact that these new 'moments' themselves only find their needed foundation in the 'pieces', not mutually in one another.

The same is the case with intuitive time-wholes. If we fragment the duration of a concrete course of events, we have fragmented this course of events itself: to the segments of time, segments of movement correspond ('movement' being understood in the widest Aristotelian sense). The same holds in the case of rest: rest too has its segments that count as 'pieces' in the sense of our pronouncements, since rest during one lapse of time, and rest during any other lapse, do not stand in any evident foundational relation to each other.

The case is quite different if, instead of limiting ourselves to the sphere of essential data to be studied by way of intuition, we rather bring our consideration to bear on empirically-real natural connections.

This transition, however, demands a widening of our notions. We have related all our conceptual constructions to the pure sphere of essence, the laws of foundation were subject to pure laws of essence, the parts were *essentially* one in the whole, as a result of *a priori* connections of the Ideas corresponding to the parts and 'moments'. But nature with all its thing-like contents certainly also has its *a priori*, whose systematic elaboration and development is the still unperformed task of an ontology of nature. It is no doubt clear from the start that natural laws in the ordinary sense do not belong to this *a priori*, this pure universal 'form' of nature, that they have the character, not of truths of essence, but of truths of fact. Their universality is not a 'pure' or 'unconditioned' universality, and just so the 'necessity' of all the thing-histories which fall under them is infected with 'contingency'. Nature with all its physical laws is a fact that could well have been otherwise. If we now treat natural laws, without regard to their infection with contingency, as true laws, and apply to them all the pure concepts we have formed, we arrive at modified Ideas of *empirical* 'foundation', of *empirical* wholes, *empirical* independence and non-independence. If, however, we conceive the Idea of a factual nature as such, of which our own nature is an individual specification, we arrive at universal Ideas, not bound down to *our* nature, of an empirical whole, empirical independence etc. These Ideas are plainly constitutive of the Idea of a nature in general, and must fit, together with the essential relations pertaining to them, into a universal ontology of nature.

All this being presumed, we return to our specific question.

While we found no example in the material sphere of essence where a fragmentation of a non-independent 'moment', e.g. of the spatial and temporal 'moment', entailed a fragmentation of the concrete whole, the matter is different in the field of all empirically real connections of coexistence and succession. This is clear if we consider the sense of empirical relations of necessity, which associate things spatially and temporally separate. If a particular causal law involves that a concrete process of change in a time-segment t_1–t_0, is necessarily succeeded by a certain new process in the neighbouring time-segment, t_2–t_1, the former thereby loses independence in regard to the latter. Let us assume now that particular laws of this sort, whose essence it is only to be knowable empirically, belong ontologically, i.e. in virtue of the Idea of Nature as such, to each concrete process of change, to which they assign certain necessary, temporally contiguous consequences, and let us make the still stronger assumption that each such process must itself be a necessary consequence of previous antecedents. To assume all this is to hold that each concrete natural process of change lacks independence in respect of the more embracing temporal whole in which it is realized, and that no fragmentation of a time-stretch therefore conditions a fragmentation of the correlated *concrete* temporal whole. But the limitation to processes of change is unnecessary and, strictly speaking, not even allowable. As mechanics treats of rest and movement from a single viewpoint, and includes rest as a special limiting case of motion in its laws, so one should proceed analogously with concepts extended in the Aristotelian manner. Even the imaginary case of fixed rest isolated from the whole world is not immune from the properly formulated principle of causality. If we conceive of any time-lapse, however small, as filled with a rigidly unchanging concrete content (if indeed the Idea of Nature permits such a conceptual possibility) and if we conceive of the whole of reality as reduced, during this period to such a changeless being, then the causal principle certainly demands that such being should persist unchanged *a parte post* for all eternity (though, *a parte ante*, it may have arisen out of eternal rest or law-governed change). In regard to these causal connections, from which nothing temporal is immune, we may therefore say that a fragmentation of its time aspects never entails a fragmentation of a concrete temporal whole. The 'moments' needed to complete its time-sections are indeed separated as these sections are, but such separation effects no fragmentation in the temporal concretum: this is prevented by the reciprocal causal 'foundation' of its temporally sundered contents.

The case is of course similar at least in regard to the spatial fragmentation of those wholes in which spatial and temporal extension are coincident, so that each fragmentation of the one 'moment' is attended by a fragmentation of the other, and vice versa. The fragmentation of the spatial aspect of a movement is as little able, as is the fragmentation of its temporal aspect, to effect a fragmentation of the movement itself.

These considerations also mean that in objective time, the time of nature, time-stretches that *in abstracto* had the character of 'pieces' in respect of each duration that embraced them, lose their mutual independence, if we treat them in relation to a concretely occupied temporal unity of which they are non-independent 'moments'. The proposition that each objective temporal duration is a mere part of time, which cannot only be extended in both directions *in infinitum*, but also *has* to be so, is, as one readily sees, a mere consequence of causality, and therefore related to the content of time. This consequence makes a temporal part non-independent, not merely in relation to its own filling, but also in relation to neighbouring parts of time and their contents. This non-independence of temporal parts, and their reciprocal 'foundation', is governed by laws which not merely associate time-stretches with time-stretches, but associate concretely occupied temporal wholes with other similar temporal wholes. Since in these laws, among the variables representing 'moments' of time-occupying contents, times or time-stretches also figure as mutually dependent variables, such time-stretches likewise acquire a mediate relation of 'foundedness' in regard to a more inclusive concrete unity. The same of course holds of bits of space in relation to more embracing spatial unities, and ultimately to the whole infinite space of nature. The proposition that each bit of space requires to be extended in all directions, or, as we should put it more precisely, requires the *real* possibility of being so extended and as far as the one infinite space goes, is a consequence of certain causal laws, more precisely of certain natural laws. The fact that we freely extend spatial and temporal stretches in imagination, that we can put ourselves in imagination at each fancied boundary of space or time while ever new spaces and times emerge before our inward gaze – all this does not prove the relative 'foundedness' of bits of space and time, and so does not prove space and time to be *really* infinite, nor even that they *can* really be so. This can only be proved by a law of causation which presupposes, and so requires, the possibility of being extended beyond any given boundary.

INVESTIGATION IV

The Distinction Between Independent and Non-Independent Meanings and the Idea of Pure Grammar

INTRODUCTION

IN the following discussions we wish to turn our gaze to a fundamental difference in the field of meanings, a difference which lies hidden behind insignificant grammatical distinctions, such as those between categorematic and syncategorematic expressions, or between closed and unclosed expressions. To clear up such distinctions will enable us to apply our general distinction between independent and non-independent objects in the special field of meanings, so that the distinction treated in our present Investigation may be called that of independent and non-independent meanings. It yields the necessary foundation for the essential categories of meaning on which, as we shall briefly show, a large number of *a priori* laws of meaning rest, laws which abstract from the objective validity, from the real (*real*) or formal truth, or objectivity of such meanings. These laws, which govern the sphere of complex meanings, and whose role it is to divide sense from nonsense, are not yet the so-called laws of logic in the pregnant sense of this term: they provide pure logic with the *possible meaning-forms*, i.e. the *a priori* forms of complex meanings significant as wholes, whose 'formal' *truth* or '*objectivity*' then depends on these pregnantly described 'logical laws'. The former laws guard against *senselessness* (*Unsinn*), the latter against formal or analytic *nonsense* (*Widersinn*) or formal absurdity. If the laws of pure logic establish *what an object's possible unity requires in virtue of its pure form*, the laws of complex meanings set forth the requirements of merely *significant unity*, i.e. the *a priori* patterns in which meanings belonging to different semantic categories can be united to form one meaning, instead of producing chaotic nonsense.

Modern grammar thinks it should build exclusively on psychology and other empirical sciences. As against this, we see that the old idea of a universal, or even of an *a priori grammar*, has unquestionably acquired a foundation and a definite sphere of validity, from our pointing out that there are *a priori* laws which determine the possible forms of meaning. The extent to which there may be other discoverable fields of the grammatical *a priori* goes beyond our present field of interest. Within pure logic, there is a field of laws indifferent to all objectivity to which, in distinction from 'logical laws' in the usual pregnant sense, the name of 'logico-grammatical laws' can be justifiably given. Even more aptly we can oppose *the pure theory of semantic forms* to *the pure theory of validity* which presupposes it.

§ 1 *Simple and complex meanings*

We start from the immediately obvious division of meanings into *simple* and *complex*, which corresponds to the grammatical distinction between simple and complex expressions or locutions. A complex expression is an expression, to the extent that it has *one* meaning; as a complex *expression* it is made up of parts which are themselves expressions, and which as such have their own meanings. If we read of 'a man of iron' or 'a king who wins the love of his subjects' etc., we are impressed by such part-expressions or part-meanings as those of *man, iron, king, love* etc.

If we now find further part-meanings in such part-meanings, meanings may again come forward as parts of these, but this can obviously not go on *in infinitum*. Continued division must ultimately lead to simple, elementary meanings. That there really are such simple meanings is shown by the indubitable case of *something*. The presentative experience we have when we understand this word is undoubtedly complex, but its meaning shows no sign of complexity.

§ 2 *Whether complexity of meanings merely reflects complexity of objects*

Clear as this seems, we are still beset by varied doubts and questions.

We may ask first whether the complexity or simplicity of meanings[1] merely reflects the complexity or simplicity of the objects which such meanings significantly present. One might at first imagine so: the presentation presents the object, and is its mental

---

[1] We could equally say: 'of presentations'. For plainly an answer to the more specialized question also answers the more general question relating to presentations or objectifying acts as such.

picture. Very little reflection will, however, show how deceptive such a picture-analogy is, both in this and in many other cases, and that its presumed parallelism holds from neither side. In the first place, complex meanings may present simple objects. An example as clear as it is decisive is the expression 'simple object' itself. It is quite indifferent whether there is, or is not, any such object.[1]

It is true, conversely, that simple meanings can 'present' complex objects, can refer to them in significant fashion. One might doubt (though I do not think correctly) whether the simple names in our above examples ('man', 'iron', 'king' etc.), really give expression to simple meanings, but we shall have to count names like 'one' and 'something' as doing so. It is clear that they, in their indefinite reference to all that is possible, will refer to every complex object, even if they refer to it quite indeterminately, or as a mere 'something'.

It is clear, further, that even where a complex meaning refers to a complex object, no part of the object need correspond to each part of the meaning, let alone the other way round. Bolzano's noteworthy example, *a land without mountains*, has indeed been disputed by Twardowski, but this is due to his identification of meaning with the direct, intuitive presentation of the subject, and to his total disregard of that notion of meaning which alone is fundamental in logic. This leads him to take constituents of the meaning (*without mountains*) as 'auxiliary presentations which resemble linguistic roots'.[2]

§3 *Complexity of meanings and complexity of the concrete act of meaning. Implied meanings*

There are, on the other hand, wide ranges of cases where doubt arises *whether a given meaning should count as complex or simple*. If we wish, e.g., to treat the meanings of proper names as simple, we face the objection that in a certain obviously good sense, we can say that a name like 'Schultze', when used of a person *known* to us, helps to present a certain human being, a being possessed of all

---

[1] Twardowski (op. cit. above p. 94) removes the whole basis for making such a distinction when he objects, as against Bolzano (whom we here follow) that there are no simple objects. Cf. Twardowski's own question where he speaks expressly of *presented* objects. We are here dealing with objects of reference as such.

[2] Twardowski, op. cit. p. 98.

the parts and attributes that we think proper to human beings, as well as many individual peculiarities which distinguish him from others. On the other hand, we hesitate to assign partial meanings within such 'proper meaning' to the successively stressed attributes of the thing the name uniquely stands for, the more or less clearly presented object, or even to identify such a 'proper meaning' with a complex meaning of the form 'an A, which is a, b, c...' which we build up step by step as we analyse the content of the idea Schultze objectively.

Closer consideration shows that we must here distinguish *two senses of simplicity and complexity*; simplicity in one sense does not exclude complexity in another. Undoubtedly we must refuse to look on a 'proper meaning' as an articulate, and so complex structure of meanings: we must nonetheless grant that our consciousness of meaning here shows a certain complexity, that surely stands in need of clarification. Everything that later explication and conceptualization coax out of the *Schultze* on whom we confer a name and a certain content, no doubt represents new meanings that were not really (*reell*) implicit as under-emphasized parts in our original meaning. Without doubt, the 'proper meaning' of *Schultze* was simple. It is plain, further, that the presentative content with which Schultze is presented when we name him, can change in many ways, while his proper name goes on performing the same significant role, always naming the same Schultze 'directly'. On the other hand, we are not here dealing with some *chance* presentational addition to our consciousness of meaning, but with facts of presentation that are necessary, even though variable in content; without them our actual meaning could not point to the object it means, and so not really *be* a meaning at all. Using the proper name significantly, we *must* present to ourselves the subject named, in this case the definite person Schultze, and as endowed with some definite content or other. However impalpably, defectively, vaguely, indefinitely we may think of him, presentational content cannot be wholly lacking. The indefiniteness which is here to a large extent inevitable – for even the most intuitively vivid and rich presentation of a real thing (*Dingrealen*) must be in principle one-sided and incomplete – can never be entirely void of content. Its essence plainly involves possibilities of further determination, and these not in *any* direction whatsoever, but in connection with the identical man Schultze whom we mean, and no other. Or what is the same: our consciousness of meaning, taken in its full concreteness, has an essence which involves possibilities of fulfilment and coincidence with *certain* ranges of intuition and no others. This consciousness, even when wholly non-intuitive, must plainly have a certain intentional content, in virtue of which the individual is not given as a quite empty somewhat, but as somehow determinate and typically determinable – determinable whether as a physical thing, an animal, a human being etc. – even if not meant in such capacities.

The consciousness of meaning which attaches to proper names therefore has a certain double-sidedness: there are two directions in which one can here talk of complexity or simplicity. One side fixes the simplicity or complexity of the meaning itself, and here we have the pure essence of meaning as such; to it alone belongs the intentional essence of our concrete, complete meaning-consciousness which, regarded *in specie, is* the meaning. In our case of 'proper meanings' this side is simple. But it necessarily presupposes a wider intentional background of content, for the very reason that the same thing, referred to in the same sense (or univocally named by the same proper name) can be very differently presented, with a variable set of determining marks, and that it *must* be presented with some such set – while the variation and complexity of this set do not touch the meaning itself.

Here we have openings for expositions and for predicative interpretations of meaning, such as we give when we try to answer the question as to how, and as what, the object called 'Schultze' is presented in a given case. Such complicating developments stand in contrast with our original consciousness of meaning, and we must therefore first clarify the essence of our present distinction: the distinction between concrete, meaning-conferring experiences, which are complex or simple as regards their meaning conceived purely *as* meaning, and such experiences as are complex or simple only in a secondary respect, through the presentative content through which one is conscious of the object meant. Plainly, as pointed out above, the meanings which emerge in predicative expositions of what is presented as such, are newly conceived meanings, not in any way really (*reell*) implicit in our original meaning, in our intrinsically simple 'proper meanings'. The proper name P names the object, or its 'proper meaning' means the object, in a single 'ray' as it were, a 'ray' intrinsically uniform, and so not capable of differentiation in respect of the same intentional object. Explicative meanings such as *E which is a*, *Ea which is b*, *Eb which is a* etc., are many-rayed meanings, or are at least put together in several steps and in varying forms, so that they can 'head for' the same object with varying content. Their plurality of levels does not disturb their *unity*: they are unified, complex meanings. The corresponding consciousness of meaning is, on its purely meaning-side, a single act, but also an act that is complex.

We assumed above that the proper name was that of a *known* person. This means that it is functioning normally, and not in the indirect sense of *a certain person called Schultze*. The latter meaning would, of course, be complex.

A similar problem and a similar attempted solution occur in many other substantial meanings, and also in certain adjectival and similar meanings: e.g. *human being, virtue, just* etc. We must observe further that *logical definition*, in which bounds are set to the difficulties of articulate analysis, and above all to shifts in verbal meanings, is of course merely a practical logical artifice, through which meaning cannot properly be said to be demarcated or inwardly articulated. Here, rather, a new meaning, articulate in content, is set over against the existent meaning, as a standard to govern judgements which rely on the meaning in question. To avoid logical dangers, we forbid all judgements in which meanings cannot be replaced by such standard equivalents, and recommend also, as far as possible, the regular use of such standard word-meanings in the work of knowing, or the regulation of the effect on knowledge of our actual meanings, by frequently measuring these latter against such standards and by appropriate habits of use.

Note. The duality of our meaning-intentions as treated in the first edition of this section has received a clearer, phenomenologically more profound treatment in the present edition. The writer had not plumbed the full sense and range of application of the distinction when he first conceived of this book. The careful reader will note that the Sixth Investigation does not give a proper account of it.

§4 *The question of the meaningfulness of 'syncategorematic' components of complex expressions*

The treatment of complex meanings leads at once to a new and fundamental division. Such meanings are, in general, only given to us as meanings of articulate word-complexes. Regarding these one may, however, ask whether each word in such a complex has its own correlated meaning, and whether all verbal articulation and form counts as expressing a corresponding semantic articulation and form. According to Bolzano, 'each word in speech stands for its own presentation, while some stand for entire propositions'.[1] He therefore, without further ado, attributes a peculiar meaning to every conjunction or preposition. On the other hand, one frequently hears of words and expressions that are merely 'synsemantic', i.e. that have no meaning by themselves, but acquire this only in conjunction with other meanings or expressions. One distinguishes between complete and incomplete expressions of presentations, and likewise between complete and incomplete expressions of judgements and of the phenomena of feeling and will, and one bases on such a distinction the notion of the *categorematic* or *syncategorematic* sign. Marty applies the expression 'categorematic sign' (or 'name') to 'all verbal means of designation, that are not merely synsemantic (as, e.g., "the father's", "around", "nonetheless" etc.) but which yet do not themselves completely express a judgement (an assertion), or a feeling or voluntary decision etc. (requests, commands, questions etc.), but merely express a presentation. "The founder of ethics", "a son who has insulted his father" are names.'[2] Since Marty and other writers employ the terms 'syncategorematic' and 'synsemantic' in the same sense of signs 'which only have complete significance together with other parts of speech, whether they help to arouse concepts as mere parts of a name, or contribute to the expression of a judgement (i.e. to a statement) or to that of an emotion or act of will (i.e. to a request or command-sentence) etc.',[3] it would have been more consistent to interpret the notion

---

[1] B. Bolzano, *Wissenschaftslehre* (Sulzbach, 1837), II, §57. 'Presentation' means for Bolzano 'self-existent presentations', which corresponds to our concept of meaning.

[2] A. Marty, 'Über subjektlose Sätze', *Vierteljahrschrift für wis. Philos.*, VIIIth year, p. 293, note.

[3] Marty, 'Über das Verhältnis von Grammatik und Logik', *Symbolae Pragenses* (1893), p. 121, n. 2.

of categorematic expression equally widely. This notion should have been made to cover all *independently significant* or complete expressions of any intentional experience (any 'psychic phenomenon' in Brentano's sense), and a division should have been made then between the categorematic expressions of presentations (i.e. names), the categorematic expressions of judgements (i.e. statements) etc. Whether such a coordination is justified, whether names, e.g., express presentations in the same sense that request-sentences express requests, wish-sentences express wishes etc., and likewise whether the things that names and sentences are said to 'express' are themselves experiences of meaning, or how they stand to meaning-intentions and meanings – all these are questions to which we shall have to devote earnest thought. However this may be, the distinction between categorematic and syncategorematic expressions, and the pleas for its introduction, certainly have justification, and so we are led to conceive syncategorematic words in a manner at variance with the above-mentioned doctrine of Bolzano. Since the distinction between categorematic and syncategorematic words is grammatical, it might seem that the situation underlying it is likewise 'merely grammatical'. We often use several words to express a 'presentation' – this, one might think, depends on chance peculiarities of one's language. The articulation of one's expression may bear no relation to the articulation of meaning. The syncategorematic words which help to build up this expression are, properly speaking, quite meaningless: only the whole expression really has a meaning.

The grammatical distinction, however, permits another interpretation, provided one decides to view the completeness or incompleteness of expressions as reflecting a certain completeness or incompleteness of meanings, the grammatical distinction as reflecting a certain essential semantic distinction.[1] Language has not been led by chance or caprice to express presentations by names involving many words, but by the need to express suitably a plurality of mutually cohering part-presentations, and dependent presentational forms, within the enclosed self-sufficiency of a

---

[1] In his last-mentioned article Marty defines a categorematic sign as one which independently arouses a *complete presentation*, through which an object is named. But the definition of the syncategorematic sign which follows (see above) does not clearly bring out that the grammatical division rests on an essential division in the field of meaning, as Marty certainly thought.

presentational unity.[1] Even a non-independent moment, an intentional form of combination through which, e.g., two presentations unite in a third, can find semantic expression, it can determine the peculiar meaning-intention of a word or complex of words. Clearly we may say that if presentations, expressible thoughts of any sort whatever, are to have their faithful reflections in the sphere of meaning-intentions, then there must be a semantic form which corresponds to each presentational form. This is in fact an *a priori* truth. And if the verbal resources of language are to be a faithful mirror of all meanings possible *a priori*, then language must have grammatical forms at its disposal which give distinct expression, i.e. sensibly distinct symbolization, to all distinguishable meaning-forms.

§ 5 *Independent and non-independent meanings. The non-independence of the sensory and expressive parts of words*

This conception is plainly the only right one. We must not merely distinguish between categorematic and syncategorematic expressions but also between categorematic and syncategorematic *meanings*.[2] It is more significant to speak of *independent* and *non-independent* meanings. It is of course possible that meaning may so shift that an unarticulated meaning replaces one that was originally articulated, so that nothing in the meaning of the total expression now corresponds to its part-expressions. But in this case the expression has ceased to be genuinely complex, and tends, in developed speech, to be telescoped into one word. We no longer count its members as syncategorematic expressions, since we do not count them as expressions at all. We only call significant signs expressions, and we only call expressions complex when they are compounded out of expressions. No one would call the word 'king' a complex expression since it consists of several sounds and syllables. As opposed to this, many-worded expressions

---

[1] The word 'presentation', carefully regarded, does not here mean 'act of presentation', but merely what is presented as such, together with the articulations and forms with which it is present in consciousness. The 'presentational form' is therefore the form of what is presented as such; we must keep this in mind in what follows.

[2] A. Marty recently wrote, in his 'Untersuchungen zur Grundlegung der allgemeinen Grammatik und Sprachphilosophie' (Halle, 1918) of 'autosemantic' and 'synsemantic' signs (pp. 205 *ff.*).

are admittedly complex, since it is part of the notion of a word to express something; the meaning of the word need not, however, be independent. Just as non-independent meanings may occur only as 'moments' of certain independent ones, so the linguistic expression of non-independent meanings may function only as formal constituents in expressions of independent meanings: they therefore become linguistically non-independent, i.e. 'incomplete' expressions.

Our first purely external impression of the difference between categorematic and syncategorematic expressions ranks the syncategorematic parts of expressions on a level with quite different parts of expressions, with the letters, sounds and syllables which are in general meaningless. I say 'in general', since there are many genuine syncategorematic expressions even among these, such as the prefixes and suffixes used in inflexion. But, in the vast majority of cases, they are not parts of an expression *qua* expression, i.e. not its significant parts; they are only parts of the expression as a sensuous phenomenon. Syncategorematic expressions are therefore understood, even when they occur in isolation; they are felt to carry definite 'moments' of meaning-content, 'moments' that look forward to a certain completion which, though it may be indeterminate materially, is formally determined together with the content in question, and is circumscribed and governed by it. But where a syncategorematic expression functions normally, and occurs in the context of an independently complete expression, it has always, as illustration will testify, a *determinate* meaning-relation to our total thought; it has as its meaning a certain non-independent part of this thought, and so makes a definite contribution to the expression as such. That we are right becomes clear when we consider that the same syncategorematic expression can occur in countless compounds in which it always plays the same semantic role. For this reason, in cases of syncategorematic ambiguity, we can reasonably consider, doubt and dispute whether the same conjunction, predicate or relational expression has the same meaning in two contexts or not. To a conjunction like 'but', or to a genitive like 'father's', we can significantly attribute a meaning, but not to a verbal fragment like 'fu'. Both come before us as needing completion, but their needs of completion differ essentially: in the one case the need principally affects the thought rather than the mere expression, in the other case it affects the expression alone or rather the fragmentary expression. The hope is it may *become* an expression, a possible spur to thought. In the successive formation of a complex verbal structure its total meaning gradually gets built up,[1] in the successive formation of a word, the word alone gets built up; only when the word is completed does it house the fleeting thought. In its own way, of course, the verbal fragment evokes thoughts: that it is, e.g., a verbal fragment, and how it may be completed; these are not, however, its meaning. And according as we complete it in differing ways (fu–futile, fuming, fugitive, furry, refuge etc.) the meaning alters, without thereby revealing an element common to this multitude of meanings, that could be taken to be *the* meaning of this common fragment. We search in vain also for a structuring of the individual word-meaning which might in part depend upon the significance of this verbal fragment. It is quite meaningless.

§6 *Other opposed distinctions. Unclosed, abnormally abbreviated and defective expressions*

We must go on to a much-needed clarification of the difference between independent and non-independent meanings, fixing its character more precisely in relation to more general concepts, and connecting with it the dominant fact, the presiding rule in the whole field of meaning. Before we do this, however, it will be useful to separate off the grammatical distinction that formed our starting point from other distinctions confused with it.

Syncategorematic expressions, *qua* non-independent, require some sort of completion, and we therefore also call them 'incomplete expressions'. Talk of 'incompleteness' has, however, another sense, which is not to be confused with the need for completion which is here in question. To show this, we first observe that a division of meanings into independent and non-independent crosses the division into simple and complex. Meanings such as, e.g., *larger than a house*; *beneath God's own sky*; *in*

---

[1] The mode of speech need not be taken as literally as Marty has done in his Untersuchungen, pp. 211 *f.*, as meaning that we build total meanings out of 'bricks' of partial meaning that could also exist separately. That this is a wrong conception is precisely the theme of my further argued doctrine of non-independent meanings. I cannot see how the exposition above can bear such an interpretation, and that it is in any way touched by Marty's objections. See the further discussions below regarding the understanding of isolated syncategorematica.

life's troubles; *but*, *Lord*, *to give thy messengers due honour*, are non-independent meanings, *unitary* despite their plurality of discernible parts. Several non-independent meanings, or meanings partly non-independent and partly independent, can be accordingly associated *in relatively closed units*, which yet manifest, *as wholes*, a character of *non-independence*. This fact of complex non-independent meanings is grammatically registered in the relatively closed unity of complex syncategorematic expressions. Each of these is a single expression, because expressive of a single meaning, and it is a complex expression, because expressive part by part of a complex meaning. It is in relation to *this* meaning that it is a complete expression. If nonetheless we call it incomplete, this depends on the fact that its *meaning*, despite its unity, is in need of completion. Since it can only exist in a wider semantic context, its linguistic expression likewise points to a wider linguistic context, to a completion in speech that shall be independent and closed.

It is quite different in the case of an abnormally abbreviated expression, which gives to thought, whether independent or non-independent, an incomplete, though possibly in the circumstances quite intelligible, expression. We can here point to *defective expressions*, where syntactical members are omitted from a continuous sentential context, although a certain mutual belong-ingness of the *disjecta membra* remains recognizable. The need for completion of such defective utterances differs in kind from the need for the completion of the syncategorematica. Not because the pertinent meaning is non-independent, but because all unitary meaning is absent, such defective talk cannot serve as finished talk, not even as talk at all. If on deciphering a fragmentary inscription we read *Caesar...qui...duabus*, external indications may point to a certain sentential and semantic unity: this indirect thought is not, however, the meaning of the fragment before us. As it stands, it is without unitary meaning, and constitutes no expression: a loose assemblage of partially independent, partially non-independent meanings, together with a side-thought relative but also strange to them, that they may be part of a certain significant unity: that is all that is given.

Talk about expressions that are unclosed, incomplete and requiring completion, therefore plainly covers quite different things. On the one hand, it covers syncategorematic expressions: on the other hand, abnormally abbreviated and, in the limit, defective expressions, which are not so much expressions as expressional fragments. These distinct notions cross one another. An abbreviated expression can be categorematic, a syncategorematic expression gapless etc., etc.

§7 *The conception of non-independent meanings as founded contents*

We have recognized that the seemingly indifferent distinction between categorematic and syncategorematic expressions corresponds to a fundamental division in the realm of meanings. We took the former as our starting-point, but the latter revealed itself as basic, as the prime foundation of the grammatical distinction.

The concept of the *expression*, or of the difference between the merely audible, or sensuous parts of an expression and its partial expressions in the true sense of the word, or, as we may say more pointedly, its *syntactical parts* (roots, prefixes, suffixes,[1] words, conjoined complexes of words), can only be fixed by recurring to a distinction among meanings. If these divide into simple and complex meanings, the expressions which fit them must also be simple or complex, and *this* complexity necessarily leads back to final significant parts, to syntactical parts and so once more to expressions. On the other hand, the analysis of expressions as mere sensuous phenomena also always yields mere sensuous parts, ones that no longer signify. The same is true of the superimposed distinction of expressions into categorematic and syncategorematic. It can at least be described by holding the former to be capable of serving as complete expressions, finished locutions by themselves, whereas the latter cannot. But if one wishes to limit the vagueness of this characterization, and to pin down the sense that is here relevant, as well as the inner ground that enables some expressions, and not others, to stand as finished locutions, one must, as we saw, go back to the semantic realm, and point out there the need of completion that attaches to certain non-independent meanings.

Having called syncategorematic meanings 'non-independent', we have already said where we think the essence of such meanings lies. In our enquiries into non-independent contents in general,

---

[1] In so far as these and the rest have not lost their articulate meanings in the evolution of speech.

we have given a general determination of the concept of non-independence: it is this same non-independence that we have to recognize in the field of meaning. Non-independent contents, we stated above (Inv. III, §§ 5–7), are contents not able to exist alone, but only as parts of more comprehensive wholes. This inability has its *a priori* governing ground in the specific essences of the contents in question. Each non-independence points to a law to the effect that a content of the sort in question, e.g. sort *A*, can exist only in the context of a whole *W* (*AB*...*M*), where *B*...*M* stand for *determinate* sorts of content. 'Determinate', we said, since no law merely asserts connection between the sort *A*, and any other sorts whatever, that an *A* only needs some completion, no matter what. Law involves specific determinateness of context: dependent and independent variables have spheres limited by fixed generic or specific characters. We have mainly employed as examples the concrete things of sensuous intuition. We could, however, have brought in other fields, those of act-experiences and their abstract contents.

Here we are only interested in meanings. We conceived these as ideal unities, but our distinction naturally passed over from the real (*real*) to the ideal realm. In the concrete act of meaning something, there is a moment which corresponds to the meaning which makes up the essential character of this act, i.e. necessarily belongs to each concrete act in which the same meaning is 'realized'. In regard to the division of acts into simple and complex, a concrete act can involve several acts; such partial acts can live in the whole, whether as independent or non-independent parts. An act of meaning, in particular, can *as such* be complex, be made up of acts of meaning. A total meaning then belongs to the whole act, and to each partial act a partial meaning (a part of the meaning that is itself a meaning). A meaning, accordingly, may be called 'independent' when it can constitute the *full, entire meaning of a concrete act of meaning*, 'non-independent', when this is not the case. It can then only be realized in a non-independent part-act in a concrete act of meaning, it can only achieve concreteness in relation to certain other complementary meanings, it can only exist in a meaningful whole. The non-independence of meaning *qua* meaning thus defined determines, in our view, the essence of the syncategorematica.

§8 Difficulties of this conception (a) Whether the non-independence of the meaning does not really only lie in the non-independence of the object meant

We must now consider the difficulties of our conception. We shall first discuss the relation between independence and non-independence of meanings, and independence and non-independence of objects meant. One might for the moment think the former distinction reducible to the latter.[1] Acts which lend meaning refer as 'presentations', as 'intentional' experiences, to objects. If some constituent of an object is non-independent, it cannot be 'presented' in isolation; the corresponding meaning therefore demands a completion, it is itself non-independent. The seemingly obvious principle emerges: categorematic expressions are directed to independent objects, syncategorematic expressions to non-independent ones.

Such a conception is readily seen to be erroneous. The very expression *non-independent moment* provides a decisive counter-example. It is a categorematic expression and yet presents a non-independent object. *Every non-independent object whatever can be made the object of an independent meaning*, and that directly, e.g. *Redness, Figure, Likeness, Size, Unity, Being*. These examples show that independent meanings correspond, not merely to *material* moments of objects, but also to their *categorial forms*, meanings peculiarly directed to these forms and making them their objects: the latter are not for that reason self-existent in the sense of being independent. The possibility of independent meanings directed to non-independent 'moments' is not at all remarkable, when we reflect on the fact that a meaning 'presents' an object, but does not therefore have the character of picturing it, that its essence consists rather in a certain intention, which can be intentionally 'directed' to anything and everything, to what is independent as much as what is non-independent. Anything, everything can be objectified as a thing meant, i.e. can become an intentional object.

[1] We dealt with an analogous, closely related question in §2.

§9 (b) The understanding of isolated syncategorematica

A serious difficulty is occasioned by our understanding of syncategorematic expressions torn from all context. If our notion is right, there can be no such thing: for us the non-independent elements of categorematically closed speech (λόγος) cannot be isolated. How can we possibly treat such elements, as Aristotle treated them, apart from all connection? Under the headings of τὰ ἄνευ συμπλοκῆς, τὰ κατὰ μηδεμίαν συμπλοκὴν λεγόμενα he covers all classes of words, including the syncategorematica.

This objection can first be met by pointing to the distinction between 'authentic' and 'so-to-speak' presentations, or what is here the same, the difference between merely intending and fulfilling meanings. We may in fact say:

Isolated syncategorematica such as *equals, together with, and, or* can achieve no fulfilment of meaning, no intuitive understanding, except in the context of a wider meaning-whole. If we wish to 'be clear' what the word 'equals' means, we must turn to an intuitive equation, we must actually (genuinely) perform a comparison, and following upon this, bring to understanding and fulfilment a sentence of the form $a = b$. If we wish to be clear as to the meaning of the word 'and', we must actually carry out an act of collection, and bring to fulfilment in the aggregate thus genuinely presented a meaning of the form *a and b*. And so in every case. The non-independent status of the fulfilling meaning, which thus necessarily forms part of a fulfilling meaning of wider content, serves to base derived talk about the non-independent status of the intending meaning.[1]

Undoubtedly we have here a correct and valuable thought. We can also express it by saying that *no syncategorematic meaning, no act of non-independent meaning-intention, can function in knowledge outside of the context of a categorematic meaning.* Instead of 'meaning', we could of course say 'expression', in the normal sense of a unity of verbal sound and meaning or sense. But we have to ask whether, since there is a unity-of-coincidence between intending and

---

[1] In our whole exposition 'fulfilment' must of course be taken to cover the opposed state of 'frustration', the phenomenologically peculiar situation in which absurdly combined meanings in a meaningful whole make their incompatibility plain in intuitive clarification and in 'bringing to insight': the intended unity is 'frustrated' in intuitive disunity.

fulfilling meaning in the state of fulfilment, we can look on a fulfilling meaning as non-independent, while an intending meaning is independent. Can we, in other words, hold that talk of non-independence in the case of *intuitively unfulfilled* meanings is merely loose, conditional on non-independence in possible fulfilment? This seems scarcely thinkable, and so we are pushed back to holding that even empty meaning-intentions – the 'non-authentic', 'symbolic' presentations which give sense to an expression apart from any knowledge-function – reveal a difference between independence and non-independence. How can we explain the indubitable fact that isolated syncategorematica, e.g. the isolated word 'and', are understood? They are non-independent as regards their meaning-intention, and this surely means that such intentions can exist only in categorematic contexts: the isolated 'and', the particle torn from its context, ought therefore to be a hollow noise.

We can only resolve our difficulty in the following manner:

A syncategorematic expression torn from context either has not got the meaning it has in categorematic contexts, or it has got it, but has also undergone a *completion of meaning* quite indefinite in content, so that it is an incomplete expression of this momentarily activated, completed meaning. We understand an isolated 'and' either because the indirect, verbally unexpressed thought of *a certain familiar conjunction* gives it an unusual meaning, or because vague, unverbalized presentations of things help us to form a thought of the type *A and B*. In the latter case, the word 'and' is functioning normally to the extent that it is really only an aspect in a complete, inwardly performed meaning-intention, the same aspect as in a combination of categorematic expressions standing for a collection. It is functioning abnormally only in not being connected with other expressions, which give normal utterance to the complementary parts of the meaning here in question.

Our difficulties are thus removed. We may assume that the difference between independent and non-independent meanings affects the realm of meaning-intentions as it affects the realm of fulfilment. We *have* the situation which the possibility of an adequate fit between intention and fulfilment necessarily requires.

§ 10 *A priori laws governing combinations of meanings*

If we relate the distinction between independent and non-independent meanings to the more general distinction between independent and non-independent objects, we are really covering one of the most fundamental facts in the realm of meaning: *that meanings are subject to a priori laws regulating their combination into new meanings.* To each case of non-independent meaning, a law of essence applies – following the principle discussed by us in relation to all non-independent objects whatever – a law regulating the meaning's need of completion by further meanings, and so pointing to the forms and kinds of context into which it must be fitted. Since meanings cannot be combined to form new meanings without the aid of connective forms, which are themselves meanings of a non-independent sort, there are obviously *a priori* laws of essence governing all meaning-combinations. The important fact here before us is not peculiar to the realm of meaning: it plays its part wherever combination occurs. All combinations whatever are subject to pure laws; this holds particularly of all material combinations limited to a single sphere of fact, where the results of combination must occupy the same sphere as the combining members. (This case is opposed to that of formal, 'analytic' combinations, e.g. collections, which are not bound up with the peculiarities of a sphere of fact, nor with the factual essence of their combining members.) In no sphere is it possible to combine items of any and every kind by way of any and every form: the sphere of items sets *a priori* limits to the number of combinatorial forms, and prescribes the general laws for filling them in. That this fact is general should not lessen our obligation to point out such general laws in each given field, and to pursue their unfolding into special laws.

As regards the field of meaning, the briefest consideration will show up our unfreedom in binding meanings to meanings, so that we cannot juggle at will with the elements of a significantly given, connected unity. Meanings only fit together in antecedently definite ways, composing other significantly unified meanings, while other possibilities of combination are excluded by laws, and yield only a heap of meanings, never a single meaning. The impossibility of their combination rests on a law of essence, and is by no means merely subjective. It is not our mere factual incapacity, the compulsion of our mental make-up, which puts it beyond us to realize such a unity. In the cases we here have in mind, the impossibility is rather objective, ideal, rooted in the pure essence of the meaning-realm, to be grasped, therefore, with apodictic self-evidence. The impossibility attaches, to be more precise, not to what is singular in the meanings to be combined, but to the essential *kinds*, the *semantic categories*, that they fall under. This or that meaning is, of course, itself a species, but, relative to a meaning-category, it only counts as an individual specification. In arithmetic, likewise, relatively to numerical forms and laws a numerically definite number is an individual specification. Wherever, therefore, we see the impossibility of combining given meanings, this impossibility points to an unconditionally general law to the effect that meanings belonging to corresponding meaning-categories, and conforming to the same pure forms, should lack a unified result. We have, in short, an *a priori* impossibility.

What we have just said holds of course of the *possibility* of significant combinations as it holds of their impossibility.

To consider an example. The expression 'This tree is green' has unified meaning. If we formalize this meaning (the independent logical proposition) and proceed to the corresponding pure form of meaning, we obtain 'This S is P', an ideal form whose range of values consists solely of independent (propositional) meanings. It is now plain that what we may call the 'materialization' of this form, its specification in definite propositions, is possible in infinitely many ways, but that we are not completely free in such specification, but work confined within definite limits. We cannot substitute any meanings we like for the variables 'S' and 'P'. Within the framework of our form we can change our example 'This tree is green' into 'This gold...', 'This algebraic number...', 'This blue raven etc., is green': any nominal material – in a wide sense of 'nominal material' – can here be inserted, and so plainly can any adjectival material replace the 'P'. In each case we have once more a meaning unified in sense, i.e. an independent proposition of the prescribed form, but if we depart from the categories of our meaning-material, the unitary sense vanishes. Where nominal material stands, any nominal material can stand, but not adjectival, nor relational, nor completed propositional material. But where we have materials from such other categories, other material of the same kind can be put, i.e. always material from the same category and not from another. This holds of all meanings whatsoever, whatever the complexity of their form.

In such free exchange of materials within each category, false, foolish, ridiculous meanings – complete propositions or elements of propositions – may result, but such results will necessarily be unified meanings, or grammatical expressions whose sense can be unitarily realized. When we transgress the bounds of categories, this is no longer true. We can string together words like 'This careless is green', 'More intense is round', 'This house is just like'; we may substitute 'horse' for 'resembles' in a relational statement of the form '*a* resembles *b*', but we achieve only a word-series, in which each word is as such significant, or points to a complete, significant context, but we do not, in principle, achieve a closed unity of sense. This is above all the case when we seek arbitrarily to exchange parts which are themselves formed units within an articulated unit of meaning, or when we replace such parts by others taken at random from other meanings, as, e.g., when we try to replace the antecedent in a hypothetical proposition (a mere element in the total unity that we call '*the* hypothetical proposition') by a nominal element, or one of the members of a disjunction by a hypothetical consequent. Instead of doing this in the concrete, we may also attempt it in the corresponding pure forms of meaning, i.e. propositional forms. We are at once made aware, through *a priori* insight into law, that such intended combinations are ruled out by the very nature of the constituents of the pure patterns in question, that such constituents can only enter into definitely constituted meaning-patterns.

It is plain, finally, that the pure elements of form in a concrete unity of meaning can never change places with the elements to which they give form, and which also give our meaning its relation to things. The specification of unified meaning-forms such as 'An S is p', 'If S is p, Q is r' etc., cannot, in principle, so proceed that abstracted elements of form take the place of the 'terms', i.e. the materials in the meaning-pattern which relate to things. We can construct verbal strings such as 'if the or is green', 'A tree is and' etc., but such strings have no graspable single meanings. It is an analytic truth that the forms in a whole cannot function as its materials, nor vice-versa, and this obviously carries over into the sphere of meanings.

In general we recognize, as we construct and think over such examples, that every concrete meaning represents a fitting together of materials and forms, that each such meaning falls under an ideal pattern that can be set forth in formal purity, and that to each such pattern an *a priori* law of meaning corresponds. This law governs the formation of unitary meanings out of syntactical materials falling under definite categories having an *a priori* place in the realm of meanings, a formation according to syntactical forms which are likewise fixed *a priori*, and which can be readily seen to constitute a fixed system of forms. Hence arises the great task equally fundamental for logic and for grammar, of setting forth the *a priori* constitution of the realm of meanings, of investigating the *a priori* system of the formal structures which leave open all material specificity of meaning, in a 'form-theory of meanings'.

§11 *Objections. Modifications of meaning which are rooted in the essence of expressions or meanings*

We must now take account of possible objections. One must not be led astray by the fact that meanings of any category, even syncategorematic forms like *and*, can be put into the subject-position otherwise occupied by substantival meanings. If one looks closely, one sees that this happens by a *modification of meaning*, so that what replaces a name is itself really nominal: a meaning differing in syntactical type (an adjectival or merely formal meaning) has not been simply transplanted. We have such a case, e.g., in statements like '*If* is a conjunction', '*And* is a non-independent meaning'. The *words* certainly occupy the subject-position, but their meaning is plainly not the same as they have in an ordinary context. That each word and expression can, by a *change of meaning*, come to occupy every place in a categorematic whole, is not remarkable. What we have in mind here is not a verbal but a semantic compounding, or a compounding of words in which meanings remain constant. Logically considered, all shifts of meaning are to be adjudged abnormal. Our logical interest, oriented towards unitary selfsameness of meaning, demands constancy in the meaning-function. It naturally happens, however, that *certain meaning-transformations belong to the grammatically normal stock-in-trade of every language*. Verbal context will at least make a modified meaning readily intelligible, and, if the motives for modification are pervasively general, rooted, e.g., in the general character of expressions, or in the pure essence of the realm of meanings, then such abnormalities will recur regularly, and their logical abnormality will win a grammatical sanction.

Here belongs the *suppositio materialis* of scholastic parlance. Every expression, whether its normal meaning is categorematic or syncategorematic, can also function as its own name, i.e. it will name itself as a grammatical phenomenon. If we say '"The earth is round" is a statement', our subject-presentation is not the meaning of the statement, but a presentation of the statement as such. We do not judge about the *fact* that the earth is round, but about the *indicative sentence*: this sentence itself functions abnormally as its own name. If we say '"And" is a conjunction', the nuance of meaning normally corresponding to the word 'and' is not put into the position of subject: this is occupied by an independent meaning directed to the *word* 'and'. In this abnormal reading, 'and' is not really a syncategorematic, but a categorematic expression: it names itself as a word.

We have an exact analogue of *suppositio materialis* when an expression has, *instead of its normal meaning, a presentation of this meaning* (i.e. a meaning directed to this meaning as object). This is the case, e.g., if we say '*And, but, greater than* are non-independent meanings'. Here we should generally say that the meanings of the words 'and', 'but', 'greater than' are non-independent. Just so in the utterance '*Man, table, house*, are thing-concepts', presentations of these concepts function as subjects, and not the concepts themselves. In these, as in the previous cases, the change of meaning regularly shows itself in our written expression: quotation marks, or what may be suitably called other *heterogrammatical modes of expression*, are employed. All expressions to which 'modifying' rather than 'determining' predicates attach, function abnormally in the above described or some similar sense: the normal sense of our utterance is to be replaced by another, in a more or less complex fashion, so that, however it may otherwise be built up, its apparent subject (on a normal interpretation) is replaced by some sort of *presentation* of itself, an ideal presentation, perhaps, in the sense of pure logic, or an empirical-psychological one, or a purely phenomenological one. We say, e.g., 'The centaur is a poetic fiction'. With a little circumlocution we can instead say: 'Our ideas of centaurs, i.e. subjective presentations with the meaning-content *centaur*, are poetic fictions'. The predicates 'is', 'is not', 'is true', 'is false' modify meaning. They do not express properties of the apparent subject, but of the corresponding subject-meaning. 'That $2+2 = 5$ is false' means that the thought is a false thought, the proposition a false proposition.

Leaving aside the examples in the last paragraph, where the modifying presentation is subjective in a psychological or a phenomenological sense, and understanding our analogue of *suppositio materialis* with its previously stated limitations, we note that we are here dealing with alterations in the content, or rather *act of meaning, that have their roots in the ideal nature of the meaning-realm itself*. They have their roots in changes of meaning, in a certain other sense of 'meaning' that abstracts from expressions, but which is not unlike that of arithmetical talk of 'transforming' arithmetical patterns. In the realm of meaning there are *a priori* laws allowing meanings to be transformed into new meanings while preserving an essential kernel. Here belongs the transformation that any meaning can undergo, by an *a priori* rule, when there is a 'direct presentation' of it, i.e. an intrinsic reference to its original meaning. Its verbal expression will then function, with modified meaning, as a 'proper name' of its original meaning. This modification, having *a priori* universality, conditions a large class of equivocations in *general grammar*, changes in the verbal act of meaning which go far beyond the peculiarities of empirical languages. In our further Investigations we shall have more chances of meeting similar modifications rooted in the essence of meanings, the important cases, e.g., where whole statements are 'nominalized' so as to appear in the subject-position, and so too in any position that requires nominal members. We may point to cases where adjectival predicates or attributes are 'nominalized', so as to dispel any doubt aroused by things said in our previous section. An adjective has, as it were, a predicative, or, more generally, an attributive role; it functions normally, in its 'original', unmodified meaning in, e.g., our above example 'This tree is green'. It remains intrinsically unchanged – apart from its syntactical role – if we say 'This green tree'. Such a change in form as opposed to the stuff of syntax, which occurs also when, e.g., a nominal presentation functioning as subject takes on the object-role, or a proposition functioning as antecedent takes on the role of a consequent, must first be pinned down: it is a central theme in describing pervasive structures in the meaning-realm. But an adjectival meaning, in the sense of syntactical material not affected by changing from a predicative to an attributive role, can yet undergo a modification when, from functioning merely as an attributive aspect of some nominal meaning, it is itself nominalized, i.e. made into a name, as, e.g., in 'Green is a colour' and 'Being green (Greenness) is a differentiation of Being coloured (of Colour)'. These two modes of speech do not mean quite the same, despite shifting ambiguities, since in one case a non-independent side of a concrete object's content may be meant, while in the other case we mean a nominalization of the being which is the correlate of the predicativity attaching to the predicate member of a categorical predication and applied to its positing of the subject. The same word 'green' therefore changes its meaning in such nominalizations: its written expression [in German] with its initial capital, indicates what is common to such modifications, which capital is by no means logically or grammatically pointless. The original and the nominalized meaning (*green* and *Green*, *is green* and *Being-green*) plainly have an essential moment, an identical kernel, in common. This kernel is an abstractum having several forms *qua* kernel: these forms are to be distinguished from the syntactical forms which already presuppose kernels, together with their forms *qua* kernels, as their syntactical materials. If the form *qua* kernel of an adjectival kernel or kernel-content yields syntactical material of nominal type, then such determinately constructed nominal meanings can perform every syntactical function which requires nominal meanings for its syntactical materials in accordance with formal meaning-laws. This will suffice as an indication. Closer treatment belongs in a systematic setting forth of our theory of forms.

§12 *Nonsense and absurdity*

One must, of course, distinguish the law-governed incompatibilities to which the study of syncategorematica has introduced us, from the other incompatibilities illustrated by the example of 'a round square'. As said in our *First Investigation*,[1] one must not

[1] §15.

confound the senseless (or nonsensical) with the absurd (or 'counter-sensical'), though we tend to exaggerate and call the latter 'senseless', when it is rather a sub-species of the significant. The combination 'a round square' really yields a unified meaning, having its mode of 'existence' or being in the *realm of ideal meanings, but it is apodictically evident* that no existent object can correspond to such an existent meaning. But if we say 'a round or', 'a man and is' etc., there exist no meanings which correspond to such verbal combinations as their expressed sense. The coordinated words give us the indirect idea of *some* unitary meaning they express, but it is apodictically clear that no such meaning can exist, that significant parts of these sorts, thus combined, cannot consist with each other in a unified meaning. This indirect notion would not itself be accepted as the meaning of such verbal complexes. When an expression functions normally, it evokes its meaning: when understanding fails, its sensuous similarity to understood, meaningful speech will evoke the inauthentic notion of a 'certain' pertinent meaning, since the meaning itself is what is precisely missing.

The difference between the two incompatibilities is plain. In the *one* case certain partial meanings fail to assort together in a unity of meaning as far as the objectivity or truth of the total meaning is concerned. An object (e.g. a thing, state of affairs) which unites all that the unified meaning conceives as pertaining to it by way of its 'incompatible' meanings, neither exists nor can exist, though the meaning itself exists. Names such as 'wooden iron' and 'round square' or sentences such as 'All squares have five angles' are names or sentences as genuine as any. In the *other* case the possibility of a unitary meaning itself excludes the possible coexistence of certain partial meanings in itself. We have then only an indirect idea, directed upon the synthesis of such partial meanings in a single meaning, and at the same time see that no object can ever correspond to such an idea, i.e. that a meaning of the intended sort cannot exist. The judgement of incompatibility is in one case connected with ideas, in another with objects; ideas of ideas enter the former unity of judgement, whereas plain ideas enter the latter.

The *grammatical* expression of the *a priori* incompatibilities and compatibilities here in question, as of the pertinent laws governing meaning-combinations, must in part be found in the grammatical rules governing the parts of speech. If we ask why our language allows certain verbal combinations and disallows others, we are to a large extent referred to contingent linguistic habits, to matters of mere fact concerning language, which develop in one way in one speech-community and another way in another. In part, however, we encounter the essential difference of independent and non-independent meanings, and, closely involved therewith, the *a priori* laws of the combination and transformation of meanings, laws which must be more or less revealed in every developed language, both in its grammar of forms and in the related class of grammatical incompatibilities.

§13 *The laws of the compounding of meanings and the pure logico-grammatical theory of forms*

The task of an accomplished science of meanings would be to investigate the law-governed, essence-bound structure of meanings and the laws of combination and modification of meaning which depend upon these, also to reduce such laws to the least number of independent elementary laws. We should obviously also need to track down the primitive meaning-patterns and their inner structures, and, in connection with these, to fix the pure categories of meaning which circumscribe the sense and range of the indeterminates – the 'variables' in a sense quite close to that of mathematics – that occur in such laws. What formal laws of combination may achieve, can be made fairly plain by arithmetic. There are definite forms of synthesis, through which, quite in general or in certain definite conditions, two numbers give rise to new numbers. The 'direct operations' $a+b$, ab, a^b yield resultant numbers unrestrictedly, the 'inverse operations, $a-b$, a/b, $b\sqrt{a}, ^b\log a$, only in certain conditions. That this is the case must be laid down by an *assertion* or rather a *law of existence*, and perhaps proved from certain primitive axioms. The little we have so far been able to indicate has made plain that there are similar laws governing the existence or non-existence of meanings in the semantic sphere, and that in these laws meanings are not free variables, but are bound down to the range of varying categories, all arising out of the nature of the sphere in question.

In the pure logic of meanings, whose higher aim is the laws of objective validity for meanings (to the extent that such validity depends purely on semantic form), *the theory of the essential meaning-structures, and the laws of their formal constitution, provide the needed foundation.* Traditional logic, with its theories of concepts and judgements, offers us a few isolated starting-points, without being clear as to the end to be aimed at, either in general or in respect of the pure Idea of meaning. Plainly the theory of the elementary structures and the concrete patterns of 'judgement' – here understood as 'propositions' – will comprise the whole form-theory of meanings, each concrete meaning-pattern being either a proposition or a possible element in propositions. We must note that the exclusion of the 'material of knowledge', to which pure logic is by its very sense committed, obliges us to keep out everything which could give semantic forms (types, patterns) a definite relation to factual spheres of being. Everywhere indefinitely general presentations of factual material, definitely determined only in respect of semantic category, e.g. nominal, adjectival, propositional etc., must do duty for contentful concepts and even for the highest of such concepts, e.g. physical thing, spatial thing, mental thing etc.

Our first task, therefore, in a purely logical form-theory of meanings, is to lay down the *primitive* forms of meaning with the requisite purity just described. *We must fix the primitive forms of independent meanings, of complete propositions with their internal articulations, and the structures contained in such articulations.* We must fix, too, the primitive forms of *compounding* and *modification* permitted by the essence of different categories of possible elements. (We must note that complete propositions can become members of other propositions.) After this, we must systematically survey a boundless multitude of further forms, all derivable by way of repeated compounding or modification.

The forms to be established are naturally 'valid', which here means that, however specified, they will yield real meanings, meanings real as meanings. To each such primitive form there belongs, therefore, *an a priori law of existence*, to the effect that each meaning-combination conforming to such a form genuinely yields a unified meaning, provided only that its terms, the Form's indeterminates or variables, belong to certain semantic categories. The *deduction of derived forms* must also *pro tanto* be a deduction of their validity, and laws of existence will, therefore, also relate to these, but they will be deduced from those relating to the primitive forms. Any two propositions yield, when combined in the form

M and N, another proposition, any two adjectives another adjective (again one meaning that can stand as a complex but unitary attribute or predicate). To any two propositions, *M*, *N*, there belong, likewise, the primitive connective forms *If M then N, M or N*, so that the result again is a proposition. To any nominal meaning *S*, and any adjectival meaning *p*, there belongs the primitive form *Sp* (e.g. *red house*), the result being a new meaning fixed by law in the category of nominal meaning. We could in this manner give many other examples of primitive connective forms. We must remember, in stating all the laws that hold here, and in conceiving categorial Ideas of *proposition, nominal presentation, adjectival presentation*, which determine the variables of the laws, to abstract from the changing syntactical forms that such meanings have in given cases, and that they have to have in some determinate form. We speak of the same name, whether it occupies the subject-position or serves as a correlated object, of the same adjective, whether used predicatively or attributively, of the same proposition, whether used as a free unit or as a conjunctive, disjunctive, or hypothetical antecedent or consequent, or whether occupying this or that place as a member in a complex propositional unity. We thus fix plainly the much used, but never scientifically clarified, talk about *terms* in traditional logic. In the formal laws which enter the purview of this logic,[1] as in our own laws of structures, such 'terms' function as variables; the categories circumscribing the range of their variability are categories of terms. The scientific pinning down of these categories is plainly one of the first tasks of our doctrine of forms.

If we now make gradual substitutions in the primitive forms set forth, and for a simple term repeatedly substitute a combination exemplifying the same forms, and if we always reapply our primitive existential law, we arrive at ever new forms, of deductively proven validity, encapsulated in one another with any degree of complexity. Thus for the conjunctive combination of propositions one can substitute:

(*M* and *N*) and *P*
(*M* and *N*) and (*P* and *Q*)
{(*M* and *N*) and *P* } and *Q*

---

[1] The genuine contribution traditional logic makes to pure logic including the whole logic of the syllogism, is part of the logic of propositional meanings (or 'apophantic' logic).

etc., etc., and so for the disjunctive and hypothetical combination of propositions, and for other modes of combinations in any other semantic categories. We see at once that the compoundings go on *in infinitum*, in a manner permitting comprehensive oversight, that each new form remains tied to the same semantic category, the same field of variability as its terms, and that, as long as we stay in this field, all framable combinations of meaning snecessarily *exist*, i.e. must represent a unified sense. We see also that the relevant existential propositions are obvious deductive consequences of an existential proposition with the primitive form. Instead of constantly reapplying the same mode of combination, we can plainly vary our procedure at will, and combine different forms of combination in our construction, always within legally allowed limits, and so conceive an infinity of complex forms legally engendered. As we formulate these facts in consciousness, we gain insight *into the a priori constitution of the meaning-realm in respect of all those forms which have their a priori origin in its basic forms*.

This insight, and the final comprehensive insight into the formal constitution of the *whole* semantic realm, is, of course, the one aim of such investigations. It would be stupid to hope for worthwhile rules for the compounding of meanings (or rules for the grammatical compounding of expressions) from the formulation of semantic types, and the existential laws relating to them. There is no temptation here to depart from the line of correctness, hence no practical interest in determining it scientifically. *Nonsense* stands so immediately revealed, with each deviation from normal forms, that we hardly fall into such deviations in the practice of thought and speech. The theoretical interest of the systematic investigation of all possible meaning-forms and primitive structures, is all the greater. We, in fact, rise to the insight that all possible meanings are subject to a fixed *typic* of categorial structures built, in *a priori* fashion, into the general Idea of meaning, that *a priori* laws govern the realm of meaning, whereby all possible concrete meaning-patterns systematically depend on a small number of primitive forms, fixed by laws of existence, out of which they flow by pure construction. This last generalization, through its *a priori*, purely categorial character, brings to scientific awareness a basic chapter in the constitution of 'theoretical reason'.

Additional note. I talked above of compounding and *modification*.

The rules of modification also have a place in the sphere we must define. What we mean is shown by the analogue of *suppositio materialis* considered above. Other instances are differences of contextual functioning, of *a priori* syntactical position, as when a name functioning as subject shifts to the object-place. These differences are not easy to elucidate: they are mixed up with empirical factors, and terminate in case-forms and syntactical forms of grammar. The difference between the attributive and predicative functioning of adjectival meanings, as well as similar matters, have here their place. (The investigation of the form-doctrine of meanings announced in our First Edition, and since expounded with many improvements in my lectures at Göttingen since 1901, will shortly, I hope, be laid before a wider public in my *Jahrbuch für Philosophie und phänomenologische Forschung*.)

§14 *Laws which discourage nonsense and laws which discourage absurdity. The Idea of a grammar of pure logic*

The formal laws of meaning just discussed, which serve merely to separate the realms of sense and nonsense, must in an extended sense certainly count as laws of formal logic. They will, however, be the last things one will think of where 'logical laws' are in question: this term only suggests the quite different laws, infinitely more interesting in our cognitive practice, that are concerned only with significant (i.e. not-nonsensical) meanings, and with their objective possibility and truth. Let us look into the relation of these two types of law.

The *a priori* laws pertinent to the constitution of the essential forms of meaning, leave quite open whether meanings built on such forms have objects or not, or whether (when they are pro-positional forms) they yield possible truth or not. As said above, these laws have the mere function of separating sense from non-sense. The word 'nonsense' – let us stress it again – must be understood in its literal, strict sense. A heap of words like 'King but or like and' cannot be understood as a unit: each word has sense in isolation, but the compound is senseless. These laws of sense, or, normatively put, laws of the avoidance of nonsense, *direct logic to the abstractly possible forms of meaning, whose objective value it then becomes its first task to determine*. This logic does by setting up the *wholly different* laws which distinguish a formally consistent from a formally inconsistent, i.e. absurd, sense.

The consistency or absurdity of meanings expresses *objective*, i.e. *a priori*, possibility (consistency, compatibility) as opposed to objective impossibility (incompatibility); it expresses, in other words, the possibility or impossibility *of the being of the objects meant* (compatibility or incompatibility of the objective determinations meant) to the extent that this depends on the intrinsic essence of meanings, and is seen from this essence with apodictic evidence. This contrast between objectively, semantically consistent sense and absurdity, has been notionally opposed and set apart from the contrast between sense and nonsense, but we must observe that, in loose, common speech, the two contrasts are confused, and every absurdity, even every affront to empirical truth, is readily called 'nonsense'. We have also to draw a line between *material* (*synthetic*) absurdity and *formal, analytic absurdity*. In the former case, concepts with content (first-order material kernels of meaning) must be given, as is the case, e.g., in the proposition 'A square is round' and in all false propositions of pure geometry, while the latter covers every purely formal, objective incompatibility, grounded in *the pure essence of the semantic categories*, without regard to any material content of knowledge. (There is an analogous division within the contrasted concept of a consistent sense.) Laws such as that of Contradiction, Double Negation or the Modus Ponens are, normatively restated, *laws of the avoidance of formal absurdity*. They show us what holds for objects in general in virtue of their pure 'thought-form', i.e. what can be said regarding the objective validity of meanings on a basis purely of the meaningful form in which we think them, and in advance of all objective matters signified. These laws may not be violated if falsehood is not to result, even before objects in their factual particularity have been taken into account. They are, in the sense of our *Third Investigation* (III, §§ 11 f.) 'analytic' laws, as opposed to the synthetic *a priori* laws which contain non-formal concepts, and depend on these for their validity. In the sphere of analytic laws as such, these formal laws, with their objective validity reposing on pure categories of meaning, are distinct from ontological-analytic laws, which rest on formal-ontological categories (such as object, property, plurality etc.) and they define sharply a second, narrower notion of the analytic. We may call it the *apophantic analytic*, the analytic of *apophantic logic*. In part, but only in part, relations of equivalence link the two sets of laws, but we cannot go into this further here.

If we now abstract from all questions of objective validity, and confine ourselves to the *a priori* which has its roots purely in the generic essence of meaning as such, if we confine ourselves to the discipline that our present Investigation has illuminated, in its probing of primitive meaning-structures, primitive articulations and combinations, as well as in the operational laws of meaning-compounding and meaning-modification which rest on these – we recognize the undoubted soundness of the idea of a *universal grammar* conceived by the rationalists of the seventeenth and eighteenth century. What has been hinted at in this regard in our *Introduction*, scarcely needs fuller exposition. The older grammarians instinctively concentrated attention on this sphere of laws, even if they were unable to bring it to full clarity. Even in the sphere of grammar there are fixed standards, *a priori* norms that may not be transgressed. As in the proper sphere of logic, the *a priori* element separates itself off from the empirically and practically logical, so in the grammatical sphere the so-called purely grammatical, i.e. the *a priori* element or 'idealized form of speech', as it is well called, separates itself off from the empirical element. In both cases the empirical element is in fact determined by universal, yet merely factual traits of human nature, partly by chance peculiarities of race, nationality and national history, or by peculiarities of the individual and his life-experience. The *a priori* in either case is, at least in its primitive forms, obvious, even trivial, but its systematic demonstration, theoretical pursuit and phenomenological clarification remains of supreme scientific and philosophical interest, and is by no means easy.

The notion of universal grammar can of course be carried beyond the *a priori* sphere, if the somewhat vague sphere of the universally human (in the empirical sense) is brought in. There can, and must, be a universal grammar in this widest of senses, and that this extended sphere is 'rich in important and well-established findings' (as A. Marty observes on page 61 of his *Untersuchungen z. Grundlegung* etc., under the strange impression that he is contradicting me) is something I do not, and never did, doubt. But here, as elsewhere where philosophical interests are concerned, it is important to separate the *a priori* sharply from the empirical, and to recognize that, within this widely conceived discipline, the findings of formal semantics relevant for grammarians have a peculiar character: they belong to an *a priori* discipline that should be kept apart in its purity. Here as elsewhere, one must subscribe to a great Kantian insight, and steep oneself in its sense: that one does not enrich, but rather subverts, the sciences if one blurs their boundaries. One must realize that a universal grammar in this widest sense is a concrete science which, like all concrete sciences, frequently brings together for explanatory purposes findings whose theoretical place lies in essentially different theoretical sciences, in empirical sciences, on the one hand, and in *a priori* sciences, on the other. Our age, oriented towards natural science, sees to it that generalizing, empirical investigations are not neglected in the grammatical field, nor in any other. What is *a priori* is not so favoured; even though all basic insights lead back to the *a priori*, our age's sense for it almost threatens to wither away. I therefore fairly take up the cudgels for the old doctrine of a *grammaire générale et raisonnée*, a philosophical grammar, for its obscure, undeveloped intention aiming at the 'rational' in speech, in the true sense of the word, and in particular at the 'logic' of speech or its semantic *a priori*.[1]

If I am right, it is of basic importance for linguistic investigations that they should become clear as to the distinctions provisionally shadowed forth here. They should possess themselves of the insight that the foundations of speech are not only to be found in physiology, psychology and the history of culture, but also in the *a priori*. The latter deals with the essential meaning-forms and their *a priori* laws of compounding or modification, and no speech is conceivable that is not in part essentially determined by this *a priori*. Every investigator of language operates with notions stemming from this field, whether he is clear on the matter or not.

We may finally say: within pure logic one must separate off what, considered in itself, forms a first, basic sphere, the pure

---

[1] I gladly accept A. Marty's objections (which I do not think otherwise fit the main features of the present Investigation or the other Investigations of this work) that I went too far, in the First Edition when I said that '*all* censure of the old doctrine of *grammaire générale et raisonnée* only affects the unclearness of its historical expressions and their mixture of the *a priori* and the empirical'. Nonetheless, the sharpest words of censure were directed against it for trying to make a rational, logical element count in speech.

theory of meaning-forms. Considered from the standpoint of grammar, it must lay bare an ideal framework which each actual language will fill up and clothe differently, in deference either to common human motives or to empirical motives that vary at random. To whatever extent the actual content and grammatical forms of historical languages are thus empirically determined, each is bound to this ideal framework: theoretical research into this framework must accordingly be one of the foundations of the final scientific clarification of all language as such. The main point to be kept in mind is this: all semantic types set forth in pure, formal semantics, and systematically explored in their articulations and structures – the basic forms of propositions, the categorical proposition with its many particular patterns and forms of members, the primitive types of propositionally complex propositions, e.g. the conjunctive, disjunctive and hypothetical propositional unities, the differences of universality and particularity, on the one hand, and of singularity, on the other, the syntactical forms of plurality, negation, the modalities etc. – all these matters are entirely *a priori*, rooted in the ideal essence of meanings as such. The same applies to the semantic formations to be conjured up by operational laws of compounding and modification out of these primitive forms. They hold prime place over against their empirical-grammatical expressions, and resemble an absolutely fixed ideal framework, more or less perfectly revealed in empirical disguises. One must have this in mind in order to be able to ask significantly: How does German, Latin, Chinese etc., express 'the' existential proposition, 'the' categorical proposition, 'the' antecedent of a hypothetical, 'the' plural, 'the' modalities of possibility and probability, 'the' negative etc.? It is no matter of indifference whether the grammarian is content with a pre-scientific personal opinion on meaning-forms, or with notions empirically contaminated by historical, e.g. by Latin grammar, or whether he keeps his eyes on a scientifically fixed, theoretically coherent system of pure meaning-forms, i.e. on our own form-theory of meanings.

Considering the fact that in this lowest field of logic questions of truth, objectivity, objective possibility are not yet relevant, and considering too its just described role of rendering intelligible the ideal essence of all speech as such, one might give this basic field of pure logic the name of pure logical grammar.

Notes

Note 1 In the First Edition I spoke of 'pure grammar', a name conceived and expressly devised to be analogous to Kant's 'pure science of nature'. Since it cannot, however, be said that pure formal semantic theory comprehends the entire *a priori* of general grammar – there is, e.g., a peculiar *a priori* governing relations of mutual understanding among minded persons, relations very important for grammar – talk of pure logical grammar is to be preferred.

Note 2 After what has been said, no one will imagine that there could be a universal grammar in the sense of a universal science comprehending all particular grammars as contingent specifications, just as a universal mathematical theory contains all possible cases *a priori* in itself, and settles them all 'in one go'. Naturally we speak of a general or purely logical grammar in a sense analogous to that in which we speak of general linguistic science. Just as the latter deals with the universal principles that can be placed before the sciences of particular languages, and mainly, therefore, with the presuppositions and foundations equally relevant to all such languages, so pure logical grammar in its *narrower* sense explores only *one* of these foundations, which has pure logic for its theoretical home-territory. Its inclusion in linguistic science naturally only serves interests of application just as, in another direction, linguistic science itself satisfied similar interests in many chapters of psychology.

Marty of course disagrees with me on these points, as also generally in regard to a theoretical classification into *a priori* and empirical researches (cf. loc. cit. §21, pp. 63 *ff*.). In the note to page 67, he holds that the logico-grammatical findings I credit to pure logic 'have, theoretically, their natural home in the psychology of language. Logic, and the nomothetic part of linguistic psychology, borrow from this what serves and suits their purpose'. To me Marty's conception is basically mistaken. On it, we should ultimately have to class arithmetic, as well as all other formal disciplines in mathematics in – psychology, if not in linguistic psychology. For pure logic in the narrower sense, i.e. the doctrine of the validity of meanings, and the connected pure theory of meaning-forms, is, I hold, essentially one with these disciplines (cf. the final chapter of the *Prolegomena*). In the essential unity of a *mathesis universalis* all these sciences must be treated, and certainly be kept quite apart from all empirical sciences, whether styled 'physics' or 'psychology'. Mathematicians in fact do this, even if in naïvely dogmatic fashion, turning their back on specifically philosophical problems, and not worrying about philosophical objections – to the great profit, in my view, of their science.

Note 3 Nothing has so much confused discussions of the question of the right relation of logic to grammar, as the constant confusion of two logical spheres, sharply distinguished by us as lower and upper, and characterized by way of their negative counterparts – the spheres of nonsense and of formal absurdity respectively. The logical sphere, in the sense of the upper sphere oriented towards formal truth and objectivity, is certainly irrelevant to grammar. This is not true of all logic whatever. If, however, one tried to discredit the lower logical sphere on account of its supposed narrow obviousness and practical uselessness, one would have to say that it ill befits the philosopher, the dedicated representative of purely theoretical interests, to let himself be guided by considerations of practical use. He must surely also know that it is precisely behind the obvious that the hardest problems lie hidden, that this is so much so, in fact, that philosophy may be paradoxically, but not unprofoundly, called the science of the trivial. In the present case at least what seems at first quite trivial, reveals itself, on closer examination, as the source of deep-lying, widely ramifying problems. These problems, though intrinsically prior in the sense of Aristotle, are not the first to make themselves felt by logicians, concerned as these are with objective validity: it is not, therefore, remarkable that, till this day, no logicians, not even Bolzano, have even formulated these problems scientifically, have formed the idea of a purely logical theory of forms. Logic accordingly lacks its prime foundation; it lacks a scientifically strict, phenomenologically clarified distinction of primitive meaning-elements and structures, and a knowledge of relevant laws of essence. We may thus explain how, in particular, the many theories of 'the concept' or 'the judgement', which in certain of their aspects belong in this field, have produced so few tenable results. This is to a large extent due to a lack of correct aims and viewpoints, to confusions of radically distinct layers of problems, and to a psychologism operative openly or in manifold disguises. Since the eye of the logician is ever on form, these defects also point to difficulties inherent in these matters themselves.

Note 4 For related but opposed conceptions one may refer to H. Steinthal's *Einleitung in die Psychologie und Sprachwissenschaft* (Introduction IV, 'Sprechen und Denken, Grammatik und Logik', pp. 44 *ff.*). I refer especially to his beautifully precise statement of the notion of W. v. Humboldt (loc. cit. pp. 63 *ff.*), from which it would seem that the views stated here are in some points close to those of the great thinker, whom Steinthal also respects. Steinthal himself sides against us, and raises many objections to our views, but our distinctions would seem to have disposed of these all so clearly, that no thoroughgoing criticism is required here.

INVESTIGATION V

On Intentional Experiences and their 'Contents'

INTRODUCTION

IN our Second Investigation we clarified the general sense of the ideality of the Species, and, together with it, the sense of the ideality of meanings with which pure logic is concerned. As with all ideal unities, there are here real possibilities, and perhaps actualities, which correspond to meanings: to meanings *in specie* correspond acts of meaning, the former being nothing but ideally apprehended aspects of the latter. New questions now arise regarding the kind of experiences in which the supreme genus Meaning has its originative source, and likewise regarding the various sorts of experiences in which essentially different sorts of meaning unfold. We wish to enquire into the originative source of the concept of Meaning and its essential specifications, so as to achieve a deeper-going, more widely ranging answer to our question than our investigations have so far given us. In very close connection with this question, certain other questions arise: meanings have to be present in meaning-intentions that can come into a certain relation to intuition. We have often spoken of the *fulfilment* of a meaning-intention through a corresponding intuition, and have said that the highest form of such fulfilment was that of self-evidence. It is therefore our task to describe this remarkable phenomenological relationship, and to lay down its role, and so to clarify the notions of knowledge which presuppose it. For an analytical investigation these tasks are not really separable from our earlier work on the essence of meaning (particularly as this last relates to the logical presentation and the logical judgement).

The present investigation will not yet embark on these tasks, since we cannot enter upon them without first performing a much more general phenomenological investigation. Experiences of meaning are classifiable as 'acts', and the meaningful element in each such single act must be sought in the act-experience, and not in its object; it must lie in that element which makes the act an 'intentional' experience, one 'directed' to objects. The essence of the fulfilling intuition likewise consists in acts, for thinking and intuiting must be different *qua* acts. Naturally, too, self-fulfilment must be reckoned a relation especially bound up with the characters of acts. No term in descriptive psychology is, however, more controversial than the term 'act', and doubt, if not quick rejection, may have been aroused by all passages in our previous Investigations where we made use of the notion of 'act' to characterize or express our conception. It is therefore important, and a precondition for carrying out all our tasks, that this concept should be clarified before all others. It will appear that the concept of act, *in the sense of an intentional experience*, circumscribes an important generic unity in the sphere of experiences (apprehended in its phenomenological purity), and that to put meaning-experiences into this genus enables us to characterize them in a truly worthwhile manner.

It is of course part of phenomenological research into the essence of acts as such, that we should clear up the difference between the *character* and the *content* of acts, and that, as regards the latter, we should point out the fundamentally different senses in which the 'content' of an act has been talked about.

The nature of acts as such cannot be satisfactorily discussed unless one goes fairly fully into the phenomenology of 'presentations'. The intimate relevance of this topic is recalled by the well-known statement, that every act is either a presentation or is founded upon presentations. We must, however, ask which of the very many concepts of 'presentation' is here the required one: to separate the closely confused phenomena underlying the ambiguities of this word thus becomes an essential part of our task.

The treatment of the problems thus roughly outlined (to which certain others will be intimately linked) is suitably connected by us with the many concepts of consciousness which are always being distinguished, and are always shading into one another in descriptive psychology. Mental acts are often called 'activities of consciousness', 'relations of consciousness to a content (object)', and 'consciousness' is, in fact, at times defined as a comprehensive expression covering mental acts of all sorts.

Consciousness as the Phenomenological Subsistence of the Ego and Consciousness as Inner Perception

---

§ 1 *Varied ambiguity of the term 'consciousness'*

IN psychology there is much talk of 'consciousness', and likewise of 'conscious contents' and 'conscious experiences': the latter are generally abbreviated to 'contents' and 'experiences'. This talk is mainly connected with the division between psychical and physical phenomena; the former being those phenomena which belong to the sphere of psychology, the latter to the sphere of the natural sciences. *Our* problem, that of circumscribing the concept of 'mental act' in its phenomenological essence, is closely connected with *this* problem of division, since the concept arose precisely in this context, as supposedly marking off the psychological sphere. *One* concept of consciousness is justifiably employed in effecting this demarcation correctly, *another* yields us the definition of a mental act. We must, in either case, distinguish between several thematically cognate, and so readily confounded, notions.

We shall, in what follows, discuss three concepts of consciousness, as having interest for our purposes:

1. Consciousness as the entire, real (*reelle*) phenomenological being of the empirical ego, as the interweaving of psychic experiences in the unified stream of consciousness.

2. Consciousness as the inner awareness of one's own psychic experiences.

3. Consciousness as a comprehensive designation for 'mental acts', or 'intentional experiences', of all sorts.

It need hardly be said that we have not exhausted *all* ambiguities of the term in question. I particularly recall, e.g., modes of speech current in non-scientific parlance such as 'entering consciousness', 'coming to consciousness', 'heightened' or 'reduced' self-consciousness, the 'awakening of self-consciousness' (the last expression quite differently used in psychology from the sense given it in ordinary life), and so forth.

Since *all* terms at all relevant for terminological differentiation are ambiguous, an unambiguous fixing of the concepts which here distinguish themselves can only be done indirectly: we must put together equivalent expressions, and oppose them to expressions to be kept apart from them, and we must employ suitable paraphrases and explanations. We shall therefore have to make use of these aids.

§ 2 *First sense: Consciousness as the real phenomenological unity of the ego's experiences. The concept of an experience*

We begin with the following summary statement. The modern psychologist defines (or could define) his science as the science of 'psychic individuals' considered as concrete conscious unities, *or* as the science of the conscious experiences of experiencing individuals; the juxtaposition of these terms in this context determines a certain concept of consciousness, and, at the same time, certain concepts of experience and content. These latter terms, 'experience' and 'content', mean for the modern psychologist the real occurrences (Wundt rightly calls them 'events') which, in flux from one moment to the next, and interconnected and interpenetrating in manifold ways, compose the real unity-of-consciousness of the individual mind. In this sense, percepts, imaginative and pictorial presentations, acts of conceptual thinking, surmises and doubts, joys and griefs, hopes and fears, wishes and acts of will etc., are, just as they flourish in our consciousness, 'experiences' or 'contents of consciousness'. And, with these experiences in their total and concrete fulness, their component parts and abstract aspects are also *experienced*: they are real contents of consciousness. Naturally, it is irrelevant whether these parts are in some manner inwardly articulated, whether they are marked off by special acts directed upon themselves, and whether, in particular, they are themselves objects of an 'inner' perception, which seizes them as they are in consciousness, and even whether they can be such objects or not.

We may now point out that *this concept of consciousness can be seen in a purely phenomenological manner*, i.e. a manner which *cuts out all relation to empirically real existence* (to persons or animals in nature): experience in the descriptive-psychological or empirically-phenomenological sense then becomes experience in the sense of pure phenomenology.[1] The clarifying illustrations that we now append may and must lead to the conviction that the required exclusion lies always in our power, and that the descriptive-psychological treatments that we have first applied or might first apply to such illustrations, are to be interpreted 'purely' in the manner sketched above, and to be understood in what follows as pure, *a priori* insights into essence. The same, of course, holds in all parallel cases.

The sense-aspect of colour, e.g., which in outer perception forms a real constituent of my concrete seeing (in the phenomenological sense of a visual perceiving or appearing) is as much an 'experienced' or 'conscious' content, as is the character of perceiving, or as the full perceptual appearing of the coloured object. As opposed to this, however, this object, though perceived, is not itself experienced nor conscious, and the same applies to the colouring perceived in it. If the object is non-existent, if the percept is open to criticism as delusive, hallucinatory, illusory etc., then the visually perceived colour, that of the object, does not exist either. Such differences of normal and abnormal, of veridical and delusive perception, do not affect the internal, purely descriptive (or phenomenological) character of perception. While the seen colour, i.e. the colour appearing upon and with the appearing object of visual perception, and seen as its property, and one with it in its present being – while this colour certainly does not exist as an experience, there is a real part (*reelles Bestandstück*) of our experience, of this appearing to perception, which corresponds to it. Our colour-sensation corresponds to it, that qualitatively determinate phenomenological colour-aspect, which receives an 'objectifying interpretation' in perception, or in an intrinsic aspect of such perception (the 'appearance of the object's colouring'). These two, the colour-sensation and the object's objective colouring, are often con-

---

[1] See my *Ideas towards a Pure Phenomenology, etc.*, in the *Jahrbuch für Philos. u. phänom. Forschung*, 1 (1913), Section 2. [The present paragraph is an insertion in the Second Edition.]

founded. In our time people have favoured a form of words according to which both are the same thing, only seen from a different standpoint, or with a different interest: psychologically or subjectively speaking, one has a sensation, physically or objectively speaking, one has a property of an external thing. Here it is enough to point to the readily grasped difference between the red of this ball, objectively seen as uniform, and the indubitable, unavoidable projective differences among the subjective colour-sensations in our percept, a difference repeated in *all* sorts of objective properties and the sense-complexes which correspond to them.

What we have said about single properties carries over to concrete wholes. It is phenomenologically false to say that the difference between a conscious content in perception, and the external object perceived (or perceptually intended) in it, is a mere difference in mode of treatment, the *same appearance* being at one time dealt with in a subjective connection (in connection with appearances which relate to an ego), and at another time in an objective connection (in connection with the things themselves). We cannot too sharply stress the equivocation which allows us to use the word '*appearance*' *both of the experience in which the object's appearing consists* (the concrete perceptual experience, in which the object itself seems present to us) and of *the object which appears as such*. The deceptive spell of this equivocation vanishes as soon as one takes phenomenological account as to how little of the object which appears is as such to be found in the experience of its appearing. The appearing of the thing (the experience) is not the thing which appears (that seems to stand before us *in propria persona*). As belonging in a conscious connection, the appearing of things is experienced by us, as belonging in the phenomenal world, things appear before us. The appearing of the things does not itself appear to us, we live through it.

If we ourselves appear to ourselves as members of the phenomenal world,[1] physical and mental things (bodies and persons) appear in physical and mental relation to our phenomenal ego.

---

[1] Which is only in question *qua* phenomenal, since we exclude all questions regarding its existence or non-existence, and that of the empirical ego which appears in it, if we wish our treatments to have, not a descriptive-psychological, but a purely phenomenological value. One should note how, up to this point and for the future, each analysis can be first conducted as mere psychology, but there really permits of that 'purification' which gives it value as 'pure' phenomenology. [Second Edition comment.]

This relation of the phenomenal object (that we also like to call a 'conscious content') *to the phenomenal subject* (myself as an empirical person, a thing) must naturally be *kept apart from the relation of a conscious content, in the sense of an experience, to consciousness in the sense of a unity of such conscious contents* (the phenomenological subsistence of an empirical ego). There we were concerned with the relation of two appearing things, here with the relation of a single experience to a complex of experiences. Just so, conversely, we must of course distinguish the relation of the appearing person I to the externally appearing thing, from *the relation of the thing's appearing* ('*qua*' *experience*) *to the thing which appears*. If we speak of the latter relation, we only make clear to ourselves that the experience is not itself what is intentionally present 'in' it: we can, e.g., make plain that what is predicated of a thing's appearing is not also predicated of the thing that appears in it. And yet another relation is the *objectifying relation* ascribed by us to the *sense-complex experienced by us when something appears to us, a relation in which the complex stands to the object which appears to us*. We concede that such a complex is experienced in the act of appearing, but say that it is in a certain manner 'interpreted' or 'apperceived', and hold that it is in the phenomenological character of such an animating interpretation of sensation that what we call the appearing of the object consists.[1]

Similar distinctions of essence to those needed by us in the case of perception, when we sought to separate off what is really 'experience' in it and really composes it, from what is only 'in' it in an 'improper' or intentional sense, will have soon to be drawn in the case of other 'acts' as well. We shall soon have to deal with such distinctions more generally. Here it is only important to guard from the start against certain misleading thought-tendencies, which might obscure the plain sense of the notions to be elucidated.

§3 *The phenomenological and the popular concept of 'experience'*

A similar aim leads us to point out that *our concept of experience does not tally* with the popular notion; here the distinction just

[1] Or what we also call its 'appearance' in the sense given above, which will also be employed in future, the sense in which a (phenomenologically understood) experience is itself styled an 'appearance'.

sketched, between real (*reellem*) and intentional content, has its part to play.

If someone says he 'experienced' the wars of 1866 and 1870, then what he has been said to have 'experienced' in this sense, is a complex of outer events, and 'experiencing' consists here in perceptions, judgements and other acts, in which these events appear as objects, and often as objects of certain assertions which relate them to the empirical ego. The experiencing ego, in the phenomenologically paradigmatic sense, has naturally not got these events in itself as things mentally lived through, as its real constituents or contents, in the way in which these events are in the things concerned in them. What it finds in itself, what are present in it as realities, are the relevant acts of perceiving, judging etc., with their variable sense-material, their interpretative content, their assertive characters etc. Experiencing in the latter sense is quite different from experiencing in the former sense. To experience outer events meant to *have* certain acts of perception, of this or that type of knowledge, directed upon them. This 'having' at once furnishes an instance of the quite different 'experiencing' in the sense of phenomenology. This merely means that certain contents help to constitute a unity of consciousness, enter into the phenomenologically unified stream of consciousness of an empirical ego. This itself is a real whole, in reality made up of manifold parts, each of which may be said to be 'experienced'. It is in this sense that what the ego or consciousness experiences, are its experience: there is no difference between the experience or conscious content and the experience itself. What is sensed is, e.g., no different from the sensation. If, however, an experience 'directs itself' to an object distinguishable from itself, as, e.g., external perception directs itself to a perceived object, a nominal presentation to an object named etc., such an object is not experienced or conscious in the sense to be established here, but perceived, named etc.

The situation justifies talk of 'contents', which is here entirely *proper*. The normal sense of the word 'content' is relative: it refers quite generally to a comprehensive unity which has its content in the sum total of its component parts. Whatever can be regarded as a part of a whole, and as truly constituting it in real fashion (*reell*), belongs to the content of that whole. In our current descriptive-psychological talk of contents, the tactitly assumed relational focus, i.e. the corresponding whole, is the real unity of consciousness. Its content is the sum total of present experiences, and 'contents' in the plural means these experiences themselves, i.e. all that as real parts constitute any phenomenological stream of consciousness.

§4 The relation between experiencing consciousness and experienced content is no phenomenologically peculiar type of relation

The foregoing exposition has made clear that the relation in which experiences are thought to stand to an experiencing consciousness (or to an experiencing 'phenomenological ego')[1] points to *no peculiar phenomenological situation*. The ego in the sense of common discourse is an empirical object, one's own ego as much as someone else's, and each ego as much as any physical thing, a house or a tree etc. Scientific elaboration may alter our ego-concept as much as it will, but, if it avoids fiction, the ego remains an individual, thinglike object, which, like all such objects, has phenomenally no other unity than that given it through its unified phenomenal properties, and which in them has its own internal make-up. If we cut out the ego-body from the empirical ego, and limit the purely mental ego to its phenomenological content, the latter reduces to a unity of consciousness, to a real experiential complex, which we (i.e. each man for his own ego) find in part evidently present, and for the rest postulate on good grounds. The phenomenologically reduced ego is therefore nothing peculiar, floating above many experiences: it is simply identical with their own interconnected unity. In the nature of its contents, and the laws they obey, certain forms of connection are grounded. They run in diverse fashions from content to content, from complex of contents to complex of contents, till in the end a unified sum total of content is constituted, which does not differ from the phenomenologically reduced ego itself. These contents have, as contents generally have, their own law-bound ways of coming together, of losing themselves in more comprehensive unities, and, in so far as they thus become and are one, the phenomenological ego or unity of consciousness is already constituted, without need of an

---

[1] In the First Edition the name 'phenomenological ego' was given to the stream of consciousness as such.

additional, peculiar ego-principle which supports all contents and unites them all once again. Here as elsewhere it is not clear what such a principle would effect.[1]

§5 *Second sense. 'Inner' consciousness as inner perception*

Our sense of the terms 'consciousness', 'experience', 'content', has been fixed in the treatments of the last three sections, a descriptive-psychological sense which, with phenomenological 'purification', becomes *purely* phenomenological. We wish to adhere to this sense in future, but only when other concepts have been expressly indicated.

A second concept of consciousness is expressed by talk of 'inner consciousness'. This is that 'inner perception' thought to accompany actually present experiences, whether in general, or in certain classes of cases, and to relate to them as its objects. The 'self-evidence' usually attributed to inner perception, shows it to be taken to be an *adequate* perception, one ascribing nothing to its objects that is not intuitively presented, and given as a real part (*reell*) of the perceptual experience, and one which, conversely, intuitively presents and posits its objects just as they are in fact experienced in and with their perception. Every perception is characterized by the intention of grasping its object as present, and *in propria persona*. To this intention perception corresponds with complete perfection, achieves *adequacy*, if the object in it is itself actually present, and in the strictest sense present *in propria persona*, is exhaustively apprehended as that which it is, and is therefore itself a real (*reell*) factor in our perceiving of it. It is accordingly clear, and evident from the mere essence of perception, that adequate perception can only be 'inner' perception, that it can only be trained upon experiences simultaneously given, and belonging to a single experience with itself. This holds, precisely stated, only for experiences in the purely phenomenological sense. One cannot, however, at all concur with the converse opinion and say, in psychological language, that each percept directed upon one's own inner experience (which would be called an 'inner' percept in the natural sense of the word) need be

---

[1] The opposition to the doctrine of a 'pure' ego, already expressed in this paragraph, is one that the author no longer approves of, as is plain from his *Ideas* cited above.

adequate. In view of the just exposed ambiguity of the expression 'inner perception', it would be best to have different terms for inner perception, as the perception of one's own experiences, and adequate or evident perception. The epistemologically confused and psychologically misused distinction of inner and outer perception would then vanish; it has been put in the place of the genuine contrast between *adequate* and *inadequate* perception which has its roots in the *pure* phenomenological essences of such experiences.

Many thinkers, as, e.g., Brentano, are led to posit a close connection between the two concepts of consciousness so far discussed, because they think that they may regard the consciousness, or the being-experienced, of contents, in the first sense, as at the same time a consciousness in the second sense. The equivocation which pushes us to treat consciousness as a sort of knowing, and in fact of intuitive knowing, may here have recommended a conception fraught with too many grave difficulties. I recall the infinite regress which sprung from the circumstance that inner perception is itself another experience, which requires a new percept, to which the same again applies etc., a regress which Brentano sought to avoid by distinguishing between a primary and a secondary direction of perception. Since our concern is here with purely phenomenological asseverations, we must leave theories of this sort on one side, so long, that is, as the need to assume the unbroken activity of inner perception cannot be phenomenologically demonstrated.

§6 *Origin of the first concept of consciousness out of the second*

Undeniably the second concept of consciousness is the more 'primitive': it has an 'intrinsic priority'. The following considerations would enable us to pass in scientific order from this last narrower concept to our former, broader one. If we consider the self-evidence of the *Cogito, ergo sum*, or rather of its simple *sum*, as one that can be sustained against all doubts, then it is plain that what here passes as ego cannot be the empirical ego. But since, on the other hand, we cannot allow the self-evidence of the proposition 'I am' to depend on the knowledge and acceptance of philosophical ideas about the ego which have always remained questionable, we can at best say: In the judgement 'I am' self-evidence attaches to a certain central kernel of our empirical ego-notion which is not bounded by a perfectly clear concept. If we now ask what could belong to this conceptually un-demarcated and therefore unutterable kernel, what may constitute the self-evidently certain, given element in the empirical ego at each moment, it comes easy to refer to judgements of inner (i.e. adequate) perception. Not only is it self-evident that I am: self-evidence also attaches to countless judgements of the form *I perceive this or that*, where I not merely think, but am also self-evidently assured, that what I perceive is given as I think of it, that I apprehend the thing itself, and for what it is – this pleasure, e.g., that fills me, this phantasm of the mind that float before me etc. All these judgements share the lot of the judgement 'I am', they elude complete conceptualization and expression, they are evident only in their living intention, which cannot be adequately imparted in words. What is adequately perceived, whether ex-pressed thus vaguely or left unexpressed, constitutes the epistemo-logically primary, absolutely certain focus yielded by the reduc-tion, at any given moment, of the phenomenal empirical ego to such of its content as can be grasped by the pure phenomenol-ogist. It is also true, conversely, that in the judgement 'I am', it is the kernel of what is adequately perceived which, ranged under the ego, first makes possible and provides a ground for this 'I am's' evidence.[1] To this primary focus more territory is added when we reduce to its past phenomenological content all that retention, essentially attached to perception, reports as having been recently present, and also all that recollection reports as having belonged to our earlier actual experience, and when we then go back through reflection to what 'in' retention and remembrance is reproductively phenomenological. We proceed similarly with what can be assumed on empirical grounds to coexist with what at each instant we adequately perceive, or with what can be assumed to have coexisted with what now forms

[1] The text as here set forth is taken over without essential change from the First Edition. It fails to do justice to the fact that the empirical ego is as much a case of transcendence as the physical thing. If the elimination of such transcendence, and the reduction to pure phenomenological data, leaves us with no residual pure ego, there can be no real (adequate) self-evidence attaching to the 'I am'. But if there is really such an adequate self-evidence – who indeed could deny it? – how can we avoid assuming a pure ego? It is precisely the ego apprehended in *carrying out* a self-evident *cogito*, and the pure carrying out *eo epso* grasps it in phenomenological purity, and necessarily grasps it as the subject of a pure experience of the type *cogito*.

the reflective substance of retention and recollection, and can be assumed to have cohered continuously with it in unity. When I say 'cohered continuously with it in unity', I refer to the unity of the concrete phenomenological whole, whose parts are either *abstract aspects*, mutually founded upon, and requiring each other in their coexistence, or *pieces* from whose nature spring forms of coexistent unity, forms which actually contribute to the content of the whole as real indwelling aspects. These 'unities of coexistence' pass continuously into one another from one moment to the next, composing a unity of change, of the stream of consciousness, which in its turn demands the continuous persistence, or no continuous change, of at least one aspect essential for its total unity, and so inseparable from it as a whole. This part is played by the presentative form of *time* which is immanent in the stream of consciousness, which latter appears as a unity in time (not in the time of the world of things, but in the time which appears together with the stream of consciousness itself, and in which the stream flows). Each instant of this time is given in a continuous projective series of (so-to-speak) 'time-sensations'; in each actual phase of the stream of consciousness the *whole* time-horizon of the stream is presented, and it thereby possesses a form overreaching all its contents, which remains the same form continuously, though its content steadily alters.

This accordingly forms the phenomenological content of the ego, of the empirical ego in the sense of the psychic subject. Phenomenological reduction yields the really self-enclosed, temporally growing unity of the stream of experience. The notion of experience has widened out from what is inwardly perceived, and that is in *this* sense conscious, to the notion of the 'phenomenological ego', by which the empirical ego is intentionally constituted.

§7 Reciprocal demarcation of psychology and natural science

(Paragraph from the First Edition, excised by Husserl from the Second Edition as being unclear and irrelevant.)

Psychology's task – descriptively – is to study the ego-experiences (or conscious contents) in their essential species and forms of combination, in order to explore – genetically – their origin and perishing, and the causal patterns and laws of their formation and trans-formation. For psychology, conscious contents are contents of an ego, and so its task is to explore the real essence of the ego (no mystical thing-in-itself but one only to be demonstrated empirically), to explore the interweaving of psychic elements in the ego, and their subsequent development and degeneration.

To empirical egos stand opposed empirical, physical things, non-egos, unities of coexistence and succession, having a claim to exist as things. To us, who are egos, they are only given as intentional unities, as things referred to in psychical experiences, as unities presented or judged about. They are not for this reason themselves mere presenta-tions, any more than the same is true of the egos alien to ourselves. Physical things are given to us, they stand before us, they are objects – this means that we have certain percepts and judgements fitted to them which are 'directed to these objects'. To the system of all such percepts and judgements corresponds its intentional correlate, the physical world. As we deal with the system of such judgements in individuals, or as the common judgement-system of a community of individuals, or in the unity of science, we should draw more precise distinctions between the world of the individual, the world of the empirical, social community, and perhaps the world of an ideal community of knowers, the world of (ideally perfected) science, the world in itself. Psychical experiences and the ego likewise document their being and their law-governed connections only in science as a system of objectively valid presentations and judgements, and they are given only as targets of intentional acts in the ego. But they are given, truly and as what they are, though in a somewhat narrower sphere than that of their being, while this never happens in the case of physical things. The doctrine of Berkeley and Hume, which reduces phenomenal bodies to bundles of ideas, fails to do justice to the fact that, even if the elementary ideas in these bundles are psychically realizable, the bundle itself, the intended complexes of elements, are never present in real fashion (*reell gegenwärtig*) in any human consciousness and never will be. No body can be inwardly perceived – not because it is 'physical', but because, e.g., its three-dimensional spatiality cannot be adequately intuited in any conscious-ness. But adequate intuition is the same as internal perception. It is the fundamental defect of phenomenalistic theories that they draw no distinction between appearance (*Erscheinung*) as intentional experience, and the apparent object (the subject of the objective predicates), and therefore identify the experienced complex of sensation with the complex of objective features. In any case the objective unities of psychology and those of natural science are not identical, at least not, as in the position of first data, they await scientific elaboration. Whether the two sciences in their full development will still be separated, depends on whether they really concern separate, or at least relatively self-sufficient realities in their mutual relation. (Such self-sufficiency does not of course entail necessary separation of the two realities by any mystical abysses.) We can turn the matter round and say: If there is such a separation, we can only learn of it as both sciences develop. It is sure, at least, that their points of origin, the original spheres of facts that they attempt to elaborate, are to a large extent mutually independent, and that this is true, further, as regards their advancing growth.

We can indeed not exclude the possibility which is presented by phenomenalism as a proven theory – to me phenomenalism has not advanced beyond vague, if by no means worthless lines of thought – that the objective bases of all talk of physical things and happenings lie merely in law-governed correlations established among the psychical experiences of many consciousnesses. The acceptance of such a theory would not, however, remove the separation of the sciences. The distinction between lived experiences, conscious contents, and the non-experiences presented in such experiences (and perceived in them or judged to exist) would remain as before the foundation for the division of the sciences as departments of reason. It would therefore be the foundation for the sort of division that alone is in question at the present stage of development of the sciences. With the demand of a 'psychology without a soul', i.e. a psychology that abandons all metaphysical presumptions in regard to the soul – and does so because they could only become insights when science was perfected – corresponds the demand of a 'natural science without bodies', i.e. a natural science that begins by rejecting all theories as to the metaphysical nature of the physical. Such a theory which puts metaphysics in bondage from the outset, is what we have in phenomenalism. But it ought not to anticipate the answer to the question as to the division of the two sciences. The division must rest on purely phenomenological ground, and I think that, in this respect, our discussions above were well suited to resolve the much-debated question in a satisfactory manner. They only make use of the most fundamental phenomenological distinctions, those between the descriptive content and the intended object of our percepts and of our 'acts' in general.

This distinction has naturally not escaped the psychologists. We find it in Hobbes, Descartes and Locke. One can say that all the greater modern thinkers have at times touched on it or treated of it. It is only a pity that they merely do so at times, instead of starting with the distinction, and taking the closest account of it at every step, instead, that is, of making it the *foundation of scientific epistemology and psychology*. Only in this manner can there be scientific correctness in our way of speech and thought, although it may make this last very prolix and inconvenient.

What we are conscious of, in the narrower sense, is something apparent, and, if one wishes to speak of such a thing, in the usual way, as a 'phenomenon', a psychic *phenomenon*. As against this, far the greater part of what we are conscious of, in the wider sense of the word, is not, properly speaking, apparent. For one would certainly not wish to assert that all psychic being is perceived, or is even perceptible (i.e. in the sense of a real possibility). The definition of psychology as the science of psychic *phenomena* must therefore be understood just as we understand the definition of natural science as the science of physical phenomena. The phenomena in question do not mean an objective scientific field which they are to exhaust, but only the nearest points of attack for our scientific researches. So understood, these definitions raise no objections.

§8 *The pure ego and being-in-consciousness* ('*Bewusstheit*')

We have not so far referred to the pure ego (the ego of 'pure apperception') which for many Kantians, and likewise for many empirical investigators, provides the unitary centre of relation, to which all conscious content is as such referred in a wholly peculiar fashion. To the fact of 'subjective experience' or consciousness, this pure ego is accordingly held to pertain essentially. 'Being-in-consciousness is relation to the ego', and whatever stands in this relation is a content of consciousness. 'We *call* anything content if it is related to an ego in consciousness: its other properties are irrelevant'. 'This relation is plainly one and the same despite manifold variation of content: it constitutes, in fact, what is common and specific to consciousness. We mark it off', says Natorp (whom we are continuously quoting),[1] 'by the special expression "being-in-consciousness" (*Bewusstheit*) to distinguish it from the total fact of consciousness.'

The ego as subjective centre of relation for all contents in my consciousness, cannot be compared to what are contrasted with it, it is not relative to them as they are to it, it is not consciously given to its

[1] Cf. the whole of §4 in Natorp's *Einleitung in die Psychologie nach kritischer Methode*, pp. 11 *f.*

contents as they are given *to* it. It reveals itself as *sui generis* in its incapacity to be in anything else's consciousness, while other things are in *its* consciousness. It cannot itself be a content, and resembles nothing that could be a content of consciousness. For this reason, it can be no further described, since all descriptive terms we might seek to employ, could be drawn only from the content of consciousness, and could not therefore hit off the ego, or a relation to the ego. Otherwise put: each *idea* we could make of the ego would turn it into an *object*, but we have ceased to think of it as an ego, if we think of it as an object. To be an ego is not to be an object, but to be something opposed to all objects, for which they are objects. The same holds of their relation to the ego. Being-in-consciousness means being-objective for an ego: such being-objective cannot in its turn be made into an object.

The fact that things are in consciousness, while it is the basic fact of psychology, can be acknowledged and specially emphasized, but it can neither be defined nor deduced from anything else.

These statements are impressive, but closer consideration fails to substantiate them. How can we assert such a 'basic fact of psychology', if we are unable to think it, and how can we think it, if not by making the ego and consciousness, both subject-matters of our assertion, into 'objects'? This might be done if we thought of this fact only in indirect, symbolic fashion. Natorp, however, wants it to be a 'basic fact', which must as such surely be given in direct intuition. He in fact tells us that it 'can be acknowledged and specially emphasized'. Surely what is acknowledged or emphasized will be content? Surely it will be made into an object? Perhaps, indeed, some narrower concept of object is excluded, but the wider concept is here relevant. A taking note of a thought, a sensation, a stirring of displeasure etc., makes these experiences objects of inner perception, without making them objects in the sense of things, just so, the ego as relational centre, and any particular relation of the ego to some content, will, if taken note of, be objectively given.

I must frankly confess, however, that I am quite unable to find this ego, this primitive, necessary centre of relations.[1] The only thing I can take note of, and therefore perceive, are the empirical ego and its empirical relations to its own experiences, or to such external objects as are receiving special attention at the moment,

---

[1] I have since managed to find it, i.e. have learnt not to be led astray from a pure grasp of the given through corrupt forms of ego-metaphysic cf. note to §6.

while much remains, whether 'without' or 'within', which has no such relation to the ego.

I can only clarify this situation by subjecting the empirical ego, with its empirical relation to objects, to phenomenological analysis, from which the above conception necessarily results. We excluded the body-ego, whose appearances resemble those of any other physical thing, and dealt with the mind-ego, which is empirically bound up with the former, and appears as belonging to it. Reduced to data that are phenomenologically actual, this yields us the complex of reflectively graspable experiences described above, a complex which stands in the same sort of relation to the mental ego as the side of a perceived external thing open to perception stands to the whole thing. The conscious intentional relation of the ego to its objects means for me simply that intentional experiences whose intentional objects are the ego-body, the personal ego-mind and therefore the entire empirical ego-subject or human person, are included in the total phenomenological being of a unity of consciousness, and that such intentional experiences also constitute an essential phenomenological kernel in the phenomenal ego.

This brings us to our *third* concept of consciousness, defined in terms of 'acts' or 'intentional experiences', which will be analysed in our next chapter. If the peculiar character of intentional experiences is contested, if one refuses to admit, what for us is most certain, that being-an-object consists phenomenologically in certain acts in which something appears, or is thought of as our object, it will not be intelligible how being-an-object can itself be objective to us. For us the matter is quite clear: there are acts 'trained upon' the character of acts in which something appears, or there are acts trained upon the empirical ego and its relation to the object. The phenomenological kernel of the empirical ego here consists of acts which bring objects to its notice, acts in which the ego directs itself to the appropriate object.

I am unable, further, to grasp the view that the relation of the ego to conscious content is bare of all difference. For if by 'content' we mean the *experience* which forms the real side of the phenomenological ego, surely the way in which contents enter the unity of experience will depend throughout on their specific nature, which is true of all parts that enter into wholes? But, if by 'content' we mean some object upon which consciousness 'directs itself', whether perceivingly, imaginingly, retrospectively, expectantly, conceptually or predicatively etc., then it plainly involves many differences, obvious even in running through the expressions just used.

Objection may be raised to our previous assertion that the ego appears to itself, enjoys a consciousness and, in particular, a perception of itself. Self-perception of the empirical ego is, however, a daily business, which involves no difficulty for understanding. We perceive the ego, just as we perceive an external thing. That the object does not offer all its parts and sides to perception is as irrelevant in this case as in that. For perception is essentially the presumptive apprehension of some object, not its adequate intuition. Perception itself, though part of the ego's phenomenological being, naturally falls, like so much else in consciousness that evades notice, beyond the glance of perception, much as ungrasped, yet apparent, aspects of a perceived external thing are not themselves perceived. Ego and thing are in either case said to be perceived, and perceived they indeed are, and in full, 'bodily' presence.

Additional Note to the Second Edition. I must expressly emphasize that the attitude here taken up to the question of the pure ego – an attitude I no longer endorse, as remarked before – *is irrelevant to the investigations of this volume.* Important as this question may be, phenomenologically or in other respects, there remain wide fields of phenomenological problems, relating more or less generally to the real content of intentional experiences, and to their relation of essence to intentional objects, which can be systematically explored without taking up any stance on the ego-issue. The present investigations are entirely confined to such problems. But since such an important work as volume I of P. Natorp's Second Edition of his *Einleitung in die Psychologie* concerns itself with what I have said above, I have not simply struck it out.

CHAPTER TWO

Consciousness as Intentional Experience

WE must now embark upon a fuller analytic discussion of our third concept of consciousness, which ranges over the same phenomenological field as the concept of 'mental act'. In connection with this, talk of conscious contents, talk in particular concerning contents of presentations, judgements etc., gains a variety of meanings, which it is all-important to sort out and to subject to the sharpest scrutiny.

§9 *The meaning of Brentano's demarcation of 'psychic' phenomena*

Among the demarcations of classes in descriptive psychology, there is none more remarkable nor more important philosophically than the one offered by Brentano under his title of 'psychical phenomena', and used by him in his well-known division of phenomena into psychical and physical. Not that I can approve of the great thinker's guiding conviction, plain from the very terms that he uses, that he had achieved an exhaustive classification of 'phenomena' through which the field of psychological research could be kept apart from that of natural science, and through which the vexed question of the right delimitation of the fields of these disciplines could be very simply solved. Possibly a good sense can be given to defining psychology as the science of psychical phenomena, and to the coordinated definition of natural science as the science of physical phenomena, but there are good reasons for disputing the view that the concepts which occur in Brentano's division are those found under like names in the definitions in question. It can be shown that not all 'psychical phenomena' in the sense of a possible definition of psychology, are psychical phenomena (i.e. mental acts) in Brentano's sense, and that, on the other hand, many genuine 'psychical phenomena'

fall under Brentano's ambiguous rubric of 'physical phenomena'.[1]
The value of Brentano's conception of a 'psychical phenomenon'
is, however, quite independent of the aims that inspired it. A
sharply defined class of experiences is here brought before us,
comprising all that enjoys mental, conscious existence in a certain
pregnant sense of these words. A real being deprived of such
experiences, merely having[2] contents inside it such as the experiences of sense, but unable to interpret these objectively, or
otherwise use them to make objects present to itself, quite
incapable, therefore, of referring to objects in further acts of
judgement, joy, grief, love, hatred, desire and loathing – such a
being would not be called 'psychical' by anyone. If one doubts
whether it is at all possible to conceive of such a being, a mere
complex of sensations, one has but to point to external phenomenal things, present to consciousness through sensational
complexes, but not appearing as such themselves, and called by us
'bodies' or 'inanimate things', since they lack all psychical
experiences in the sense of our examples. Turning aside from
psychology, and entering the field of the philosophical disciplines
proper, we perceive the fundamental importance of our class of
experiences, since only its members are relevant in the highest
ranks of the normative sciences. They alone, seized in their
phenomenological purity, furnish concrete bases for abstracting
the fundamental notions that function systematically in logic,
ethics and aesthetics, and that enter into the ideal laws of these
sciences. Our mention of logic recalls the particular interest which
has inspired our whole probing into such experiences.

§ 10 *Descriptive characterization of acts as 'intentional' experiences*

We must now dig down to the essence of Brentano's demarcation
of phenomenal classes, of his concept of consciousness in the
sense of psychical act. Moved by the interest in classification just

[1] My deviations from Brentano are not on the same lines as the qualifications that
he found necessary to add to the inadequate simplifications of which he was clearly
conscious (See *Psychologie*, I, pp. 127 *ff.*). This will be plain from the discussions in
App. 2 at the end of this volume.

[2] We could not say 'experiencing contents', since the concept of 'experience' has
its prime source in the field of 'psychic acts'. Even if this concept has been widened
to include non-acts, these for us stand connected with, ranged beside and attached to
acts, in a unity of consciousness so essential that, were it to fall away, talk of
'experiencing' would lose its point.

mentioned, Brentano conducts his enquiry in the form of a two-edged separation of the two main classes of 'phenomena' that he recognizes, the psychical and the physical. He arrives at a sixfold differentiation in which only two heads are relevant for our purpose, since in all the others misleading ambiguities do their destructive work, rendering untenable his notion of 'phenomenon' in general and of 'physical phenomenon' in particular, as well as his concepts of internal and external perception.[1]

Of his two principal differentiations, one directly reveals the *essence* of psychical phenomena or acts. This strikes us unmistakably in any illustration we choose. In perception something is perceived, in imagination, something imagined, in a statement something stated, in love something loved, in hate hated, in desire desired etc. Brentano looks to what is graspably common to such instances, and says that 'every mental phenomenon is characterized by what the mediaeval schoolmen called the intentional (or mental) inexistence of an object, and by what we, not without ambiguity, call the relation to a content, the direction to an object (by which a reality is not to be understood) or an immanent objectivity. Each mental phenomenon contains something as object in itself, though not all in the same manner.'[2] This 'manner in which consciousness refers to an object' (an expression used by Brentano in other passages) is presentative in a presentation, judicial in a judgement etc. etc. Brentano's attempted classification of mental phenomena into presentations, judgements and emotions ('phenomena of love and hate') is plainly based upon this 'manner of reference', of which three basically different kinds are distinguished (each admitting of many further specifications).

Whether we think Brentano's classification of 'psychical' phenomena successful, and whether we think it basically significant for the whole treatment of psychology, as Brentano claims it is, does not matter here. Only one point has importance for us: that there are essential, specific differences of intentional relation or intention (the generic descriptive character of 'acts'). The manner in which a 'mere presentation' refers to its object, differs from the manner of a judgement, which treats the same state of affairs as true or false. Quite different again is the manner of a

[1] See further the *Appendix* referred to above.
[2] *Psychologie*, I, 115.

surmise or doubt, the manner of a hope or a fear, of approval or disapproval, of desire or aversion; of the resolution of a theoretical doubt (judgemental decision) or of a practical doubt (voluntary decision in the case of deliberate choice); of the confirmation of a theoretical opinion (fulfilment of a judgemental intention), or of a voluntary intention (fulfilment of what we mean to do). Most, if not all, acts are complex experiences, very often involving intentions which are themselves multiple. Emotional intentions are built upon presentative or judging intentions etc. We cannot, however, doubt that to resolve such complexes is always to come down on primitive intentional characters whose descriptive essence precludes reduction into other types of experience, and that the unity of the descriptive genus 'intention' ('act-character') displays specific differences, flowing from its pure essence, which take *a priori* precedence over empirical, psychological matters-of-fact. There are essentially different species and subspecies of intention. We cannot, in particular, reduce all differences in acts into differences in the presentations or judgements they involve, with help only from elements not of an intentional kind. Aesthetic approval or disapproval, e.g., is evidently and essentially a peculiar mode of intentional relation as opposed to the mere presentation or theoretical assessment of the aesthetic object. Aesthetic approval and aesthetic predicates may be asserted, and their assertion is a judgement, and as such includes presentations. But the aesthetic intention and its objects are then *objects* of presentations and judgements: it remains essentially distinct from these theoretical acts. To evaluate a judgement as valid, an emotional experience as elevated etc., presupposes analogous, closely related, not specifically identical intentions. Just so in comparisons of judgemental with voluntary decisions etc.

We take intentional relation, understood in purely descriptive fashion as an inward peculiarity of certain experiences, to be the essential feature of 'psychical phenomena' or 'acts', seeing in Brentano's definition of them as 'phenomena intentionally containing objects in themselves' a circumscription of essence, whose 'reality' (in the traditional sense) is of course ensured by examples.[1]

---

[1] We are not therefore troubled by such vexed questions as to whether all mental phenomena, e.g. the phenomena of feeling, have the peculiarity in question. We must ask instead whether the phenomena in question *are* mental phenomena. The oddness of the question springs from the unsuitability of its wording. More about this later.

Differently put in terms of pure phenomenology: Ideation performed in exemplary cases of such experiences – and so performed as to leave empirical-psychological conception and existential affirmation of being out of account, and to deal only with the real phenomenological content of these experiences – yields us the pure, phenomenological generic Idea of *intentional experience* or *act*, and of its various pure species.[1] That not all experiences are intentional is proved by sensations and sensational complexes. Any piece of a sensed visual field, full as it is of visual contents, is an experience containing many part-contents, which are neither referred to, nor intentionally objective, in the whole.

The discussions which follow will give precision and clarity to the fundamentally different uses of the word 'content'. Everywhere it will appear that what one grasped in the analysis and comparison of instances of the two sorts of contents, can be ideationally seen as a pure distinction of essence. The phenomenological assertions we aim at, are all meant by us (even without special pointing) as assertions of essence.

A second characterization of mental phenomena by Brentano that has value for us is the formula 'that they are either presentations or founded upon presentations'.[2] 'Nothing can be judged about, nothing can likewise be desired, nothing can be hoped or feared, if it is not presented.'[3] In this characterization the term 'presentation' does not of course mean the presented content or object, but the act of presenting this.

This characterization does not seem a suitable starting-point for our researches, since it presupposes a concept of 'presentation' that has yet to be worked out: it is hard to draw distinctions among the word's highly ambiguous uses. The discussion of the concept of 'act' will lead us naturally on to this. But the characterization is an important utterance, whose content prompts further investigations: we shall have to come back to it later.

---

[1] Within the framework of psychological apperception, the purely phenomenological concept of experience fuses with that of mental reality, or rather, it turns into the concept of the mental state of an animal being (either in actual nature or in an ideally possible nature with ideally possible animals, i.e. without existential implications). Later on the pure *phenomenological* generic Idea *intentional experience* transforms itself into the parallel, nearly related *psychological* generic concept. According as psychological apperception is kept out or kept in, the same sort of analysis has phenomenological or psychological import.

[2] *Psychologie*, p. 111 (end of 3).

[3] *Psychologie*, p. 109.

§11 *Avoidance of verbally tempting misunderstandings.*
(a) The 'mental' or 'immanent' object

While we adhere to Brentano's essential characterization, our departures from his opinions force us to abandon his terminology. It will be as well to drop talk of 'psychical phenomena', or of 'phenomena' at all, where we are dealing with experiences of the class in question. 'Psychical phenomena' is a justifiable phrase only on Brentano's view that it fairly circumscribes the psychological field of research: on our view all experiences are in this respect on a level. The term 'phenomenon' is likewise fraught with most dangerous ambiguities, and insinuates a quite doubtful theoretical persuasion, expressly professed by Brentano, that each intentional experience is a phenomenon. As 'phenomenon' in its dominant use (which is also Brentano's) means an appearing object as such, this implies that each intentional experience is not only directed upon objects, but is itself the object of certain intentional experiences. One thinks here, mainly, of the experiences in which things 'appear' in the most special sense, i.e. perceptions: 'every psychical phenomenon is an object of inner consciousness'. We have already mentioned the grave misgivings that keep us from assenting to this.

Further objections surround the expressions used by Brentano as parallel with, or roughly circumscribing, his term 'psychical phenomenon', and which are also in general use. It is always quite questionable, and frequently misleading, to say that perceived, imagined, asserted or desired objects etc., 'enter consciousness' (or do so in perceptual, presentative fashion etc.), or to say conversely that 'consciousness', 'the ego' enters into this or that sort of relation to them, or to say that such objects 'are taken up into consciousness' in this or that way, or to say, similarly, that intentional experiences 'contain something as their object in themselves' etc. etc.[1] Such expressions promote *two misunderstandings*: first, that we are dealing with a real (*realen*) event or a real (*reales*) relationship, taking place between 'consciousness' or 'the ego', on the one hand, and the thing of which there is consciousness, on the other; secondly, that we are dealing with a relation between two things, both present in equally real fashion (*reell*) in consciousness, an act and an intentional object, or with a sort of box-within-box structure of mental contents. If talk of a *relation*

[1] Cf. Brentano, *Psychologie*, pp. 266–7, 295 and *passim*.

is here inescapable, we must avoid expressions which tempt us to regard such a relation as having psychological reality (*Realität*), as belonging to the real (*reellen*) content of an experience.

Let us first discuss our *second* misunderstanding more closely. It is particularly suggested by the expression 'immanent objectivity' used to name the essential peculiarity of intentional experiences, and likewise by the equivalent scholastic expressions 'intentional' or 'mental inexistence' of an object. Intentional experiences have the peculiarity of directing themselves in varying fashion to presented objects, but they do so in an *intentional* sense. An object is 'referred to'[1] or 'aimed at' in them, and in presentative or judging or other fashion. This means no more than that certain experiences are present, intentional in character and, more specifically, presentatively, judgingly, desiringly or otherwise intentional. There are (to ignore certain exceptions) not two things present in experience, we do not experience the object and beside it the intentional experience directed upon it, there are not even two things present in the sense of a part and a whole which contains it: only one thing is present, the intentional experience, whose essential descriptive character is the intention in question. According to its particular specification, it constitutes the full and sole presentation, judgement etc. etc., of this object. If this experience is present, then, *eo ipso* and through its own essence (we must insist), the intentional 'relation' to an object is achieved, and an object is 'intentionally present'; these two phrases mean precisely the same. And of course such an experience may be present in consciousness together with its intention, although its object does not exist at all, and is perhaps incapable of existence. The object is 'meant', i.e. to 'mean' it is an experience, but it is then merely entertained in thought, and is nothing in reality.

If I have an idea of the god Jupiter, this god is my presented object, he is 'immanently present' in my act, he has 'mental inexistence' in the latter, or whatever expression we may use to disguise our true meaning. I have an idea of the god Jupiter: this means that I have a certain presentative experience, the presentation-of-the-god-Jupiter is realized in my consciousness. This intentional experience may be dismembered as one chooses in descriptive analysis, but the god Jupiter naturally will not be

---

[1] No reference to selective attention or notice is included in the sense of the 'reference' involved in our 'intention'. See also §13.

found in it. The 'immanent', 'mental object' is not therefore part of the descriptive or real make-up (*deskriptiven reellen Bestand*) of the experience, it is in truth not really immanent or mental. But it also does not exist extramentally, it does not exist at all. This does not prevent our-idea-of-the-god-Jupiter from being actual, a particular sort of experience or particular mode of mindedness (*Zumutesein*), such that he who experiences it may rightly say that the mythical king of the gods is present to him, concerning whom there are such and such stories. If, however, the intended object exists, nothing becomes phenomenologically different. It makes no essential difference to an object presented and given to consciousness whether it exists, or is fictitious, or is perhaps completely absurd. I think of Jupiter as I think of Bismarck, of the tower of Babel as I think of Cologne Cathedral, of a regular thousand-sided polygon as of a regular thousand-faced solid.[1]

These so-called immanent contents are therefore merely intended or intentional, while truly *immanent contents*, which belong to the real make-up (*reellen Bestande*) of the intentional experiences, are *not intentional*: they constitute the act, provide necessary *points d'appui* which render possible an intention, but are not themselves intended, not the objects presented in the act. I do not see colour-sensations but coloured things, I do not hear tone-sensations but the singer's song etc. etc.[2]

What is true of presentations is true also of other intentional experiences that are built upon them. To represent an object, e.g. the Schloss at Berlin, to oneself, is, we said, to be minded in this or that descriptively determinate fashion. To *judge* about this Schloss, to delight in its architectural beauty, to cherish the wish that one could do so etc. etc., are new experiences, characterized in novel phenomenological terms. All have this in common, that

---

[1] We may here ignore the various possible assertive traits involved in the believed being of what is presented. One should again recall that it is possible to leave out all presupposing of natural reality, persons and other conscious animals included therein in our completed studies, so that they are understood as discussions of *ideal* possibilities. One finally sees them in the light of methodological exclusions, which cut out whatever is matter of transcendent apperception and assertion, so as to bring out what is *really* part of an experience and of its essence. Experience has then become the pure experience of phenomenology, from which psychological apperception has likewise dropped away.

[2] As regards the seemingly obvious distinction between immanent and transcendent objects, modelled on the traditional schema of inner conscious image *v.* extraconscious self-existence, cf. the Appendix at the end of this chapter.

they are modes of objective intention, which cannot be otherwise expressed than by saying that the Schloss is perceived, imagined, pictorially represented, judged about, delighted in, wished for etc. etc.

We shall need more elaborate investigation to determine the justification of talking figuratively about the object presented in a presentation, judged in a judgement etc., as well as the full sense of talk about the relation of acts to objects. It is clear, at least, as far as we now have penetrated, that it will be well to avoid all talk of immanent objectivity. It is readily dispensed with, since we have the expression 'intentional object' which is not exposed to similar objections.

As regards misleading talk of the intentional 'containment' of objects in acts, it is undeniable that the parallel, equivalent locutions – 'the object is a conscious datum', 'is in consciousness', 'is immanent in consciousness' etc. – suffer from a most damaging ambiguity; 'being conscious' (*bewusst*) here means something quite different from the possible senses given to it in the two previously discussed meanings of 'consciousness'. All modern psychology and epistemology have been confused by these and similar equivocations. With psychological thought and terminology as influential as they are now, it would be ill-advised to set up our own terms in opposition to those of contemporary psychology. Our first concept of consciousness, given an empirical-psychological slant, covers the whole stream of experience which makes up the individual mind's real unity, together with all aspects that enter into the constitution of this stream. This conception shows signs of spreading to psychology, and we therefore decided in our last chapter to give the preference to it, though we did so in phenomenological purity and not from a properly psychological angle. We must therefore exercise some necessary care in talking of consciousness as inner perception, or in talking of it as intentional relation, even if we do not altogether avoid such 'uses', which would scarcely be practicable.

§ 12 (*b*) *The act and the relation of consciousness or the ego to the object*

The situation is similar as regards the first misunderstanding we mentioned, where it is imagined that consciousness, on the one hand, and the 'matter in consciousness' on the other, become related to one another in a real sense. ('The ego' is here often put in the place of 'consciousness'.) In *natural reflection*, in fact, it is not the single act which appears, but the ego as one pole of the relation in question, while the other pole is the object. If one then studies an act-experience, which last tempts one to make of the ego an essential, selfsame point of unity in every act. This would, however, bring us back to the view of the ego as a relational centre which we repudiated before.

But if we simply 'live' in the act in question, become absorbed, e.g., in the perceptual 'taking in' of some event happening before us, in some play of fancy, in reading a story, in carrying out a mathematical proof etc., the ego as relational centre of our performances becomes quite elusive. The idea of the ego may be specially *ready* to come to the fore, or rather to be recreated anew, but only when it is really so recreated, and built into our act, do *we* refer to the object in a manner to which something descriptively ostensible corresponds. We have here, in the actual experience described, a correspondingly complex act which presents the ego, on the one hand, and the presentation, judgement, wish etc., of the moment, with its relevant subject-matter, on the other. From an *objective* standpoint (and so, too, from the standpoint of natural reflection) it is doubtless the case that in each act the ego is intentionally directed to some object. This is quite obvious since the ego is either no more than the 'conscious unity', or contemporary 'bundle', of experiences, or, in a more natural empirically-real (*realer*) perspective, the continuous thing-like unity, constituted in the unity of consciousness as the personal subject of our experiences, the ego whose mental states these experiences are, that performs the intention, percept, or judgement in question. If such and such an intentional experience is present, the ego *eo ipso* has the corresponding intention.

The sentences 'The ego represents an object to itself', 'The ego refers presentatively to an object', 'The ego has something as an intentional object of its presentation' therefore mean the same as 'In the phenomenological ego, a concrete complex of experiences, a certain experience said, in virtue of its specific nature, to be a presentation of object X, is really (*reell*) present'. Just so the sentence 'The ego judges about the object' means the same as 'such and such an experience of judging is present in the ego' etc. etc. In our *description* relation to an experiencing ego is inescapable, but the experience described is not itself an experiential complex having the ego-presentation as its part. We perform the description after an objectifying act of reflection, in which reflection on the ego is combined with reflection on the experienced act to yield a relational act, in which the ego appears as itself related to its act's object through its act. Plainly an essential descriptive change has occurred. The original act is no longer simply there, we no longer live in it, but *we attend to it and pass judgement on it.*

We must therefore avoid the misunderstanding which our present discussion has just ruled out, that of treating relation to an ego as of the essence of an intentional experience itself.[1]

§ 13 *The fixing of our terminology*

After these critical prolegomena, we shall now fix our own terminology, excluding as far as we can, and in their light, all conflicting assumptions and confusing ambiguities. We shall avoid the term 'psychical phenomenon' entirely, and shall talk of 'intentional experiences' wherever accuracy requires it. 'Experience' must be understood in the phenomenological sense fixed above. The qualifying adjective 'intentional' names the essence common to the class of experiences we wish to mark off, the peculiarity of *intending*, of referring to what is objective, in a presentative or other analogous fashion. As a briefer expression, in harmony with our own and foreign verbal usage, we shall use the term 'act'.

These expressions certainly have their defects. We speak of 'intending' [not, of course, in English: *Trans.*] in the sense of specially noticing, or attending to something. *An intentional object need not, however, always be noticed or attended to.* Several acts may be present and interwoven with one another, but attention is emphatically active in one of them. We experience them all together, but we 'go all out' (as it were) in this particular one. But it is not unfitting, in view of the traditional use of the term 'intentional object', to which Brentano has given renewed currency, to speak in a correlative sense of 'intention', especially when we have the term 'attending' to do the work of 'intention'

[1] Cf. the additional note to ch. 1, p. 363, and my *Ideen zu einer reinen Phänomenologie*, l.c.

in the other sense; we shall find reason to hold that attention does not involve a peculiar act.[1] Another ambiguity, however, confronts us. The term 'intention' hits off the peculiarity of acts by imagining them to *aim* at something, and so fits the numerous cases that are naturally and understandably ranked as cases of theoretical aiming. But the metaphor does not fit all acts equally, and if we study the examples enumerated in § 10, we cannot avoid distinguishing a *narrower* and a *wider* concept of intention. In our metaphor an act of *hitting the mark* corresponds to that of aiming, and just so certain acts correspond as 'achievements' or 'fulfilments' to other acts as 'intentions' (whether of the judging or the desiring sort). The image therefore fits these latter acts quite perfectly; fulfilments are, however, themselves acts, i.e. 'intentions', though they are not intentions – at least not in general – in that narrower sense *which points to corresponding fulfilments*. This ambiguity, once recognized, becomes harmless. But of course, where the narrower concept is wanted, this must be expressly stated. The equivalent term 'act-character' will also help to avoid misunderstandings.

In talking of 'acts', on the other hand, we must steer clear of the word's original meaning: *all thought of activity must be rigidly excluded*.[2] The term 'act' is so firmly fixed in the usage of many psychologists, and so wellworn and loosed from its original sense that, after these express reservations, we can go on using it without concern. If we do not wish to introduce artificial novelties, strange alike to our living speech-sense and to historical tradition, we can hardly avoid inconvenience of the just-mentioned sort.

§ 14 *Difficulties which surround the assumption of acts as a descriptively based class of experiences*

In all these terminological discussions, we have gone deep into descriptive analyses of a sort required by our interests in logic and epistemology. Before we go deeper, however, we shall have to

---

[1] Cf. § 19.

[2] We are in complete agreement with Natorp (*Einleitung in die Psychologie*, ed. i, p. 21) when he objects to fully serious talk about 'mental activities', or 'activities of consciousness', or 'activities of the ego', by saying that 'consciousness only appears as a doing, and its subject as a doer, because it is often or always accompanied by conation'. We too reject the 'mythology of activities': we define 'acts' as intentional experiences, not as mental activities.

consider some objections which affect the bases of our descriptions.

There are a group of thinkers who absolutely reject any marking-off of a class of experiences which have been described by us as 'acts' or 'intentional experiences'. In this connection Brentano's original introduction of the distinction, and his aims in introducing it, have, with some surreptitious misunderstandings, produced confusion: they have kept the distinction's extraordinarily valuable descriptive content from being rightly assessed. Natorp, e.g., rejects it decisively. But when this distinguished thinker objects by saying that[1] 'I can deal with a tone by itself or in relation to other contents of consciousness, without also paying regard to its being for an ego, but I cannot deal with myself and my hearing by themselves, without thinking of the tone', we find nothing in this that could confuse. Hearing certainly cannot be torn out of the hearing of a tone, as if it were something apart from the tone it hears. But this does not mean that two things are not to be distinguished: the tone heard, the object of perception, and the hearing of the tone, the perceptual act. Natorp is quite right in saying of the former: 'Its existence for me is my consciousness of it. If anyone can catch his consciousness in anything else than the existence of a content for him, I am unable to follow him.' It seems to me, however, that the 'existence of something for me', is a thing both permitting and requiring further phenomenological analysis. Consider, first, differences in the mode of attention. A content is differently present to me, according as I note it implicitly, not relieved in some whole, or see it in relief, according as I see it marginally, or have specially turned my focussing gaze upon it. More important still are differences between the existence of a content in consciousness in the sense in which a sensation so exists, without being itself made a perceptual object, and of a content which *is* made such an object. The choice of a tone as an instance slightly obscures the distinction without altogether removing it. 'I hear' can mean in psychology 'I am having sensations': in ordinary speech it means 'I am perceiving'; I hear the adagio of the violin, the twittering of the birds etc. Different acts can perceive the same object and yet involve quite different sensations. The same tone is

[1] P. Natorp, *Einleitung in die Psychologie*, ed. 1, p. 18.

at one moment heard close at hand, at another far away. The same sensational contents are likewise 'taken' now in this, and now in that manner. What is most emphasized in the doctrine of apperception is generally the fact that consistency of stimulus does not involve constancy of sensational content; what the stimulus really provokes is overlaid by features springing from actualized dispositions left behind them by previous experiences. Such notions are, however, inadequate, and, above all, phenomenologically irrelevant. Whatever the origin of the experienced contents now present in consciousness, we can think that the same sensational contents should be present with a differing interpretation, i.e. that the same contents should serve to ground perceptions of different objects. Interpretation itself can never be reduced to an influx of new sensations; it is an act-character, a mode of consciousness, of 'mindedness' (*Zumuteseins*). We call the experiencing of sensations in this conscious manner the perception of the object in question. What has here been made plain, in a context of natural existence, and by methods appropriate to psychology and natural science, will yield up its phenomenological substance if we abstract from the empirically real (*Realen*). If we consider pure experiences and their own essential content, we form Ideas of pure species and specific situations, in this case the pure species of Sensation, Interpretation, Perception in relation to its *perceptum*, and the relations of essence among these. We then see it to be a fact of essence that the being of a sensational content differs from that of the perceived object presented by it, which is not a reality in consciousness (*reell bewusst*).[1]

All this becomes clear if we change our field of illustration for that of vision. Let us lay the following considerations before a sceptic. I see a thing, e.g. this box, but I do not see my sensations. I always see *one and the same box*, however *it* may be turned and tilted. I have always the *same* 'content of consciousness' – if I care to call the perceived object a content of consciousness. But each turn yields a *new* 'content of consciousness', if I call experienced contents 'contents of consciousness', in a much more appropriate use of words. Very different contents are therefore experienced, though the same object is perceived. The experienced content, generally speaking, is not the perceived object. We must note, further, that the object's real being or non-being is irrelevant

---

[1] Last three sentences added in Edition II.

to the true essence of the perceptual experience, and to its essence as a perceiving of an object as thus and thus appearing, and as thus and thus thought of. In the flux of experienced content, we imagine ourselves to be in perceptual touch with one and the same object; this itself belongs to the sphere of what we experience. For we experience a 'consciousness of identity', i.e. a claim to apprehend identity. On what does this consciousness depend? Must we not reply that different sensational contents are given, but that we apperceive or 'take' them 'in the same sense', and that *to take them in this sense is an experienced character through which the 'being of the object for me' is first constituted*. Must we not say, further, that the consciousness of identity is framed on a basis of these two sorts of experienced characters, as the immediate consciousness that they *mean the same*? And is this consciousness not again an act in our defined sense, whose objective correlate lies in the identity it refers to? These questions, I think, call for an affirmative and evident answer. I find nothing more plain than the distinction here apparent between contents and acts, between perceptual contents in the sense of presentative sensations, and perceptual acts in the sense of interpretative intentions overlaid with various additional characters. Such intentions, united with the sensations they interpret, make up the full concrete act of perception. Intentional characters and complete intentional acts are, of course, contents of consciousness in the widest descriptive sense of experiences: all differences predicable at all, are in this sense *eo ipso* differences of content. But within this widest sphere of what can be experienced, we believe we have found an evident difference between intentional experiences, in whose case *objective intentions* arise through *immanent characters* of the experiences in question, and experiences in whose case this does not occur, contents that may serve as the building-stones of acts *without being acts themselves*.

Examples that will serve to elucidate this distinction, and also to show up various characters of acts, are provided by comparing perception with memory, or comparing either with presentations by means of physical images (paintings, statues etc.), or of signs. Verbal expressions yield the best examples of all. Let us imagine that certain arabesques or figures have affected us aesthetically, and that we then suddenly see that we are dealing with symbols or verbal signs. In what does this difference consist? Or let us take the case of an attentive man hearing some totally strange word as a sound-complex without even dreaming it is a word, and compare this with the case of the same man afterwards hearing the word, in the course of conversation, and now acquainted with its meaning, but not illustrating it intuitively? What in general is the surplus element distinguishing the understanding of a symbolically functioning expression from the uncomprehended verbal sound? What is the difference between simply looking at a concrete object *A*, and treating it as representative of 'any *A* whatsoever'? In this and countless similar cases it is act-characters that differ. All logical differences, and differences in categorial form, are constituted in logical acts in the sense of intentions.

In analysing such cases the inadequacies of the modern theory of apperception become plain: it overlooks points decisive from a logical or epistemological standpoint. It does not do justice to phenomenological fact; it does not even attempt to analyse or describe it. Differences of interpretation are above all *descriptive* differences, and these alone, rather than obscure, hypothetical events in the soul's unconscious depths, or in the sphere of physiological happenings, concern the epistemologist. These alone permit of a purely phenomenological treatment, excluding all transcendent affirmations, such as the critique of knowledge presupposes. Apperception is our surplus, which is found in experience itself, in its descriptive content as opposed to the raw existence of sense: it is the act-character which as it were ensouls sense, and is in essence such as to make us perceive this or that object, see this tree, e.g., hear this ringing, smell this scent of flowers etc. etc. *Sensations*, and the acts 'interpreting' them or apperceiving them, are alike experienced, *but they do not appear as objects*: they are not seen, heard or *perceived* by any sense. *Objects* on the other hand, appear and are perceived, but they are not *experienced*. Naturally we exclude the case of adequate perception.

The same holds in other cases: it holds, e.g., in the case of the 'sensations' (or however we choose to call contents serving as bases to interpretation) which are found in acts of simple or representative imagining. It is an imaging interpretation that sets an imagined rather than a perceptual appearance before us, where experienced sensations mediate the appearance of a pictorially presented object (e.g. a centaur in a painting).[1] One sees at once

[1] The much discussed dispute as to the relation between perceptual and imaginative presentation can have no satisfactory outcome in default of a properly prepared

that the very same thing which, in relation to the intentional object, is called its *presentation*, i.e. the perceiving, remembering, picturing, symbolizing intention directed towards it, is also called an *interpretation, conception, apperception* in relation to the sensations really present in this act.

I also regard it as relevantly evident, in regard to the examples just cited, that there are different 'manners of consciousness', different intentional relations to objects: the character of our intention is specifically different in the case of perceiving, of direct 'reproductive' recall, of pictorial representation (in the ordinary sense of the interpretation of statues, pictures etc.), and again in the case of a presentation through signs. Each logically distinct way of entertaining an object in thought corresponds to a difference in intention. To me it seems irrefragable that we only know of such differences because we envisage them in particular cases (apprehend them adequately and immediately), can then compare them and range them under concepts, and can thus make them into objects of varying acts of intuition and thought. From such 'seeing' we can, through abstract Ideation, progress toward an adequate grasp of the pure species they exemplify, and of the connections of essence among these latter. When Natorp remarks that 'all richness, all multiplicity of consciousness pertains rather to contents alone. Consciousness of a simple sensation does not differ, *qua* consciousness, from consciousness of a world: the "being in consciousness" is entirely the same in both; their difference lies solely in their content', he seems to me not to be keeping apart quite distinct notions of consciousness and content, and to be erecting his identification into an epistemological principle. We have explained the sense in which we too teach that all multiplicity of consciousness depends on content. Content must mean experience, a real part of consciousness: consciousness itself must be the complex formed by experiences. The world, however, never is a thinker's experience. To refer to the world may be an experience, but the world itself is the object intended. It is immaterial, from the point of view of our distinction, what attitude one takes up to the question of the make-up of objective

phenomenological foundation and consequent clarity in concepts and questions. The like holds of enquiries as to the relation of simple perception to representational or sign-consciousness. It can be readily shown, I think, that act-characters differ in such cases in pictorial representation, e.g. an essentially new mode of intention, is experienced.

being, of the true, real inner being of the world or of any other object, or of the relation of objective being, as a 'unity', to our 'manifold' thought-approaches, or of the sense in which one may metaphysically oppose immanent to transcendent being. The distinction in question is prior to all metaphysics, and lies at the very gates of the theory of knowledge: it presupposes no answers to the questions that this theory must be the first to provide.

§ 15 *Whether experiences of one and the same phenomenological kind (of the genus* Feeling *in particular) can consist partly of acts and partly of non-acts*

A new difficulty arises in regard to the generic unity of intentional experiences.

It might be thought that the standpoint from which we divide experiences into intentional and non-intentional, is a merely external one, that the same experiences, or experiences of the same phenomenological class, may at times have an intentional relation to some object, and at times have none. The examples used to attest either concept, and also, in part, the attempted solutions of the problem, have already been discussed in literary fashion in regard to the debated issue as to whether the 'intentional relation' suffices to demarcate 'psychical phenomena' (the domain of psychology) or not. The debate centred chiefly in phenomena from the sphere of *feeling*. Since the intentionality of other feelings seemed obvious, two doubts were possible: one wondered whether intentionality might not perhaps attach loosely to the *acts* of feeling in question, belonging really to the presentations fused with them, or whether intentionality could be essential to the class of feelings, since one allowed it to some feelings while denying it to others. The connection between this commonly debated question and our present question has thus been made clear.

We must first see whether any sorts of feeling-experience are essentially intentional, and then whether other sorts of feeling-experience lack this property.

(*a*) *Are there any intentional feelings?*

Many experiences commonly classed as 'feelings' have an undeniable, real relation to something objective. This is the case, e.g., when we are pleased by a melody, displeased at a shrill blast etc. etc. It seems obvious, in general, that every joy or sorrow, that is joy or sorrow *about* something we think of, is a directed act. Instead of joy we can speak of pleased delight in something, instead of sorrow we can speak of displeased or painful dislike of it, aversion from it etc. etc.

Those who question the intentionality of feeling say: Feelings are mere states, not acts, intentions. Where they relate to objects, they owe their relation to a complication with presentations.

No intrinsic objection is involved in this last position. Brentano who defends the intentionality of feelings, also maintains without inconsistency that feelings, like all acts that are not themselves presentations, have presentations as their foundations.[1] We can only direct ourselves feelingly to objects that are presented to us by inwoven presentations. No difference emerges between the disputing parties until someone is really prepared to maintain that feeling, considered in itself, involves nothing intentional, that it does not point beyond itself to a felt object, that only its union with a presentation gives it a certain relation to an object, a relation only intentional by way of *this* connection and not intrinsically so. This is just what the other party disputes.

Brentano thinks we have here two intentions built on one another: the underlying, founding intention gives us the *presented* object, the founded intention the *felt* object. The former is separable from the latter, the latter inseparable from the former. His opponents think there is only *one* intention here, the presenting one.

If we subject the situation to a careful phenomenological review, Brentano's conception seems definitely to be preferred. Whether we turn with pleasure to something, or whether its unpleasantness repels us, an object is presented. But we do not merely have a presentation, with an added feeling *associatively* tacked on to it, and not intrinsically related to it, but pleasure or distaste *direct* themselves to the presented object, and could not exist without such a direction. If two psychical experiences, e.g. two presentations, are associated in an objective-psychological sense, there is a phenomenologically discernible type of associative unity among the reproduced experiences which corresponds to the objective dispositions which govern them. Side by side with the intentional elation which each has to its object, there is also a phenomeno-

[1] *Psychologie*, I, pp. 116 ff.

logical mode of connection: one idea, e.g. that of Naples, carries with it the idea of Vesuvius, the one is peculiarly bound up with the other, so that we say in regard to the objects presented – the mode of their presentation here essentially requires further description – that the one reminds us of the other. (This sentence is being used to express a phenomenological situation.) It is easily seen, however, that though all this in a sense constitutes a new intentional relationship, it does not turn each associated member into an object of the other's intention. The intentional relationships remain unconfused in their association. How indeed could they furnish an object, borrowed from an associated intention, to something not itself intentional? It is clear, further, that such a phenomenologically associative relation is extrinsic, not at all to be put on a level with the relation of pleasure to the pleasant. The presentation which reproduces is quite possible without such a reproductive function. But pleasure without anything pleasant is unthinkable. And it is unthinkable, not because we are here dealing with correlative expressions, as when we say, e.g., that a cause without an effect, or a father without a child, is unthinkable, but because *the specific essence of pleasure demands a relation to something pleasing*. Just so the feature known as conviction is unthinkable apart from something of which we are convinced. There is, similarly, no desire whose specific character can do without something desired, no agreement or approval without something agreed on or approved etc. etc. These are all intentions, genuine acts in our sense. They all 'owe' their intentional relation to certain underlying presentations. But it is part of what we mean by such 'owing' that they themselves really now *have* what they owe to something else.

It is plain, too, that the relation between founding (underlying) presentation and founded act cannot be correctly described by saying that the former *produces* the latter. We say that the object arouses our pleasure, just as we say in other cases that some circumstance inspires doubt, compels agreement, provokes desire etc. But the result of such apparent causation, the pleasure, doubt or agreement provoked, is itself through and through intentional. We are not dealing with an external causal relation where the effect conceivably could be what it intrinsically is without the cause, or where the cause brings something forth that could have existed independently.

Closer consideration shows it to be absurd in principle, here or in like cases, to treat an intentional as a causal relation, to give it the sense of an empirical, substantial-causal case of necessary connection. For the intentional object, here thought of as 'provocative', is only in question as an intentional, not as an external reality, which really and psycho-physically determines my mental life. A battle of centaurs, seen in a picture or framed in fancy, 'provokes' my approval just like some beautiful, real landscape: if I look on the latter psycho-physically as the real cause of my mentally provoked state of pleasure, this 'causation' is altogether different from the causation we have when we see the visible landscape – in virtue of such and such a mode of appearing and such and such pictured colours and forms – as the 'source', 'ground' or 'cause' of my pleasure. Pleasantness or pleasure do not belong as effect to this landscape considered as a physical reality, but only to it *as appearing in this or that manner*, perhaps as thus and thus judged of or as reminding us of this or that, in the conscious act here in question: it is as such that the landscape 'demands', 'arouses' such feelings.[1]

(b) Are there non-intentional feelings? Distinction between feeling-sensations and feeling-acts.

We may now ask more generally whether, in addition to the intentional varieties of feeling, there are not other *non*-intentional species. It may seem at first that an obvious 'Yes' is the right answer. In the wide field of so-called sensory feelings, no intentional characters can be found. The sensible pain of a burn can certainly not be classed beside a conviction, a surmise, a volition etc. etc., but beside sensory contents like rough or smooth, red or blue etc. If we recall such pains, or any sensory pleasures (the fragrance of a rose, the relish of certain foods etc. etc.), we find that our sensory feelings are blended with the sensations from the various sense-fields, just as these latter are blended with one another.

Every sensory feeling, e.g. the pain of burning oneself or of being burnt, is no doubt after a fashion referred to an object: it is referred, on the one hand, to the ego and its burnt bodily member, on the other hand, to the object which inflicts the burn. In all these

[1] [Paragraph added in Edition II.]

respects there is conformity with other sensations: tactual sensations, e.g., are referred in just this manner to the bodily member which touches, and to the external body which is touched. And though this reference is realized in intentional experiences, no one would think of calling the referred sensations intentional. It is rather the case that our sensations are here functioning as presentative contents in perceptual acts, or (to use a possibly misleading phrase) that our sensations here receive an objective 'interpretation' or 'taking-up'. They themselves are not acts, but acts are constituted through them, wherever, that is, intentional characters like a perceptual interpretation lay hold of them, and as it were animate them. In just this manner it seems that a burning, piercing, boring pain, fused as it is from the start with certain tactual sensations, must itself count as a sensation. It functions at least as other sensations do, in providing a foothold for empirical, objective interpretations.

All this seems unobjectionable, and the whole question disposed of. We seem to have shown that *some* feelings are to be reckoned among intentional experiences, while others are non-intentional.

But we are led to doubt, then, whether two such sorts of 'feelings' really form a single class. We spoke previously of 'feelings' of liking and dislike, of approval and disapproval, of valuation and disvaluation – experiences obviously akin to theoretical acts of assent and rejection, of taking something to be probable or improbable, or to deliberative acts of judgemental or voluntary decision etc. Here we have a *kind*, a plain unity of essence, which included nothing but acts, where such sensations of pain and pleasure have no place: descriptively the latter belong, in virtue of their specific essence, among tactual, gustatory, olfactory and other sensations. Being at best presentative contents of objects of intention, but not themselves intentions, they manifest descriptive differences so essential, that we cannot seriously believe in the unity of a genuine class. In both cases of course, we speak of 'feelings', i.e. in the case of the above-mentioned acts of liking as in the case of the above-mentioned sensations. This fact need not perplex, any more than our ordinary talk of 'feeling', in the sense of touching, need lead us astray in the case of tactile sensations.

Brentano has already pointed to the ambiguity here dealt with, in discussing the intentionality of feelings. He draws a distinction, in sense if not in words, between *sensations* of pain and pleasure (feeling-sensations) and pain and pleasure in the sense of *feelings*. The contents of the former – or, as I should simply say, the former[1] – are in this terminology 'physical', while the latter are 'psychical phenomena', and they belong therefore to essentially different genera. This notion I regard as quite correct, but only doubt, whether the meaning of the word 'feeling' does not lean predominantly towards 'feeling-sensation', and whether the many acts we call 'feelings' do not owe their name to the feeling-sensations with which they are essentially interwoven. One must of course not mix up questions of suitable terminology with questions regarding the factual correctness of Brentano's distinction.

Our distinction should constantly be kept in mind and fruitfully applied in analysing all complexes of feeling-sensations and feeling-acts. Joy, e.g., concerning some happy event, is certainly an act. But this act, which is not merely an intentional character, but a concrete and therefore complex experience, does not merely hold in its unity an idea of the happy event and an act-character of liking which relates to it: a sensation of pleasure attaches to the idea, a sensation at once seen and located as an emotional excitement in the psycho-physical feeling-subject, and also as an objective property – the event seems as if bathed in a rosy gleam. The event thus pleasingly painted now serves as the first foundation for the joyful approach, the liking for, the being charmed, or however one's state may be described. A sad event, likewise, is not merely seen in its thinglike content and context, in the respects which make it an event: it seems clothed and coloured with sadness. The same unpleasing sensations which the empirical ego refers to and locates in itself – the pang in the heart – are referred in one's emotional conception to the thing itself. *These* relations are purely presentational: we first have an essentially new type of intention in hostile repugnance, in active dislike etc. Sensations of pleasure and pain may continue, though the act-characters built upon them may lapse. When the facts which provoke pleasure sink into the background, are no longer apperceived as emotionally coloured, and perhaps cease to be intentional objects at all, the pleasurable excitement may linger on for a

[1] Here as elsewhere I identify the pain-sensation with its 'content', since I do not recognize peculiar sensing acts. Naturally I reject Brentano's doctrine that presentative acts, in the term of acts of feeling-sensation, underlie acts of feeling.

while: it may itself be felt as agreeable. Instead of representing a pleasant property of the object, it is referred merely to the feeling-subject, or is itself presented and pleases.

Much the same holds in the sphere of desire and volition.[1] If difficulty is felt in the fact that desire does not always seem to require conscious reference to what is desired, that we are often moved by obscure drives or pressures towards unrepresented goals, and if one points especially to the wide sphere of natural instinct, where goal-consciousness is at least absent at the start, one may say: This is a case of mere sensations – we may speak analogically of 'desire-sensations' – without needing to affirm the existence of an essentially new class of sensations – i.e. of experiences really lacking intentional reference, and so also remote in kind from the essential character of intentional desire. Alternatively one may say: Here we are dealing with intentional experiences, but with such as are characterized by indeterminateness of objective direction, an 'indeterminateness' which does not amount to a privation, but which stands for a descriptive character of one's presentation. The idea we have when 'something' stirs, when there is a rustling, a ring at the door, etc., an idea had before we give it verbal expression, has indeterminateness of direction, and this indeterminateness is of the intention's essence, it is determined as presenting an indeterminate 'something'.

Our one concept of desire might fit many cases, and our other concept others, and we might have to allow, not a relation of generic community between intentional and non-intentional urges or desires, but one of mere equivocation.

We must observe, also, that our classification is oriented to the concretely complex, and that the total character of such unities may at one time seem to depend on sensational features (e.g. pleasure on urge-sensations), at another on act-intentions which rest on these. The formation and use of our expressions will at times therefore point to sensory contents, at times to act-intentions, so giving rise to the equivocations in question.

Additional Note. The obvious tendency of our conception is to attribute primary, genuine differences in intensity to underlying sensations, and to concrete acts only in a secondary manner, in so

[1] I point here, for purposes of comparison, and perhaps completion, to H. Schwarz's *Psychologie des Willens* (Leipzig, 1900) which in §12 deals with similar questions.

far as their concrete total character involves differences of intensity in their sensational basis. *Act-intentions*, the inseparable aspects which give acts their essential distinctive peculiarities, or which characterize them severally as judgements, feelings etc., *must be without intrinsic intensity*. Deeper analyses are, however, required here.

§16 *Distinction between descriptive and intentional content*

We have buttressed our notion of the essence of acts against objection, and given them a generic unity of essence in their character as intentions, as consciousnesses in the unique descriptive sense. We now introduce an important phenomeno-logical distinction, obvious after our previous discussions, between the *real (reellen)*[1] and the *intentional* content of an act.

By the real phenomenological content of an act we mean the sum total of its concrete or abstract parts, in other words, the sum total of the *partial experiences* that really constitute it. To point out and describe such parts is the task of pure descriptive psycho-logical analysis operating from an empirical, natural-scientific point of view. Such analysis is in all cases concerned to dismember what we inwardly experience as it in itself is, and as it is really *(reell)* given in experience, without regard either to genetic connections, or to extrinsic meaning and valid application. Purely descriptive psychological analysis of an articulated sound-pattern finds only sounds and abstract parts or unifying forms of sounds, it finds no sound-vibrations or organs of hearing etc.; it also never finds anything that resembles the ideal sense that makes the sound-

---

[1] In the First Edition I wrote 'real *or* phenomenological' for 'real'. The word 'phenomenological' like the word 'descriptive' was used in the First Edition only in connection with *real (reelle)* elements of experience, and in the present edition it has so far been used predominately in this sense. This corresponds to one's natural starting with the psychological point of view. It became plainer and plainer, however, as I reviewed the completed Investigations and pondered on their themes more deeply – particularly from this point onwards – that the description of intentional objectivity as such, as we are conscious of it in the concrete act-experience, represents a distinct descriptive dimension where purely intuitive description may be adequately practised, a dimension opposed to that of real *(reellen)* act-constituents, but which also deserves to be called 'phenomenological'. These methodological extensions lead to important extensions of the field of problems now opening before us and considerable improvements due to a fully conscious separation of descriptive levels. Cf. my *Ideen zu einer reinen Phänomenologie*, Book I, and particularly what is said of *Noesis* and *Noema* in Section III.

pattern to be a name, nor the person to whom the name may apply. Our example suffices to make our intention clear. The real (*reell*) contents of acts are of course only known through descriptive analyses of this kind. That obscurities of intuition or inadequacies of descriptive conception – faults, in short, of method – may lead to much 'manufacture' of sensations (to use Volkelt's phrase) cannot be denied. This, however, only concerns the legitimacy of particular cases of descriptive analysis. It is clear, if anything is clear, that intentional experiences contain distinguishable parts and aspects, and this alone is of importance here.

Let us now shift from our natural-scientific, psychological standpoint to an ideal-scientific, phenomenological one. We must exclude all empirical interpretations and existential affirmations, we must take what is inwardly experienced or otherwise inwardly intuited (e.g. in pure fancy) as pure experiences, as our exemplary basis for acts of Ideation. We must ideate universal essences and essential connections in such experiences – ideal Species of experiencing of differing levels of generality, and ideally valid truths of essence which apply *a priori*, and with unlimited generality, to possible experiences of these species. We thus achieve insights in a pure phenomenology which is here oriented to *real* (*reellen*) constituents, whose descriptions are in every way 'ideal' and free from 'experience', i.e. from presupposition of real *existence*. When we speak simply of the real (*reellen*), and in general of the phenomenological analysis and description of experiences, the tie-up of our discussions to psychological material is (we must keep on stressing) merely transitional, since none of its empirically real (*reellen*) conceptions and assertions of existence (e.g. of experiences as states of animal beings having experiences in a real (*realen*), space-time world) are at all operative, that *pure* phenomenological validity of essence is aimed at and claimed.[1]

Content in the real (*reellen*) sense is the mere application of the most general notion of content, valid in all fields to intentional experiences. If we now oppose *intentional*[2] to real (*reell*) content, the word shows that the peculiarity of intentional experiences (or

---

[1] Paragraph added in the Second Edition.

[2] *Real* would sound much better alongside 'intentional' but it definitely keeps the notion of thinglike transcendence which the reduction to *real* (*reell*) immanence in experience is meant to exclude. It is well to maintain a conscious association of the *real* with the thinglike.

acts) is now in question. Here, however, there are several concepts, all grounded in the *specific* nature of acts, which may be equally covered by the rubric 'intentional content', and are often so covered. We shall first have to distinguish *three* concepts of the intentional content: the *intentional object* of the act, its *intentional material* (as opposed to its *intentional quality*) and, lastly its *intentional essence*. These distinctions will become familiar in the course of the following very general analyses, which are also essential to the more restricted aim of clarifying the essence of knowledge.

§17 *The intentional content in the sense of the intentional object*

Our first concept of intentional content needs no elaborate preliminaries. It concerns the intentional object, e.g. a house when a house is presented. That the intentional object does not generally fall within the real (*reellen*) content of an act, but rather differs completely from this, has been already discussed. This is not only true of acts pointing intentionally to 'outer' things; it is also true in part of acts that point to our own present experiences, as when I speak of, e.g., my actually present, but 'background' conscious experiences. Partial coincidence is only found where an intuition actually points to something 'lived through' in the intentional act itself, as, e.g., in acts of adequate perception.

We must distinguish, in relation to the intentional content taken as object of the act, between *the object as it is intended*, and the *object* (period) *which* is intended. In each act an object is presented as determined in this or that manner, and as such it may be the target of varying intentions, judgemental, emotional, desiderative etc. Known connections, actual or possible, entirely external to the reality of the act, may be so cemented with it in intentional unity as to be held to attribute objective properties to the same presented object, properties not in the scope of the intention in question. Many new presentations may arise, all claiming, in virtue of an objective unity of knowledge, to be presenting the same object. In all of them the object *which* we intend is the same, but in each our intention differs, each means the object in a different way. The idea, e.g., of the German Emperor, presents its object as an Emperor, and as the Emperor of Germany. The man himself is the son of the Emperor Frederick III, the grandson of Queen

Victoria, and has many other properties neither named nor presented. One can therefore quite consistently speak of the intentional and extra-intentional content of the object of some presentation, and one can use many other suitable, non-technical expressions, e.g. what we intend in the object, that would not lead to misunderstandings.

Another, yet more important, distinction goes with the distinction just drawn, that between *the objective reference of the act, taken in its entirety,* and the *objects to which its various partial, constituent acts refer.* Each act has its own appropriate, intentional, objective reference: this is as true of complex as of simple acts. *Whatever the composition of an act out of partial acts may be, if it is an act at all, it must have a single objective correlate,* to which we say it is 'directed', in the *full, primary* sense of the world. Its partial acts (if they really are acts entering the complex act as parts, and not mere parts *of* this act) likewise point to objects, which will, in general, not be the same as the object of the whole act, though they may occasionally be the same. In a *secondary* sense, no doubt, the whole act may be said to refer to these objects also, but its intention only terminates on them inasmuch as its constituent acts primarily intend them. Or, seen from the other side, they are only the act's objects in so far as they help to make up its true object, in the manner in which this is intended. They function as terms of relations in which the primary object is seen as the correlated term. The act, e.g., corresponding to the name 'the knife on the table' is plainly complex: the object of the whole act is a knife, of one of its part-acts, a table. But, as the whole nominal act refers to the knife as on the table, presents it in this relative position to the latter, one can say that the table is in a secondary sense an intentional object of the whole act. Again, to illustrate another important class of cases, the knife is the object *about* which we judge or make a statement, when we say that the knife is on the table; the knife is not, however, the primary or full object of the judgement, but only the object of its subject. The full and entire object corresponding to the whole judgement is the *state of affairs* judged: the same state of affairs is presented in a mere presentation, wished in a wish, asked after in a question, doubted in a doubt etc. The wish that the knife were on the table, which coincides (in object) with the judgement, is concerned with the knife, but we don't in it wish the knife, but that the knife should be on the table, that this should be so. The state of affairs must obviously not be confused with the judging of it, nor with the presentation of this judgement: I plainly do not wish for a judgement, nor for any presentation. Just so there is a corresponding question regarding the knife, but the knife is not (nonsensically) what we ask; we ask regarding the knife's position on the table, whether this actually is the case. So much for the first sense in which we speak of intentional contents. Since such talk is so highly ambiguous, we shall do well never to speak of an intentional content where an intentional object is meant, but to call the latter the intentional object of the act in question.

§ 18 *Simple and complex, underlying and founded acts*

We have so far only learnt to attach one meaning to the term 'intentional contents'. Further meanings will develop in our ensuing investigations, where we shall attempt to seize on certain important peculiarities of the phenomenological essence of acts, and to throw light on the ideal unities rooted in these.

We start with the difference, previously noted, between simple and compound acts. Not every unitary experience compounded out of acts is for that reason a *compound* act, just as every concatenation of machines is not a compound machine. Our comparison illuminates our further requirements. A compound machine is a machine compounded out of machines, but so compounded, that it has a total performance into which the performances of the partial machines flow, and the like is the case in regard to compounded acts. Each partial act has its particular intentional reference, each its unitary object, and its way of referring to it. These manifold part-acts are, however, summed up in one total act, whose total achievement lies in the unity of its intentional reference. To this the individual acts contribute their individual performances: the unity of what is objectively presented, and the whole manner of the intentional reference to it, are not set up *alongside* of the partial acts, but *in* them, in the way in which they are combined, a way which realizes a unity of *act*, and not merely a unity of experience. The object of this total act could not appear as it does, unless the partial acts presented their objects in their fashion: their general function is to present parts, or to present externally related terms, or to present relational forms of the object etc. The same is true of the non-presentative aspects of the act that make out of the unified qualities in the partial acts the quality of whole acts, and so determine the specifically different ways in which the objects concerned in either sort of act are 'taken up into consciousness'.

We may take as an example the unity of categorical or hypothetical predication, where the total acts are plainly put together out of partial acts. The subject-member of a categorical assertion is an underlying act, a positing of a subject, on which the positing of a predicate, its attribution or denial, reposes. Just so the antecedent of a hypothetical assertion is constituent in a clearly demarcated part-act, upon which the conditional assertion is built. The total experience is in each case plainly one act, one judgement, whose single, total object is a single state of affairs. As the judgement does not exist alongside of, or between, the subject-positing and the predicating acts, but exists in them as their dominant unity, so, on the correlative side, the objective unity is the state of affairs judged, an appearance emergent out of subject and predicate, or out of antecedent and consequent.

The situation may be yet more complex. On such a structured act (whose members may themselves be further structured) a new act may be built, e.g. a joy may be built on the assertion of a state of affairs, a joy *in* that state of affairs. The joy is not a concrete act in its own right, and the judgement an act set up beside it: the judgement rather underlies the joy, fixes its content, realizes its abstract possibility for, without some such foundation, there could be no joy at all.[1] Judgements may similarly serve as foundations for surmises, doubts, questions, wishes, acts of will etc., and the latter acts may likewise serve to found other acts in their turn. There are therefore manifold ways in which acts may be combined into total acts. The briefest consideration makes plain that there are deep differences in the ways in which acts are concretely woven into other acts, or based upon underlying acts, and made possible by such concretion: the systematic investigation of such ways, even in descriptive, psychological fashion, is as yet hardly in its beginnings.

[1] We have here a case of 'foundation' in the strict sense of our Third Investigation. We only use the term in this strict sense.

§ 19 *The function of attention in complex acts. Instance of the phenomenological relation of verbal sound to sense*

How far differences go in this direction will be plain from an example previously considered: the whole which is formed by expression and sense.[1] This will be quite as interesting as the examples just analysed. Further considerations will also illustrate the obvious to anyone, the fact that there are great differences in the energy, so to speak, with which acts assert themselves in an act-complex. Generally the greatest energy will be displayed by the act-character which comprehends and subsumes all partial acts in its unity – whether it be a particular act-intention like joy, or a form of unity that pervades all parts of the whole act. In this act, we live, as it were, principally; in the subordinate acts only in proportion to the importance of their achievements for the whole act and its intention. But plainly to talk of such differences of importance, is just to use other words to cover the 'preferential living' in question, which some acts enjoy and others not.

Let us now consider our example. It concerns a union of the acts in which an expression, treated as a sensuous verbal sound, is constituted, with the quite different act constitutive of its meaning, an essentially different connection, we may note, to that of the last-mentioned acts with the acts in which they have an immediate or a more remote intuitive fulfilment. Not only is the mode of union here essentially different, but also the energy with which certain acts are performed. The expression is indeed perceived, but our interest does not live in this perception; we attend, when not distracted, to the signified rather than the signs. Dominant energy resides in the sense-giving acts. The intuitive acts which perhaps accompany, and are inwoven into the total act's unity, lending it evidence, or illustrating it, or otherwise functioning in it, absorb our dominant interest in varying degree. They may be prominent, as in the perceptual judgement, or the analogously constituted picture-judgement, where our one wish is to express the perception or imagination in which we live, and likewise in the completely evident judgement of necessary law. They may recede and come to seem quite subsidiary, as in cases of imperfect or wholly unsuitable illustration of some dominant thought. They may then be a vanishing phantasm, to which

[1] *Investigation* I, §§9, 10.

practically no interest attaches. (In extreme cases one may even doubt whether accompanying picture-ideas really enter the unity of the expressive act at all, whether they are not mere accompaniments; coexisting with the acts in question but not forming a single act with them.)

For us it is especially important to get as much clarity as we can on this situation of expressions: we shall therefore dwell on some points in more detail.

Expression and sense are two objective unities, laid before us by certain acts. An expression itself, e.g. a written word, is, as our *First Investigation* showed,[1] as much a physical object as any penscratch or ink-blot on paper. It is 'given' to us in the same sense as a physical object, i.e. it appears, and that it appears merely means, as it means elsewhere, that a certain act is experienced, in which certain sensory experiences are 'apperceived' in a certain manner. The acts in question are naturally perceptual or imaginative presentations: in these the expression (as physically meant) is constituted.

What make the expression an expression are, we know, the acts attaching to it. These are not outside of it or beside it, or merely simultaneous in consciousness; they are one with it, and so one, that we can scarce avoid regarding them all as making up a *unitary total act*. (By the word 'expression' we mean, with natural and convenient looseness, the act-unity which presents it.) A statement, an assertion, e.g., we should at once say, is a strictly unitary experience, which belongs to the genus Judgement. We do not find in ourselves a mere sum of acts, but a single act in which, as it were, a bodily and spiritual side are distinct. Just so an expressed wish is no mere *ensemble* of expression and wish – with perhaps an additional, debatable judgement regarding the wish – but a whole, an act, which we unhesitatingly call a wish. The physical expression, the verbal sound, may seem unessential to this unity, and it is unessential inasmuch as any other verbal sound might have replaced it and done duty for it: it could even have been wholly dispensed with. But if it is there, and serves as a verbal sound, it will be fused with the accompanying acts in a single act. Plainly the connection is in a certain sense extrinsic, since the expression as such, i.e. the manifest verbal sound or written sign etc., is not seen as part of the object meant in the

[1] Cf. §10.

whole act, nor even as really determining it, nor as having really to do with it. The contribution made by the acts constituting the verbal sound of a statement, differs characteristically from the contribution of the underlying acts illustrated and discussed above, or of the partial acts which pertain to the predicative members of complete predications. We must not, however, despite all this, question the presence of a certain intentional linkage between word and thing. Inasmuch, e.g., as the word names the thing, it once more appears as in some sense one with it, as belonging to it, even if not as materially part of it, or one of its material properties. Its material unrelatedness does not exclude a certain intentional unity, correlated with the interconnection of the corresponding acts to form a single act. This is confirmed if we recall the deep-set tendency to exaggerate the bond between word and thing, to invest it with objectivity, perhaps even to insinuate something of mystic unity into it.

In the compound act which includes both appearing-expression and sense-giving acts, it is plainly the latter, or the act-unity which dominates both, which essentially fixes the character of the whole act. It is for this reason that we call experiences, whether expressed or unexpressed, by the same names: i.e., 'judgement', 'wish', etc. Certain acts in the compound are therefore peculiarly prominent, a fact incidentally noted when we said that, when we normally express something, we do not, *qua* expressing it, live in the acts constituting the expression as a physical object – we are not interested in this object – but we live in the acts which give it sense: we are exclusively *turned* to the object that appears in such acts, we *aim* at it, we *mean* it in the special, *pregnant* sense. We pointed out, also, that, while a special orientation to the physical expression is possible, it essentially changes the character of our experience: this no longer is 'expressive' in the ordinary sense of the word.

Plainly we are here concerned with a case of the general fact of *attention*, to which long effort has not yet brought sufficient clearness.[1] Nothing has so hindered right views in this field as the by-passing of the fact that *attention is an emphatic function which belongs among acts in the above defined sense of intentional experiences*, and which is not descriptively graspable as long as 'being experi-

---

[1] We encountered this fact in criticizing the prevailing theory of abstraction. See Inv. II, §22.

enced', in the sense of the mere existence of a content in consciousness, is confused with intentional objectivity. *Acts* must be present, before we can *live* in them or be *absorbed* in performing them, and when we are so absorbed (in various manners requiring further description) we mind the *objects* of these acts, we are primarily or secondarily oriented towards them, perhaps thematically concerned with them. Absorption in acts and minding objects are the same thing expressed from different angles.

As opposed to this, men speak of attention as if it were a name for modes of special relief imparted to *experienced* contents. At the same time there is still talk of these contents (the contemporary experiences themselves) as if they were the things to which we ordinarily say we are attending. We do not of course dispute the possibility of attending to experienced contents, but when this happens, such contents become objects of *internal* perception: such perception is not the mere being of the content in a conscious setting, but an *act* in which the content is rendered *objective*. *Intentional* objects of acts, and only intentional objects, are the things to which we are at any time attentive, and to which we can be so attentive. This accords with ordinary usage, whose true sense should be plain on the briefest reflection. To ordinary usage the objects of attention are always objects of inward or outward perception, objects of memory, of expectation, perhaps states of affairs in a scientific discussion, etc. Certainly we can only speak of attention where what we attend to is 'in consciousness'. What is not a 'content of consciousness' cannot attract or hold attention nor become a theme of consciousness. The danger of this obvious truth lies in the equivocal term 'content of consciousness'. For the obvious truth does not mean that attention is necessarily directed to conscious contents in the sense of *experiences*, as if no one could attend to things, and to other real (*reale*) or ideal objects, which are not experiences. It means, rather, that there must be a basic act in which what we attend to becomes objective, becomes presented in the widest sense of this word. Such *presentation* can be non-intuitive as well as intuitive, can be utterly inadequate as much as adequate. One might, however, consider, from another angle, whether the *preference* an act enjoys over its fellows when we 'live' in it, when we are primarily or secondarily 'turned' towards its objects, are perhaps 'specially concerned' with them, *should itself be reckoned as an act*. Such a view would make all dominant facts *eo ipso* complex. Should we not rather regard the phenomena of attention as mere ways – requiring much more detailed description of their several varieties – in which acts may be carried out? This would seem to be undoubtedly right.

But we do not wish to work out a 'theory' of attention here, but to discuss the important role played by it in complex acts, in putting certain act-characters into relief, and so essentially influencing the phenomenological pattern of these acts.

§20 *The difference between the quality and the matter of an act*

We now turn from the distinction between the acts in which we 'live' and the acts which proceed 'on the side', to another extremely important, seemingly plain distinction lying in a quite different direction. This is the distinction between the general act-character, which stamps an act as merely presentative, judgemental, emotional, desiderative etc., and its 'content' which stamps it as presenting *this*, as judging *that* etc. etc. The two assertions '$2 \times 2 = 4$' and 'Ibsen is the principal founder of modern dramatic realism', are both, *qua* assertions, of one kind; each is qualified as an assertion, and their common feature is their *judgement-quality*. The one, however, judges one content and the other another content. To distinguish such 'contents' from other notions of 'content' we shall speak here of the *matter* (material) of judgements. We shall draw similar distinctions between *quality* and *matter* in the case of all acts.

Under the rubric of 'matter' we shall not divide, and then reassemble in unity, constituents of an act such as the subject-act, the predicate-act etc.: this would make the unified total content the act itself. What we here have in mind is something totally different. Content in the sense of 'matter' is a component of the concrete act-experience, which it may share with acts of quite different quality. It comes out most clearly if we set up a series of identical utterances, where the act-qualities change, while the matter remains identical. All this is not hard to provide. We recall familiar talk to the effect that *the same content* may now be the content of a mere presentation, now of a judgement, now of a question, now of a doubt, a wish etc. etc. A man who frames the presentation 'There are intelligent beings on Mars' frames the same presentation as the man who asserts 'There are intelligent beings on Mars', and the same as the man who asks 'Are there intelligent beings on Mars?', or the man who wishes 'If only there are intelligent beings on Mars!' etc. etc. We have deliberately written out the closely correspondent expressions in full. To be alike in 'content', while differing in act-quality has its visible grammatical expression; the harmony of grammatical forms points the way to our analysis.

What do we mean by the 'same content'? Plainly the intentional objectivity of the various acts is the same. One and the same state of affairs is presented in the presentation, put as valid in the judgement, wished for in the wish, asked about in the question. This observation does not, however, go far enough, as we shall now show. In real (*reell*) phenomenological treatment, objectivity counts as nothing: in general, it transcends the act. *It makes no difference what sort of being we give our object, or with what sense or justification we do so, whether this being is real* (real) *or ideal, genuine, possible or impossible, the act remains 'directed upon' its object.* If one now asks how something non-existent or transcendent can be the intentional object in an act in which it has no being, one can only give the answer we gave above, which is also a wholly sufficient one. The object is an intentional object: this means there is an act having a determinate intention, and determinate in a way which makes it an intention towards this object. This 'reference to an object' belongs peculiarly and intrinsically to an act-experience, and the experiences manifesting it are by definition intentional experiences or acts.[1] *All differences in mode of objective reference are descriptive differences in intentional experiences.*

We must note, however, that this peculiarity revealed in the phenomenological essence of acts, of directing themselves to a *certain* object and not another, will not exhaust the phenomenological essence in question. We spoke of differences in mode of objective reference, but this lumps together totally distinct, independently variable differences. Some are differences in *act-quality*, as when we speak of such different ways of being intentional as being presented, being judged, being asked etc. Such variation intersects with the *other*, wholly independent variation in objective reference: one act may point to this, another to that object, regardless as to whether the acts are alike or different in

[1] Cf. the Appendix to this chapter.

quality. *Every quality can be combined with every objective reference.* This second variation therefore points to a second *side in the phenomenological content of acts, differing from their quality.*

In the case of this latter variation, which concerns the changing direction to objects, one does not speak of different 'manners of objective reference', though the differentia of this direction lies in the act itself.

Looking more closely, we see another possibility of variation independent of quality which certainly prompts talk of different ways of referring to objects. We see, too, that the twofold variation just distinguished is not quite in a position to effect a neat separation of what must be defined as 'matter' from quality. Our distinction posited two sides in every act: its quality, which stamped it as, e.g., presentation or judgement, and its matter, that lent it direction to an object, which made a presentation, e.g., present *this* object and no other. This is quite right, and yet is to some extent misleading. For one is at first tempted to interpret the situation simply: matter is that part of an act which gives it direction to this object and no other. Acts are therefore unambiguously determined by their quality, on the one hand, and by the object they will intend, on the other. This seeming obviousness is, however, delusive. One can readily see, in fact, that *even if quality and objective direction are both fixed at the same time, certain variations remain possible.* Two identically qualified acts, e.g. two presentations, may appear directed, and evidently directed, to the same object, without full agreement in intentional essence. The ideas *equilateral triangle* and *equiangular triangle* differ in content, though both are directed, and evidently directed, to the same object: they present the same object, although 'in a different fashion'. The same is true of such presentations as *a length of a + b units* and *a length of b + a units*; it is also true of statements, in other respects synonymous, which differ only in 'equivalent' concepts. The same holds if we compare other types of equivalent assertions, e.g. *We shall have rain* and *The weather is becoming rainy*. If we consider a series of acts like the judgement *It will rain today*, the surmise *It may well rain today*, the question *Will it rain today?* and the wish *Oh that it would rain today!*, we see that it exemplified identity not only as regards objective reference in general, but also *as regards a new sense of objective reference*, a sense not fixed by the quality of the act.

Quality only determines whether what is already presented *in definite fashion* is intentionally present as wished, asked, posited in judgement etc. The matter, therefore, must be *that element in an act which first gives it reference to an object, and reference so wholly definite that it not merely fixes the object meant in a general way, but also the precise way in which it is meant.*[1] The matter – to carry clearness a little further – is that peculiar side of an act's phenomenological content that not only determines *that* it grasps the object but also *as what* it grasps it, the properties, relations, categorial forms, that it itself attributes to it. It is the act's matter that makes its object count as this object and no other, it is *the objective, the interpretative sense (Sinn der gegenständlichen Auffassung, Auffassungssinn)* which serves as basis for the act's quality (while indifferent to such qualitative differences). Identical matters can never yield distinct objective references, as the above examples prove. Differences of equivalent, but not tautologically equivalent expressions, certainly affect matter. Such differences must not be thought to correspond to any fragmentation of matter: there is not one piece of matter corresponding to an identical object, another to the differing mode of presenting it. Reference to objects is possible *a priori* only as being a definite manner of reference: it arises only if the matter is fully determined.

To this we may add an observation: act-quality is undoubtedly *an abstract aspect of acts*, unthinkable apart from all matter. Could we hold an experience possible which was a judging without definite subject-matter? This would take from the judgement its character as intentional experience, which is evidently part of its essence.

The same holds of matter. A matter that was not matter for presentation, nor for judgement, nor for...etc. etc., would be held to be unthinkable.

Talk about the manner of objective reference is ambiguous: at times it points to differences of quality, at times to differences of matter. We shall henceforth counteract such ambiguity by

---

[1] Confusion results from unavoidable ambiguities in talk of the definite and the indefinite. One speaks, e.g., of the indefiniteness of perceptual judgements, which consists in the fact that the rear side of a perceived object is subsidiarily meant, but indefinitely, whereas the clearly seen front side seems definite. Or one speaks of the indefiniteness of 'particular' assertions, e.g. *An A is B, Some A's are B's*, as opposed to the definiteness of the singular assertion 'This *A* is *B*'. Such definitenesses and indefinitenesses differ in sense from those in the text: they belong among the particularities of possible 'matters', as will be plainer in what follows.

suitable locutions involving the terms 'quality' and 'matter'. That such talk has yet other important meanings will appear in due course.

§ 21 *The intentional and the semantic essence*

We shall postpone investigation of the difficult problems here involved, to treat of a new distinction, in which a new concept of intentional content arises, which has to be separated off from the full descriptive content of the act.

In each act's descriptive content we have distinguished quality and matter as two mutually dependent aspects. If both are taken together, it would at first seem, the act in question will merely have been reconstituted. Looked at more closely, however, another conception distinguishes itself from whose point of view *the two aspects, brought to unity, do not make up the concrete, complete act.* Two acts may in fact agree in respect of their quality and their matter, and yet differ descriptively. In so far as quality and matter now count for us (as will be shown later) as the wholly essential, and so never to be dispensed with, constituents of an act, it would be suitable to call the union of both, forming one part of the complete act, the act's *intentional essence*. To pin down this term, and the conception of the matter it goes with, we simultaneously introduce a second term. To the extent that we deal with acts, functioning in expressions in sense-giving fashion, or capable of so functioning – whether all acts are so capable must be considered later – we shall speak more specifically of the *semantic essence* of the act. The ideational abstraction of this essence yields a 'meaning' in our ideal sense.

In justification of our conceptual ruling, we may point to the following new series of identifications. We may say generally, and with good sense, that a man may, at different times, and that several men may, at the same or different times, have the same presentation, memory, expectation, perception, utter the same assertion or wish, cherish the same hope etc. etc.

To have the same presentation means, but does not mean as much as, having a presentation of the same object. The presentation I have of Greenland's icy wastes certainly differs from the presentation Nansen has of it, yet the object is the same. Just so the ideal objects *straight line* and *shortest line* are identical, but the presentations – 'straight' being suitably defined – different.

Talk about the same presentation, judgement etc. points to no individual sameness of acts, as if my consciousness were in some way conjoined with someone else's. It also means no relation of perfect likeness, of indiscernibility as regards inner constituents, as if the one act merely duplicated the other. We have the same presentation of a thing, when we have presentations in which the thing is not merely presented, but presented as exactly the same: following our previous treatment we may add 'presented with the same interpretative sense' or 'based on the same matter'. In our 'essence' we really have the same presentation despite other phenomenological differences. Such essential identity comes out most clearly when we reflect how presentations function in forming higher acts. For essential identity can be equivalently defined if we say: Two presentations are in essence the same, if exactly the same statements, and no others, can be made on the basis of either regarding the presented thing (either presentation being taken alone, i.e. analytically). The same holds in regard to other species of acts. Two judgements are essentially the same judgement when (in virtue of their content alone) everything that the one judgement tells us of the state of affairs judged, would also be told us by the other, and nothing more is told us by either. Their truth-value is identical, and this is clear to us when 'the' judgement, the intentional essence uniting judgement-quality and judgement-matter, is the same.

Let us now be quite clear that *the intentional essence does not exhaust the act phenomenologically.* An imaginative presentation, qualified *as* merely imaginative, is unessentially altered in manner, if the fulness and vividness of the sensuous contents helping to build it up is increased or decreased, or, objectively put, if the object now appears with greater clearness and definiteness, now becomes lost in a mist, now becomes paler in colour etc. Whether or not one here assumes intensive differences, whether one concedes or denies a basic likeness between the sensory phantasms here present and the sensational elements in perception, all this makes little difference to the absolute qualities, forms etc. of the act, in so far as the act's intention, its *meaning*, stays unchanged, identically determined (identity of matter). We attribute these changes, not to the object, but to its 'appearance'; we 'mean' the object as constant and persistent, and we 'mean' this in merely 'feigning' fashion (identity of quality). As opposed to this, the *matter* of a unitary presentation changes if its object is given as changing (despite any overreaching form of unity to which the intentional object's identity-in-variety corresponds). The same is true when new features enrich our conception of an object, which is constantly before consciousness, features not previously part of the object's intentional content, of the object of our presentation as such.

The case of perception is similar. If many persons share the 'same' percept, or repeat a previous one, we have merely an identity of matter, of intentional essence, which does not at all exclude change in the descriptive content of the experience. The same holds of the variable part played, or that can be played, by imagination in perception, in the putting of a perceived object before us. Whether or not images of the back of the cigarette-box float in front of me, with this or that degree of fulness, steadiness and vividness, is quite irrelevant to the essential content, the interpretative sense of my percept, to that side of it, in short which, suitably understood, explains and justifies talk of the 'same percept' in opposition to a multiplicity of pheno-menologically distinct perceptual acts. In each of such cases the object is presupposed as identical, is seen clothed with the same array of properties: it is 'meant' or 'apprehended' and posited in perceptual fashion.

A percept may, further, have the same matter as a flight of fancy: the latter may present an object or state of affairs in imagination as being 'just the same' as it is perceptually appre-hended in the percept. Nothing may be objectively ascribed in the one case which is not likewise ascribed in the other. Since the *quality* of the presentation may be identical (e.g. in the case of memory), we see that the specific differences of intuitive acts do not depend on their intentional essence.

Much the same may be said of any sort of act. Many persons cherish the *same* wish, when their optative intention is the same. This wish may in one person be fully expressed, in another unexpressed, in one person it may bring to full intuitive clarity its basic presentative content, in another it may be more or less 'notional' etc. In each case the identity of essence plainly lies in the two aspects distinguished above, in an identity of act-quality and of matter. The same may be claimed for expressive acts, for the acts in particular which *lend meaning* to expressions: as said above by anticipation, their *semantic essence*, i.e. the really present (*reell*) phenomenological correlate of their meaning, coincides with their intentional essence.

We may confirm our notion of semantic essence (the act of meaning *in concreto*) by recalling the series of identities used above in Investigation I (§12) in order to draw a distinction between a unity of meaning and a unity of object, and the numerous examples of expressive experience which there illustrated our general notion of intentional essence. The identity of 'the' judgement or of 'the' statement consists in an identity of meaning repeated *as* the same in the many individual acts, and represented in them by their semantic essence. This leaves room for important descriptive difference in regard to other constituents of these acts, as we have pointed out in detail.[1]

Appendix to §11 *and* §20

Critique of the 'image-theory' and of the doctrine of the 'immanent' objects of acts

There are two fundamental, well-nigh ineradicable errors that have to be guarded against in the phenomenological interpretation of the relationship between act and subject:

   1. The erroneous *image-theory*, which thinks it has sufficiently explained the fact of presentation – fully present in each act – by saying that: '*Outside* the thing itself is there (or is at times there); in consciousness there is an image which does duty for it.'

To this notion we must object that it entirely ignores a most weighty point: that in a representation by images the *represented* object (the original) is *meant*, and meant by way of its image as an apparent object. This representative character is, however, no 'real predicate', no intrinsic character of the object which functions as image: an object is not representative as, e.g., it is red and spherical. What therefore enables us to go beyond the image which alone is present in consciousness, and to refer to the latter *as* an image to a certain extraconscious object? To point to the resemblance between image and thing will not help. It is doubtless present, as an objective matter-of-fact, when the thing actually exists. But for consciousness, which is assumed only to possess

---

[1] Cf. §§17, 30.

the image,[1] this fact means nothing: it can throw no light on the essence of the representative relation to the object, to the original, which is external to itself. Resemblance between two objects, however precise, does not make the one be an image of the other. Only a presenting ego's power to use a similar as an image-representative of a similar – the first similar had intuitively, while the second similar is nonetheless *meant* in its place – makes the image *be* an image. This can only mean that the constitution of the image as image takes place in a peculiar intentional consciousness, whose *inner* character, whose *specifically* peculiar mode of apperception, not only constitutes what we call image-representation as such, but also, through its particular inner determinateness, constitutes the image-representation of this or that *definite* object. The reflective, relational opposition of image to original does not, however, point to two genuinely apparent objects in the imaginative act itself, but rather to possible cognitive consummations, which new acts must realize, both fulfilling the imaginal intention and achieving a synthesis between the image and the thing it represents. Inaccurate oppositions of inner likenesses to outer objects cannot be allowed in a descriptive psychology, and much less in a pure phenomenology. A painting only is a likeness for a likeness-constituting consciousness, whose imaginative apperception, basing itself on a percept, first gives to its primary, perceptually apparent object the status and meaning of an image. Since the interpretation of anything as an image presupposes an object intentionally given to consciousness, we should plainly have a *regressus in infinitum* were we again to let this latter object be itself constituted through an image, or to speak seriously of a 'perceptual image' immanent in a simple percept, *by way of which* it refers to the 'thing itself'. We must come to see, moreover, the general need for a constitution of presented objects *for* and *in* consciousness, in consciousness's own circle of essential being. We must realize that a transcendent object is not present to consciousness merely because a content rather similar to it simply somehow *is* in consciousness – a supposition which, fully thought out, reduces to utter nonsense – but that all relation to an object is part and parcel of the phenomenological essence of consciousness, and can in principle be found in nothing else,

---

[1] For the moment we permit ourselves this improper mode of expression, which in its proper interpretation assorts ill with the image-theory.

even when such a relation points to some 'transcendent' matter. This pointing is 'direct' in the case of a straightforward presentation: it is mediate in the case of a 'founded' presentation, e.g. one by way of images.

One should not talk and think as if an image stood in the same relation to consciousness as a statue does to a room in which it is set up, or as if the least light could be shed on the matter by inventing a hotch-potch of two objects. One must rise to the fundamental insight that one can only achieve the understanding one wants through a phenomenological analysis of the essences of the acts concerned, which are acts of the 'imagination' in the wide, traditional sense of Kant and Hume. The essential and *a priori* peculiarity of such acts consists in the fact that in them 'an object appears', sometimes straightforwardly and directly, and sometimes as 'counting' as a 'representation by images' of an object that resembles it. Here we must not forget that the representative image, like any apparent object, is itself constituted in an act in which the prime source of its representative character is to be sought.

Our exposition extends, *mutatis mutandis*, to the theory of representation in the wider sense of a *theory of signs*. To be a sign, likewise, is no real (*real*) predicate; it requires a founded conscious act, a reference to certain novel characters of acts, which are all that is phenomenologically relevant, and, in consequence of this last predicate, all that is really (*reell*) phenomenological.

2. It is a serious error to draw a real (*reell*) distinction between 'merely immanent' or 'intentional' objects, on the one hand, and 'transcendent', 'actual' objects, which may correspond to them on the other. It is an error whether one makes the distinction one between a sign or image really (*reell*) present in consciousness and the thing it stands for or images, or whether one substitutes for the 'immanent object' some other real (*reelles*) datum of consciousness, a content, e.g., as a sense-giving factor. Such errors have dragged on through the centuries – one has only to think of Anselm's ontological argument – they have their source in factual difficulties, but their support lies in equivocal talk concerning 'immanence' and the like. It need only be said to be acknowledged *that the intentional object of a presentation is the same as its actual object, and on occasion as its external object, and that it is absurd to distinguish between them.* The transcendent object would not be the object of

this presentation, if it was not *its* intentional object. This is plainly a merely analytic proposition. The object of the presentation, of the 'intention', *is* and *means* what is presented, the intentional object. If I represent God to myself, or an angel, or an intelligible thing-in-itself, or a physical thing or a round square etc., I mean the transcendent object named in each case, in other words my intentional object: it makes no difference whether this object exists or is imaginary or absurd. 'The object is merely intentional' does not, of course, mean that it exists, but only in an intention, of which it is a real *(reelles)* part, or that some shadow of it exists. It means rather that the intention, the reference[1] to an object so qualified, exists, but not that the object does. If the intentional object exists, the intention, the reference, does not exist alone, but the thing referred to exists also. But enough of these truisms, which so many philosophers still manage to obfuscate so completely.

What we have said above does not, of course, stop us from distinguishing, as we said previously, between the object *tout court* which is intended on a given occasion, and the object *as* it is then intended – what interpretative slant is put upon it and with what possible fulness of intuition – and in the latter case peculiar analyses and descriptions will be appropriate.

---

[1] Which does not mean, we must repeat, that the object is noticed, or that we are thematically occupied with it, though such things are included in our ordinary talk about 'referring'.

CHAPTER THREE

The Matter of the Act and its
Underlying Presentation

---

§22 *The question of the relation between the matter and quality of an act*

WE wind up our general probe into the phenomenological structure of intentional experience with a discussion which throws important light on the main problems in our special field of meaning. It deals with the relation of *quality* to *matter*, and so with the sense in which each act both needs and also includes in itself a presentation which serves as its basis. We here at once come up against fundamental difficulties, scarce noticed before[1] and certainly not put into words. The gap in our phenomenological knowledge is all the more grievous since, while it remains unfilled, we can have no real insight into the essential make-up of intentional experiences, and none therefore into meanings.

Quality and matter were distinguished by us as two 'moments', two inner constituents of all acts. We did so quite properly. If, e.g., we call an experience one of 'judgement', there must be some inner determination, not some mere outwardly attached mark, that distinguishes it as a judgement from wishes, hopes and other sorts of acts. This determination it shares with all judgements: what distinguishes it from all other judgements (i.e. judgements other *in essence*) is above all its matter (disregarding certain other 'moments' to be investigated later). This matter also is an inner moment of the act. This is not so much directly apparent – quality and matter are not readily prised apart in the analysis of, e.g., an isolated judgement – but appears when we set qualitatively different acts side by side, and compare them in respect of certain correspondent identities, when we find an identical matter as a moment common to them all, much as in the

---

[1] At the time, of course, of the appearance of this work's First Edition.

sensory realm we come upon like intensities or colours. *What we only have to ask is what this identical element is and how it stands to the moment of quality.* Are we dealing with two *separate albeit abstract constituents of acts*, such as colour and shape in sensuous intuition, or are they otherwise related, as, e.g., *genus* and *differentia* etc.? This question is all the more weighty since the matter of acts is that aspect of them which gives them their *determinate objective reference*. To be as clear as one can in regard to the nature of such reference is of fundamental interest for epistemology, since all thinking takes place in acts.

§23 *The view of 'matter' as a basic act of 'mere presentation'*

The first answer to our question is furnished by the well-known proposition, used among others by Brentano to circumscribe his 'psychical phenomena', that each such phenomenon – in our terminology and definition *each intentional experience – is either a presentation or based upon underlying presentations.* More precisely, this remarkable proposition means that in each act the intentional object is *presented in an act of presentation*, and that, whenever we have no case of 'mere' presentation, we have a case of presentation so peculiarly and intimately inwoven with one or more further acts or rather act-characters, that the presented objects become the object judged about, wished for, hoped for etc. Such plurality of intentional reference is not achieved in a linked concomitance or sequence of acts, in each of which the object has a novel, i.e. a recurrent, intentional presence, but in a single strictly unitary act, in which a single object is only *once* apparent, but is in this single appearance the target of a complex intention. We can, in other words, interpret our proposition as saying that an intentional experience only gains objective reference by incorporating an experienced act of presentation in itself, through which *the object is presented to it.* The object would be nothing to consciousness if consciousness did not set it before itself as an object, and if it did not further permit the object to become an object of feeling, of desire etc.

These added intentional characters are plainly not to be regarded as *complete* and *independent acts*: they cannot be conceived apart from the act of objectifying presentation, on which they are accordingly based. That an object or state of affairs should be desired, without being presented in and with such desire, is not merely not the case in fact, but is entirely inconceivable, and the same holds in every similar case. The matter before us therefore claims to be *a priori*, and the proposition asserting it is a self-evident *law of essence*. The addition of, e.g., desire to some underlying presentation, is not the addition of something that exists independently, with its own independent direction to some object: we must see it as the addition of a non-independent factor, intentional no doubt as having real reference to an object, and unthinkable *a priori* without it, but only able to develop or gain such reference through intimate *liaison* with a presentation. But *this last is more than a mere act-quality*: unlike the quality of desire based upon it, it is quite capable of independent existence as a concrete intentional experience, as an act of 'mere' presentation.

We round off these explanations with an observation which must be kept in mind in future discussions: that among cases of 'mere presentation' we must include, following Brentano, all cases of mere imagination, where the apparent object has neither being nor non-being asserted of it, and where no further acts concern it, as well as all cases where an expression, e.g. a statement, is well understood without prompting us either to belief or disbelief. It is mainly by contrast with such a 'belief-character', whose addition perfects judgement, that the notion of mere presentation can be elucidated. It is well-known how important a part this contrast plays in the modern theory of judgement.

Returning to our proposition, we are tempted (as said at the beginning) to apply the principle there expressed and here set forth, to explain the relation between matter and quality. Identity of matter accompanying change of quality rests, we may say, on the 'essential' identity of the underlying presentation. Or otherwise put: acts having the same 'content', and differing only in intentional essence, inasmuch as one judges, one wishes, one doubts etc., this same content, have 'in essence' the same presentation as their basis. If this presentation underlies a judgement, it yields (in its present sense as 'matter') the content of a judgement. If it underlies a desire, it yields the content of a desire etc. etc.

We spoke of '*essentially* the same presentation'. We are not to be taken as saying that matter and underlying presentation are actually one and the same, since 'matter' is merely an abstr act 'moment' in an act. In talking of 'essentially the same presentation' we rather meant, following previous discussion, presentations with one and the same matter, which may, of course, be phenomenologically differentiated by further 'moments' which have nothing to do with matter. Since quality is also the same, all these presentations have the same 'intentional essence'.

The following is the outcome: that, while every other intentional essence is a complex of quality and matter, the intentional essence of a presentation is pure matter – or is pure quality, however one may choose to call it. Otherwise put, it is only because all other acts have a complex intentional essence, and necessarily include a presentative factor among their essential constituents, that talk of the difference between quality and matter arises. The word 'matter' refers to the necessary, basic presentative constituent. In the case of simple acts, which are also *eo ipso* presentative, the whole distinction necessarily falls away. One should then say: the difference between quality and matter represents no basic difference among the kinds of abstract moments found in acts. *Matters*, treated in and for themselves, *do not differ from qualities*: they are *qualities of presentation*. What we call the intentional essence of an act is its total qualitative being: this is what is essential to it, as opposed to what varies accidentally.

The matter could also be put in the following manner:

If an act is simple, i.e. is a pure presentation, its quality coincides with what we have called its intentional essence. If it is complex – and all acts that are not mere presentations, as well as all complex presentations, belong here – its complex intentional essence is merely a complex of qualities brought together in unity, from which a unitary total quality emerges, in such a way, however, that each primitive or complex quality in the pattern, which is not itself a presentative quality, rests upon such a presentative quality, which in this function yields, or is called, the corresponding matter, or the total matter in relation to the complex total act.

§24 *Difficulties. The problem of the differentiation of qualitative kinds*

Evident as this whole interpretation seems, and based on an irrefragable support, it is yet not such as to exclude other possibilities. Brentano's principle is undoubtedly self-evident, but things have perhaps been read into it which are not truly part of it.

We note at least the peculiar stress laid on presentations[1] as the one class of intentional experiences whose intentional essence (or, what now is the same, whose intentional quality) could be truly simple. In connection with this *a problem arises as to the interpretation of the last specific differences of the various types of intentional essence* (or briefly of 'intentions'). When we judge, e.g., is our full judgement-intention, the aspect in the act of assertion which corresponds to our asserted sentence's meaning, a complex whole made up, on the one hand, of a presentative intention, which merely gives 'presence' to some state of affairs, and a corresponding, strictly judgemental intention, which sees it in the further aspect of what really is? What is the position, we may ask, in regard to last specific differences of such added intentions? The *summum genus* of Intention specifies itself, mediately or immediately, in the species of Judgement-intention (the latter of course conceived 'for itself', and in abstraction from its supposedly underlying presentative intention). Is this species, we may ask, an ultimate specific difference?

To preserve clarity let us compare our case with a plain case where generic essence is differentiated. The genus Quality is essentially specified in the species Colour, and this in its turn has the species Red ranged under it, as well as this determinate shade of Red. This last is a last specific difference, permitting of no differentiation which remains within its generic limits. All that is still possible are alliances with determinations which belong to other genera, which are themselves last differences in their own class. Such alliances add definiteness to content, but they do not, properly speaking, differentiate.[2] The same Red, e.g., can be extended in this or that shape. We modify the moment of Red, not *qua* quality, but in respect of the new genus Extension, a moment essentially belonging to it, since it is of the essence of colour that it cannot be without extension.

Returning to our present case, how shall we hold that the superadded character of judging stands to its presentational basis in a concrete judgement? Is it quite the same in all judgements, and is the Species Judgement-intention (understood in ideal

---

[1] 'Mere' presentations, we iterate, as opposed to acts of *belief*. How the sense of Brentano's proposition stands up to changes in our concept of presentation will be thoroughly investigated in the next two chapters.
[2] See Inv. III, §§4 ff.

isolation, uncomplicated by presentations) truly a lowest specific difference?[1] We should not hesitate to say so. But if we do say so, and if we then try to argue similarly in the case of *all kinds of intention*, we encounter serious difficulties in the case of presentations. For, if no further differentiation of the species Presentation is possible, the difference between this or that presentation *in specie*, e.g. the difference between the presentation *Emperor* and the presentation *Pope*, will not affect the presentative intention as such. What then will differentiate these presentations, or rather these intentional essences or presentational *meanings*? They must plainly be complexes of the character or quality *Presentation* together with another, generically different character, and, since all difference of objective reference is absent from the former, this second character must introduce such difference into the complete meaning. In other words, the intentional essence of the presentation (its meaning, in our example) cannot be the last specific difference in the presentative intention; a wholly new determination of some other sort must be added to the fully differentiated intention. The meaning of each presentation will then consist of *Presentative Intention* compounded with *Content*, two generically different ideal unities woven together in unity. Returning to our old terms we must say: If we hold it obvious, as we did above, that intentions of all sorts must be differentiated in like manner, we must again opt for an essential distinction between act-quality and act-matter. We cannot maintain the view that what we called 'matter' is identical with the intentional essence of an underlying presentation, and that this in its turn is identical with a mere quality of presentation.

§ 25 *Closer analysis of our two possible solutions*

Many will here ask in amazement why we are so prolix in removing the difficulties that we ourselves have put in our path. The whole matter is quite simple. Each act of presentation has of course the general act-character of the Species Presentation, which permits no further genuine differentiation. What differentiates

---

[1] I have here ignored the disputed sub-species of Affirmative and Negative Judgement. If anyone accepts them he can everywhere substitute 'Affirmative Judgement' for 'Judgement' in the present discussion, while those who reject them, may take our words as they stand. It makes no essential difference to our argument.

presentation from presentation? Their content, of course. The presentation *Pope* presents the Pope, the presentation *Emperor* the Emperor.

Such 'obviousnesses' will satisfy nobody who has grasped the phenomenological distinctions of kind which obtain here, and which derive from ideal unities, and especially the fundamental cleft between 'content' as object and 'content' as matter (interpretative sense or meaning). It will only satisfy those who, at this point where it is so all-important, fail to feel the force of the truth that the object is, properly speaking, nothing at all 'in' a presentation.

Our prolixity was therefore quite necessary. *Objects, that are nothing in a presentation are also unable to create differences among presentations*, and especially not the differences so familiar to us from the proper content of each presentation in respect of *what* it presents. If we think of this last as a 'content', both distinct from the intended object and immanent in the presentation, it is not clear what we could mean by it. Only two possibilities seem open to us, which were indicated above and which we now wish to set forth as sharply as possible.

We may assume, as one possibility, that it is the quality of the presentation, differentiated in this or that fashion, which constitutes the variable intentional essence, and with it the variable objective reference, in the real (*reellen*) content of the presentation. The presentations *Pope* and *Emperor* (not Pope and Emperor themselves) differ from one another in the very same way that the colour Red differs from the colour Blue (both thought of as wholly definite 'shades'). Our universal is Presentation, our particular is Presentation in the full determinateness and complete differentiation that its semantic essence permits. In the compared case the universal is Colour, the particular this or that definite colour, this shade of Red, that shade of Blue. That a presentation refers to a certain object in a certain manner, is not due to its acting on some external, independent object, 'directing' itself to it in some literal sense, or doing something to it or with it, as a hand writes with a pen. It is due to nothing that stays outside of the presentation, but to its own inner peculiarity alone. This last holds on any view, but, on the present view, a given presentation presents *this object in this manner* in view of its *peculiarly differentiated presentational quality*.

Or we may hold, as the *second* possibility open to us, that the full intentional essence (in our cases the full semantic essence) that achieves Abstract Ideation in talk of '*The* (ideally-single) Presentation *Pope*' or of 'The Meaning of the word "Pope",' is essentially complex, and divides into two abstract moments: Presentational Quality, on the one hand, the Act-Quality of presentation conceived in universal selfsameness and purity, and 'Content' or Matter, on the other hand, which does not pertain to the inner essence of Presentation as a differentiating feature, but accedes to it and perfects it into a total meaning. The relation of Presentational Quality to Matter is therefore like that of Determinate Shade of Colour to Extension, in our parallel example. Each colour is the colour of a certain extension: each presentation likewise is the presentation of a certain content. In neither case is the connection contingent, but has *a priori* necessity.

Our comparison shows how we wish to conceive this kind of combination, and how we must conceive it from our present point of view. It is a form of combination that still lacks a suitable name. Brentano and certain kindred thinkers call it a combination of 'metaphysical parts': Stumpf prefers to speak of 'attributive parts'. The connections of inner properties in the unity of external phenomenal things yield the typical examples on which the Idea of this form of combination must be conceived. We must, however, note that the completing character which adds determining content to the Pure Character of Presentative Quality (only abstractly separable from such content) must be seen as truly belonging to a *new genus*. If we again regarded it as a qualitative character, the difficulties we are now seeking to remove would surge up once more, and only names would have been altered.

If we therefore decide to exclude 'Content' or 'Matter' from the genus Act-Quality, we shall have to say: The qualitative character which is such as to make a presentation a presentation, and the qualitative characters, consequently, which are such as to make judgements judgements, desires desires etc., have in their *inner* essence no relation to an object. But an ideally necessary relation *is grounded in this essence*: this character cannot be without complementary 'matter', through which the relation to the object first enters the complete intentional essence and the concrete intentional experience itself. This carries over *eo ipso* to the semantic essence of expressive experiences, what makes us speak, e.g., of the 'same judgement' as asserted by different persons. This semantic essence, this meaning in the ideal sense, is, in the concrete judgement-experience, the Act-character of Judgemental Position (the abstract Judgement-quality), attributively bound up with the 'content' (the Matter of Judgement) through which the relation to the 'object', i.e. the state of affairs, is consummated. This Judgemental Assertion may be seen *a priori* to be unthinkable without a Content, as a colour is unthinkable without extension.

§26 *Consideration and rejection of the proposed conception*

How shall we decide among these opposed possibilities, both pondered over with equal care?

If we accept the *first* possibility Presentation stands as an unacceptable exception in a series of intentional experiences. Within the essential genus Intentional Quality, which includes as coordinated species the Qualities of Presentation, Judgement, Wish, Will etc., the species Presentation is differentiated into all the varieties classed as presentations of this or that 'content' (or matter), while qualities of Judgement, Wishing, Willing etc., are last differences: differences of content are in their case mere differences in the presentational qualities which are combined with, or underlie, their own quality. The matter can be seen in another way. One cannot restore uniformity by treating the distinguishing contents of different judgements, wishes, willings etc., as differences of the qualitative species Judgement, Wish, Will etc., since different pure species cannot share the *same* lowest difference. Is this anomaly not exchanged for another if we accept different species at the same level, of which some have lowest differences *under them*, while others themselves *are* such lowest differences?

But if we adopt the *second* possibility it seems to force us to change our conception yet further. Have we good ground left for adhering to the principle that every intentional experience is either a 'mere' presentation, or implies presentations as its necessary basis? Such priority for presentations – as acts – and such complication in all acts not themselves presentations, seem an almost gratuitous assumption. On the view now set up as correct, the 'contents' are thought of as experiences *sui generis*, only entering into combinatory unity with the act-character of Presentation. (This combinatory unity may be very intimate and may connect intrinsic, positive properties.) But if such a manner of combination can here produce what we call an act-with-a-given-content, why should the case be different for other types of act, or at least why *must* it be different? The combinatory form here in question makes out of Presentative Quality and 'Content' a whole entitled 'Presentation with a given Content'. Why should not the same combinatory form do the same for other acts, and in the case, e.g., of the Judgement, make out of Judgement-Quality and Content, the whole entitled 'Judgement with a given Content'?

The peculiar character of many sorts of acts may of necessity require mediation: many act-qualities may only make their appearance in combination with other act-qualities, e.g. that of presentation, which underlie them in the total act, and which relate to the same matter, so that they are mediately linked with this matter. But that this must always be so, and that the Act-species of Mere Presentation plays this all-important role, so that every act not itself a mere presentation gets its matter only through a mediating presentation: all this appears neither obvious nor initially likely.

§27 *The testimony of direct intuition. Perceptual presentation and perception*

We close our argument with the 'testimony of inner perception', which should come first in exploring controversial questions of description, though we see reason to prefer speaking of immediate intuitive analysis of the essences of intentional experiences. Such a reversal of *expository* order is permitted and in certain circumstances necessary. We wish in epistemology to render all due honour to the evidence of a rightly understood, immanent inspection of essence which is falsely credited to 'internal perception'. But this testimony, when appealed to, must be conceptually apprehended and asserted, and will thereby lose much authority and permit of well-founded doubts. Different people all appeal to such 'internal perception', and come to quite opposite results: they read different things into it or out of it. This is true in the case before us. The analyses just done enable us to recognize this fact, and to distinguish and appraise various

illusions which arise in interpretations of the data of phenomenological inspections of essence. The same holds in regard to the
evidence of general principles based on our inner intuition of
individual cases, based on this evidence, i.e., and not on interpretative interpolations.

We said above that it was wrong to talk of 'internal perception'
instead of 'immanent inspection of essences' in making the usual
appeals to the 'evidence of internal perception'. For, if one
examines the matter, all such appeals either serve to establish
facts of essence belonging to the pure phenomenological sphere,
or mere transfers of such facts to the sphere of psychological
reality. Assertions of phenomenological fact can never be epistemologically grounded in *psychological experience (Erfahrung)*,
nor in *internal perception* in the ordinary sense of the word, but
only in *ideational, phenomenological inspection of essence*. The latter
has its illustrative start in inner intuition, but such inner intuition
need not be actual internal perception or other inner experience
(*Erfahrung*), e.g. recollection: its purposes are as well or even
better served by any free fictions of inner imagination provided
they have enough intuitive clarity. Phenomenological intuition,
however, as often stressed, fundamentally excludes all psychological apperception and real (*reale*) assertion of existence, all positings
of psycho-physical nature with its actual things, bodies and
persons, including one's own empirical ego, as well as all that
transcends pure consciousness. This exclusion is achieved *eo ipso*,
since the phenomenological inspection of essence, in its turning
of immanent ideation upon our inner intuitions, only turns its
ideating gaze on what is *proper* to the real (*reellen*) or intentional
being of the experiences inspected, and only brings to an adequate
focus the specific modes of experience which such individual
experiences exemplify, and the *a priori* ideal laws which relate to
them. It is of the greatest importance to be quite clear on this
matter. Men are misled by a mere illusion when they think, in
conducting epistemological discussions, or in psychological
discussions which base general principles of conscious data on
apodictic evidence, that the source of such evidence lies in inner
experience (*Erfahrung*), and in particular in internal perception,
i.e. in acts which *assert existence*. This cardinal error infects that
style of psychologism which thinks it has satisfied the requirements of pure logic, ethics and epistemology and that it has gone

beyond extreme empiricism, merely because it speaks of 'apodictic evidence' and even of '*a priori* insights', without ever leaving the ground of internal experience (*Erfahrung*) and psychology. It is in principle impossible to go beyond Hume in this manner, since he too acknowledges the *a priori* in the form of 'relations of ideas', and yet is so far from distinguishing in principle between inner experience (*Erfahrung*) and Ideation, that he interprets the latter nominalistically as a set of contingent facts. [Second Edition comment. *Trans.*]

Going into more detail, it is, of course, evident that each intentional experience has its basis in a presentation. It is evident that we cannot judge if the state of affairs about which we judge is not present to our minds, and the same is true of enquiring, doubting, surmising, desiring etc. But does a 'presentation' here mean what it means in other contexts? May we not be thralls to an equivocation when we expand this evidence into the principle: 'Each act-experience is either a mere presentation, or has its basis in presentations'. We are put on our guard by the fact that, if we confront our experiences in sternly descriptive fashion, we do not by any means always find it possible to analyse the acts which are not 'mere presentations' into the partial acts which supposedly make them up. Let us contrast a case where intentional reference is plainly compound, and in relation to the same matter, with one or other of our dubious cases. I cannot rejoice in anything unless what I rejoice in stands before me in the hues of existence, in the perceptual, the reminiscent, possibly also the judgemental and assertive manner. Here the compounding is indubitable. If, e.g., I see and rejoice, the act-character of my joy has its basis in a percept with its own act-character, which makes its matter into matter for my joy. The character of my joy may fall away while my percept remains unaltered. Without doubt, therefore, it forms part of the concretely complete experience of joy.

Perception offers an example of the dubious compounding of acts. Here as in all acts we distinguish between quality and matter. Comparison with a corresponding mere presentation, one, e.g., of mere imagination, shows how the same object can be present *as* the same (with the same 'interpretative sense'), and yet present in an entirely different 'manner'. In perception the object seemed to achieve full-bodied presence, to be there *in propria persona.* In the imaginative presentation it merely 'floats before us', it is 'represented' without achieving full-bodied presence. This is not, however, the difference that concerns us: ours is a difference of mere 'moments', involving neither matter nor quality, just like, e.g., the difference between perceiving and recollecting one selfsame object which is present to mind with the same interpretative sense etc. Let us therefore compare a percept with a mere presentation that corresponds to it, while *abstracting* from all such differences. On our conception, a 'matter' is abstractly common to both cases, given in each case in different fashion, and with a differing act-quality. On the other conception which we were questioning, the matter which underlies perception is itself a second act-quality, that of an underlying act of mere presentation. Does analysis reveal anything of the sort? Can we look on a percept as a compound act in which an independent act of mere presentation can be really isolated?

Perhaps someone will here point to the possibility of an exactly correspondent illusion, and will hold that, once exposed as illusion, it can be seen as the isolated mere presentation, inwrought without change into our percept and providing it with its matter. Illusion, while not recognized as illusion, was simple perception. But, later, its perceptual character, the act-quality of belief, fell away, and the mere perceptual presentation remained. The same compounding must be assumed to obtain in all percepts: everywhere the underlying perceptual presentation – whose quality forms the matter of perception – will be completed by a belief-character.

Let us discuss the matter more closely in the light of a concrete example. Wandering about in the Panopticum Waxworks we meet on the stairs a charming lady whom we do not know and who seems to know us, and who is in fact the well-known joke of the place: we have for a moment been tricked by a waxwork figure. As long as we *are* tricked, we experience a perfectly good percept: we see a lady and not a waxwork figure. When the illusion vanishes, we see exactly the opposite, a waxwork figure that only *represents* a lady. Such talk of 'representing' does not of course mean that the waxwork figure is modelled on a lady as in the same waxworks there are figure-models *of* Napoleon, *of* Bismarck etc. The percept of the wax-figure as a thing does not therefore underlie our awareness of the same figure as representing the lady. The lady, rather, makes her appearance together with the wax-figure and in union with it. Two perceptual interpretations, or two appearances of a thing, interpenetrate, coinciding as it were in part in their perceptual content. And they interpenetrate in conflicting fashion, so that our observation wanders from one to another of the apparent objects each barring the other from existence.

It can now be argued that while the original perceptual presentation does not achieve an entirely detached existence, but appears in conjunction with the new percept of the wax-figure, it does not serve to found a genuine percept: only the wax-figure is perceived, it alone is believed to be really there. The isolation is achieved after a fashion, which suffices for the present purpose. But it would only really suffice if we could truly speak of isolation in this case, if we could, in other words, assume the presentation of the lady in the second case to be really contained in the original percept of the same lady. But, when the fraud is exposed, presentation amounts to perceptual consciousness resolved in conflict. But a consciousness qualified in this fashion is naturally not part of the original percept. Certainly both have something in common: they are as like one another in our illustration, which cannot in this respect be improved upon, as percept and corresponding presentation can possibly be. Certainly both share the same *matter*, for which such far-reaching likeness is by no means needed. It is the same lady who appears on both occasions, and who appears endowed with the same set of phenomenal properties. But in the one case she stands before us as real, in the other case as a fiction, with a full-bodied appearance which yet amounts to nothing. The difference lies in the qualities of our acts. It is almost exactly as if she herself were present, a genuine, actual person: the unusual likeness in matter and other non-qualitative constituents of our acts certainly inclines us to slip from a representational into a perceptual mode of consciousness. It is only the contradiction which this tendency towards believing perception encounters, as it directs itself upon the beckoning lady, that prevents us from really yielding to it, a contradiction due to the percept of the mere wax-doll, which in part coincides with our lady and in other respects rules her out, and due especially to the note of belief which informs this latter percept. The difference is, however, plainly of a sort that excludes the thought that the presentation should be contained in the percept. The same matter is at one time matter for a percept, and at another time matter for a mere perceptual fiction, but both can evidently not be combined. A percept cannot also fictitiously construct what it perceives, and a fiction cannot also perceive what it constructs.

Descriptive analysis does not, therefore, favour the view, so obvious to many, that each percept is a compound, in which a moment of belief, the characteristic quality of perception, is imposed on a *complete* act of perceptual presentation, endowed with its own independent quality.

§28 *Special investigation of the matter in the case of judgement*

The situation is similar in the case of judgements, a class of acts of particular interest to the logician. *We here employ this word in its principal sense, which connects it with assertions (predications),* and so excludes percepts, remembrances and similar acts (despite their not unessential descriptive affinity). In the judgement *a state of affairs* 'appears' before us, or, put more plainly, becomes intentionally objective to us. A state of affairs, even one concerning what is sensibly perceived, is not, however, an object that could be sensibly perceived and apparent (whether to our 'outward' or to our 'inward' sensibility). In perception an object is given to us as having full-bodied existence. We *call* it something which now is, in so far as our percept serves as our basis for judging *that it is. In this judgement,* which can continue essentially unaltered even when the percept falls away, what appears or intentionally is 'in consciousness', is not the existent sensible object, but the fact *that this is.* In the judgement it further seems to us that something has such and such properties, and this 'seeming', which we must not of course conceive as a case of doubtful surmise, but as one of firm opinion, of certainty, of conviction as in the ordinary sense of 'judgement', may be realized in many forms which vary in content. It may be an opinion that S is or is not, that S is p or is not p, that either S is p or Q is r etc.

What plays the part of object to judgement and opinion we call the *state of affairs judged*: we distinguish this in reflex knowledge from the *judging* itself, the *act* in which this or that appears thus or thus, just as in the case of perception we distinguish the perceived object from the perception as act. Following this analogy, we must ask ourselves whether what constitutes the *matter* of our judgement, what *makes it the judgement of a given state of affairs, lies in an underlying act of presentation*. The state of affairs will then be first presented through this presentation, and, thus presented, will become the target or a new act, or rather act-quality, of judgemental positing which is built upon this presentation.

No one would question that, for every judgement, conceived *a priori* in essential generality, there is a presentation endowed with the same matter, and therefore presenting the same thing in exactly the same manner, as the judgement judges about it. To the judgement, e.g., *The earth's mass is about 1/325,000 of the sun's mass*, corresponds, as 'mere' presentation, the act performed by someone who hears and understands this statement, but sees no reason to pronounce any judgement upon it. We now ask ourselves: Is this very act of mere presentation a constituent of the judgement, and does the latter merely differ in respect of a superadded, deciding note of judgement which *supervenes* upon the mere presentation? I for my part, try as I may, can find no confirmation of this view in descriptive analysis. I can find no trace of the required duplicity in act-quality. One cannot of course base a pretended analysis on the fact that one *talks* of 'mere presentation'. The word 'mere' points to a deficiency, as it does everywhere, but not every deficiency is remedied by an addition. We oppose, e.g., 'mere' imagination to perception, thereby according a preference to the former, without crediting it with a *plus*. Just so, in the verbal opposition of mere presentation to judgement, a preference for the former corresponds to a deficiency in the latter, the preferential status of having come to a decision, a judgement, in regard to what formerly was a merely presented state of affairs.

§29 Continuation: 'acceptance' or 'assent' given to the mere presentation of the state of affairs

Others may think that the complications that escape our notice are in certain cases extremely clear. For they recall the familiar experiences where a mere idea first floats before our mind, without leading to an immediate decision in judgement, and to which an obviously novel act of assent or acceptance (or denial or rejection) only afterwards accrues.

We shall not, of course, dispute these plain facts, but we shall try to see them, and the whole matter before us, in a somewhat different light. Undoubtedly a new act terminates our 'mere presentation', follows upon the latter and maintains itself in consciousness. What is questionable, however, is that *the new act really contains the old act whole and entire in itself*, and that, to be more precise, it simply grows out of the old one through the association of the note of belief, the specific quality of judgement, with the mere presentation, thereby completing the concrete experience of judging – much as the act-quality of joy associates itself with a perceptual act and so completes the concrete act of rejoicing. Undoubtedly when the new act thus emerges from the old, an identical element persists which includes what we called their 'matter'. This identical element need not, however, be a complete act of presentation, the only change being the emergence of a new quality based upon it. We can also interpret what happens as involving the *supersession* of the specific note of presentation in the original merely presentative act by the note of judgement, while the 'identical element' was only an abstract 'moment' not amounting to a full act.

We must, however, be more precise. Only part of the situation is to some degree described by the above line of thought: what justifies talk of 'assent' is precisely absent. We shall base a more careful description on a case where the word 'assent' is specially apposite: we assent to a judgement that another pronounces. His words do not then immediately arouse a concordant judgement in us: to *judge concordantly*, simply to accept a communication, is not to assent to it. Assent rather involves an original understanding of a statement which we do not ourselves judge true: what is said is 'merely entertained' in consciousness, is *pondered* and *considered*. Plainly all these acts are involved in the mere presentation, to which assent is added. We dwell ponderingly on the speaker's opinion, for what is merely entertained must not remain thus merely entertained. We face the issue, we mean to decide it. Then the decision, the affirmative adoption supervenes: we ourselves pass judgement and concordantly with the other person. The previous 'mere presentation', the mental train of brooding suspension and questioning, are certainly not contained in this judgement. Assent is rather achieved when a judgement is pronounced that accords with the speaker's judgement and with the pondered question, which has the same 'matter'. I assent to a judgement means that I judge likewise, my judgement bases itself on the same matter. I answer 'yes' to the question means that I precisely hold what the question questions: my act again has an identical matter.

Regarded more narrowly, however, this analysis still betrays incompleteness: what is specific to assent is really omitted. The sequence of question and concordant judgement, or of judgement and concordant judgement, does not complete the whole, i.e. that of a judgement which assents to a question or a judgement. Plainly a certain transitional experience mediates or rather connects the two distinct members. The pondering and question 'intention' is fulfilled in the assenting decision, and in this fulfilling unit of *response* (which has the phenomenological character of a moment of union) the two acts are not merely successive but mutually related in the most intimate unity. The answer *fits* the question: the decision says 'It is so', just so, in fact, as it was previously pondered over as being.

Where our pondering thoughts swing to and fro like a balance, where question wakes counter-question and the latter the former (Is this so or not?), our intention is duplex, and the whole pondering experience is fulfilled by either of two possible decisions: that it is so or that it is not so. The fulfilling answer, of course, specially concerns the corresponding half of the pondered question. In simpler cases decisions with opposing fulfilments exemplify negative fulfilment or (as it were) disappointment. This automatically carries over to manifold disjunctions which are not limited to a 'Yes' and a 'No'. Negative fulfilment then lies in the decision: 'Neither A nor B, nor C etc.'

Plainly such talk of an assenting judgement – assenting in relation to another judgement uttered by a speaker – has its source in this experience of fulfilment, the resolution of a kind of tension, which is related to a pondered question. The speaker conceives of his auditor, whose concordant judgement he cannot simply count upon, as pondering the matter, and requests his agreement: even when a like judgement has occurred without pondering, agreement is felt as assent, especially since prior pondering will enhance its worth. The auditor in his turn is pleased to pose to his interlocutor as pondering and assenting, even when he has had no occasion to ponder: he hopes to give

his interlocutor the joy of assent obtained. Straightforward agreement often is thought of as assent, while true assent consists in
the complex experience where a perceived or presented judgement leads to a phase of questioning, which in its turn finds fulfilment in the corresponding actual judgement (or, in the contrary
case, in its frustration or rejection).

These considerations lead us to look on *assent as the same sort of
transitional experience as the fulfilment of a surmise, an expectation, a
wish and similar 'directed' intentions.* We have, e.g., in the fulfilment
of wishes, no mere sequence of wishful intention and wished-for
consummation but a characteristically unitary consciousness of
fulfilment. Here too there is agreement in 'material', but such
agreement alone is insufficient: otherwise any two acts with the
same material would yield a 'fulfilment'. It is the consciousness
of fulfilment which first coordinates the wish that S should be P
with the judgemental experience that S is P, giving to the latter
the relative character of the *fulfilling act*, and to the wish the
character of a pregnantly *intending, directed* act.

Our analysis shows plainly – as we observe for later Investigations – that any 'theory of judgement', or, more properly, any
purely phenomenological characterization of the judgement,
which identifies its peculiar quality with an assent or acceptance,
or a denial or rejection, of some presented state of affairs (or of
some presented object in general), is not on the right path.
*Supervenient assent is not an act-quality supervening upon a prior act
of mere presentation*: what analysis really discovers is first mere
presentation (which here includes the interrelated acts of mere
entertainment, putting the question and consideration) passing
over by way of fulfilment into a judgement of like material. The
judgement is not intrinsically the acceptance of a previously given
mere presentation: it is accepting, assertive only in a context of
fulfilment. Only in this context has it this relational character, just
as in it alone the 'presentation' (or pondering) has the relational
character of an intention directing itself to such assent. The
analogy with other sorts of fulfilment, e.g. of wish-fulfilment, is
here most illuminating. The 'turning up' of the wished-for
consummation, or rather our belief in its turning up – we are
concerned not with an objective turning up but with our knowledge or conviction about it – has in itself no character of wish-
fulfilment. No one would here wish to describe the experience of

fulfilment as the mere addition of a new act-quality to the original wish, or would dream of treating the fulfilling conviction, the goal of the process, as a compound which includes the wish as an underlying partial act.

After all this, we can no longer argue from an experience of assent subsequently added to a mere presentation, to that constitution of intentional experiences that we have found so dubious, at least not in the field of the judgement.

Additional Note

We have not of course overlooked the fact that there is generally a wish-intention woven into the pondering which precedes assent, an intention directed to a judgemental decision. But we should think it quite wrong to identify the fulfilment involved in the (so to say) theoretical question (in which the appearance of questionableness is constituted) with the fulfilment of the wish or *wish-question* which rests upon this. It would seem that the word 'question' has two senses. In one sense it stands for a definite wish, in another for a peculiar act presupposed by each such wish. Our wish aims at 'judgemental decision', i.e., it aims at a judgement which will decide a *question*, or which in the case of a two-sided disjunction, will resolve a *doubt*. The wish, in brief, strives for *an answering of the question*: this last is not therefore itself the wish.

The *doubt* just mentioned is, likewise, no emotional act. It is not in fact an act distinct from a theoretical question nor on occasion woven into it, but is simply the special case of a disjunctive question, in our present theoretical sense.

§30 *The conception of the identical understanding of a word or a sentence as a case of 'mere presentation'*

The following general argument may suggest itself as against our doubt.

The same words and verbal patterns preserve their identical sense in the most varied contexts and are partial expressions for quite different acts. There must therefore be *some uniform experience* which *in all cases* corresponds to them, which can only be regarded as an *act of presentation* underlying them all.

One man says '*S* is *P*' to express a judgement, another man hears and understands his words without himself judging. The same words function in the same sense: they are used and grasped with a similar understanding. The difference is plain: in the second case, there is only an understanding of the words, in the first something more as well. Our understanding is the same in the two cases, but judgement is something additional. Widening the range of our samples, different persons may wish, hope, surmise, doubt etc., that *S* is *P*, all performing appropriate acts of expression. They all understand a common set of words; all share with the man who judges what he shares with the man who merely understands. This last man experiences *in isolation* what in the other man appears coloured with conviction, desire, hope etc. *Mere understanding is here mere presentation* which furnishes a uniform basis for a series of acts having the same 'matter'. The same notion can of course be transferred from verbally expressed acts to acts without such expression.

This is certainly a specious argument. Talk of a sameness of sense, of sameness of understanding of words and sentences, certainly points to something which does not vary in the varied acts thus brought to expression. This something is not merely what leads us to attribute a 'stance', an active response of conviction, desire, hope, etc., to ourselves, but something that we think also consists purely in an activity, an active achievement of understanding. Much of this may point back to peculiarities of character having genuine phenomenological interest, but we must remind ourselves that the concept of act was not defined by us in terms of activity, but that we meant to use the word merely to abbreviate the locution 'intentional experience'. By this last we understood any concrete experience that 'refers' intentionally to an object, in one of the familiar modes of consciousness that can be elucidated only by examples. Such sameness of understanding therefore offers two possibilities of interpretation. *Either* we are dealing with a common element which is not a complete act, but is something *in* an act which gives it definiteness of objective direction. This common element will occur with differing act-qualities, through which the total intentional essence of each act is completed. *Or* our common element consists in a complete intentional essence, and there is a peculiar act of understanding underlying all the acts of a close-knit group, serving as a basis for this or that sort of act or rather act-quality. In this way, e.g., a judgement arises when mere presentation is enriched by the quality of judging, a wish when it is enriched by the quality of wishing etc. etc.

We cannot, however, be sure that the proposed isolation of a basic act of the mere understanding of a statement represents a true isolation, in the sense that is here relevant. Closer consideration rather proves that *such understanding stands to actual judgement much as a mere idea of imagination stands to a precisely similar memory.* There are different modes of intentional reference to one and the same object of which we are in an identical sense 'conscious', and this means that we have *two acts similar in matter but differing in quality.* One of them is not, as a real part, enclosed in the other, in the sense merely that, in the latter, a new qualification has been added to it.

§31 A last objection to our view. Mere presentations and isolated 'matters'

If one immerses oneself without bias in descriptive relations, and frees oneself from delusive prejudices and equivocations, one will be led to the conviction that 'presentations', conceived as 'mere presentations' in isolation from and in opposition to judgements as a peculiar species of acts, play no such dominant role in knowledge as has been supposed. What is ascribed to them – the 'making present' in each act of its intentional object – is in fact performed by *non-independent experiences, which are necessarily found in all acts, since they are abstract aspects of their intentional essence.*

The opponents of this view remain silently beguiled by the following argument: If an intentional character is to have reference to something objective, this last must be 'present' to us. How can I believe, wish, doubt etc., a state of affairs, if it is not at all present to me? But what gives 'presence' to objects is precisely an underlying presentation.

There is nothing factually wrong in all this. What is here said is quite true, only it is no objection to our view. Every intentional experience certainly houses a component, a side, that looks after the presentation of a thing. That this component is a complete act is, however, just what is in question. And it is in question

above all in the case of the judgement and its immanent component, the presentation of the state of affairs judged, which are
our special concern. We felt forced to the conclusion that this
component, in respect of the essential feature through which the
'presenting' of the state of affairs was managed, must differ
essentially in kind from the characters elsewhere called 'act-
qualities', the familiar characters in virtue of which the presented
thing is judged, wished etc. Among these characters we count
also that of 'mere presentation' mentioned above, but not the
abiding, self-identical moment of 'content' or 'matter', however
much the latter, or the whole underlying act-component, may
likewise be called a presentation or a presenting.

The following route of evasion still seems open. Having
admitted that 'contents' are not act-qualities, one might still
think it possible that the very same contents which at one time
make their appearance in acts, i.e. in conjunction with complementary act-qualities, may at other times also appear by themselves, i.e. in concrete experiences quite free from act-qualities.
Genuine cases of mere presentation would arise in the latter
manner, as concrete experiences which are yet not 'acts', if we
hold, that is, to the notion of acts as involving, among other
things, the presence of an act-quality.

Careful inspection of the essences of the experiences concerned
forces us, however, to treat mere presentation as a genuine act.
Exemplary intuition will convince us that the involvement of
matters with act-qualities is an involvement of abstract 'moments'.
But matters cannot occur in isolation: they can only achieve
concretion if supplemented by certain moments which fall under
the supreme genus 'act-quality' and are subject to its limiting
laws. Mere understanding, mere entertainment as such, certainly
differs totally from the 'assertion' of belief, or from our other
attitudes of surmise, wish etc. We must accordingly acknowledge
differences in the comprehensive Genus Act-quality, and pin
these down phenomenologically.[1]

[1] Cf. my *Ideas*, Book I, Section 2, §109. A deeper knowledge of the peculiarity of
'qualitative modification' ('neutrality-modification') requires extensions of the
doctrine of act-quality. These leave the essential content of our discussions in this
chapter untouched, but involve a partial reinterpretation of their outcome.

CHAPTER FOUR

Study of Underlying Presentations with Special Regard to the Theory of Judgement

§32 *An ambiguity in the word 'presentation', and the supposed self-evidence of the principle that every act is founded on an act of presentation*

IF we may take the results of our last chapter as assured, we must distinguish *two* concepts of Presentation. Presentation in Sense One is an act (or a peculiar act-quality) on a level with Judgement, Wish, Question etc. We have examples of this concept in all cases where isolated words, or where complete sentences not functioning normally, are merely understood: we understand indicative, interrogative and optative sentences without ourselves judging, asking or wishing. The same applies to any unexpressed, merely floating thoughts where no 'attitude' is taken up, or any mere imaginations etc.

In Sense Two, 'Presentation' is no act, but the matter for an act, constituting one side of the intentional essence of each complete act, or, more concretely, this matter united with the remaining moments needed for full concreteness – what we shall later call 'representation'. This 'presentation' underlies every act, and so also underlies the act of presentation (in Sense One). If this happens, the matter which can function as self-identical in acts of different sorts, is given with the peculiar act-quality of 'presentation', in a peculiar 'mode of consciousness'.

If we model the meaning of talk about acts of mere presentation on the above examples, we can in the case of such acts undoubtedly carry out a phenomenological analysis in terms of quality and matter just as we could in the case of other acts. In the case of judgement we distinguish between the specific character of conviction, and the contents of the conviction: here we distinguish between the peculiar mental state of mere understanding, pure

620

entertainment, and the determination which lays down what we understand. The same plainly holds whatever set of examples one selects to elucidate Mere Presentation or to bring out its notion. It must always be kept in mind that our present analysis attempts no resolution of acts into parts, only a distinction of *abstract* moments or 'sides' in them. These appear as acts are compared, they are moments contained in the essence of the acts themselves, they condition the possibility of arranging acts serially according to their likeness and difference. The likeness and difference intuitively shown in such a series plainly are the 'sides' in question, e.g. quality and matter. In the same way no one can break up a motion into direction, acceleration etc.: he can only distinguish these properties in it.

That each intentional experience is either itself a (mere) presentation, or is based on such a presentation, is a proposition that our previous investigations have shown to have a merely *pretended self-evidence*. The mistake rested on the just discussed ambiguity of 'presentation'. In its first half, the proposition, correctly interpreted, speaks of 'presentation' in the sense of a certain *sort of act*, in its second half in the sense of the mere *matter of acts* (completed in the manner indicated above). This second half by itself, i.e. *every intentional experience is based on a presentation*, has genuine self-evidence, if 'presentation' is interpreted as completed matter. The false proposition we reject arises if 'presentation' is here given the sense of an act as well.

An objection here warns us to take care. Is there only one way in which 'presentation' can be interpreted as an act? The questionable proposition perhaps admits of other interpretations which are not open to our objection. In that case our treatment would be right as regards the concept of presentation taken over from ordinary explanations of the word, but not right in regard to other concepts of presentation, nor to the consequently arising new interpretations of our proposition, with its ever shifting senses.

§33 *Re-establishment of our proposition by means of a new notion of presentation. Naming and asserting*

We must now ask whether our proposition cannot be completely sustained on the basis of another notion of presentation.

The unity of an act corresponds in each case to the correlated objective unity of the 'object' (understood in the widest sense) to which it refers 'intentionally'. We had doubts regarding the proposition under discussion in so far as it meant by 'presentation' a certain *act* underlying another act, and directing itself upon the total objective unity of the latter act. The state of affairs opined in the judgement, wished in the wish, surmised in the surmise etc., is necessarily 'presented', and presented in a peculiar act of 'presentation'. By the term 'presentation' we understood 'mere' presentation, a kind of act illustrated by the case of the mere understanding of isolated words, or of statements heard, but to which a 'wholly neutral' attitude is adopted. But our proposition at once achieves a new and unobjectionable sense, if a new concept is made to underlie the term 'presentation', one not strange and remote, since talk of *names as expressing presentations* leads up to it. We must indeed then cease to demand that our 'presentation' should intentionally cover the whole objective unity of the act in question. But we can *employ the term to cover acts in which something becomes objective to us in a certain narrower sense of the word*, one borrowed from the manner in which percepts and similar intuitions grasp their objects in a single 'snatch', or in a single 'ray of meaning', or borrowed, likewise, from the one-term subject-acts in categorical statements, or from acts of straightforward hypothesis, serving as antecedents in acts of hypothetical assertion etc.

We here have in view the following most important descriptive difference:

When we make a judgement, an act of complete predication, something seems to us either to be or not to be, e.g. that S is P. But the same being which thus becomes 'present' to us, can plainly become present in quite different fashion when we speak of 'the P-ness of S'. The state of affairs S *is* P likewise comes before consciousness in quite different fashion when we simply judge and assert 'S is P', and when it occurs in the *subject-act* of another judgement, as when we say 'the fact that S is P', or simply 'That S is P – has as a consequence...is delightful, is doubtful' etc. The same is true when we say, in the *antecedent* of some hypothetical or causal proposition, 'If (Since) S is P', or, in the second or later member of a disjunction, 'or S is P'. In all these cases the state of affairs – *not the judgement* – is our object in a different sense, and is seen in the light of different meanings, from what it is for the judgement whose full objective correlate it is. Plainly the state of affairs is 'objective' in much the same sense as a thing caught in single 'mental ray' of perception or imagination or representation, although a state of affairs is of course no thing, and cannot be perceived, imagined or represented in the stricter, narrower sense of these words.

I said above in passing that *propositions functioning as subjects* were not *presentations of judgements*, but of the corresponding *states of affairs*. This point must be noted. Judgements as concrete experiences can, like things, be objects of possible perception, imagination and perhaps of some non-physical representation. They can then function as subject-objects in judgements, as happens when we *judge about judgements*. When such subordinate judgements are expressed, and not merely indirectly referred to (e.g. as 'this judgement', 'your judgement' etc.) *a sentence will occupy the subject-position*. But where a sentence occupies this position, it will not always serve to *name a judgement*. Judging *about judgements differs from judging about states of affairs*: having a presentation of or naming a judgement is likewise different *from having a presentation of, or naming some state of affairs as a logical subject*. If I say, e.g., 'That *S* is *P* is delightful' I do not think that my judgement is delightful. It makes no difference in this connection whether we mean by 'judgement' the individual act, or the proposition or judgement *qua* Species. What is delightful, is rather that such and such is the case, the objective state of affairs, the fact. This is shown by the objectively equivalent transformation (which however differs in meaning), 'The *P*-ness of *S* (the victory of the righteous cause) is delightful'.

If one builds upon this changed notion of presentation, and also lets drop, as suggested above, the claim that the presentation underlying an act must also cover *all* the matter of the act that it underlies, it would seem that our discarded principle – that each act not itself a presentation must be founded upon presentations – acquires a valuable content, for which self-evidence may very well be claimed. We shall have to give it more precision in the following form: each act is either itself a presentation, or is founded on *one* or *more* presentations. Examples illustrating the first part of this sentence are one-termed (one-rayed) acts of perception, memory, anticipation, imagination, etc.: these are now our 'mere' presentations. Examples illustrating its second half are predicative judgements, and mere presentations in the sense just stated as their correspondent images. A judgement is based on at least one presentation, just as each expressed statement contains at least one name. On the prevailing view which cites S is P as the normal form of simple judgements, we should have to accept a basis of at least two presentations (or two names). There is, however, no maximal upper limit to such presentations. Indefinitely many presentations can nest in a single judgement. It makes no difference if one here brings in compound judgements, since each compound judgement undoubtedly also is a judgement.

The same seems to hold for all other acts, to the extent that they are full and complete. The wish 'May S be P', 'May truth triumph' etc., has as its presentations 'S' and 'P'; 'truth' is straightforwardly posited as subject, and our wish arises out of its predicatively presented triumph. The same holds of all similarly constituted acts, and of the simpler acts immediately based on intuitions, e.g. my rejoicing in something perceived.

We may finally add the proposition that the *ultimately underlying* acts in each act-complex are necessarily presentations.

§34 *Difficulties. The concept of the name. Positing and non-positing names*

Our new concept of presentation is by no means free from difficulties. That our ultimate, underlying acts genuinely have it in common to make objects 'present', in a peculiar, pregnant sense, cannot be doubted. But whether 'presentations' in this sense stand for an *essential genus* of intentional experiences, whose generic unity is purely determined by *act-quality*, so that the acts excluded from their sphere necessarily belong to *qualitatively* different genera: all this is not established. It is not at all easy to decide in what the community consists.

In this connection the following elaborations are necessary. Where *names* are said, as they usually are, to be *expressions of presentations*, our present concept of presentation really is in question. All presentations expressed by names certainly form a unity, which must now be examined. Different senses in which one can speak of 'expression' involve that by 'presentations' one can mean both nominal meaning-*intentions* and also the corresponding fulfilments of meaning. Both non-intuitive and intuitive acts alike fall under the notion here demarcated. By 'names' we should not understand mere nouns, which by themselves do not express complete acts. If we wish to see clearly what names are and mean we should look at contexts, particularly statements, in which names function in their normal meaning. Here we note that words and word-groupings that are to count as names only express complete acts when they either stand for some *complete simple subject of a statement* (thereby expressing a complete subject-act), or at least *could* perform such a simple subject-function in a statement without change in their intentional essence.[1] (Syntactical formations are here disregarded.) It is not therefore a mere *noun*, perhaps even coupled with an attributive or relative clause, that makes a full name: we must also add the definite or indefinite article, which has a most important semantic function. 'The horse', 'a bunch of flowers', 'a house built of sandstone', 'the opening of the Reichstag', also expressions like 'that the Reichstag has been opened', are names.

We now note a remarkable difference. In many, but plainly not all cases, names and nominal presentations are such as to intend and mean objects as *actually existent*, without thereby being more than mere names, without in other words counting as full assertions. This last is excluded by the fact that assertions can never take the subject-position without a change in meaning. Judgements may function as subjects of judgements in the sense of objects judged about, but never, without a certain change of meaning, as subject-acts of other judgements, as 'presentations'. This important proposition must not, however, be conceded without further argument, which we shall provide in what follows. Let us for the time being ignore cases where full statements apparently serve as subjects, and deal with names such as 'Prince Henry', 'the statue of Roland in the market-place', 'the postman hurrying by' etc. Someone who uses these names in their normal sense in genuine discourse 'knows' that Prince Henry is a real, and not a mythic, person, that a statue of Roland does stand in the market-place, that the postman is hurrying by etc. The objects named certainly confront him differently from imaginary objects: not only do they appear to him as existent,

---

[1] Conjunctive or disjunctive plurality on the subject side, as illustrated by '*A* and *B* are *P*', '*A* or *B* is *P*' are therefore excluded. We may also say: the subject-function is *as such* singular, while predication is not *plural* in a wider sense of the word.

but their expression also treats them as such. Nothing of all this is, however, said in the act of naming: exceptionally existence may be expressed attributively in some such form as 'the really existent S', as, in the opposed case, one may say 'the supposed S', 'the imaginary S' etc. But existential positing is achieved, even in the case of such a grammatically enriched name – we shall not enquire whether its sense has been essentially modified or merely extended – in that aspect of the act expressed by the definite article, and only the matter is altered. Even now we have not said *that S exists*, only that S, possibly in an altered sense, is presented as *really existent*, that it is also posited and therefore called 'the really existent S', and even here naming differs in sense from saying.

If this is conceded, we have two different sorts of names and nominal acts, *those that give what they name the status of an existent*, and those that do *not* do this. An example of the latter, if any is needed, is yielded by the nominal material of a discussion of existence, which genuinely starts without an existential commitment.

Plainly there are similar differences in other underlying acts, as a comparison of an *if*-protasis with a *since*-protasis shows: this was only to be expected, since these acts have an essential affinity with nominal ones. The difference between positing and non-positing acts ranges over *the whole field of presentation* in our present sense, and far beyond that of strictly nominal presentation. Among the intuitive presentations which belong here, which, not themselves nominal, have the logical vocation of fulfilling nominal acts of meaning, there are certain positing acts, sense-perception, recollection and anticipation, which all catch their object in a single ray of positing reference. The corresponding abnormal perceptions lack existential commitment, e.g. illusions freed from attitudes towards the reality of the apparent, and all cases of mere fancy. *To each positing act there corresponds a possible non-positing act having the same matter, and vice versa.*

This characteristic difference is plainly a difference in *act-quality*, which imports a certain duality into the notion of presentation. Can we still speak of a *genus* of presentations in the strict sense, and dare we think that positing and non-positing presentations are species or differentiations of this unitary genus?

Our difficulty would be at once removed, could we treat

positing acts as acts founded on other acts, not as mere presentations, but as acts founded on presentations, a new positing
character being then presumably added on to the mere presentation. (One would then have to consider whether this new character was not obviously of the same kind as judgement-quality.)

The analyses performed above make such a notion most
questionable. As little as one can separate off an act of mere
presentation from a percept, or an act of mere, unjudging understanding from an actual assertion, so little can one, e.g., separate
off a non-positing act of nominal meaning from a positing one. A
perfect analogy must obtain between nominal and propositional
acts, since it is clear *a priori* that to each complete, positing
nominal act a possible complete assertion corresponds, and that to
each non-positing nominal act a correlated act of modified
assertion (mere understanding of an assertion) corresponds.
Analysis would therefore reveal, even in this wider sphere, that
what is common to positing and non-positing acts of like content
is no full act, but the mere matter for an act, that occurs in the
two cases with a different act-quality. A name may be merely
understood, but such mere understanding is not part of the
positing use of the name. There seems no way, therefore to span
the deep cleft now yawning among presentations in our present
sense of nominal acts.

§35 *Nominal positing and judgement. Where judgements can be parts of nominal acts*

Let us now go back to the question raised above as to the affinity
and true *relationship between positing presentations and predicative
judgements*. One might try to look on the difference of the two
sorts of act as unessential, and to say: a positing may be no
assertion, i.e. no independent predication, no expression of self-
sufficient judgement. But it still yields a judgement, one, however,
that will serve as a presupposition or basis of another act that will
be built upon it. This role, though *making no difference to the judgement's intentional content*, makes a difference to the judgement's
verbal form. If someone says 'the postman hurrying by...' he
implies the judgement 'The postman is hurrying by'. The nominal
form merely indicates the thetic subject-function, which points
towards the predicative positing which follows.

13-2

We can scarcely approve such a total externalization of the difference under discussion – as if new acts simply attached themselves to some self-identical judgement, and the grammatical name-form merely gave an indirect indication of this sort of attachment. Most logicians, among them the profound Bolzano, saw the distinction between names and assertions as one of essence, and a maturer science will support them. Something may very well be common to both cases, but views of the difference as merely external must be disputed. One must, more precisely, be clear that nominal acts and complete judgements never can have the same intentional essence, and that every switch from one function to the other, though preserving communities, necessarily works changes in this essence.

What most leads us astray at this point is the circumstance that true predications, *complete assertions*, can *in a certain sense really function as logical subjects*. Though not themselves subject-acts, they are built into these last in a certain fashion as judgements determining subjects otherwise already given in them, e.g. 'the Minister – he is now driving up – will make the decision'. We can replace our parenthetic assertion without change of sense by speaking of 'the Minister who is now driving up' or 'the Minister now driving up'. It can be seen, however, that such a conception is not always suitable. Attribution often represents a determining predication, but, even if it invariably did so, which it certainly does not, it would only concern part of the subject-name. After the removal of such determining additions, a complete name would be left over, corresponding to which it would be vain to look for some judgement functioning as logical subject. In our example the determining predication attaches to the name 'the Minister', from which no second predication can be separated. What could the underlying judgement be in this case, and how would we formulate it independently? Is 'the Minister' equivalent to 'he – he is a Minister'? In that case 'he' would be a complete name and would require its own judgement. But how can this be uttered? Is it perhaps the judgement which, expressed independently, would run 'He exists'? Here again we encounter the same subject 'he', and so are involved in an infinite regress.

Undoubtedly many names, including all attributive names, have 'arisen' directly or indirectly out of judgements, and accordingly 'refer back' to judgements. But such talk of 'arising' and 'referring back' implies that names and judgements are different. The difference is so sharp, that it should not be played down for the sake of theoretical prejudice or hoped-for simplifications in the theory of presentation and judgement. The prior judgement is not as yet the nominal meaning that grows out of it. *What in the name remains as a deposit of judgement is not a judgement but a modification sharply differing from it.* The carrying out of the modified act does not include the unmodified one. If we have found out or seen that the town Halle is on the Saale, or that π is a transcendent number, we may go on to talk of Halle-on-the-Saale or of the transcendent number π, but we shall not be judging any longer, or at least we need not be doing so, and *such a judgement, should it arise on the side, makes no contribution to our act of nominal reference.* And so in every case.

We said above that judgements could function in determining fashion, but this is not strictly or properly so. Better regarded, their function consists solely in setting before our eyes an attribution which enriches the name. *Judging itself is not an attributive function, and cannot take over such a function*: it will only provide the soil out of which an attributive meaning will phenomenologically grow. This function once performed, the judgement can fall away, and the attribute with its significant content remain over. Our exceptional cases are therefore cases of compounding: *the attributive function is combined with the predicative.* The latter gives rise to the former, but still wants to count independently and 'on the side' – hence the normal parenthetic expression. Ordinary cases of attribution are free from such complication. A man who speaks of 'the German Emperor' or 'the transcendent number π', does not mean to say 'the Emperor – he is the Emperor of Germany' nor 'π – it is a transcendent number'.

What has been said is only fully intelligible with an important addition. The performance of the modified act, we said, no longer contains the 'original' one: this is at best present as an unnecessary, subsidiary complication. This does not remove the fact that the 'original' judgement is in some sense logically implicit in the modified act. We must here stress that talk of 'origin' and 'modification' are not to be *understood in an empirical-psychological, biological sense, but as expressing a peculiar relation of essence grounded in the phenomenological content of the experiences.* It is part and parcel of the essential content of the nominal, attributive presentation that its intention 'refers back' to the corresponding judgement, and that it intrinsically presents itself as a 'modification' of this judgement. If we wish to 'realize' the sense of presentations of the form 'the S which is P' (the transcendent number π), and to do this with complete clarity and authenticity, if we wish to enter the path of demonstrative fulfilment of what the expression 'means', we must appeal as it were to the corresponding predicative judgement, we must carry this out, and take our nominal presentations from it as from a source, let them proceed from it, derive them from it. The same plainly holds, *mutatis mutandis*, of non-positing attributive presentations, their 'proper' carrying out requires phenomenologically predicative acts of qualitatively modified type (the counterparts of the actual judgements) out of which they may then 'originate'. A certain mediacy therefore enters phenomenologically into the essence of the attributive presentation, which our talk of origination, derivation and also of 'referring back' expresses. It is therefore true *a priori* that the grounded validation of each nominal attribution leads back to that of the corresponding judgement. Correlatively, we may likewise say that the nominal object, whatever its categorial interpretation, derives from the corresponding state of affairs, which has an intrinsic priority as regards authenticity.

After saying all this, we may maintain generally that *there are differences between names and assertions which affect their 'semantic essence'*, or that rest on the essential difference of presentations and judgements. *It is not the same, in terms of intentional essence, whether one perceives an existent or judges that it exists, so it is not the same if one names an existent as existent, or says or predicates of it that it exists.*

We may now note that *to every positing name a possible judgement self-evidently corresponds, or that to every attribution a possible predication corresponds and vice versa.* After we have rejected the essential sameness of these acts, we can assume only that we have here a case of law-governed connection, and of connection governed by *ideal law*. Ideal connections do not point to the causal genesis or the empirical concomitance of the acts they coordinate, but to a certain ideally governed, operative belongingness of the ideatively graspable act-essences[1] in question, which have their 'being' and law-governed ontological order, in the realm of

---

[1] Here we have, in a pure logico-grammatical context, a certain sort of significant modification grounded in the pure essence of Meaning (cf. Inv. iv).

phenomenological ideality, just as pure numbers and pure specifications of geometric patterns have theirs respectively in the
realms of arithmetical and geometrical ideality. If we enter the
a priori reaches of pure Ideas, we can likewise say that 'one' (in
pure, i.e. unconditional universality) could not perform the one
set of acts without being able to perform those coordinated with
them, and this on account of the specific semantic essence of the
acts concerned. We may say, further, that there are coordinations,
interesting from the point of view of logical validity, law-governed
equivalences, rendering it impossible or rather irrational to
start with the words 'this *S*' without 'potentially' conceding that
there are *S*'s. In other words, that propositions containing positing names should be true, and that the existential judgements
which correspond to such names should be false, involves an
a priori inconsistency. This is one of the ideal, analytic truths which
are rooted in the 'mere form' of our thought, or in the categories
or specific Ideas which belong to the possible forms of thinking
proper.

§36 *Continuation. Whether assertions can function complete as names*

We have yet another important class of instances to consider
and shall use them to confirm our notion of the relation of
nominal acts and judgements. We are concerned with cases where
declarative sentences are not merely used with determining
intent, and so seem, as actual assertions, to be parts of names,
but where they seem to function as full and complete names, e.g.
'That rain has set in at last will delight the farmers'. It seems
impossible to avoid the admission that the subject-sentence is
here a complete assertion. For it means that rain has really set in.
The modified expression of the judgements by way of a subordinate clause-form here only serves to show that our assertion is
functioning as a subject, that it provides the basic act on which a
predicative assertion may be imposed.

All this sounds very nice. If the disputed conception had real
support in our class of instances, and were really allowable there,
a doubt would arise whether, despite all previous objections, it
might not apply even over a wider field.

Let us consider our example more closely. If asked what the
farmers are glad about, one replies with a 'that so-and-so' or

'about the *fact* that rain has at length fallen'. The fact, therefore, the state of affairs posited as existent, is the object of the gladness, is the subject about which we are making an assertion. This fact can be variously named. We can simply say 'this', as in the case of all other objects, we can also say 'this fact', or, more definitely, 'the fact of the set-in rain, of the setting in of the rain' etc. We can also say, as above, 'that the rain has set in'. Our coordination shows that this clause is a name in exactly the same sense as all other nominal expressions of acts, that it does not differ essentially in sense-giving backing from other acts. It *names* exactly as they do, and in naming *presents*; as other names name other things, properties etc., so it names or presents a *state of affairs*, which in particular is an empirical fact.

What is the difference between such *naming* and the independent *assertion of the state of affairs*, when, e.g., we make the assertion: 'Rain has at last set in'?

It sometimes happens that we first assert something absolutely, and then proceed to name the state of affairs: 'Rain has at last set in. That will delight the farmers'. Here we can study an undeniable contrast. The state of affairs is in both cases the same, but it is our object in quite a different manner. In the straightforward assertion we judge about the rain, and about its having set in: both are in a pregnant sense objective to us, *presented*. But we do not enact a mere sequence of presentations, but a *judgement*, a peculiar 'unity of consciousness', that binds these together. In this binding together the consciousness of the *state of affairs* is constituted: *to execute judgement, and to be conscious of a state of affairs, in this synthetic positing of something as referred to something, are one and the same*. A thesis is enacted, and on it a second dependent thesis is based, so that, in this basing of thesis on thesis, the synthetic unity of the state of affairs is intentionally constituted. Such a synthetic consciousness is plainly quite different from *setting something before one in a single-rayed thesis, in a possible, direct subject-act, in a presentation*. One may compare the ways in which the rain 'comes to consciousness', the assertedness of the state of affairs, and the presentational, naming way which in our example succeeds it, and which applies to the same state of affairs: 'That will delight the farmers'. 'That', as it were, points a finger to the state of affairs: it therefore means this same state of affairs. But this reference is not the judgement itself, which has preceded it as a thus and thus qualified mental happening now passed away: it is a *new act of a new kind*, which in pointing to the state of affairs previously constituted in synthetic, many-rayed fashion, now simply confronts this state of affairs with a single-rayed thesis, and so makes it an object in a sense quite different from the way the judgement does so. The state of affairs comes more 'primitively' to consciousness in the judgement: the single-rayed intention towards the state of affairs presupposes the many-rayed judgemental intention, and a reference to the latter is part of its intrinsic sense. But in each many-rayed conscious approach there is rooted, in *a priori* fashion, an essential, ideal possibility of transformation into the single-rayed approach, in which a state of affairs will be pregnantly 'objective' or 'presented'. (Just as there is an *a priori* possibility, resting on the ideal essence of geometrical figures, that 'one' can turn them about in space, distort them into certain other figures etc.) It is now at all events quite clear that the manner in which we are conscious of something, or in which it is our intentional object, is different in each case. Otherwise put, we are dealing with 'essentially' different acts, or with acts differing in intentional essence.

If we ignore pointing proper, what is essential in the 'That' of our previous example is also present in the thought of the *mere sentence occupying a subject-position* (and any other position in a context which demands presentation), and is necessarily absent from the thought of a genuine and independent assertion. *As soon as the semantic moment which underlies the definite article comes alive, a presentation in our present sense is enacted.* Whether a language or dialect actually employs the article or not, whether one speaks of *der Mensch* or *homo*, of *Karl* or *der Karl* is irrelevant. That this moment of meaning attaches to the sentence 'That S is P', functioning as subject, is easily seen. For 'That S is P' means what we mean by 'This, that S is P', or, a little more elaborately, 'The fact, the circumstance that S is P'.

The situation is not of a kind, after all this, to encourage us to speak of judgements, actual predications, that could be logical *subjects* or *nominal acts*. We rather see that there is a difference of intentional essence between sentences serving to name states of affairs, and the corresponding assertions of states of affairs, a gulf bridged by ideal relations of law. *An assertion can never function as a name, nor a name as an assertion, without changing its essential nature,* i.e., its semantic essence, and therewith its very meaning.

This does not of course mean that the corresponding acts are descriptively alien. The matter of the assertion is in part the same as that of the nominal act, in both the same state of affairs is intended in the same terms, though in a different form. The great affinity of expressive form is no matter of chance, but has semantic roots. If occasionally the expression stays unchanged, despite a change in semantic function, we are dealing with a particular case of equivocation, which belongs to the broad class of cases where expressions have anomalous meanings. These anomalies, arising from the pure essence of the semantic field, resemble the anomalies of *pure grammar*.[1] Our conception accordingly admits of a consistent working-out: we differentiate in all cases between presentations and judgements, and, among presentations, between such as are positing and existentially committed, and such as are not. We shall accordingly not hesitate to deny judgement-status to antecedents of the form 'Because S is P' which *state causes*: *we shall put them in the same relation to hypothetical antecedents that we have recognized as obtaining between positing and non-positing names*. The 'because' may point back to a judgement that asserted S to be P, but this judgement is not again enacted with the causal sentence itself. We no longer assert that S is P, but we impose on a purely presentative substructure, that of an antecedent characterized in its very sense as a modified judging synthesis, a second consequential thesis which is grounded upon, and which 'looks to', the former. The whole is a new form of judgemental synthesis, whose sense, a little elaborated, can be said to be: the *conditioning* of the being of one state of affairs by that of another which grounds it. Only as so combined, moreover, antecedent and consequent function as a judgement, as when we assert 'S is P', and because this is so, 'Q is R'. Here it is not enough to establish such a sequence synthetically, but to have and to hold the two states of affairs 'S is P' and 'Q is R' judgementally together, in our relating, synthetic consciousness itself.

Note. The extensions just made show that nominal presentations in the strict, narrow sense merely represent a wider, but still limited class of 'thetic' or 'single-rayed positing' acts. This must be remembered in what follows, even when we connect our

[1] See Inv. IV, §11, and the additional note to §13.

treatments with genuinely nominal presentations. The term 'nominal presentation', understood as a class-term, must accordingly be given a much widened sense.

Our standards of terminology must also be noted, according to which a 'judgement' means a complete, independent assertion. That such a meaning cannot without intrinsic change become the meaning of a hypothetical or causal antecedent or indeed any nominal meaning, is the thesis established above.

Further Contributions to the Theory of Judgement. 'Presentation' as a Qualitatively Unitary Genus of Nominal and Propositional Acts

§37 *The aim of the following investigation. The concept of an objectifying act*

THE investigations just completed have not done with the question raised at the beginning of §34. Our result was that presentations and judgements are essentially different acts. Since the ambiguity of words again needs the help of standard-setting concepts, we mean by 'presentations' nominal acts, and by 'judgements' assertions that are normally performed and complete. Naming and asserting do not merely differ grammatically, but 'in essence', which means that the acts which confer or fulfil meaning for each, differ in *intentional essence*, and therefore in *act-species*. Have we thereby shown that presentation and judgement, the acts which lend meaning and semantic fulfilment to naming and assertion, belong to different *basic classes* of intentional experience?

Obviously our answer must be negative: nothing points to such a thing. We must recall that intentional essence is made up of the two aspects of *matter* and *quality*, and that a distinction of 'basic class' obviously relates only to act-qualities. We must further recall that our exposition does not at all entail that nominal and propositional acts *differ in quality*, much less that they differ *generically* as regards quality.

This latter point should not arouse objection. The matter of acts is in our sense no alien, external attachment, but an internal moment, an inseparable side of the act-intention, of the intentional essence itself. Talk about the differing 'ways of consciousness', in which we can be aware of the same state of affairs, should not mislead us. It points to a distinction of acts, but not one of act-qualities. Quality may remain identical – so much has guided us since we formed the Idea of matter – while the same object remains differently present to consciousness. One may think, e.g., of equivalent positing presentations, which point by way of differing matters to the same object. The essential change of meaning which an assertion undergoes when it passes over into the nominal (or other parallel) function, a point whose proof we found so important above, may involve no more than a *change of matter*; *quality or at least qualitative genus* (according to the kind of nominal modification) *may remain unchanged*.

That this describes the actual situation becomes plain if we carefully attend to the matters themselves. Completion by nominally significant articles like 'the circumstance that', 'the fact that', where a propositional meaning is made to function as subject, has been shown by the above examples to be necessary. The examples introduce us to contexts where transformed sense goes with a transfer of unchanged, essential, material content, and where, therefore, interpretative functions are present which the original assertion lacks, or for which it has substitutes. The essential moments which agree in the two cases, also undergo, as we can see in each case, a different 'categorial structuring'. One may compare, e.g., the form '*S* is *P*' with its nominal modification '*S* which is *P*'.

The following treatments will show, on the other hand, that there is a *qualitative* community between nominal and propositional acts; we shall therefore end by *demarcating yet another new concept of presentation, wider and more significant than the former*, which will give us a new, most important interpretation of the principle that each act has its basis in presentations.

To keep our present two concepts of 'presentation' apart, we shall – without making final recommendations as to terminology – speak of 'nominal acts' in the case of the narrower concept, and of 'objectifying acts' in the case of the wider. We need hardly stress, after our whole introduction of the concept of 'nominal presentation' in the last chapter, that the expression does not merely cover acts attached to nominal expressions, and conferring or fulfilling their meaning, but also all acts that function analogously, even if not performing the same grammatical role.

§38 *Qualitative and material differentiation of objectifying acts*

Among nominal acts we distinguish positing from non-positing acts. The former were after a fashion existence-meanings: they were either sensuous percepts, or percepts in the wider sense of pretended apprehensions of what is, or other acts which, without claiming to seize an object 'itself', in 'full-bodied' or intuitive fashion, yet refer to it as *existent*.[1] The other acts leave the existence of their object unsettled: the object may, objectively considered, exist, but it is not referred to as existent in them, it does not *count* as actual, but rather as 'merely presented'. In all this there is a law to the effect that to each positing nominal act a non-positing act, a 'mere presentation' of like matter, corresponds, and vice versa, this correspondence being understood in the sense of the ideally possible.

A certain *modification*, as we may also express the matter, makes each positing nominal act pass over into a mere presentation with like matter. We find exactly the same modification in the case of judgements. Each judgement has its modified form, an act which merely presents what the judgement takes to be true, which has an object without a decision as to truth and falsity.[2] Phenomenologically regarded, this modification of judgements is quite of the same sort as that of positing nominal acts. Judgements as *positing propositional acts* have therefore their merely presentative correlates in *non-positing propositional acts*. The corresponding acts have in both cases the same matter and a differing quality. But just as we count positing and non-positing nominal acts as *one* genus of quality, we do the same for propositional acts in regard to judgements and their modified counterparts. The qualitative differences are in both cases the same, and not to be regarded as differentiations of any higher genera of quality. To pass from the positing to the modified act is not to pass to a heterogeneous class, as in the case of passing from any nominal act to a desire or act of will. But in the passage from a positing nominal act to an act of affirmative assertion, we are not tempted to see a qualitative difference; the same holds if we compare the corresponding 'mere presentations'. Matter alone, in the sense fixed for the present investigation, constitutes both differences: it alone

---

[1] Cf. the examples in §34.
[2] It must be noted that this mode of expression is a circumlocution.

determines the unity of the nominal, and the unity of the propositional acts.

This suffices to mark off a comprehensive class of intentional experiences which includes all the acts hitherto dealt with in their qualitative essence, and determines the widest concept that the term 'presentation' can stand for within the total class of intentional experiences. We ourselves would like to call this qualitatively unitary class, taken in its natural width, the class of *objectifying acts*. It yields (to put the matter clearly in front of us):

1. through qualitative differentiation, the division into positing acts – acts of belief or judgement in the sense of Mill and Brentano respectively – and non-positing acts, acts 'modified' as regards positing, the corresponding 'mere presentations'. How far the concept of positing belief extends, and how it is specified, remains undetermined;

2. through differentiation of matter, it yields the difference of nominal and propositional acts, though we still must consider whether this difference is not merely one of many equally valid material differences.

A glance over the analyses of the last chapter,[1] makes us aware of the truly pervasive opposition between *synthetic, many-rayed act-unities* and *single-rayed acts, acts which posit or entertain something in a single thesis*. We must note, however, that predicative synthesis is only an especially favoured form (or complete system of forms) of synthesis, to which other frequently inwoven forms stand opposed, e.g. the form of conjunctive or disjunctive synthesis. We have, for example, in the plural predication '*A* and *B* and *C* are *P*' a unitary predication terminating in three predicative layers on the same predicate *P*. 'Upon' the basic positing of *A*, the secondary positing of *B*, and the tertiary positing of *C*, the predicate *P*, kept identical throughout, is posited in a single, three-layered act. Our act of judgement is as it were articulated by a 'caesura' into a subject- and a predicate-positing, but so that the one subject-member is in its turn a unitary conjunction of three nominal members. These are united in the conjunction, but they do not come together in one nominal presentation. But it is true of the 'conjunctive' (or better 'collective') synthesis, as it is true of the predicative synthesis, that it permits of nominalization, in which case the collective object constituted by the

---

[1] [§38, from this point onwards, is mainly a Second Edition supplement.]

synthesis, becomes the simply presented object of a new 'single-rayed' act, and so is made 'objective' in the pregnant sense of the word. The nominal presentation of the collection now again refers back in its own sense (in the matter from the original act that it takes over and modifies) to the matter (or the consciousness) which originally constituted it. Closer examination reveals in all synthesis what we noted in the case of the predicative synthesis – when we kept, moreover, to the basic predicative form of categorical synthesis – that we can always perform the *fundamental operation of nominalization, the transformation of many-rayed synthesis into single-rayed naming with an appropriate backward reference in our material.*

Our general treatment of ideally possible objectifying acts therefore brings us back to the basic distinction of 'thetic' and 'synthetic' acts, of 'single-rayed' and 'many-rayed' acts. The single-rayed acts are not articulate, the many-rayed acts are articulate. Each member has its objectifying quality (its peculiar stance towards being, or the corresponding qualitative modification of this stance) and its matter. The whole synthesis as a single objectifying act has likewise a quality and a matter, the latter articulate. To analyse such a whole is, on the one hand, to come upon members, and, on the other, upon syntactical forms of synthesis. The members in their turn may be simple or complete. They may themselves be articulate and synthetically unified, as in our above example of the conjunctive subjects of plural predications, or as in the case of conjoined antecedents in hypothetical predications, or as in the corresponding disjunctions in either case etc.

We at length come down to simple members, *single-rayed in their objectification, but not necessarily primitive in some ultimate sense.* For such single-rayed members may still be nominalized syntheses, nominal presentations of states of affairs or *collectiva* or *disjunctiva*, whose members may again be states of affairs etc. Our matter will therefore contain *backward references* of a more or less complex sort, and therefore, in a peculiarly modified, indirect sense, *implicit* articulations and synthetic forms. If the members no longer refer back, they are also simple in this respect. This is, e.g., plainly true of all proper name-presentations, and of single-membered percepts, imaginations, etc., which are not split up by explanatory syntheses. Such wholly straightforward objectifications are free from all 'categorial forms'. Plainly the analysis of each act that is *not* straightforward in its objectifications, must pursue the series of backward references contained in its nominalizations, until it comes down upon *such straightforward act-members, simple both in form and in matter*. We may finally note that the general treatment of possible articulations and synthetic formations leads to the pure *logico-grammatical laws* discussed in our Fourth Investigation. In this respect only *matters* (objectifying act-senses) are relevant, and in these all forms of structured objectifying synthesis express themselves. Here the principle obtains that our self-contained objectifying matter (and therefore any possible non-dependent meaning) can function as a member in every synthesis of every possible form. This entails the particular principle that each such matter is either a complete propositional (predicative) matter or a possible member of such a matter. If we now bring in qualities, we can affirm the principle that, ideally regarded, any objectifying matter can be combined with any quality.

If we now look at the special difference between nominal and propositional acts, which is of such particular interest in our present Investigation, the just-mentioned possibility of combining any quality with any matter can be readily confirmed. In the analyses of previous sections, it has not been made universally plain, since we confined ourselves to modifications of the judgement, i.e. a *positing* propositional act, into a nominal act. Undeniably, however, each judgement modified into a 'mere' presentation can be transformed into a corresponding nominal act. Thus '$2 \times 2 = 5$', uttered to express understanding and not to take up an assertive stance, can be changed into the name 'that $2 \times 2 = 5$'. Since 'modifications' are spoken of in the case of such transformations of propositions into names as leave qualities unaffected, i.e. in the case of mere transformations of propositional or other synthetic *matters*, it will be well to reserve the name 'qualitative modification' for the quite different type of modification which affects *qualities* (transforming of positing names and statements into non-positing ones). Where the matter, which alone gives form or underlies formal distinctions, either remains, or is meant to remain constant, where a name stays a name, a proposition a proposition, in all their internal articulations and forms, we shall also have to speak of *conformative modifications* of positing acts. But if the notion of conformative modification is widened, by a natural extension, so as to cover *every modification not affecting act-material*, then (as we shall presently see) it will be a *wider* notion than our present concept of qualitative modification.

§39 *Presentation in the sense of an objectifying act, and its qualitative modification*

When we grouped objectifying acts into a single class, we were decisively moved by the fact that this whole class is characterized by one qualitative opposition: just as there is a 'merely presentative' counterpart to each nominal belief, so there is one in the case of each propositional belief, each complete judgement. We may now doubt, however, whether this qualitative modification really characterizes a *class*, whether it does not rather govern the whole sphere of such experiences, and provide a basis for dividing them. An obvious argument favours this last: there is a mere presentation corresponding to every intentional experience, to a wish the mere idea of a wish, to a hate the mere idea of a hate, to a volition the mere idea of willing etc. – just as there are mere presentations corresponding to actual cases of naming and assertion.

One should not, however, mix up quite different things. To each possible act, to each possible experience, to each possible object in general, there is a presentation which relates to it, and which can as readily be qualified as positing as non-positing (as 'mere' presentation). Fundamentally, however, we have not here one, but a whole multitude of presentations of different sorts: this is true even if we restrict ourselves (as we would seem tacitly to have done) to presentations of nominal type. Such a presentation can present its object intuitively or notionally, directly or by way of attributes, and can do so very differently. But it suffices for our purposes to speak of *one* presentation, or to high-light any one variety of presentation, e.g. the imaginative, since all varieties of presentation are in each case and in the same way possible.

To each object, therefore, corresponds the presentation of that object, to a house the presentation of a house, to a presentation the presentation of the presentation, to a judgement the presentation of a judgement etc. Here we must note, however, as indicated above, that the presentation of the judgement is not the presentation of the state of affairs judged. Just so, more generally, the presentation of a positing is not the presentation of the positingly presented object. Different objects are presented in each case. The will, e.g., to realize a state of affairs, differs from the will to realize a judgement or the nominal positing of this state of affairs. A positing act's qualitative counterpart corresponds to it in quite different fashion from the fashion in which its presentation, or any act's presentation, corresponds to that act. *Modifying an act qualitatively is quite a different 'operation', as it were, from producing a presentation 'of' this act.* The true difference between these operations comes out in the fact that the *operation of presentative objectification*, shown symbolically in the sequence O, $P(O)$, $P(P(O))$... where O is any object and $P(O)$ its presentation, admits of iteration, *whereas qualitative modification does not*, and in the further fact that *presentative objectification applies to all objects whatever, whereas qualitative modification only makes sense in the case of acts*. It also comes out in the fact that, in the one order of modifications, 'presentations' are exclusively *nominal*, whereas the other order is not so restricted, and in the further fact that, in the first order, *qualities remain irrelevant*, and modification only affects *matters*, whereas, in the other order of modification, it is precisely *quality* that is modified. Each act of belief has a 'mere presentation' as its counterpart, which presents the same object in precisely the same manner, i.e. on the ground of the same matter, and only differs from the former act in that it leaves the presented object *in suspense*, and does not refer to it positingly as existent. Such a modification can of course not be repeated, as little as it makes sense in the case of acts not ranged under the notion of belief. It therefore creates a quite peculiar connection between acts of this quality and their counterparts. A positing percept or recollection, e.g., has its counterpart in a corresponding act of 'mere' imagination having the same matter, as in, e.g., the intuitive percept of an image, the consideration of a painting that we allow to influence us purely artistically, without in any way responding to the existence or non-existence of what is represented, or the intuition of some mental picture where we drop all stances towards existence and lose ourselves in fantasy. 'Mere' presentation has here no further counterpart: it is unintelligible what such a presentation could mean or achieve. If belief has been transformed into mere presentation, we can at best *return* to belief: There is no modification that can be repeated in the *same* sense, and carried on further.

The case is different if we pass from the operation of qualitative modification to that of nominalizing, presentative objectification. Here there is an evident possibility of iteration. This is most simply shown in the relation of acts to the ego, and their division among different persons and points of time. At one time I perceive something, at another I present to myself that I am perceiving it, at yet another I present to myself that I am presenting to myself that I am perceiving it etc.[1] Or another example: *A* is painted, a second painting represents the first painting, a third the second etc. The differences are obvious in these cases, and they are of course not merely differences in sense-contents, but in the interpretative act-characters (and their intentional 'matters') without which it would be quite senseless to talk of mental images, paintings etc. These differences are immanently apprehended, are *phenomenologically* certain, as soon as the corresponding experiences have been had, and their intentional differences reflected upon. This happens, e.g., when a man draws distinctions and says: I am now perceiving *A*, picturing *B*, while *C* is represented in this painting etc. A man who has become clear regarding these relations, will not fall into the error of those who think *presentations of presentations* phenomenologically undiscoverable, in fact mere *fictions*. Such judgements confuse the two operations distinguished here: they substitute the presentation *of* a mere presentation for the utterly impossible qualitative modification of this presentation.

We may now, it seems, assume a community of *kind*[2] among qualities coordinated by conformative modification, and may think it true that one or other of these qualities pertains to all acts, entering essentially into the unitary structure of each qualitatively unmodified or modified judgement, whether we consider acts of mere significant intention or acts which fulfil meaning. It is obvious, further, that the mere presentations of any act whatever, which we distinguished above from the qualitative counterparts possible only in the case of positing acts, are, as

---

[1] All this must of course not be understood in an empirical-psychological manner. We are concerned here (as everywhere in this investigation) with *a priori* possibilities rooted in pure essence, which are as such grasped by us with apodictic self-evidence.

[2] Cf. however the interpretation of a 'community of kind' as a peculiar relation of 'essence and counter-essence' in my *Ideas*, p. 233. The further pursuit of the results of this investigation has generally led to many essential deepenings and improvements. Cf, in particular, *Ideas*, §§ 109–14, 117 on the modification.

mere presentations, themselves qualitative counterparts, but not to their acts of origin, which are rather their presented objects. The mere presentation of a wish is no counterpart of a wish, but of any positing act, e.g. a percept, directed upon this wish. This pair, percept and mere presentation of a wish, are of one kind, whereas the wish and its percept or imagination or any other presentation which relates to it, differ in kind.

§40 Continuation. Qualitative and imaginative modification

One is readily led to call positing acts *affirmative* (*fürwahrhaltende*), their counterparts *imaginative*. Both expressions have at first blush their objections, which especially impede the terminological fixation of the latter. The discussion of these objections will prompt us to make certain not unimportant additions.

The whole tradition of logic only speaks of affirmation in the case of judgements, i.e. the meanings of statements, but now we wish to call all percepts, recollections, anticipations, and all acts of normally expressed positing, 'affirmations'. The word 'imagination', likewise, normally means a non-positing act, but we should have to extend its original meaning beyond the sphere of sensuous imagination, so as to cover all possible counterparts of affirmations. Its meaning will also require restriction, since we must exclude all thought of imaginations as conscious fictions, as objectless presentations or false opinions. Often enough we understand narrations without decision as to their truth or falsity. Even when we read novels, this is normally the case: we know we are dealing with aesthetic fictions, but this knowledge remains inoperative in the purely aesthetic effect.[1] In such cases all expressions express non-positing acts, 'imaginings' in the sense of our proposed terminology, both in respect of significant intentions and of fancied fulfilments. This also affects complete assertions. Judgements are passed in a certain manner, but they lack the character of genuine judgements: we neither believe, deny or doubt what is told us – mere 'imaginings' replace genuine judgements. Such talk must not be taken to mean that *imagined judgements here take the place of actual ones*. We rather enact, instead of a judgement affirming a state of affairs, the *qualitative* modifi-

[1] The same is of course true of other act-products, e.g. the aesthetic consideration of pictures.

cation, the neutral putting in suspense of the same state of affairs, which cannot be identified with any picturing of it.

The name 'imagination' has an inconvenience which seriously blocks its use as a term: it suggests an imaginative or fanciful conception, pictorial in the stricter sense, while we can by no means say that *all non-positing acts involve imagining*, and that *all positing acts are non-imagining*. This last is immediately clear. A pictured sensuous object can as readily come before us posited as existent, as merely imagined in modified fashion. This can be so, while the representative content of its intuition remains identical, the content which not merely gives the intuition its determinate relation to *this object*, but also the character of imaginative, i.e. of fanciful or pictorial representation, of it. The phenomenal content of a painting, with its painted figures etc., remains, e.g., the same, whether we regard these as representing real objects, or allow them to influence us aesthetically without positing anything. It is most doubtful whether anything similar occurs in its purity in normal perception: whether perception can preserve the rest of its phenomenological features, but be qualitatively modified, so as to lose its normal positing character. It may be doubted whether the characteristic perceptual view of the object as *itself* present in full-bodied reality, would not at once pass over into a picture-view, where the object, much as in the case of normal perceptual picture-consciousness (paintings and the like) appears portrayed rather than as itself given. Yet one might here point to many sensible appearances, e.g. stereoscopic phenomena, which one can treat, like aesthetic objects, as 'mere phenomena', without adopting an existential stance, and yet treat as 'themselves', and not as portraits of something else. It suffices that perception can pass over into a corresponding picturing (an act with like 'matter' differently interpreted) yet without change in its positing character.

We see that two conformative modifications may here be distinguished: one *qualitative* and one *imaginative*. In both the 'matter' remains unchanged. But with matter unchanged, more than quality can alter in an act. Quality and matter we took to be absolutely essential to acts, since inseparable from them, and relevant to their meaning, but we originally pointed out that other aspects could be distinguished in them. Our next investigation will show more precisely the relevance of these last two distinctions between non-intuitive objectification and intuition, and between perception and imagination.

When the descriptive relations are clarified, it is plainly a purely terminological issue whether one limits the word 'judgement', in the sense of tradition, to the unmodified meaning of statements, or applies it throughout the sphere of acts of belief. In the former case no 'ground-class' of acts, not even a lowest qualitative difference, is completely covered, since the 'matter' – which for us covers the 'is not' as well as the 'is' – assists in the demarcation. All this is, however, irrelevant. Since 'judgement' is a logical term, it is for logical interests and logical tradition alone to decide what concept will be its meaning. It has to be said, in this connection, that a notion so fundamental as that of an (ideal) propositional meaning, being the ultimate point of unity to which all things logical must relate, must retain its natural, traditional expression. The term 'act of judging' must therefore be confined to corresponding types of act, to the significant intentions behind complete statements, and to the fulfilments which fit in with these and share their semantic essence. To call all positing acts 'judgements' tends to obscure the essential distinction, despite all qualitative community, between nominal and propositional acts, and so to confuse an array of important relationships. The case of the term 'presentation' resembles that of the term 'judgement'. Logical requirements must decide what logic is to mean by it. Heed must be paid to the (mutually) exclusive separation of presentation and judgement, and to the fact that a 'presentation' claims to be something from which a complete judgement may possibly be built up. Shall one then accept the notion of presentation, as comprehending *all possible part-meanings of logical judgement*, which Bolzano made basic for his treatment of *Wissenschaftslehre*? Or shall one limit one's notion to what are, phenomenologically speaking, relatively independent meanings of this type, complete members of judgements, and, in particular, *nominal acts*? Or shall one not follow another route of division, and treat as presentations the mere *representations*, i.e. the total content of all acts that survives the abstraction of quality, and only preserves the 'matter' out of their intentional essence? These are difficult questions which can certainly not be decided here.

§41 *New interpretation of the principle that makes presentations the bases of all acts. The objectifying act as the primary bearer of 'matter'*

Several thinkers in olden and more modern times have interpreted the term 'presentation' so widely as to include 'affirmative' acts, particularly judgements, as well as 'merely presentative' acts, in its purview, and so to include in this *the whole sphere of objectifying acts*. If we now base ourselves on this important concept, which sums up a closed class of quality, our proposition regarding basic presentations gains a highly significant, novel sense – as pointed out above – of which the former sense based on the nominal concept of presentation, is merely a secondary offshoot. For we may say: *Each intentional experience is either an objectifying act or has its basis in such an act*, i.e. it must, in the latter case, contain an objectifying act among its constituents, whose total matter is individually the same as *its* total matter. What we previously said,[1] in expounding the sense of this as yet unclarified proposition, can now be practically used word for word in justification of the term 'objectifying act'. If no act, or act-quality, not objectifying by nature, can acquire 'matter' except through an objectifying act that is inwoven with it in unity, objectifying acts have the unique function of first providing other acts with presented objects, to which they may then refer in their novel ways. The reference to an object is, in general terms, constituted in an act's 'matter'. But all matter, according to our principle, *is the matter of an objectifying act*, and only through the latter can it become matter for a new act-quality founded upon this. We must after a fashion distinguish between *secondary* and *primary intentions*, the latter owing their intentionality to their foundation on the former. Whether primary objectifying acts are of a positing, affirming, believing character, or of a non-positing, merely presenting, neutral character, does not affect this function. Many secondary acts invariably require affirmations, as, e.g. joy and sorrow: for others mere modifications suffice, e.g. for wishes or aesthetic feelings. Quite often there is a complex underlying objectifying act, including acts of both sorts.

[1] §23.

§42 *Further developments. Basic principles of complex acts*

To cast more light on this remarkable situation, we add the following remarks.

Each complex act is *eo ipso* qualitatively complex: it has as many qualities, whether of differing or identical sort, as it has distinguishable individual acts in itself. Each complex act is further a founded act: its total quality is no mere sum of the qualities of part-acts, but a *single* quality, with a unity resting on those constitutive qualities, just as the unity of the total 'matter' is no mere sum of the matters of the part-acts, but is founded, to the extent that this 'matter' is really divided among these part-acts, in the partial 'matters'. The manner, however, in which an act can be qualitatively complex and founded upon other acts, differs profoundly, and this as regards the varied ways in which differing qualities stand to one another, and stand to the unitary total matter and to possible part-matters, ways in which they achieve unity through varied sorts of elementary foundedness.

An act can be complex in such fashion that its complex total quality divides into *several qualities*, each having *individually the same* common matter, e.g. in joy over some fact, the specific quality of the joy is compounded with that of the affirmation in which the fact becomes 'present' to us. This might lead one to think that each of these qualities, bar one chosen at random, could fall away, while a concrete complete act was left standing. One might also think that qualities of any kind could be bound up with a single matter in the manner in question. Our law asserts that all this is not possible, that in each act there must necessarily be an act-quality of the objectifying kind, since there can be no matter that is not the matter of an objectifying act.

Qualities of other kinds are accordingly always founded on objectifying qualities; they can never be immediately associated with matter in their own right. Where the former are present, the total act must be qualitatively *multiform*, i.e. must involve qualities differing in kind, in such a way that a complete objectifying act can be (one-sidedly) separated from it, an act having the whole matter of the total act as its total matter. Acts *uniform* in a corresponding sense need not be simple. All uniform acts are objectifying acts, and, conversely, all objectifying acts may be held to be uniform, but objectifying acts may nonetheless be complex. The matters of the part-acts are then mere parts of the matter of the total act: in this total act the total matter is constituted inasmuch as its parts belong to the part-acts, while the unifying element of the total matter belongs to the unifying element of the total quality. The division into parts can, further, be an explicit articulation, but matters nominalized in the previously described fashion, may also reveal as implicit articulations all the forms otherwise possible in free syntheses. To their members correspond underlying part-acts with their part-matters, while founded act-characters (and together with them founded moments of the total matter) correspond to the connective forms, to the *is* or the *is not*, the *if* and the *then*, the *and*, the *or* etc. In all this compounding the act remains uniform: *there can be no more than a single objectifying quality related to a single 'matter' considered as a whole.*

From such uniformity multiformity arises if the objectifying total act becomes associated with new kinds of quality referred to its total matter, or if such qualities merely accompany single part-acts, as when, on the basis of one unified, articulate intuition, liking becomes directed to one member and dislike to another. It is plain, conversely, that in each complex act *involving non-objectifying act-qualities*, which rest either on the total matter or its parts, these latter act-qualities can all as it were be eliminated. A complete objectifying act is then left, containing the total matter of the original act.

A further consequence of the law which prevails here is that the *ultimate underlying acts* in every complex act (or the *ultimately implied* acts in its nominal members) must be objectifying acts. These must all be *nominal acts*, and the ultimate implied acts are in every respect *simple* nominal acts, straightforward combinations of a simple quality with a simple matter. We may also assert the proposition that all simple acts are nominal. The converse, of course, does not hold; not all nominal acts are simple. When articulate material is present in an objectifying act, a categorial form must also be present in it, and it is of the essence of all categorial forms to be constituted in founded acts, as we shall discuss more fully later on.

Note. In this treatment and the immediately following, 'matter' need not be taken to mean the mere abstract moment of intentional essence: we could replace this by the whole act, in abstraction from its quality, i.e. by something we shall call 'representation' in our next investigation. Everything essential will then be unaffected.

§43 Backward glance to our previous interpretation of the principle under discussion

It can now be understood why we said above[1] *that Brentano's principle interpreted in terms of the nominal concept of presentation is merely a secondary consequence of the same proposition in our new interpretation.* If every non-objectifying, or not purely objectifying act, is founded on objectifying acts, it is plain that it must ultimately also be founded on nominal acts. For every objectifying act is, as we said, either simple, and so *eo ipso* nominal, or complex, and so founded upon simple, i.e. again on nominal acts. The new interpretation is plainly much more significant, since in it alone essential relations of grounding receive pure expression. *On the other interpretation, though it states nothing false, two utterly different modes of foundation are at confused cross-purposes*:

1. The founding of non-objectifying acts such as joys, wishes, volitions on objectifying acts (presentations, affirmations): here one act-quality has its primary foundation in another act-quality, and is only mediately founded on 'matter'.

2. The founding of objectifying acts on other objectifying acts, where an act-material is primarily founded on other act-materials, e.g. the act-material of a predicative statement on those of the underlying nominal acts. For we can see the matter in this way also. The fact that no 'matter' is possible without objectifying quality, has as an automatic consequence that where one matter is founded on others, an objectifying act having the former matter is founded on just such acts as have the latter 'matters'. *The fact, therefore, that each act is always founded on nominal acts, has a variety of sources.* The original source is always that each simple 'matter', involving no further material foundations, is nominal, and that therefore each ultimately underlying objectifying act is nominal. But since all other act-qualities are founded on objectifying acts, this last foundation upon nominal acts carries over from objectifying acts to all acts whatever.

[1] §38.

Summing-Up of the Most Important Ambiguities in the Terms 'Presentation' and 'Content'

§44 *'Presentation'*

IN the last chapter we have encountered a fourfold or fivefold ambiguity attaching to the word 'presentation'.

1. Presentation as *act-material* or *matter*, which can be readily completed into: Presentation as the *representation* underlying the act, i.e. the full content of the act exclusive of quality. This concept also played a part in our treatment, though our special interest in the relation between quality and matter made it important for us to lay special stress on the latter. The matter tells us, as it were, what object is meant in the act, and in what sense it is there meant. 'Representation' brings in the additional moments lying outside of the intentional essence which determine whether the object is referred to in, e.g., a perceptually intuitive or imaginatively intuitive fashion, or in a merely non-intuitive mode of reference. Comprehensive analyses will be devoted to all this in the first section of the next Investigation.

2. Presentation as 'mere presentation', as qualitative modification of any form of belief, e.g. as *mere* understanding of propositions, without an inner decision leading to assent or dissent, surmise or doubt etc.

3. Presentation as *nominal act*, e.g. as the subject-presentation of an act of assertion.

4. Presentation as *objectifying act*, i.e. in the sense of an act-class necessarily represented in every complete act since every 'matter' (or 'representation') must be given primarily as the matter of such an act. This qualitative ground-class includes acts of belief, whether nominal or propositional, as well as their counterparts, so that all presentations in the second and third of our above senses are included here.

The more precise analysis of these concepts of presentation or the experiences they comprise, and the final determination of their mutual relations, will be a task for further phenomenological investigations. Here we shall only try to add some further equivocations to those affecting the term under discussion. To keep them sharply apart is of fundamental importance in our logical and epistemological endeavours. The phenomenological analyses indispensably needed to resolve these equivocations, have only been partially encountered in our previous expositions. What is missing has, however, often been touched upon, and indicated to an extent that makes a brief list of headings possible. We therefore continue our enumeration as follows:

5. Presentation is often opposed to mere thinking. The same difference is then operative that we also call the difference between *intuition* and *concept*. Of an ellipsoid I have a presentation, though not of a surface of Kummer: through suitable drawings, models or theoretically guided flights of fancy I can also achieve a presentation of the latter. A round square, a regular icosahedron[1] and similar *a priori* impossibilia are in this sense 'unpresentable'. The same holds of a completely demarcated piece of a Euclidean manifold of more than three dimensions, of the number π, and of other constructs quite free from contradiction. In all these cases of non-presentability 'mere concepts' are given to us: more precisely, we have nominal expressions inspired by significant intentions in which the objects of our reference are 'thought' more or less indefinitely, and particularly in the indefinite attributive form of *an A* as the mere bearer of definitely named attributes. To mere thinking 'presentation' is opposed: plainly this means the intuition which gives fulfilment, and adequate fulfilment, to the mere meaning-intention. The new class of cases is favoured because in it 'corresponding intuitions' are added member by member and from all sides to thought-presentations – whether these are purely symbolic meaning-intentions or fragmentarily and inadequately mixed with intuitions – presentations which leave our deepest cognitive cravings unsatisfied. What we intuit stands *before our eyes in perception or imagination* just as we intended it in our thought. *To present something to oneself means therefore to achieve a corresponding intuition of what one merely thought of or what one meant but only at best very inadequately intuited.*

[1] Not a good example of the impossible, but a slip. *Translator.*

6. A very common concept of presentation concerns the opposition of *imagination* to perception. This notion of presentation dominates ordinary discourse. If I see St Peter's Church, I do not have an 'idea', a presentation of it. But I do have the latter, when I picture it in my memory, or when it stands before me in a painting or drawing etc.

7. A presentation has just been identified with the *concrete act of imagination*. But, looked at more narrowly, a physical thing-image is also called a presentation or representation of what it depicts, as, e.g., in the words 'This photograph represents St Peter's Church'. The word 'presentation' is also applied to the apparent image-object, in distinction from the image-subject or thing represented. This is here the thing appearing in photographic colours, not the photographed church (image-subject), and it only presents (represents) the latter. These ambiguities carry over into the straightforward pictured presence of *memory* or *mere imagination*. The appearance of the fancied object as such in experience is naïvely interpreted as the real containment of an image in consciousness. What appears, in its mode of appearing, counts as an inner picture, like a painted picture presenting the imagined object. In all this it is not realized that the inner 'picture' is *intentionally* constituted, and that so is the way in which it and other possible pictures present one and the same thing, and that it cannot be counted as a real moment in the imaginative experience.[1]

8. In all cases of this ambiguous talk of presentation, where a picturing relation is supposed, the following thought also seems active. A very inadequate picture 'represents' a thing and also recalls it, is a sign of it, and this last in the sense that it is able to introduce a direct presentation of it that is richer in content. A photograph recalls an original, and also is its representative, in a manner its surrogate. Its pictorial presentation makes many judgements possible, that would otherwise need a basis in a percept of the original. A sign remote in content from a thing often fulfils similar functions, e.g. an algebraic symbol. It arouses the presentation of what it stands for, even if this is something non-intuitive, an integral etc.; it turns our thought towards this, as when we represent to ourselves the complete definitory sense of the integral. At the same time, the sign functions 'representa-

[1] See the criticism of the picture-theory in §21, Additional Note.

tively', surrogatively, in a context of mathematical operations: one operates with it in additions, multiplications etc., as if the symbolized were directly given in it. Previous discussions have shown this mode of expression to be rather crude,[1] but it expresses the governing notion in our use of 'presentation', which here means representation in *the double sense of provoking presentations and doing duty for them*. Thus the mathematician drawing on the blackboard says: 'Let *OX* represent (present) the asymptote of the hyperbola', or, calculating, 'Let *x* represent (present) the root of the equation $f(x) = O$'. A sign, whether it depicts or names, is called the 'representation' ('presentation') of what it stands for.

Our present talk of representation (which we do not wish to erect into a fixed terminology) relates to *objects*. These 'representative objects' are constituted in certain acts, and acquire a representative character for *new objects* in certain new acts of transcendent (*hinausdeutenden*) presentation. Another, more primitive sense of 'representation' was mentioned under (1): this made 'representatives' experienced contents receiving an objectifying *interpretation* in such representation, and in this manner helping to present objects, without becoming objective themselves.

This leads to a new ambiguity.

9. The distinction between *perception* and *imagination* (which latter itself shows important descriptive differences) is always confused with the distinction between *sensations* and *images*. The former is a distinction of acts, the latter of non-acts, which receive interpretation in acts of perception or imagination. (If one wishes to call *all* contents which are in this sense 'representative', 'sensations', we shall have to have the distinct terms 'impressional' and 'reproductive sensations'.) If there are essential descriptive differences between sensations and images, if the usually mentioned differences of liveliness, constancy, elusiveness etc., are sufficient, or if a varying mode of consciousness must be brought in, cannot be discussed here. Anyhow we are sure that possible distinctions of content do not make up the difference between *perception* and *imagination*, which analysis shows, with indubitable clarity, to be a difference of acts *qua* acts. We cannot regard what is descriptively given in perception or imagination

[1] Cf. Inv. i, §20. Also Inv. ii, §20, and the chapter on 'Abstraction and Representation'.

as a mere complex of experienced sensations or images. The all too common confusion between them is, however, grounded in the fact that at one time a 'presentation' is understood as an imaginative idea (in the sense of (6) and (7)), at another time as a corresponding image (the complex of representative contents or imagery), so that a new ambiguity arises.

10. The confusion between an appearance (e.g., a concrete imaginative experience or a 'mental picture'), and what appears in it, leads us to call the presented object a presentation (idea). This applies to perceptions, and generally to presentations in the sense of mere intuitions or logically interpreted intuitions, e.g. 'The world is my idea'.

11. The notion that all conscious experiences (contents in the real (*reellen*)[1] phenomenological sense) are 'in consciousness', in the sense of inner perception or some other inner orientation (consciousness, original apperception), and that with this orientation a presentation is *eo ipso* given (consciousness or the ego represents the content to itself), led to all contents of consciousness being called 'presentations'. These are the 'ideas' of the English empiricist philosophy since Locke. (Hume calls them 'perceptions'.) *To have an experience and to experience a content*: these expressions are often used as equivalent.

In logic it is very important to separate the specifically logical concepts of presentation (idea) from other concepts of it. That there are several such concepts has already been indicated in passing. We may again mention one not included in our list so far, Bolzano's notion of the 'presentation in itself', which we interpreted as equal to every independent or dependent part-meaning within a complete assertion.

In connection with all purely logical concepts of presentation, we must, on the one hand, distinguish the ideal presentation from the real (*realen*)[1] one, e.g. the nominal presentation in the purely logical sense and the *acts* in which it is realized. And, on the other hand, we must distinguish between the mere *meaning-intentions* and the experiences which fulfil them more or less adequately, i.e. presentations in the sense of intuitions.

13. Beside the aforementioned ambiguities, whose danger is obvious to all who seriously absorb themselves in the pheno-

[1] *Reell* applies to a thing's actual parts as opposed to what it merely intends or means. *Real* is the being of real things in the world.

menology of the thought-experiences, there are others which are in part less important. We may for instance mention talk of presentation (idea) in the sense of Opinion (δόξα). This is an ambiguity which arose through gradual transformations as occurs in all similar terms. I recall the verbally manifold, but always equivalent phrases: It is a widely held opinion, idea, view, conception etc.

§45 The 'content' of presentations

Expressions correlative to 'presentation' naturally have a correspondent ambiguity. This is particularly the case in regard to talk about 'what is presented in a presentation', i.e. about the 'content' of a presentation. That a mere distinction between content and object of presentations, like the one recommended by Twardowski following Zimmerman, will not remotely suffice – however meritorious it may have been to dig down to any form-differences in this field – is clear from our analyses up to this point. In the logical sphere – to which these authors limit themselves without being aware of their limitation – there is not *one* thing which can be distinguished as 'content' from the *object named*; there are several things which can and must be so distinguished. Above all, we can mean by 'content', in the case, e.g., of a nominal presentation, its *meaning* as an ideal unity: the presentation in the sense of pure logic. To this corresponds, as a real (*reelles*) moment in the *real* (*reellen*) *content* of the presentative act, the *intentional essence* with its presentative quality and matter. We can further distinguish, in this real (*reellen*) content, the separable contents not belonging to the intentional essence: the 'contents' which receive their interpretation in the act-consciousness (in the intentional essence), i.e. the *sensations* and *images*. To these are again added, in the case of many presentations, variously meant differences of *form* and *content*: particularly important is here the difference of *matter* (in a totally new sense) and *categorial form*, with which we shall have to concern ourselves a great deal. With this is connected the by no means univocal talk concerning the *content of concepts*: content = sum total of 'properties', in distinction from their mode of combination. How dubious 'blanket' talk about 'content' can be, when we merely oppose act, content and object, is shown by the difficulties and confusions into which Twardowski fell, and which have in part been exposed above.

We may point particularly to his talk of 'presentative activity moving in two directions', his complete ignoring of meaning in the ideal sense, his psychologistic elimination of plain differences of meaning by recourse to etymological distinctions, and, lastly, his treatment of the doctrine of 'intentional inexistence' and the doctrine of universal objects.

Note. In recent times a view has often been expressed which denies the difference between presentation and presented content, or at least denies its phenomenological ostensibility. One's attitude to this rejection naturally depends on one's interpretation of the words 'presentation' and 'content'. If these are interpreted as the mere having of sensations and images, and the phenomenological moment of interpretation is ignored or discounted, it is right to deny a distinct act of presentation: presentation and presented are one and the same. The mere having of the content, as a mere experiencing of an experience, is no intentional experience, directing itself upon an object by way of an interpretative sense: it is, in particular, not an introspective percept. For this reason we identified a sensation with a sensational content. But can anyone doubt, once he has distinguished the various concepts of presentation, that a concept so delimited is impossible to sustain, and has arisen merely through a misinterpretation of original, intentional notions of presentation? However the notion of presentation is defined, it is universally seen as a pivotal concept, not only for psychology, but also for epistemology and logic, and particularly for pure logic. A man who admits this, and yet bases himself on the above rejection, has *eo ipso* involved himself in confusion. For this concept has no part to play in epistemology and pure logic.

Only through this confusion can I explain how a thinker as penetrating as v. Ehrenfels, on occasion maintained (*Zeitschr. f. Psychologie u. Physiologie der Sinnesorgane, XVI*, 1897) that we cannot dispense with a distinction between act and content of presentation since without it we should be unable to state the psychological difference between the presentation of an object *A*, and the presentation of a presentation of this object. For the rest, he informs us, he has no direct assurance of the existence of such a phenomenon. I myself should say that an act of presentation is as such directly intuited, precisely where this distinction between a presentation and a presentation of this presentation is *phenomen-*

ologically drawn. Were there no such cases, no earthly argument could possibly provide an indirect justification of the distinction in question. Just so, I believe, we have directly established the existence of an act of presentation in becoming clear as to the difference between a mere sound-pattern and the same pattern understood as a name etc.

FOREWORD

(To Volume Two, Part Two of the Second German Edition)

THE present new edition of the final part of my *Logical Investigations* does not correspond, unfortunately, with the notice in the Preface added in 1913 to the first volume of the Second Edition. I was forced to a decision to publish the old text, only essentially improved in a few sections, instead of the radical revision of which a considerable portion was already in print at the time. Once again the old proverb came true: that books have their destinies. The exhaustion naturally consequent on a period of overwork first forced me to interrupt the printing. Theoretical difficulties that had made themselves felt as the printing progressed, called for revolutionary transformations of the newly planned text, for which fresher mental powers were necessary. In the war years which followed, I was unable to muster, on behalf of the phenomenology of logic, that passionate engagement without which fruitful work is impossible for me. I could only bear the war and the ensuing 'peace' by absorption in the most general philosophical reflections, and by again taking up my works devoted to the methodological and material elaboration of the Idea of a phenomenological philosophy, to the systematic sketch of its foundations, to the arrangement of its work-problems and the continuation of such concrete investigations as were in these connections indispensable. My new teaching activity at Freiburg favoured a direction of my interest to dominant generalities and to system. Only very recently have these systematic studies led me back into the territories where my phenomenological researches originated, and have recalled me to my old work on the foundations of pure logic which has so long awaited completion and publication. Divided as I am between intensive teaching and research, it is uncertain when I shall be in a position to adapt my old writings to the advances since made, and to recast their literary form. It is also uncertain whether I shall use the text of the Sixth Investigation for this purpose, or shall give my plans, whose content already goes far beyond the text, the form of an entirely new book.

As things stand, I have yielded to the pressures of the friends of the present work, and have decided to make its last part once more accessible, at least in its old form.

The First Section, that I could not revise in detail without endangering the style of the whole, I have allowed to be reprinted practically *verbatim*. But in the Second Section on *Sensibility and Understanding* by which I set particular store, I have, on the other hand, continually intervened to improve the form of the text. I remain of the opinion that the chapter on 'Sensuous and Categorial Intuition', together with the preparatory arguments of the preceding chapters, has opened the way for a phenomenological clarification of *logical* self-evidence (and *eo ipso* of its parallels in the axiological and practical sphere). Many misunderstandings of my *Ideas towards a Pure Phenomenology* would not have been possible had these chapters been attended to. Quite obviously, the *immediacy* of the vision of universal essences spoken of in the *Ideas*, implies, like the immediacy of any other categorial intuition, an opposition to the mediacy of a non-intuitive, e.g. an emptily symbolic thought. But people have substituted for *this* immediacy, the immediacy of intuition in the ordinary sense of the word, just because they were unacquainted with the distinction, fundamental to any theory of reason, of sensible and categorial intuition. I think it shows something about the contemporary state of philosophical science that straightforward statements of such incisive meaning, presented in a work that for nearly two decades has been much attacked, but also much used, should have remained without noticeable literary effect.

The position is similar in the case of the textually improved chapter on 'The *A Priori* Laws of Authentic and Inauthentic Thinking'. It at least offers a blueprint for the first radical worsting of psychologism in the theory of Reason. This blueprint makes its 'breakthrough' within the framework of an Investigation exclusively concerned with formal logic, and is therefore restricted to the Reason of formal logic. With how little deep attention this chapter is read, is shown by the often heard, but to my mind grotesque reproach, that I may have rejected psychologism sharply in the first volume of my work, but that I fell back into psychologism in the second. It does not affect what I have said to add that, after twenty years of further work, I should not write at many points as I then wrote, and that I do not approve of much that I then wrote, e.g. the doctrine of categorial representation. Nonetheless, I think I can say that even the immature and misguided elements in my work deserve a close pondering. For everything and all that is there said, derives from a research which actually reaches up to the things themselves, which orients itself towards their intuitive self-givenness, and which also has that eidetic-phenomenological attitude to pure consciousness through which alone a fruitful theory of reason becomes possible. Anyone who here, as also in the *Ideas*, wishes to grasp the *sense* of my arguments, must not be afraid of considerable efforts, including the efforts of 'bracketing' his own notions and convictions upon the same, or the putatively same, themes. These efforts are demanded by the nature of the things themselves. One who is not afraid, will find sufficient opportunity for improving on my positions, and, if he cares to, for censuring their imperfections. Only if he entrenches himself in a superficial reading drawn from an extra-phenomenological sphere of thought, will he refuse to attempt this, if he is not to be disavowed by all who truly understand the matter. How readily many authors employ critical rejections, with what conscientiousness they read my writings, what nonsense they have the audacity to attribute to me and to phenomenology, are shown in the *Allgemeine Erkenntnislehre* of Moritz Schlick. On page 121 of this work it is said that my *Ideas* 'asserts the existence of a peculiar intuition, that is *not a real psychical act*, and that if someone fails to find *such an "experience", which does not fall within the domain of psychology*, this indicates that he has not understood the doctrine, that he has not yet penetrated to the correct attitude of experience and thought, for this requires "peculiar, strenuous studies"'. The total impossibility that I should have *been able* to utter so insane an assertion as that attributed to me by Schlick in the above italicized sentences, and the falsity of the rest of his exposition of the meaning of phenomenology, must be plain to anyone familiar with this meaning. Of course I have always repeated my demand for 'strenuous studies'. But not otherwise than, e.g., the mathematician demands them of anyone who wishes to *share in talk* of mathematical matters, or who even presumes to criticize the value of mathematical science. In any case, to devote less study to a doctrine than is necessary to master its meaning, and yet to criticize it, surely violates the eternal laws of the literary conscience. No amount of learning in natural science or psychology or historical philosophies, will make it unnecessary to make these efforts in penetrating into phenomenology, or can do more than lighten them. Everyone, however, who has made these efforts, and who has risen to a very seldom exercised lack of prejudice, has achieved an indubitable certainty regarding the givenness of its scientific *foundation* and the inherent justification of the *method* demanded by it, a method which here, as in other sciences, renders possible a common set of conceptually definite work-problems, as well as definite decisions as to truth or falsehood. I must expressly observe that, in the case of M. Schlick, one is not dealing with irrelevant slips, but with sense-distorting substitutions on which all his criticism is built up.

After these words of defence, I must also observe, in regard to Section III, that I changed my position on the problem of the phenomenological interpretation of interrogative and optative sentences shortly after the first edition of the work, and that there would be no place for small revisions, which were all that could be undertaken at the time. The text therefore remained unaltered. I could be less conservative as regards the much used *Appendix* on 'Outward and Inward Perception'. Though the text's essential content has been preserved, it now appears in a considerably improved form.

The desideratum of an Index for the whole work could unfortunately not be realized, since my promising pupil, Dr Rudolf Clemens, who had undertaken to prepare it, had died for his country.

E. HUSSERL

Freiburg-im-Breisgau, October 1920

INVESTIGATION VI

Elements of a Phenomenological Elucidation of Knowledge

INTRODUCTION

OUR last Investigation may have seemed at first to lose itself in remote questions of descriptive psychology: it has, however, been of considerable help in our attempted elucidation of knowledge. All thought, and in particular all theoretical thought and knowledge, is carried on by way of certain 'acts', which occur in a context of expressive discourse. In these acts lies the source of all those unities-of-validity which confront the thinker as objects of thought and knowledge, or as the explanatory grounds and principles, the theories or sciences of the latter. In these acts, therefore, lies the source, also, of the pure, universal Ideas connected with such objects, whose ideally governed combinations pure logic attempts to set forth, and whose elucidation is the supreme aim of epistemological criticism. Plainly we shall have gone far in our elucidation of knowledge, once we have established the phenomenological peculiarities of *acts* as such, that much debated, little understood class of experiences. By putting our logical experiences into this class, we shall have taken an important step towards the demarcation of an analysis which will 'make sense' of the logical sphere and of the fundamental concepts which concern knowledge. In the course of our Investigation we were led to distinguish various concepts of *content* which tend to become confusedly mixed up whenever acts, and the ideal unities pertaining to acts, are in question. Differences which had already struck us in our First Investigation, in the narrower context of meanings and of acts conferring meaning, appeared once more in a wider context and in the most general forms. Even the highly noteworthy notion of content, that of 'intentional essence', which emerged as a novel gain from our last Investigation, was not without this relation to the logical sphere: for the same series of identities, previously employed to illustrate the unity of meaning, now yielded, suitably generalized, a certain identity, that of 'intentional essence', which applied to all acts whatsoever. By thus linking up, or subordinating, the ideal unities and phenomenological characters of the logical realm, to

667

the quite general characters and unities of the sphere of acts, we importantly deepened our phenomenological and critical understanding of the former.

The investigations carried out in the last chapter, basing themselves on the distinction of act-quality and act-material within the unity of intentional essence, again led us far into the zone of logical interest. We were forced to enquire into the relation of such intentional material to the presentational foundation essential to every act, and were compelled to hold apart several important, constantly confounded concepts of presentation, and so to work out a fundamental part of the 'theory of judgement'. Here as elsewhere a vast amount remains to be done: we have barely made a beginning.

We have not yet even been successful in our more immediate task, that of laying bare the source of the Idea of Meaning. Undeniably and importantly, the meaning of expressions must lie in the intentional essence of the relevant acts, but we have not at all considered the sorts of acts that can thus function in meaning, and whether all types of acts may not be in this respect on a level. But when we seek to tackle this question, we at once encounter – as the next paragraphs will demonstrate – *the relation between meaning-intention and meaning-fulfilment*, or to speak traditionally, and in fact ambiguously, the relation between 'concept' or 'thought' on the one hand, understood as mere meaning without intuitive fulfilment, and 'corresponding intuition', on the other.

It is most important that this distinction, touched on even in our First Investigation, should be most minutely explored. In carrying out the appropriate analyses, and, in the first instance, attaching them to the simplest naming-intentions, we at once perceive that our whole treatment calls for a *natural extension and general circumscription*. The widest class of acts, in which we meet with distinctions between intention and intention-fulfilment (or intention-frustration), extends far beyond the logical sphere. This is itself demarcated by a peculiarity in the relation of fulfilment. A class of acts – those known as 'objectifying' – are in fact marked off from all others, in that the fulfilment-syntheses appropriate to their sphere have the character of *knowings*, of *identifications*, of a 'putting-together' of things congruent, while their syntheses of frustration, similarly, have the correlative character of a setting apart of things conflicting. Within this widest sphere of objectifying acts, we shall have to study *all the relations relevant to the unity of knowledge*. We shall not have to limit ourselves to the fulfilment of such peculiar meaning-intentions as attach to our verbal expressions, since similar intentions also turn up without grammatical support. Our intuitions, further, themselves mostly have the character of intentions, which both require, and very often sustain a further fulfilment.

We shall provide a phenomenological characterization of the quite general notions of *signification* and *intuition* in relation to the phenomena of fulfilment, and we shall pursue the analysis of *various sorts of intuition*, starting with sensuous intuition, an enquiry basic to the elucidation of knowledge. We shall then embark upon the phenomenology of the varying degrees of knowledge, giving clearness and definite form to a related series of fundamental epistemological concepts. Here certain novel notions of content, barely glanced at in our previous analyses, will take the centre of the stage: the concept of *intuitive content* and the concept of *representing* (*interpreted*) content. We shall range the notion of *epistemic essence* alongside of our previous notion of intentional essence, and within the former we shall draw a distinction between intentional quality and intentional matter, the latter being divided into *interpretative sense*, *interpretative form* and interpreted (apperceived, or representing) content. We shall thereby pin down the concept of *Interpretation* (*Auffassung*) or *Representation*, as the unity of material and representing content by way of interpretative form.

In connection with the graded transition from intention to fulfilment, we shall recognize distinctions of greater or less *mediacy in an intention itself*, which exclude straightforward fulfilment, and which require rather a graded sequence of fulfilments: this will lead to an understanding of the all-important, hitherto unclarified sense of talk about 'indirect presentations'. We then follow up the differences of greater or lesser adequacy of intention to the intuitive experiences which fuse with it, and which fulfil it in knowledge, and point to the case of an *objectively complete adequacy* of the one to the others. In this connection we strive towards an ultimate phenomenological clarification of the concepts of Possibility and Impossibility (harmony, compatibility – conflict, incompatibility), and of the ideal axioms relating to these. Bringing back into consideration the act-qualities that we have for a while neglected, we then deal with the distinction, applicable to thetic acts, of a *provisional* and a *final fulfilment*. This final fulfilment represents an ideal of perfection. It always consists in a corresponding percept (we of course take for granted a necessary widening of the notion of perception beyond the bounds of sense). The synthesis of fulfilment achieved in this limiting case is *self-evidence or knowledge in the pregnant sense of the word*. Here we have *being in the sense of truth*, 'correspondence' rightly understood, the *adaequatio rei ac intellectus*: here this *adaequatio* is itself given, to be directly seized and gazed upon. The *varying notions of truth*, which all must be built up on one single, selfsame phenomenological situation, here reach complete clearness. The same holds of the correlative ideal of imperfection and therefore of the case of *absurdity*, and as regards the 'conflict' and the non-being, experienced therewith, of falsehood.

The natural course of our Investigation, which at first only concerns itself with such intentions as are meanings, has as a consequence that our treatments all begin with the simplest meanings, and in so doing abstract from *formal differences* among such meanings. The complementary Investigations of our Second Section will then make these differences their main theme, and will at once lead to *a totally new concept of matter or material*, to a basic contrast between *sensuous stuff* and *categorial form* or – abandoning an objective for a phenomenological stance – to a contrast between *sensuous* and *categorial acts*. In close connection with this last, we have the important distinction between sensuous (real) and categorial objects, determinations, combinations etc., regarding which last it becomes clear that they can only be 'perceptually' given in acts *which are founded* upon other acts, and in the last resort, on acts of sensibility. In general we may say that the intuitive, and accordingly likewise the imaginative, fulfilment of categorial acts, is founded on acts of sense. *Mere* sense, however, never fulfils categorial acts, or intentions which include categorial forms: fulfilment lies rather, in every case, in a sensibility structured by categorial acts. With this goes an *unavoidable extension of the originally sense-turned concepts of intuition and perception*, which permits us to speak of *categorial*, and, in particular, of *universal intuition*. The distinction between *sensuous* and *purely categorial* abstraction then leads to a distinction between *sensuous concepts* and *categories*. The old epistemological contrast between *sensibility* and *understanding* achieves a much-needed clarity through a distinction between straightforward or sensuous, and founded or categorial intuition. The same is true of the contrast between *thinking* and *seeing* (intuiting), which confuses philosophical parlance by confounding the relations of signification to fulfilling intuition, on the one hand, with the relations of sensuous and categorial acts, on the other. All talk of *logical form* concerns what is purely categorial in the meanings and meaning-fulfilments in question. But the 'matter' of logic, the 'intention' of terms, itself admits, through a graded superimposition of categorial intentions, of distinctions of *matter* and *form*, so that the *logical* antithesis of matter and form points the way to a readily understandable 'relativization' of our absolute distinction.

We shall end the main body of this Investigation by discussing the factors which limit freedom in the actual categorial shaping of given matter. We shall become aware of the *analytic rules of authentic thinking*, which, grounded in pure categories, do not depend on the specificity of their materials. Similar factors limit thought *in the inauthentic sense*, i.e. pure acts of meaning to the extent that they might lend themselves to authentic cases of expression, resting on *a priori* principles and not dependent on subject-matters to be expressed. From this demand springs the function of the laws of authentic thinking to provide norms for our acts of mere meaning.

We raised a question at the beginning of this Investigation as to the natural circumscription of sense-giving and sense-fulfilling acts: this is answered by ranging such acts under objectifying acts, and by subdividing the latter into acts of signification and acts of intuition. Having successfully clarified the phenomenological relations which concern fulfilment, we are at last in a position to evaluate the arguments for, and the arguments against, Aristotle's view of optative and imperative sentences as special cases of predication. The last section of the present Investigation is devoted to clearing up this controversial issue.

The aims just sketched are not the final, highest aims of a phenomenological elucidation of knowledge in general. Our analyses, comprehensive as they are, leave untilled the extremely fruitful field of *mediate* thought and knowledge: the nature of *mediate* evidence, and of its correlated *idealia*, remains insufficiently illuminated. We consider, however, that our aims have not been too trivial, and we hope that we may have dug down to the genuinely first, underlying foundations of a critique of knowledge. Even such a critique demands of us an exercise of the modesty essential to all strict, scientific research. If this last aims at a real, full completion of the tasks at hand, if it has given up the dream of solving the great problems of knowledge by merely criticizing traditional philosophical assertions or by probable argumentation, if it has at last seen that matters can be advanced and transformed only by getting to close grips with them, it must then also reconcile itself to tackling the problems of knowledge, not in their higher or their highest, and therefore their most interesting developments, but in their comparatively simplest forms, in the lowest grades of development accessible to us. That even such a modest epistemological enquiry has vastly many difficulties to surmount, that it has in fact still got all its achievements ahead of it, will become clear in the course of the ensuing analyses.

OBJECTIFYING INTENTIONS AND THEIR FULFILMENTS: KNOWLEDGE AS A SYNTHESIS OF FULFILMENT AND ITS GRADATIONS

CHAPTER ONE

Meaning-Intention and Meaning-Fulfilment

§ 1 *Whether every type of mental act, or only certain types, can function as carriers of meaning*

WE shall now go on with the question raised in our Introduction: whether meaning-something is exclusively the prerogative of certain restricted sorts of mental acts. It might seem at first plain that no such restrictions can exist, and that any and every act might operate in sense-giving fashion. For it seems plain that we can verbally *express* acts of every kind – whether presentations, judgements, surmises, questions, wishes etc. – and that, when we do this, they yield us the meanings of the forms of speech in question, the meanings of names, of statements, of interrogative or optative sentences etc.

The opposite view can, however, lay claim to the same obviousness, particularly in a form that restricts meanings to a single, narrow class of acts. All acts are certainly expressible, if language is sufficiently rich, each has its own appropriate speech-form: sentence-forms, e.g., differentiate themselves into indicative, interrogative, imperative etc., and among the first of these we have categorical, hypothetical, disjunctive and other sentence-forms. In each case the act, in so far as it achieves *expression* in this or that speech-form, must be known for the sort of act it is, the question as a question, the wish as a wish, the judgement as a judgement etc. This will apply also to the partial acts constitutive of such acts, in so far as these too are expressed. Acts cannot, it seems, find their own appropriate expressive forms till their form and content have been apperceived and known. The expressive role in speech lies, accordingly, not in mere words, but in *expressive acts*: these create for the correlated acts to be expressed by them a new expressive material in which they can be given *thinking expression*, the general essence of which constitutes the meaning of the speech-form in question.

A striking confirmation of this view seems to lie in the possibility of a purely symbolic functioning of expressions. The interior (*geistige*) expression, the thinking counterpart of the act to be expressed, attaches to the verbal expression, and can be brought to life by the latter even when the act itself is not performed by the person who understands the expression. We understand the expression of an act of perception without ourselves perceiving anything, of a question without ourselves asking anything etc. We experience more than the mere words, we enjoy the thought-forms or the expressions. In the opposed case, where the intended acts are themselves actually present, the expression comes to coincidence with what it has to express, the meaning which clings to the words fits itself into what it means, its thought-intention finds in the latter its fulfilling intuition.

It is plainly in close connection with these opposed viewpoints that we have the old dispute as to whether or not the peculiar forms of interrogative, optative, imperative and similar sentences are to count as statements, and their meanings as *judgements*. Aristotle's doctrine places the meaning of all complete sentences in the varied array of psychic experiences, experiences of judging, wishing, commanding and so forth. As against this, another more modern and increasingly influential doctrine locates meaning exclusively in our judgements (or in their purely presentative modifications). An interrogative sentence in a sense expresses a question, but only in so far as this question is realized to be a question, in so far as it is referred in thought to a speaker, and so judged to be *his* experience. And so similarly in other cases. Each meaning is, on this view, either a name-meaning or a propositional meaning, i.e. either the meaning of a complete indicative sentence or a possible part of such a meaning. Indicative sentences are here to be understood as predicative sentences, since judgements are, on this view, generally thought of as *predicative acts*: we shall see, however, that the controversy still has a sense even when judgements are looked on as *positing acts in general*.

To find the right stance towards the questions here raised would call for more exact discussion than the above, superficial argumentations have attempted. It will become plain, when we look at the matter more closely, that the appeals to sheer obviousness on one side or the other conceal obscurity and even error.

§2 *That all acts may be expressed does not decide the issue. There are two senses to talk about expressing an act*

All acts it has been agreed are *expressible*. This cannot, of course, be questioned, but it does not therefore follow, as might be surreptitiously suggested, that all acts for that reason also function as *carriers of meaning*. Talk of 'expressing' is, as we argued earlier,[1] ambiguous, and it remains so even when we connect it with the *acts* to be expressed. What are expressed may be, on the one hand, said to be the sense-*giving* acts, to which, in the narrower sense, 'voice' is given. But there are other acts which can also be said to be expressed, though this is the case, naturally, in a different sense. I refer here to the very frequent cases in which we *name acts we are now experiencing*, and through such naming manage *to say that we are experiencing them*. In this sense I 'express' a wish through the words 'I wish that...', a question through the words 'I am asking whether...', a judgement through the words 'I judge that...', and so on. Naturally we can pass judgement on our own inner experiences just as we can pass judgement on outward things, and, when we do the former, the meanings of the relevant sentences will reside in our *judgements* upon such experiences, and not in the experiences themselves, our wishes, questions etc. Just so, the meanings of statements about external things do not reside in these things (the horses, houses etc.), but in the judgements we inwardly pass upon them (or in the presentations that help to build up such judgements). That the objects judged about in one case transcend consciousness (or purport to do so), in another case are taken to be immanent in consciousness, makes no real difference. Naturally when I express the wish that now fills me, it is concretely one with my act of judgement, but it does not really contribute to the latter. The wish is apprehended in an act of reflex perception, subsumed under the concept of wishing, and named by way of this concept and of the further determining presentation of the wish-content. Thus the conceptual *presentation* makes the same sort of direct contribution to the judgement about the wish (and the corresponding wish-*name* to the wish-statement), that the presentation of Man makes to a judgement about Man (or the name 'Man' to a statement about Man). Substitute for the subject word 'I' in the

---

[1] *Log. Inv.* i, pp. 286-7.

sentence 'I wish that. . .' the relevant proper name, and the sense of the sentence remains unaffected in its remaining parts. It is, however, undeniable that the wish-statement can now be understood without change of sense by someone who hears it, and can be imitatively re-judged by him, even though he *does not share the wish at all*. We see, therefore, that, even when a wish chances to form a unity with an act of judgement directed upon it, it does not really form part of the meaning of the latter. A truly sense-giving experience can never be absent if the living sense of the expression is to survive change.

It becomes clear, therefore, that the expressibility of all acts is without relevance to the question whether all acts can function in sense-giving fashion, so far, that is, as such 'expressibility' means no more than the possibility of making certain statements about such acts. For in this connection acts are just not functioning as carriers of meaning at all.

§3 *A third sense of talk about the 'expression' of acts. Formulation of our theme*

We have just distinguished two senses in which there can be talk about 'acts expressed'. Either they are acts in which the sense, the meaning of the relevant expression is constituted, or they are acts that the speaker attributes to himself as items in his recent experience. This latter conception may be appropriately widened. Plainly the situation that it covers would not differ in any essential respect, were an expressed act *not* to be attributed to the experiencing ego, but to other objects, and it would not differ for any conceivable form of expression that really (*reell*) named this act as something experienced, even if it did not do it so as to mark the act off as the subject- or object-member of a predication. The main point is that the act, whether directly named or otherwise 'expressed', should appear as the actually present *object of discourse*, (or of the objectifying, positing activity behind discourse), whereas this is *not* the case in regard to our sense-giving acts.

There is a *third* sense of the same talk of 'expression' in which we deal, as in our second sense, with a judgement or other objectification related to the acts in question, but not with a judgement *about* the latter – not, therefore, with an objectification of these acts by way of presentations and naming-acts which refer to them; we have rather a judgement *grounded* upon such acts, which does not demand their objectification. That I express my percept of something may, e.g., mean that I attribute this or that content to it: it may also mean that I derive my judgement from my percept, that I do not merely assert but also perceive the matter of fact in question, and that I assert it as I perceive it. My judgement is not here concerned with the perceiving but with the thing perceived. By 'judgements of perception' *tout court* we generally mean judgements belonging to this last class.

In a similar manner we can give expression to other intuitive acts, whether imaginings, remembering or expectations.

In the case of utterances grounded on imagination we may indeed doubt whether a genuine judgement is present: it is in fact plain that this is *not* then present. We are here thinking of cases where we allow our imagination to 'run away' with us, and where we employ ordinary statements, appropriate to things perceived, in giving a name to what then appears to us, or of the narrative form in which story-tellers, novelists etc., 'express', not real circumstances, but the creations of their artistic fancy. As we saw in our last Investigation, we are here dealing with conformably modified acts which serve as *counterparts* which correspond to the actual judgements that might be expressed in the same words, just as intuitive imaginations correspond to perceptions, and perhaps also to rememberings and expectations. We shall leave aside all such distinctions for the present.

In connection with the above class of cases, and in connection with the thereby defined new sense of 'expressed act', we wish to make clear the whole relation between meaning and expressed intuition. We wish to consider whether such an intuition may not itself be the act constitutive of meaning, or if this is not the case, how the relation between them may be best understood and systematically classified. We are now heading towards a more general question: Do the acts which *give* expression in general, and the acts which in general are capable of *receiving* expression, belong to essentially different spheres, and thereby to firmly delimited act-species? And do they nonetheless take their tone from an overarching, unifying genus of acts, in which all acts *capable of functioning 'meaningfully', in the widest sense of the word* – whether as meanings proper, or as 'fulfilments' of meanings – can be brought together and set apart, so that all other genera of acts can *eo ipso*, in law-governed fashion, be excluded from such functions? This, we may say, is the immediate aim of our Investigation. And as our considerations advance, there will be an obvious widening of our sphere of treatment so as to render self-evident the relation of the questions here raised to a general 'sense-making' of knowledge. New and higher aims will then enter our field of view.

§4 *The expression of a percept ('judgement of perception'). Its meaning cannot lie in perception, but must lie in peculiar expressive acts*

Let us consider an example. I have just looked out into the garden and now give expression to my percept in the words: 'There flies a blackbird!' *What is here the act in which my meaning resides?* I think we may say, in harmony with points established in our First Investigation, that it does not reside in perception, at least not in perception alone. It seems plain that we cannot describe the situation before us as if there were nothing else in it – apart from the sound of the words – which decides the meaningfulness of the expression, but the percept to which it attaches. For we could base different statements on the *same percept*, and thereby unfold *quite different senses*. I could, e.g., have remarked: 'That is black!', 'That is a black bird!', 'There flies that black bird!', 'There it soars!', and so forth. And conversely, the sound of my words and their sense might have remained the same, though my percept varied in a number of ways. Every chance alteration of the perceiver's relative position alters his percept, and different persons, who perceive the same object simultaneously, never have exactly the same percepts. No such differences are relevant to the meaning of a perceptual statement. One may at times pay special attention to them, but one's statement will then be correspondingly different.

One might, however, maintain that this objection only showed meaning to be unaffected by such differences in *individual* percepts: it might still be held to reside in something *common* to the whole multitude of perceptual acts which centre in a single object.

To this we reply, that percepts may not only vary, but may also vanish altogether, without causing an expression to lose all its meaning. A listener may understand my words, and my sentence as a whole, without looking into the garden: confident in my veracity, he may bring forth the same judgement without the percept. Possibly he is helped by an imaginative re-enactment, but perhaps this too is absent, or occurs in so mutilated, so inadequate a form, as to be no fit counterpart of what appears perceptually, at least not in respect of the features 'expressed' in my statement.

But if the sense of a statement survives the elimination of perception, and is the same sense as before, we cannot suppose that perception is the act in which the sense of a perceptual statement, its expressive intention, is achieved. The acts which are united with the sound of our words are phenomenologically quite different according as these words have a purely symbolic, or an intuitively fulfilled significance, or according as they have a merely fancied or a perceptually realizing basis: we cannot believe that signification is now achieved in *this* sort of act, and now in *that*. We shall rather have to conceive that the function of meaning pertains in all cases to one and the same sort of act, a type of act free from the limitations of the perception or the imagination which so often fail us, and which, in all cases where an expression authentically 'expresses', merely becomes one with the act expressed.

It remains, of course, incontestable that, in 'judgements of perception', perception is internally related to our statements' sense. We have good reason to say: the statement *expresses the percept*, i.e. brings out what is perceptually '*given*'. The same percept may serve as a foundation for several statements, but, however the sense of such statements may vary, it addresses itself to the phenomenal content of perception. It is now one, now another, part of our unified, total percept – a part, no doubt, in a non-independent, attributive sense – which gives our judgement its specific basis, without thereby becoming the true carrier of its meaning, as the possibility of eliminating percepts has just shown us.

We must accordingly say: *This 'expression' of a percept* – more objectively phrased, of a perceived thing as such – *is no affair of the sound of words, but of certain expressive acts*. 'Expression' in this context means verbal expression informed with its full sense, which is here put in a certain relation to perception, through which relation the latter is in its turn said to be 'expressed'. This means, at the same time, that *between* percept and sound of words another act (or pattern of acts) is *intercalated*. I call it an act, since the expressive experience, whether or not accompanied by a percept, always has an intentional direction to something objective. This mediating act must be the true giver of meaning, must pertain to the significantly functioning expression as its essential constituent, and must determine its possession of an identical sense, whether or not this is associated with a confirming percept.

The rest of our investigation will show ever more clearly that our conception is workable.

§5 *Continuation. Perception as an act which determines meaning, without embodying it*

We can go no further without discussing a doubt which crops up at this point. Our treatment seems to demand a definite narrowing down: it appears to cover more than can be fully justified. If perception never constitutes the full meaning of a statement grounded on perception, it seems nonetheless to make a contribution to this meaning, and to do so in cases of the sort just dealt with. This will become clearer if we slightly modify our example, and instead of speaking quite indefinitely of *a* blackbird, proceed to speak of *this* blackbird. 'This' is an essentially occasional expression which only becomes fully significant when we have regard to the circumstances of utterance, in this case to an actually performed percept. The perceived object, as it is given in perception, is what the word 'this' signifies. The present tense in the grammatic form of a verb likewise expresses a relation to what is actually *present*, and so again to perception. Plainly the same holds of our original example: to say 'There flies a blackbird' is not to say that some blackbird in general is flying by, but that a blackbird is flying by here and now.

It is clear, of course, that the meaning in question is not attached to the word-sound of 'this'; it does not belong among the meanings firmly and generally bound up with this word. We must, however, allow that the sense of a unified statement is to be found in the total act of meaning which in a given case underlies it – whether or not this may be completely expressed through the universal meanings of its words. It seems, therefore, that we must allow that perception contributes to the significant content of a judgement, in all cases where such perception gives intuitive presence to the fact to which our statement gives judgemental expression. It is of course a contribution that can perhaps also be made by other acts, in an essentially similar manner. The listener does not perceive the garden, but he is perhaps acquainted with it, has an intuitive idea of it, places the imagined blackbird and reported event in it, and so, through the mere picture-work of fantasy, achieves an understanding which follows the intention and which agrees in sense with the speaker's.

The situation permits, however, of another reading. Intuition may indeed be allowed to contribute to the meaning of a perceptual statement, but only in the sense that the meaning could not acquire a *determinate* relation to the object it means without some intuitive aid. But this does not imply that the intuitive act is itself a carrier of meaning, or that it really makes *contributions* to this meaning, contributions *discoverable* among the constituents of the completed meaning. Genuinely occasional expressions have no doubt a meaning which varies from case to case, but in all such changes a common element is left over, which distinguishes *their* ambiguity from that of a casual equivocation.[1] The addition of intuition has as effect that this common element of meaning, indeterminate in its abstraction, can determine itself. Intuition in fact gives it complete determinateness of objective reference, and thereby its last difference. This achievement does not entail that a part of the meaning must itself lie in the intuitive sphere.

I say 'this', and now mean the paper lying before me. Perception is responsible for the relation of my word to *this* object, but my meaning does not lie in perception. When I say 'this', I do not merely perceive, but a *new act of pointing (of this-meaning) builds itself on my perception, an act directed upon the latter and dependent on it, despite its difference. In this pointing reference, and in it alone, our meaning resides.* Without a percept – or some correspondingly functioning act – the pointing would be empty, without definite differentiation, impossible in the concrete. For of course the indeterminate thought of the *speaker as pointing to something* – which the hearer may entertain before he knows *what* object we wish to indicate by our 'this' – is not the thought we enact in the actual pointing, with which the determinate thought of the thing pointed to has been merely associated. One should not confuse the

---

[1] See *Log. Inv.* I, §26.

general character of actual pointing as such with the indefinite presentation of 'a certain' act of pointing.

Perception accordingly *realizes the possibility* of an unfolding of my act of this-meaning with its definite relation to the object, e.g. to this paper before my eyes. But it does not, on our view, itself constitute this meaning, nor even part of it.

In so far as the act-character of a pointing act is oriented to intuition, it achieves a definiteness of intention which fulfils itself in intuition, in accordance with a general feature of acts which may be called their *intentional essence*. For a pointing reference remains the same, whichever out of a multitude of mutually belonging percepts may underlie it, in all of which the same, and *recognizably* the same, object appears. The meaning of 'this' is again the same when, instead of a percept, some act from our range of imaginative presentation is substituted for it, an act presenting the same object through a picture in a recognizably identical manner. It changes, however, when intuitions from other perceptual or imaginative spheres are substituted. We are once more referring to a *this*, but the general character of the reference which obtains here, that of direct, attributively unmediated aiming at an object, is otherwise differentiated: the intention to another object attaches to it, just as physical pointing becomes spatially different with each change in spatial direction.

We hold, therefore, that *perception is an act which determines, but does not embody meaning.* This view is confirmed by the fact that essentially occasional expressions like 'this' can often be used and understood without an appropriate intuitive foundation. Once the intention to an object has been formed on a suitable intuitive basis, it can be revived and exactly reproduced *without* the help of a suitable act of perception or imagination.

Genuinely occasional expressions are accordingly much like *proper names*, in so far as the latter function with their authentic meaning. For a proper name also names an object 'directly'. It refers to it, not attributively, as the bearer of these or those properties, but without such 'conceptual' mediation, as what it *itself* is, just as perception might set it before our eyes. The meaning of a proper name lies accordingly in a direct reference-to-this-object, a reference that perception only *fulfils*, as imagination does provisionally and illustratively, but which is not identical with these intuitive acts. It is just in this manner that perception gives an object to the word 'this' (where it is directed to objects of possible perception): our reference to 'this' is fulfilled in perception, but is not perception itself. And naturally the meaning of both types of directly naming expressions has an intuitive origin, from which their naming intentions first orient themselves towards an individual object. In other respects they are different. As 'this' is infected with the thought of a pointing, it imports (as we showed) a mediation and a complication, i.e. a peculiar form absent from the proper name. The proper name also belongs as a fixed appellation to its object; to this constant pertinence corresponds something in the manner of its relation to that object. This is shown in the fact of our knowing a person or thing by name, as something *called* so-and-so: I know Hans as *Hans*, Berlin as *Berlin*. We have, in our treatment, no doubt ignored the case of all those proper names which are *significant in derivative fashion*. When proper names have once been formed in direct application (and so on a basis of intuitions which *give* things to us), we can, by employing the concept of 'being called', itself formed by reflection on the use of proper names, give proper names to objects, or take cognizance of their proper names, even though such objects are not directly given or known to us, but are only described indirectly as the bearers of certain properties. *The capital of Spain*, e.g., *is called* (i.e. has the proper name) '*Madrid*'. A person unacquainted with the town Madrid itself, thereby achieves both knowledge of its name and the power to name it correctly, and yet not thereby the individual meaning of the word 'Madrid'. Instead of the direct reference, which only an actual seeing of the city could arouse, he must make do with an indirect pointing to this reference, operating through characteristic ideas of properties and the conception of 'being called' such and such.

If we may trust our arguments, we must not only draw a general distinction between the perceptual and the significant element in the statement of perception; we must also locate *no part of the meaning in the percept itself.* The percept, *which presents the object, and the statement which, by way of the judgement* (or by the thought-act inwoven into the unity of the judgement) *thinks and expresses it, must be rigorously kept apart,* even though, in the case of the perceptual judgement now being considered, they stand to each other in the most intimate relation of mutual *coincidence,* or in the unity of fulfilment.

685

We need not dwell on the fact that a like result applies also to other intuitive judgements, and thus also to statements which, in a sense analogous to that which applies to perceptual judgements, 'express' the intuitive content of an imagination, a remembering, an expectation etc.

Addendum. In the exposition of §§ 2–6 of Investigation I we began with the understanding of the hearer, and drew a distinction between the 'indicating' (*anzeigende*) and the 'indicated' (*angezeigte*) meaning of an essentially occasional expression, and, in particular, of the word 'this'. For the hearer, in whose momentary field of vision the thing that we wish to point out is perhaps not present, only this indefinitely general thought is at first aroused: Something is being pointed out. Only when a presentation is added (an intuitive presentation if the thing dealt with demands an intuitive pointing out), is a definite reference constituted for him, and so a full, authentic meaning for the demonstrative pronoun. For the speaker there is no such sequence: he has no need of the indefinitely referential idea which functions as 'index' for the hearer. Not the idea of an indication, but an indication itself, is given in his case, and it is *eo ipso* determinately directed thingward: from the first the speaker enjoys the 'indicated' meaning, and enjoys it in a presentative intention immediately oriented towards intuition. If the thing meant cannot be intuitively picked out, as in a reference to a theorem in a mathematical proof, the conceptual thought in question plays the part of an intuition: the indicative intuition could derive fulfilment from an actual re-living of this past thought. In each case we observe a *duplicity* in the indicative intention: the character of the indication seems in the first case to espouse the directly objective intention, as a result of which we have an intention directed upon a definite object that we are intuiting here and now. Our other case does not differ. If the previous conceptual thought is not now being performed, an intention which corresponds to it survives in memory; this attaches itself to the act-character of the indication, thereby lending it definiteness of direction.

What we have just said about *indicating* and *indicated meaning* can have *two* meanings. It can mean (1) the two mutually resolving thoughts which characterize the hearer's successive understanding: *first* the indeterminate idea of something or other referred to by 'this', *then* the act of definitely directed indication into which a completing presentation transforms it. In the latter act we have the indicated, in the former the indicating meaning. (2) If we confine ourselves to the complete, definitely directed indication which the speaker has from the beginning, we can again see something double about it: the general character of indication as such, and the feature which determines this, which narrows it down to an indication of 'this thing there'. The former can again be called an indicating meaning, or rather the indicating element in the indissoluble unity of meaning, in so far as it is what the hearer can immediately grasp by virtue of its expressive generality, and can use to indicate what is referred to. If I say 'this', the hearer at least knows that something is being pointed at. (Just so in the case of other essentially occasional expressions. If I say 'here', I have to do with something in my nearer or further spatial environment, etc.) On the other hand, the true aim of my talk lies not in this general element, but in the direct intending of the object in question. Towards it and its fulness of content I am directed, and these empty generalities do little or nothing towards determining the latter. In this sense a direct intention is the primary, indicated meaning.

This second distinction is the one laid down by our definition in our previous exposition. (*Inv.* I, §§ 3–4). The distinctions achieved in this section, and our much clearer treatment, will probably have helped towards a further clarification of this difficult matter.

§ 6 *The static union of expressive thought and expressed intuition.*
Recognition (das Erkennen)

We shall now absorb ourselves in a closer investigation of the relations holding among intuitive acts, on the one hand, and expressive acts, on the other. We shall confine ourselves, in the present section entirely, to the range of the simplest possible cases, and so naturally to expressions and significant intentions which belong to the sphere of *naming*. We shall make, for the rest, no claim to treat this field exhaustively. We are concerned with nominal expressions, which refer themselves in the most perspicuous of possible fashions to 'corresponding' percepts and other forms of intuition.

Let us first glance in this field at a *relationship of static union, where a sense-giving thought has based itself on intuition, and is thereby related to its object.* I speak, e.g., of my *inkpot*, and my inkpot also stands before me: I see it. The name names the object of my percept, and is enabled to name it by the significant act which expresses its character and its form in the form of the name. The relation between name and thing named, has, in this state of union, a certain *descriptive character*, that we previously noticed: the name 'my inkpot' seems to *overlay* the perceived object, to belong *sensibly* to it. This belonging is of a peculiar kind. The words do not belong to the objective context of physical thing-hood that they express: in this context they have no place, they are not referred to as something in or attaching to the things that they name. If we turn to the experiences involved, we have, on the one hand, as said before,[1] the acts in which the words appear, on the other hand, the similar acts in which the things appear. As regards the latter, the inkpot confronts us in perception. Follow-ing our repeated demonstration of the descriptive essence of perception, this means no more phenomenologically then that we undergo a certain sequence of experiences of the class of sensa-tions, sensuously unified in a peculiar serial pattern, and informed by a certain act-character of 'interpretation' (*Auffassung*), which endows it with an objective sense. This act-character is responsible for the fact that an *object*, i.e. this inkpot, is perceptually apparent to us. In similar fashion, the phenomenal word is constituted for us in an act of perception or imaginative presentation.

Not word *and* inkpot, therefore, but the act-experiences just described, in which they make their appearance, are here brought into relation: in these word and inkpot appear, while yet being nothing whatever *in* the acts in question. But how does this happen? What brings these acts into unity? The answer seems clear. The relation, as one of naming, is mediated, not merely by acts of meaning, but by acts of recognition (*Erkennen*), which are here also acts of *classification*. The perceived object is *recognized* for an inkpot, known as one, and in so far as the act of meaning is most intimately one with an act of classification, and this latter, as recognition of the perceived object, is again intimately one with the act of perception, the expression seems to be *applied* to the thing and to clothe it like a garment.

Ordinarily we speak of recognizing and classifying the object of

---

[1] *Log. Inv.* i, §§2, 10.

perception, as if our act busied itself with this *object*. But we have seen that there is no object in the experience, only a perception, a thus and thus determinate mindedness (*Zumutesein*): *the recognitive act in the experience must accordingly base itself on the act of perception*. One must not of course misunderstand the matter, and raise the objection that we are putting the matter as if perception was classified rather than its object. We are not doing this at all. Such a performance would involve acts of a quite different, much more complex constitution, expressible through expressions of corresponding complexity, e.g. 'the perception of the inkpot'. It follows that the recognitive experience of this thing as 'my inkpot', is nothing but a recognition which, in a definite and direct fashion, fuses an expressive experience, on the one hand, with the relevant percept, on the other.

The same holds of cases in which *picture-presentations* serve in place of percepts. The imaginatively apparent object, e.g. the identical inkpot in memory or in fancy, is felt to bear the expression which names it. This means, phenomenologically speaking, that a recognitive act in union with an expressive experience is so related to an imaginative act as to be, in objective parlance, spoken of as the recognition of an imaginatively presented object as, e.g., our inkpot. The imagined object, too, is absolutely nothing in our presentation of it, our experience is rather a certain blend of images, fancied sensations, informed by a certain interpretative act-character. To live through this act, and to have an imaginative presentation of the object, are one and the same. If we therefore express the situation in the words 'I have before me an image, the image of an inkpot', we have plainly coupled *new* acts with our expressions, and, in particular, a *recognitive* act which is intimately one with our act of imagining.

§7 *Recognition as a character of acts, and the 'generality of words'*

The following more exact argument would seem to show conclusively that, in all cases where a name is applied to a thing intuitively given, we may presume the presence of a recognitive act-character mediating between the appearance of the word-sounds, on the one hand, (or the complete sense-informed word), and the intuition of the thing on the other. One often hears of the *generality of words*, and usually understands by this highly ambiguous phrase that a word is not bound to an individual intuition, but belongs rather to an endless array of possible intuitions.

In what, however, does this belonging consist?

Let us deal with an extremely simple example, that of the name 'red'. In so far as it names a phenomenal object as red, it belongs to this object in virtue of the aspect of red that appears in this object. And each object that bears an aspect of like sort in itself, justifies the same appellation: the same name belongs to each, and does so by way of an identical sense.

But in what does this appellation by way of an identical sense consist?

We observe first that the word does not attach externally, and merely through hidden mental mechanisms, to the individual, specifically similar traits of our intuitions. It is not enough, manifestly, to acknowledge the bare fact that, wherever such and such an individual trait appears in our intuition, the word also *accompanies* it as a mere pattern of sound. A mere concomitance, a mere external going with or following on one another would not forge any internal bond among them, and certainly not an intentional bond. Yet plainly we have here such an intentional bond, and one of quite peculiar phenomenological character. The word *calls* the red thing red. The red appearing before us is what is *referred* to by the name, and is referred to as '*red*'. In this mode of naming reference, the name appears as *belonging* to the named and as *one* with it.

On the other hand, however, the word has its sense quite apart from an attachment to this intuition, and without attachment to *any* 'corresponding' intuition. Since this sense is everywhere the same, it is plain that it is not the mere phoneme, rather the true, complete word, endowed on all occasions with the constant character of its sense, that must be held to underlie the naming relation. Even then it will not be enough to describe the union of meaningful word and corresponding intuition in terms of mere concomitance. Take the word, present in consciousness and *understood as a mere symbol* without being actually used to name anything, and set the corresponding intuition beside it: these two phenomena may at once, for genetic reasons, be brought together in the phenomenological unity of naming. Their mere togetherness is, however, not as yet this unity, which *grows out of it* with plain novelty. It is conceivable, *a priori*, that no such unity should emerge, that the coexistent phenomena should be phenomeno-logically disjoined, that the object before us should not be the thing meant or named by the meaningful word, and that the word should not *belong* to the object as its name, and so name it.

Phenomenologically we find before us no mere aggregate, but an intimate, in fact intentional, unity: we can rightly say that the two acts, the one setting up the complete word, and the other the thing, are intentionally combined in a single *unity of act*. What here lies before us can be naturally described, with equal cor-rectness, by saying that *the name 'red' calls the object red*, or that *the red object is recognized (known) as red, and called 'red' as a result of this recognition*. To 'call something red' – in the fully actual sense of 'calling' which presupposes an underlying intuition of the thing so called – and to 'recognize something as red', are in reality *synonymous* expressions: they only differ in so far as the latter brings out more clearly that we have here no mere duality, but a unity engineered by a single act-character. In the intimacy of this fusion, we must nonetheless admit, the various factors implicit in our unity – the physical word-phenomenon with its ensouling meaning, the aspect of recognition and the intuiting of what one names – do not separate themselves off clearly, but our discussion compels us to presume them all to be there. We shall have more to say on this point later on.

It is plain that the recognitive character of certain acts, which gives them their significant relation to objects of intuition, does not pertain to words as noises, but to words in their meaningful, their *semantic (bedeutungsmässigen)* essence. Very different verbal sounds, e.g. the 'same' word in different languages, may involve an identical recognitive relation: the object is essentially known for the same, though with the aid of quite different noises. Natu-rally the complete recognition of something red, being equivalent to the actually used name, must include the noise 'red' as a part. The members of different speech-communities feel different verbal sounds to be fitting, and include these in the unity of 'knowing something'. But the meaning attaching to such words, and the recognitive act actually attaching this meaning to its object, remains everywhere the same, so that these verbal differences are rightly regarded as irrelevant.

The 'generality of the word' means, therefore, that the unified sense of one and the same word covers (or, in the case of a nonsense-word, purports to cover) an ideally delimited manifold of possible intuitions, each of which could serve as the basis for an act of recognitive naming endowed with the same sense. To the word 'red', e.g., corresponds the possibility of both knowing as, and calling 'red', all red objects that might be given in possible intuitions. This possibility leads on, with an *a priori* guarantee, to the further possibility of becoming aware, through an *identifying synthesis* of all such naming recognitions, of a sameness of meaning of one with the other: this A is red, and that A is *the same*, i.e. *also* red: the two intuited singulars belong under the same 'concept'.

A dubious point emerges here. We said above that a word could be understood even if not actually used to name anything. Must we not, however, grant that a word must at least have the *possibility* of functioning as the actual name of something and so of achieving an actual recognitive relation to corresponding intuition? Must we not say that without such a possibility it could not be a word at all? The answer, of course, is that this possibility depends on the possibility of the recognitions, the 'knowings', in question. Not all intended knowing is possible, not all nominal meaning can be *realized*. 'Imaginary' names may be names, but they cannot *actually* be used to name anything, they have, properly speaking, no extension, they are *without generality in the sense of the possible and the true*. Their generality is *empty pretension*. But how these last forms of speech are themselves to be made clear, what phenomenological facts lie behind them, will be a matter for further investigation.

What we have said applies to *all* expressions, and not merely to such as have generality of meaning in the manner of a *class-concept*. It applies also to expressions having *individual reference*, such as proper names. The fact spoken of as the 'generality of verbal meaning' does not point to the generality accorded to generic, as opposed to individual concepts, but, on the contrary, embraces either indifferently. The 'recognition', the 'knowing', of which we speak when a significantly functioning expression encounters corresponding intuition, must not, therefore, be conceived as an actual *classification*, the ranging of an intuitively or cogitatively presented object in a *class*, a ranging necessarily based on general concepts and verbally mediated by general names. Proper names, too, have their generality, though, when actually used to name anything, they can *eo ipso* not be said to classify it. Proper names, like other names, cannot name anything, without thereby also 'knowing' it. That their relation to corresponding intuition is, in fact, as indirect as that of any other expression, can be shown by a treatment exactly analogous to the one conducted above. Each and every name obviously belongs to no definite percept, nor to a definite imagination nor to any other pictorial illustration. The same person can make his appearance in countless possible intuitions, and all these appearances have no merely intuitive but also a recognitive unity. Each appearance from such an intuitive manifold will justify a precisely synonymous use of the proper name. Whichever appearance is given, the man using the name means one and the same person or thing. And he means this not merely in being intuitively oriented to it, as when he deals with an object personally strange to him; he knows it as this definite person or thing. He knows Hans as *Hans*, Berlin as *Berlin*. To recognize a person as this person, or a city as this city, is again an act not tied to the particular sensuous content of this or that word-appearance. It is identically the same act in the case of a variety (in possibility of an infinite variety) of verbal noises, as, e.g., when several different proper names apply to the same thing.

This generality of the proper name, and of the peculiar meaning which corresponds to it, is plainly quite different in kind from that of the *general name*.

The former consists in the fact that a synthesis of possible intuitions belongs to a *single* individual object, intuitions made one by the common intentional character imparted by every relation to the same object, despite all phenomenal differences among individual intuitions. On this unified basis, the particular unity of recognitive knowing reposes, which belongs to the 'generality of verbal meaning', to its range of ideally possible realizations. In this way the naming word has a recognitive relation to a boundless multitude of intuitions, whose identical object it both knows and thereby names.

The case of the *class-name* is quite different. Its generality covers a *range of objects*, to each of which, *considered apart*, a possible synthesis of percepts, a possible individual meaning and proper name belongs. The general name 'covers' this range through being able to name each item in the whole range in general fashion, i.e. not by individually recognizing it in the manner of the proper name, but by classifying it, in the manner of the common name. The thing that is either directly given, or known in its authentic self-being (*Eigenheit*), or known through its properties, is now known as *an A* and named accordingly.

§ 8 *The dynamic unity of expression and expressed intuition. The consciousness of fulfilment and that of identity*

From the tranquil, as it were *static* coincidence of meaning and intuition, we now turn to that *dynamic* coincidence where an expression first functions in merely symbolic fashion, and then is accompanied by a 'more or less' corresponding intuition. Where this happens, we experience a descriptively peculiar *consciousness of fulfilment*:[1] the act of pure meaning, like a goal-seeking intention, finds its fulfilment in the act which renders the matter intuitive. In this transitional experience, the *mutual belongingness* of the two acts, the act of meaning, on the one hand, and the intuition which more or less corresponds to it, on the other, reveals its phenomenological roots. We experience how *the same* objective item which was 'merely thought of' in symbol is now presented in intuition, and that it is intuited as being precisely the determinate so-and-so that it was at first merely thought or meant to be. We are merely expressing the same fact if we say that *the intentional essence of the act of intuition* gets more or less perfectly *fitted into the semantic essence of the act of expression.*

In the previously considered static relation among acts of meaning and intuition, we spoke of a *recognition*, a *knowing*. This represents the sense-informed relation of the name to the intuitive datum that it names. But the element of meaning is not here itself the act of recognition. In the purely symbolic understanding of a word, an act of meaning is performed (the word means something to us) but nothing is thereby known, recognized. The difference lies, as the foregoing paragraphs have established, not in the mere accompanying presence of the intuition of the thing named, but in the phenomenologically peculiar form of unity. What is characteristic about this unity of knowing, of recognition, is now

[1] Cf. my *Psych. Studies of elementary Logic*, II, 'Concerning Intuitions and Representations', *Philos. Monatshefte*, 1894, p. 176. I have given up the concept of intuition supported there, as the present work makes plain.

shown up by the dynamic relationship before us. In it there is at first the meaning-intention, quite on its own: then the corresponding intuition comes to join it. At the same time we have the phenomenological unity which is now stamped as a consciousness of fulfilment. Talk about recognizing objects, and talk about fulfilling a meaning-intention, therefore express the same fact, merely from differing standpoints. The former adopts the standpoint of the object meant, while the latter has the two acts as its foci of interest. Phenomenologically the acts are always present, while the objects are sometimes non-existent. Talk of fulfilment therefore characterizes the phenomenological essence of the recognitive relation more satisfactorily. It is a primitive phenomenological fact, that acts of signification[1] and acts of intuition can enter into this peculiar relation. Where they do so, where some act of meaning-intention fulfils itself in an intuition, we also say: 'The object of intuition is known through its concept' or 'The correct name has been applied to the object appearing before us'.

We can readily do justice to the obvious phenomenological difference between the static and the dynamic fulfilment or recognition. In the dynamic relationship the members of the relation, and the act of recognition which relates them, are disjoined in time: they unfold themselves in a temporal pattern. In the static relationship, which represents the lasting outcome of this temporal transaction, they occur in temporal and material (*sachlicher*) coincidence. *There* we have a first stage of mere thought (of pure conception or mere signification), a meaning-intention wholly unsatisfied, to which a second stage of more or less adequate fulfilment is added, where thoughts repose as if satisfied in the sight of their object, which presents itself, *in virtue of* this consciousness of unity, as what is thought of in this thought, what it refers to, as the more or less perfectly attained goal of thinking. In the static relationship, on the other hand, we have this consciousness of unity alone, perhaps with no noticeably marked-off,

---

[1] I use this expression without specially introducing it as a term, since it is the mere translation of 'meaning'. I shall accordingly often speak of *significative* or *signitive acts*, instead of acts of meaning-intention, of meaning etc. 'Meaning-acts' can scarcely be talked of, since *expressions* are used as the normal subjects of meaning. 'Signitive' also offers us a suitable terminological opposite to 'intuitive'. A synonym for 'signitive' is 'symbolic', to the extent that the modern abuse of a word 'symbol' obtains – an abuse already denounced by Kant – which equates a symbol with a 'sign', quite against its original and still indispensable sense.

precedent stage of unfulfilled intention. The fulfilment of the intention is not here an event of self-fulfilment, but a tranquil state of being-fulfilled, not a coming into coincidence, but a being coincident.

From an objective point of view we may here also speak of a *unity of identity*. If we compare both components of a unity of fulfilment – whether treating them in dynamic transition into one another, or holding them apart analytically in their static unity, only to see them at once flowing back into one another – we assert their *objective identity*. For we said, and said with self-evidence, that the object of intuition is the *same* as the object of the thought which fulfils itself in it, and, where the fit is exact, that the object is seen as being exactly the same as it is thought of or, (what always says the same in this context) meant. Identity, it is plain, is not first dragged in through comparative, cogitatively mediated reflection: it is there from the start as experience, as unexpressed, unconceptualized experience. In other words, the thing which, from the point of view of our acts is phenomenologically described as fulfilment, will also, from the point of view of the two objects involved in it, the intuited object, on the one hand, and the thought object, on the other, be expressively styled 'experience of identity', 'consciousness of identity', or 'act of identification'. A more or less complete *identity* is the *objective datum which corresponds to the act of fulfilment*, which 'appears in it'. This means that, not only signification and intuition, but also their mutual adequation, their union of fulfilment, can be called an act, since it has its own peculiar intentional correlate, an objective something to which it is 'directed'. Another side of the same situation is again, we saw above, expressed in talk about *recognizing* or *knowing*. The fact that our meaning-intention is united with intuition in a fulfilling manner, gives to the *object* which appears in such intuition, when it primarily concerns us, the character of a thing known. If we try to say more exactly 'as what' we recognize something, our objective reflection points, not to our *act* of meaning (*Bedeutens*), but to the meaning (*Bedeutung*), the self-identical 'concept' itself; talk of recognition therefore expresses our view of the same unified state from the standpoint of the object of intuition (or of the fulfilling act), in its relations to the meaning-concept of the signitive act. Conversely we say, though perhaps in more special contexts, that our thought 'grasps' (*begreife*) the matter, that it is the latter's concept (*Begriff*) or 'grasp'. After our exposition it is obvious that recognition, like fulfilment – the former is in fact only another name for the latter – can be called an act of identification.

Addendum. I cannot here suppress a difficulty connected with the otherwise illuminating notion of the unity of identity or recognition, as an *act* of identification or recognition. This is particularly the case, since this difficulty will reveal itself as a serious one as our clarifications proceed and progress, and will inspire fruitful discussions. Closer analysis makes it plain that, in the cases detailed above, where a name is actually applied to an object of intuition, we refer to the intuited and named *object*, but not to the *identity* of this object, as something at once intuited and named. Shall we say that an emphasis of attention decides the matter? Or ought we not rather to grant that there is not here a fully consti-tuted act of identification: the nucleus of this act, the connective union of significant intention and corresponding intuition is really present, but it 'represents' no objectifying interpretation (*Auffassung*). On the experienced unity of coincidence *no act of relational identification* is founded, no intentional consciousness of identity, in which identity, as a unity referred to, first gains objective status. In our reflection on the unity of fulfilment, in analysing and opposing its mutually connected acts, we naturally, and indeed necessarily, also framed that relational interpretation which the form of its union, with *a priori* necessity, permits. Our second section will deal with this question in its widest form which concerns the categorial characters of acts (see Chapter vi, §48, and the whole of Chapter vii). Meanwhile we shall continue to treat the sort of unity in question as a full act, or we shall at least not differentiate it expressly from a full act. This will not affect the essential point in our treatment, in so far as the passage from a consciousness of unity to a relational identification always remains open, has a possibility guaranteed *a priori*, so that we are entitled to say that an identifying coincidence has been *expe-rienced*, even if there is no *conscious intention* directed to identity, and no *relational* identification.

§9 *The differing character of an intention inside and outside the unity of fulfilment*

Our introduction of dynamic fulfilment, or of fulfilment strung out in an articulated process, to help interpret the static act of recognition, removes a difficulty which threatens to blur our clear grasp of the relation between significant intention and the full act of recognition. Can we really say that all these factors can be distinguished in the unity of recognition, the verbal expression, the acts of meaning and intuition, and, finally, the overarching character of recognitive unity or fulfilment? One might hold that analysis only lays bare *verbal expressions*, particularly names, on the one hand, and intuition, on the other, both unified through the character of recognitive naming. One might reject the idea of an *act of meaning* bound up with the verbal expression, an element distinct from recognitive character and fulfilling intuition, and identifiable with the 'understanding' as opposed to the 'knowing' character of the expression: this would seem, at least, to be an unnecessary assumption.

This doubt affects, therefore, the central conception which in §4 we took to be most intelligible, before we embarked on our analysis of the unity of recognition. We must accordingly re-emphasize the following points in our discussion:

1. If we compare expressions used in recognizing objects with those used outside of such recognition, it is plain that both have the very same meaning. Whether I understand the word 'tree' as a mere symbol, or use it in connection with my intuition of a tree, it is plain that I mean something by the word, and mean the same thing on both occasions.

2. It is plain that it is the significant intention of the expression that 'fulfils' itself in the process of fulfilment, and so achieves 'coincidence' with an intuition, and that the recognition which stems from this process of coincidence is itself this unity of coincidence. The notion of this unity of coincidence plainly involves that we are not here concerned with a divided duality but with a seamless unity, which only acquires articulation when drawn out in time. We must, therefore, maintain that the same act of meaning-intention which occurs in an empty symbolic presentation is also part of the complex act of recognition, but that a meaning-intention that was 'free', is now 'bound' and 'neutral-

ized' in the stage of coincidence. It is so peculiarly inwrought and infused in this combination that, while its semantic essence remains intact, it nonetheless undergoes a certain change of character.

The same holds wherever contents are first studied apart, and then seen in their connection with other contents, as parts knit into wholes. Connections would not connect if they made no difference to what they connected. Certain changes necessarily occur, and these are naturally such specific connectednesses as constitute the phenomenological correlatives of what are objectively *relational* properties. Consider, for example, a line set apart, perhaps on a bare white background, and the same line as part of a figure. In the latter case, it *impinges* on other lines, is *touched*, *cut* by them etc. If we turn from mathematical ideals to empirically intuited linear stretches, these are phenomenological characters that help determine the appearance of linearity. The same stretch – 'same' in internal content – appears ever different according as it enters into this or that phenomenal context, and, if incorporated in a line or surface qualitatively identical with it, melts indistinguishably into this background, losing its phenomenal separateness and independence.

§ 10 *The wider class of experiences of fulfilment. Intuitions as intentions which require fulfilment*

We may now further characterize the consciousness of fulfilment by seeing in it an experiential form which plays a part in many other fields of mental life. We have only to think of the opposition between wishful intention and wish-fulfilment, between voluntary intention and execution, of the fulfilment of hopes and fears, the resolution of doubts, the confirmation of surmises etc., to be clear that essentially the same opposition is to be found in very different classes of intentional experiences: the opposition between significant intention and fulfilment of meaning is merely a special case of it. We have dealt with this point previously,[1] and delimited a class of intentional experience under the more pregnant name of 'intentions': their peculiarity lies in being able to provide the basis for relations of fulfilment. In this class are ranged all the acts which are in a narrower or wider sense 'logical', including the *intuitive*, whose role it is to fulfil other intuitions in knowledge.

[1] Cf. § 13 of the previous Investigation.

When, e.g., a familiar melody begins, it stirs up definite intentions which find their fulfilment in the melody's gradual unfolding. The same is the case even when the melody is unfamiliar. The regularities governing melody as such, determine intentions, which may be lacking in complete objective definiteness, but which nonetheless find or can find their fulfilments. As concrete experiences, these intentions are of course fully definite: the 'indefiniteness' of what they intend is plainly a descriptive peculiarity pertaining to their character. We may say, in fact, with correct paradox (as we did before in a similar case) that 'indefiniteness' (i.e. the peculiarity of demanding an incompletely determined completion, which lies in a 'sphere' circumscribed by a law) is a definite feature of such an intention. Such an intention has not merely a range of possible fulfilment, but imports a common fulfilment-character into each actual fulfilment from this range. The fulfilment of acts which have definite or indefinite intentions is phenomenologically different, and the same holds of fulfilments of intentions whose indefiniteness points in this or that direction of possible fulfilment.

In our previous example there is also a relation between *expectation* and *fulfilment of expectation*. It would, however, be quite wrong to think, conversely, that every relation of an intention to its fulfilment was a relationship involving expectation. *Intention is not expectancy*, it is not of its essence to be directed to future appearances. If I see an incomplete pattern, e.g. in this carpet partially covered over by furniture, the piece I see seems clothed with intentions pointing to further completions – we feel as if the lines and coloured shapes go on 'in the sense' of what we see – but we expect nothing. It would be possible for us to expect something, if movement promised us further views. But possible expectations, or occasions for possible expectations, are not themselves expectations.

The external perceptions of the senses offer us an indefinite number of relevant examples. The features which enter into perception always point to completing features, which themselves might appear in other possible percepts, and that definitely or more or less indefinitely, according to the degree of our 'empirical acquaintance' with the object. Every percept, and every perceptual context, reveals itself, on closer analysis, as made up of components which are to be understood as ranged under two standpoints of intention and (actual or possible) fulfilment. The same applies to the parallel acts of imagining and picture-thought in general. In the normal case intentions lack the character of expectancy, they lack it in all cases of tranquil perceiving or picturing, and they acquire it only when perception is in flux, when it is spread out into a continuous series of percepts, all belonging to the perceptual manifold of one and the same object. Objectively put: the object then shows itself from a variety of sides. What was pictorially suggested from one side, becomes confirmed in full perception from another; what was merely adumbrated or given indirectly and subsidiarily as background, from one side, at least receives a portrait-sketch from another, it appears perspectively foreshortened and projected, only to appear 'just as it is' from another side. All perceiving and imagining is, on our view, a web of partial intentions, fused together in the unity of a single total intention. The correlate of this last intention is the thing, while the correlate of its partial intentions are *the thing's parts and aspects*. Only in this way can we understand how consciousness reaches out beyond what it actually experiences. It can so to say mean beyond itself, and its meaning can be fulfilled.

§11 *Frustration and conflict. The synthesis of distinction*

In the wider sphere of the acts to which distinctions of intention and fulfilment apply, *frustration* may be set beside fulfilment, as its incompatible contrary. The negative expression that we normally use in this case, e.g. even the term 'non-fulfilment', has no merely privative meaning: it points to a new descriptive fact, a form of synthesis as peculiar as fulfilment. This is so even in the narrower case of significant intentions as they stand to intuitive intentions. The synthesis of recognition, of 'knowing', is the consciousness of a certain agreement. The possibility correlated with agreement is, however, 'disagreement' or 'conflict': intuition may not accord with a significant intention, but may 'quarrel' with it. Conflict 'separates', but the experience of conflict puts things into relation and unity: it is a form of *synthesis*. If the previously studied synthesis was one of *identification*, this new synthesis is one of *distinction* (unfortunately we possess no other positive name). This 'distinction' must not be confused with the other 'distinction' which stands opposed to a positive likening.

The oppositions between 'identification and distinction' and between 'likening and distinction' are not the same, though it is clear that a close phenomenological affinity explains our use of the same word. In the 'distinction' which is here in question, the *object* of the frustrating act appears *not the same as*, *distinct from* the object of the intending act. These distinctions point to wider classes of cases than we have hitherto preferred to deal with. Not only significative, but even intuitive intentions are fulfilled in identifications and frustrated in conflicts. We shall have to explore the whole question of the natural circumscription of the acts to which the terms 'same' and 'other' (we can as well say 'is' and 'is not') have application.

The two syntheses are not, however, completely parallel. Each conflict presupposes something which directs its intention to the object of the conflicting act; only a synthesis of fulfilment can give it this direction. Conflict, we may say, presupposes a certain basis of agreement. If I think A to be *red*, when it shows itself to be 'in fact' green, an intention to red quarrels with an intention to green in this showing forth, i.e. in this application to intuition. Undeniably, however, this can only be the case because A has been identified in the two acts of signification and intuition. Were this not so, the intention would not relate to the intuition. The total intention points to an A which is red, and intuition reveals an A which is green. It is in the coincidence of meaning and intuition in their direction to an identical A, that the moments intended in union with A in the two cases, come into conflict. The presumed red (i.e. red of A) fails to agree with the intuited green. It is through identity that such non-coincident aspects *correspond* with each other: instead of being 'combined' by fulfilment, they are 'sundered' by conflict. An intention is referred to an appropriate aspect in intuition from which it is also turned away.

What we have here said with special regard to significant intentions and the frustrations they encounter, applies also to our whole previously sketched class of objectifying intentions. We may generally say: *An intention can only be frustrated in conflict in so far as it forms part of a wider intention whose completing part is fulfilled.* We can therefore not talk of conflict in the case of simple, i.e. isolated, acts.

§12 *Total and partial identification and distinction as the common phenomenological foundations of predicative and determining forms of expression*

The relation between intention (in particular, meaning-intention) and fulfilment that we have so far considered, was that of total agreement. This was a limitation due to our aim of maximum simplicity: to achieve this, we abstracted from all form, even from the form that announces itself in the little word 'is'. In the relation of an expression to external or internal intuition, we considered only those parts of the expression that fit what we intuit like a garment. But by bringing in conflict as the possibility opposed to the case of total agreement – conflict that could therefore, somewhat misleadingly, be called 'total conflict' – we are made aware of certain new possibilities, the important cases of *partial agreement* and *disagreement* between an intention and the act which fulfils or frustrates it.

We shall, from the start, keep the closer treatment of these possibilities so general, that the validity of all essential results will be clear for intentions of the above indicated wider class, and not merely, therefore, for meaning-intentions.

All conflict pointed to the fact that the frustrated intention in question was part of a more comprehensive intention, which partially fulfilled itself (i.e. in the supplementary parts) while the original part was estranged. In every conflict there is, accordingly, in a certain fashion, both partial agreement and partial conflict. Our attention to objective relations should have revealed these possibilities, since wherever we can talk of coincidence, we can talk about the correlated possibilities of exclusion, inclusion and intersection.

If we keep to the case of conflict, the following additional points suggest themselves:

If a θ is frustrated in a $\bar{\theta}$ in that θ is associated with other intentions $\eta, \iota \ldots$ which are fulfilled, these latter need not be so united with θ, that the whole Θ ($\theta; \eta; \iota \ldots$) deserves to be called an act constituted on its own, one 'in which we live', and to whose unified object we 'pay heed'. In the texture of conscious, intentional experience, there are many possibilities of pointing selection of acts and act-complexes, which remain for the most part unrealized. And only such pointed unities are relevant when we are speaking of individual acts and their syntheses. The case of *pure and complete frustration* therefore consists in the fact that θ alone, not Θ, is emphasized or at least mainly emphasized, and that a pointed consciousness of conflict establishes unity only between θ and $\bar{\theta}$. Our interest in other words, is specially directed to the objects corresponding to θ and $\bar{\theta}$. This happens when a green-intention is frustrated by an intuited red, and the green and red are alone attended to. If the clashing intuition of the red is expressed at all, i.e. by a verbal intention fulfilled in it, we should perhaps say: 'This (red) is not green'. (Of course this sentence does not have the same meaning as the sentence 'The verbal intention "green" is frustrated by the intuition of red'. For the new expression renders *objective* the relation of acts which concerns us, and turns new meaning-intentions upon the latter in total fulfilment.)

It can also be the case that a Θ (θ; η; ι...) enters synthesis as a whole, and is herewith either associated with a corresponding whole Θ ($\bar{\theta}$; η; ι...) or specially associated with its isolated part $\bar{\theta}$. In the former case there is in part coincidence among the combined elements, i.e. among η, ι...and in part total conflict, (θ, $\bar{\theta}$). The whole synthesis has the character of a total conflict, but of conflict not pure, but mixed. In the other case $\bar{\theta}$ alone stands out as the corresponding act, for the reason, perhaps, that in mixed conflict the unity of Θ ($\bar{\theta}$; η; ι...) is resolved. The special synthesis of conflict unites Θ ($\bar{\theta}$; η; ι...) and ($\bar{\theta}$), which is appropriately expressed by 'This (whole object, the red-tiled roof) is not green'. This important relation may be called one of *exclusion* (*Ausscheidung*). Its central character is plainly unaffected, when θ and $\bar{\theta}$ are themselves complex, so that we can distinguish between *pure* and *mixed* exclusion. Roughly speaking, the latter may be illustrated by the example 'This (red-tiled roof) is no green-tiled roof'.

Let us now consider the case of inclusion. An intention can be fulfilled in an act which contains *more* than its fulfilment needs, in so far as the latter presents an object which contains the intention's object, either as a common-or-garden part, or as a 'moment' explicitly or implicitly thought of as belonging to it. We are of course ignoring the acts in which a more comprehensive objective field is set up as an objective background, acts not delimited as unities nor as preferential carriers of attention: otherwise we should be brought back to the synthesis of total coincidence. Let us suppose that a red-tiled roof is presented to us, and that the meaning-intention behind the word 'red' is fulfilled in it. The verbal meaning is here fulfilled with complete coincidence in the intuited red, but the *total intuition* of the red-tiled roof, relieved sharply as a single item from the background, through the work of attention, still enters into a peculiar sort of synthetic unity *with the meaning-intention* Red: '(This) is red'. We speak here of a relation of 'subsumption' (*Einordnung*), the opposite of the exclusion mentioned above. Subsumption can obviously only be pure.

The act of subsumptive synthesis, as the act which puts together the intending and fulfilling acts in its total unity, has its objective correlate in the relation of *partial identity of the corresponding objects*. Talk of subsumption points in this direction: it pictures our grasp of the relation as an activity which subsumes the part in the whole. The same objective relationship is, with a change of conceptual standpoint – pointing to unnoticed phenomenological differences casually revealed in our form of expression – expressed in the words: 'Θ_g has θ_g' or 'θ_g pertains to Θ_g'. The index g makes us aware that it is the intentional objects of the acts in question which enter into these relations; we stress the *intentional* objects, the objects as they are referred to in these acts. The application of these remarks to the case of exclusion, and to the expressions 'has not' or 'does not pertain', is obvious.

To the mere 'is' objective identity belongs in all cases, to the 'is not' non-identity (conflict). That we are specially dealing with a relation of subsumption or exclusion requires other means of expression, e.g. the *adjectival form*, which marks off *what is had* or *what pertains* as such, just as the *substantival form* expresses its correlative, the *thing which has as such*, i.e. in its function as 'subject' of an identification. In the attributive, or more generally determining form of expression (even complete identity determines), being is hidden in the inflexion of the adjective, to the extent that it is not explicitly and separately expressed in a relative clause, or, *per contra*, not wholly suppressed ('this philosopher Socrates'). Whether the always mediate expression of non-identity, whether in cases of predication or attribution, or in substantival forms such as 'non-identity', 'non-agreement', expresses a necessary relation of actual 'negation' to an affirmation which, if not actual, is at least present in modified form, would lead to discussions into which we do not now care to enter.

All normal statements are accordingly statements of identity or non-identity, and expressions of the same wherever there is a relation to 'corresponding intuition', i.e. where the intention towards identity or non-identity fulfils itself in a completely achieved identification or distinction. 'The tiled roof', as we would say in our previous case provided a *mere* intention went before, 'is *really* red'. The predicate-intention fits the subject which is presented and intuited as, e.g., 'this tiled roof'. In the opposite case we say: 'It is not *really* red'; the predicate does not pertain to the subject.

But if the meaning of 'is' finds a fulfilment based on an actual identification (which often has the character of a fulfilment), it is clear that we are here passing beyond the sphere on which we had hitherto always kept our eye, without being quite clear as to its limits, the sphere namely of expressions that can really be fulfilled through corresponding *intuition*. Or rather we are made aware that intuition, in the common-or-garden sense of external or internal 'sensibility', which we took as an obvious basis in our treatment, is not the only function that can rightly be styled 'intuitive', and can be regarded as capable of carrying out the work of fulfilment. We leave the closer exploration of this emerging difference to the Second Section of the present Investigation.

We must stress, in conclusion, that the above exposition has not provided a complete analysis of the judgement, but a mere fragment of the same. We have ignored the quality of the synthetic act, the differences between attribution and predication etc.

CHAPTER TWO

Indirect Characterization of Objectifying Intentions and their Essential Varieties through Differences in the Syntheses of Fulfilment

§13 *The synthesis of knowing (recognition) as the characteristic form of fulfilment for objectifying acts. Subsumption of acts of meaning under the class of objectifying acts*

WE have, in the above treatment, classed meaning-intentions in the wider class of 'intentions' in the pregnant sense of the word. All intentions have corresponding possibilities of fulfilment (or of opposed frustration): these themselves are peculiar transitional experiences, characterizable as acts, which permit each act to 'reach its goal' in an act specially correlated with it. These latter acts, inasmuch as they fulfil intentions, may be called 'fulfilling acts', but they are called so only on account of the synthetic act of fulfilment, or rather of self-fulfilment. *Such transitional experience is not always the same in character.* In the case of meaning-intentions, and not less clearly in the case of intuitive intentions, such experiences are unities of knowing, or unities of identification in respect of their objects. This need not be so in the wider class of intentions in general. Everywhere we may speak of coincidences, and everywhere we shall meet with identifications. But the latter often depend on an inwrought act of a sort which permits of a unity of identification and also serves as the foundation of one in the contexts in question.

An example will clarify the matter. The self-fulfilment of a wish is achieved in an act which includes an identification, and includes it as a necessary component. For there is a law which ties the quality of wishing to an underlying presentation, i.e. to an objectifying act, and more precisely to a 'mere presentation', and this leads to a complementary law tying a wish-fulfilment to an underlying act, which incorporates this presentation in its identifying grasp. A wishful intention can only find its fulfilling satisfaction in so far as the underlying mere presentation of the thing wished for becomes transformed into the corresponding percept. What we have, however, is not this mere transformation, the mere fact of imagination dissolved in perception: both enter in unity into the character of an act of identifying coincidence. In this synthetic character, we have it constituted that *a thing is really and truly so* (i.e. as we had previously merely pictured and wished): this of course does not exclude the possibility that such 'really being so' is merely putative, and especially, in most cases, that it is inadequately presented. If a wish is based on a purely signitive presentation, this identification can of course involve the more special coincidence described above, in which meaning is fulfilled by an intuition that fits it. The same could plainly be said of all intentions that, as objectifying acts, are based on presentations, and what applies to fulfilment carries over, *mutatis mutandis*, to the case of frustration.

It is clear accordingly, to stick to our example, that even if the fulfilment of a wish is founded on an identification, and perhaps on an act of intuitive recognition, this latter act never exhausts the fulfilment of the wish, but merely provides its basis. The self-satisfaction of the specific wish-quality is a peculiar, act-character, different in kind. It is by a mere analogy that we extend talk of satisfaction, and even of fulfilment, beyond the sphere of emotional intentionality.

The peculiar character of an intention accordingly goes with the peculiar character of its fulfilling coincidence. Not only does *every nuance of an intention correspond to some nuance of the correlated fulfilment*, and likewise of the self-fulfilling activity in the sense of a synthetic act, but to the *essentially different classes of intention there also correspond pervasive class-differences in fulfilment* (in the twofold sense mentioned above). And obviously *the members which belong to these parallel series belong also to a single class of acts*. The syntheses of fulfilment in the case of wish- and will-intentions certainly show close affinities, and differ deeply from those occurring, e.g., in the case of meaning-intentions. On the other hand, the fulfilments of meaning-intentions and of intuitive acts are definitely of the same character, and so in the case of all acts that we classed as 'objectifying'. We may say of this class of acts which alone concerns us here, *that in them unity of fulfilment has the character of unity of identification*, possibly the narrower character of a unity of knowing, i.e. of an act to which objective identity is the corresponding correlate.

We must here emphasize the following point: As pointed out above, every fulfilment of a 'signitive' by an intuitive act has the character of a synthesis of identification. But it is not the case, conversely, that, in each synthesis of identification, a meaning-intention is fulfilled, and fulfilled by a corresponding intuition. In the widest sense, certainly, we do ordinarily speak of every actual identification as a recognition. But, in a narrower sense, what is clearly felt to be at issue is an approach to a goal of knowledge, and, in the narrowest sense of a critique of knowledge, the arrival at that goal. To turn this mere feeling into clear insight, and to define the precise sense of this approach or arrival, will yet be our task. Meanwhile we shall maintain that the *unity of identification*, and thereby all *unity of knowing* in the narrower and the narrowest sense, has *its place of origin in the sphere of objectifying acts*.

Their peculiar manner of fulfilment will therefore suffice to characterize the unified class of acts to which it essentially belongs. We can accordingly *define* objectifying acts as those whose syntheses of fulfilment have a character of identification, while their synthesis of frustration has a character of distinction. We can also define them as acts which can function phenomenologically as members of possible syntheses of identification and distinction. Lastly, presuming a law as yet unformulated, we can define them as the intending, fulfilling or frustrating acts which have a possible knowledge-function. *To this class belong also the synthetic acts of identification and distinction themselves*: they are themselves either a merely *putative* grasp of identity or non-identity, or a corresponding *real* grasp of the one or the other. This putative grasp can be either 'confirmed' or 'refuted' in an act of knowing (in the pregnant sense of the word): identity is really grasped, i.e. 'adequately perceived', in the former case, as non-identity in the latter.

Our analyses have been lightly sketched rather than thoroughly executed, but they lead to the result that *both meaning-intentions and acts of meaning-fulfilment*, acts of 'thought' and acts of intuition, *belong to a single class of objectifying acts*. We establish thereby *that acts of another sort can never exercise any sense-giving function*, and that they can be 'expressed' only in so far as the meaning-intentions which attach to words are fulfilled in percepts or imaginations which have as *objects* the acts requiring expression. While, therefore, where acts function meaningfully, and achieve expression in this sense, a 'signitive' or intuitive relation to objects is constituted in them, in the other cases *the acts are mere objects*, and objects, of course, for other acts which here function as the authentic carriers of meaning.

Before we discuss this matter more closely, and seek to refute many plausible counter-arguments – see the final Section of this Investigation – we must explore the remarkable facts of fulfilment somewhat more carefully, and in the sphere of objectifying acts.

§14 *Phenomenological characterization of the distinction between signitive and intuitive intentions through peculiarities of fulfilment*

(a) *Sign, Image and Self-presentation*

In the course of the last discussion we have been led to note how the generic character of an intention closely coheres with that of its synthesis of fulfilment, so that the whole class of objectifying acts can be defined through the identification generically characteristic of their syntheses of fulfilment, whose nature we take to be familiar. This thought leads us on to ask whether the specific differences *within* this class of objectifications, may not likewise rest upon corresponding differences in the mode of fulfilment. Objectifying intentions are basically divided into *significative* and *intuitive* intentions: let us try to give an account of the difference between these types of act.

Since the starting point of our treatment lay in expressed acts, we took *signitive intentions* to be the significations, the meanings of expressions. If we leave aside the question whether the same acts which give sense to expressions can also function outside of the sphere of meaning, these signitive intentions always have intuitive support in the sensuous side of the expression, but not on that account intuitive *content*. Though in a manner one with intuitive acts, they yet differ from them in kind.

We can readily grasp the distinction between expressed and purely intuitive intentions if we contrast *signs* with *likenesses* or *images*.

The sign has in general no community of content with the thing it signifies; it can stand as readily for what is heterogeneous, as for what is homogeneous with itself. The likeness on the other hand is related to the thing by *similarity*: where there is no similarity, there can be no talk of a likeness, an image. The sign as object is constituted for us in an act of appearing. This act is not significant: it needs, as we held in former analyses, to be tied up with a new intention, a new way of taking things, through which a novel, signified object takes the place of the old, intuitively apparent one. The likeness similarly, e.g. the marble bust, is as much a thing as anything else: the new way of regarding it first makes it a *likeness*. Not merely a thing of marble appears before us, but we have, based on this appearance, a reference to a person through a likeness.

The intentions attaching to the phenomenal content are, in either case, not externally tied up with it, but essentially based upon it, and in such a way that the character of the intention is determined thereby. It would be a descriptively wrong notion of the matter, to think of the whole difference as lying in the fact that the same intention which, in the one case is tied to the appearance of an object *like* the object referred to, is in the other case tied to the appearance of an object *unlike* it. For the sign, too, can be like what it signifies, even entirely like it: the sign-presentation is not thereby made into a presentation by way of a likeness. A photograph of the sign A is immediately taken to be a picture of the sign. But when we use the sign A as a sign of the sign A, as when we write 'A is a letter of the Latin written alphabet', we treat A, despite its representational similarity, as a sign, and not as a likeness.

The objective fact of similarity between what appears and what is meant, is accordingly irrelevant: it is not, however, irrelevant where something is presented by way of a likeness. This shows itself in the possibility of fulfilment: it was only the recollection of this possibility which allowed us to bring in 'objective' similarity in this context. The likeness-presentation plainly has the peculiarity that, when it achieves fulfilment, the object which appears before it as likeness gets identified through similarity with the object *given* in the fulfilling act. Having held this to be the peculiarity of a presentation by way of likeness, we have admitted that *fulfilment of like by like internally fixes the character of a synthesis of fulfilment as imaginative*. But, when, on the other hand, casual likeness between sign and thing signified leads to a knowledge of their mutual resemblance, this knowledge is not at all a case of the peculiar consciousness of identity, when similar is referred to similar and made to coincide with it in the manner of likeness and original thing. It is rather of the very essence of a *significative* intention, that in it the apparent objects of intending and fulfilling acts (e.g. name and thing named in their fully achieved unity) 'have nothing to do with one another'. It is clear, therefore, that descriptively distinct modes of fulfilment, being rooted in the descriptively distinct character of our intention, can help us to detect these latter differences, and to find definitions for them.

We have so far only considered the difference between signitive and imaginative intentions. If we ignore less weighty distinctions within the wider sphere of imaginative acts – we have preferred to consider representation by way of physical images, instead of stressing those of fantasy – we must still consider the case of *percepts*.

As opposed to imagination, perception is characterized by the fact that in it, as we are wont to express the matter, the object 'itself' appears, and does not merely appear 'in a likeness'. In this we at once recognize characteristic differences in *syntheses of fulfilment*. Imagination fulfils itself through the peculiar synthesis of image-resemblance, perception through the *synthesis of identical thinghood (sachlichen Identität)*. The thing establishes itself through its very self, in so far as it shows itself from varying sides while remaining one and the same.

(b) The perceptual and imaginative 'shadowing forth' of the object

We must, however, pay heed to the following distinction. Perception, so far as it claims to give us the object 'itself', really claims thereby to be no mere intention, but an act, which may indeed be capable of offering fulfilment to other acts, but which itself requires no further fulfilment. But generally, and in all cases of 'external' perception, this remains a mere pretension. The object is not actually given, it is not given wholly and entirely as that which it itself is. It is only given 'from the front', only 'perspectivally foreshortened and projected' etc. While many of its properties are illustrated in the nuclear content of the percept, at least in the (perspectival) manner which the last expressions indicate, many others are not present in the percept in such illustrated form: the elements of the invisible rear side, the interior etc., are no doubt subsidiarily intended in more or less definite fashion, symbolically suggested by what is primarily apparent, but are not themselves part of the intuitive, i.e. of the perceptual or imaginative content, of the percept. On this hinges the possibility of indefinitely many percepts of the same object, all differing in content. If percepts were always the actual, genuine self-presentations of objects that they pretend to be, there could be only a single percept for each object, since its peculiar essence would be exhausted in such self-presentation.

We must, however, note that the object, as it is *in itself* – in the only sense relevant and understandable in our context, the sense which the fulfilment of the perceptual intention would carry out – is *not wholly different* from the object realized, however imperfectly, in the percept. It is part so-to-say of a percept's inherent sense to be the self-appearance of the object. Even if, for phenomenological purposes, ordinary perception is composed of countless intentions, some purely perceptual, some merely imaginative, and some even sigitive, it yet, as a *total act*, grasps the object itself, even if only by way of an aspect. If we may conceive of a percept put into a relation of fulfilment to the adequate percept that would *offer us the object itself*, in the ideally strict and most authentic sense, then we may say that a percept so intends its object that this ideal synthesis would have the character of a *partial coincidence* of the purely perceptual contents of intending and fulfilling acts, and also the character of a complete coincidence of both complete perceptual intentions. The 'purely perceptual' content in 'external' perception is what remains over when we abstract from all purely imaginative and symbolic components: it is the 'sensed' content to which its own, immediate, purely perceptual interpretation is given, which evaluates all its parts and moments as self-projections or corresponding parts and moments of the perceptual object, and so imparts to its total content the character of a 'perceptual picture', a perceptual projection of the object. In the ideal, limiting case of adequate perception, this self-presenting sensed content coincides with the perceived object. This common relation to the object 'in itself', i.e. to the ideal of adequation, enters into the sense of all perception, and is also manifest in the phenomenological mutual belongingness of the manifold percepts pertaining to a single object. In one percept the object appears from this side, in another from that side; now it appears close, now at a distance etc. In each percept, despite these differences, one and the same object is 'there', in each it is intended in the complete range of its familiar and of its perceptually present properties. To this corresponds phenomenologically a continuous flux of fulfilment or identification, in the steady serialization of the percepts 'pertaining to the same object'. Each individual percept is a mixture of fulfilled and unfulfilled intentions. To the former corresponds that part of the object which is given in more or less perfect projection in *this* individual percept, to the latter that part of the object that is not yet given, that new percepts would bring to actual, fulfilling presence. All such syntheses of fulfilment are marked by a common character: they are identifications binding self-manifestations of an object to self-manifestations of the same object.

It is at once clear that similar distinctions apply in the case of imaginative presentation. Here too the same object is pictured, now from this and now from that side. Corresponding to the synthesis of manifold perceptions, where the same object always presents *itself*, we have the parallel synthesis of manifold imaginations, in which the same object appears *in a likeness*. To the changing perceptual projections of the object there are corresponding imaginative projections, and in the ideal of perfect copying the projection would coincide with the complete likeness. If imaginative acts are at one time fulfilled in imaginative contexts, and at another time through corresponding percepts, the difference lies plainly in the character of their synthesis of fulfilment: the passage from likeness to likeness has a different character from the passage from likeness to original thing.

The above analysis will be of use for the further investigations to be carried on in the next chapter; they also show the mutual affinity of percepts and imaginations, and their common opposition to 'signitive' intentions. In all cases we distinguish between an actually given, appearing content, which is *not* what we mean, and an object which *is* what we mean – whether we signify, represent or perceive it – or between a sign-content on the one hand, and the imaginative or perceptual projection of the object on the other. But while sign and thing signified 'have nothing to do with one another', there are inner affinities between a thing's imaginative and perceptual projections and the thing itself, affinities which are part of the very sense of our use of such words. These relationships are phenomenologically documented in differences in their constitutive intentions, and not less in their syntheses of fulfilment.

This account does not, of course, affect our interpretation of *every* fulfilment as being an identification. *In all cases* an intention comes into coincidence with the act which offers it *fulness*, i.e. the object which is meant in it is the same as the object meant in the fulfilling act. We were not, however, comparing these objects of meaning-reference, but signs and projections in their relations to such objects, or to what corresponds phenomenologically to these relationships.

Our interest in the preceding paragraphs was primarily directed to peculiarities in syntheses of fulfilment: these enable us to differentiate intuitive and signitive acts in a merely *indirect* manner. Only in the further course of our investigation – in §26 – shall we be able to give a *direct* characterization, based on an analysis of the intentions, and without regard to their possible fulfilments.

§15 *Signitive intentions beyond the limits of the meaning-function*

In our last discussion we have pinned down certain components of intuitive acts as signitive intentions. But in the whole of our investigations up to this point, signitive acts were for us acts of *meaning*, sense-giving factors attached to expressions. The terms 'signification' and 'signitive intention' were for us synonymous. It is now time to ask ourselves whether the same acts, or acts essentially similar to those found to function in meaning, may not occur quite divorced from this function and from all expressions.

That this question must be answered affirmatively, is shown by certain cases of wordless recognition, which exhibit the precise character of verbal recognition, although words, in their sensuous-signitive content, are not actually present at all. We recognize an object, e.g. as an ancient Roman milestone, its scratchings as weather-worn inscriptions, although no words are aroused at once, or indeed at all. We recognize a tool as a drill, but its name will not come back to us etc. Genetically expressed, present in-

tuitions stir up an associative disposition directed to the significant expression. But the meaning-component of this last alone
is actualized, and this now radiates backwards into the intuition
which aroused it, and overflows into the latter with the character
of a fulfilled intention. These cases of wordless recognition are
none other than fulfilments of meaning-intentions, but phenomenologically divorced from the signitive contents which otherwise
pertain to them. Comparable examples are furnished by reflection
on the normal interweavings of scientific pondering. We observe
here how trains of thought sweep on to a large extent without
bondage to appropriate words, set off by a flood of intuitive
imagery or by their own associative interconnections.

With this is connected the further fact that *expressive* speech
goes so far beyond the intuitive data necessary for the actual
appropriateness of the expression of acquaintance. This has, no
doubt, an opposed ground in the extraordinary ease with which
verbal images are revived by intuitions, and can themselves then
revive symbolic thoughts without corresponding intuitions. But
we must also observe, contrariwise, how the reproduction of
imaged words often lags quite far behind the trains of thought
revived by each present intuition. In both these ways a large
number of inadequate expressions arise, which do not apply in a
straightforward manner to the primary intuitions actually present,
nor to the synthetic formations actually built upon them, but
range far beyond what is thus given. Curious mixtures of acts
result. Objects are, strictly speaking, only 'known', as they are
given in their actual intuitive foundation, but, since the unity of
our intention ranges further, objects appear to be known as what
they are for this total intention. *The character of knowing is accordingly somewhat broadened.* Thus we recognize (know) a person
as an adjutant of the Kaiser, a handwriting as Goethe's, a mathematical expression as the Cardanian formula, and so on. Here our
recognition can of course not apply itself to what is given in
perception, at best it permits possible application to intuitive
sequences, which need not themselves be actualized at all. In this
manner recognitions, and sequences of recognitions, are possible
on a basis of partial intuitions, which would on *a priori* grounds,
not at all be possible on a basis of complete actual intuitions,
since they combine incompatibles in themselves. There are, and
are only too many, *false and even absurd recognitions*. But 'really'

they are not recognitions, i.e. not logically worthwhile, complete 'knowings', not recognitions in the strong sense. To say this is to anticipate later discussions. For we have not yet clarified the ordering of the levels of knowledge (a matter here touched upon), nor the ideals which limit these.

So far we had to do with signitive intentions, which exist identically, and just as they are, both within and without the function of meaning. But countless signitive intentions lack either a fixed or a passing tie with expressions, though their essential character puts them in a class with meaning-intentions. I here recur to the perceptual or imaginative course of a melody, or of some other familiar type of event, and to the definite or indefinite intentions and fulfilments which arise in such a course. I refer likewise to the empirical arrangement and connection of things in their phenomenal coexistence, in regard to whatever gives the things appearing in this order, and especially the parts in each unified individual thing, the character of a *unity involving precisely this order and this form*. Representation and recognition through analogy may unite likeness and original (analogon and analogizatum), and may make them seem to belong together, but they cannot unite what is not merely contiguously given together, but what appears as belonging together. And even if, in the realization of representations through contiguity, images anticipating what is signitively represented are confirmed by their fulfilling originals, the unity among such contiguous representatives and what is represented through them can be given by no relation of picturing (since such a relation is not operative among them) but only through the entirely peculiar relation of signitive representation by way of contiguity.

We may therefore rightly see, in inadequate percepts and imaginations, interwoven masses of primitive intentions, among which, in addition to perceptual and imaginative elements, there are also intentions of a signitive kind. We may therefore maintain, in general, that all phenomenological differences in objectifying acts reduce to their constituent elementary intentions and fulfilments, the former bound to the latter through syntheses of fulfilment. On the side of intentions, the only last differences are those between signitive intentions, as intentions by way of contiguity, and imaginative intentions, as intentions by way of analogy, each plain and pure in their own kind. On the side of fulfilment, intentions of either sort again function as components, but on occasion (as in the case of perception) we have components which cannot be called intentions, since they only fulfil but require no fulfilment, *self*-presentations of the object meant by them in the strictest sense of the word. The character of the elementary acts then determines the characters of the syntheses of fulfilment, which in their turn determine the homogeneous unity of the complex act. The emphatic power of attention helps to transfer the character of this or that elementary act to the unity of the act as a whole: this whole act becomes imagination or signification or pure perception. And where two such unified acts enter into relation, relationships of agreement and conflict arise, whose character is determined by the total acts underlying such relations, and ultimately by their elements.

In the next chapter these relationships will be further tracked down, within the limits in which they can be phenomenologically ascertained and epistemologically evaluated. We shall keep strictly to phenomenologically given unities, and to the sense inherent in these and declared in their fulfilment. We shall thus avoid the temptation to embark on hypothetical construction, with whose doubts a clarification of knowledge should in no way be burdened.

CHAPTER THREE

The Phenomenology of the Levels of Knowledge

---

§16 *Simple identification and fulfilment*

IN describing the relation of significant intention to fulfilling intuition we began with the verbal expression of a percept, and said that the intentional essence of the intuitive act fitted in with, or *belonged* to, the semantic essence of the significative act. This is plainly so in every case of total identification, where acts of like quality, i.e. *both* assertive or *both* unassertive, are synthetically unified; where the acts are of unlike quality, the identification is solely based on their *materials*. This carries over, *mutatis mutandis*, to cases of partial identification, so that we may hold that the *material* or *matter* is the aspect of the character of each act which comes up for synthesis, that is essential for identification (and naturally also for distinction).

In the case of identification, the 'matters' are the special carriers of the synthesis, without themselves being identified. For talk of identification is, in virtue of its sense, concerned with the *objects* presented by such 'matters'. On the other hand, in the act of identification, the matters themselves achieve coincidence. Every example shows, however, that even where qualities are alike, the acts need not become quite alike: this is due to the fact that an act is not exhausted by its intentional essence. What remains over will reveal its importance in a careful phenomenological investigation of the levels of knowledge, which will be our task. It is clear from the start that, if knowledge admits of degrees of perfection, even when matter is constant, matter cannot be responsible for such differences of perfection, and cannot therefore determine the peculiar essence of knowledge as against any identification whatever. We shall tie our further investigation to a discussion of the previously studied difference of *mere identification and fulfilment*.

We equated fulfilment with knowledge (in the narrower sense

of the word) indicating that we were only talking of certain forms of identification which brought us nearer to the *goal of knowledge*. What this means may be elucidated by saying: In each fulfilment there is more or less complete *intuitive illustration* (*Veranschaulichung*). What the intention means, but presents only in more or less inauthentic and inadequate manner, the fulfilment – the act attaching itself to an intention, and offering it 'fulness' in the synthesis of fulfilment – *sets directly before us*, or at least more directly than the intention does. In fulfilment our experience is represented by the words: 'This is the thing *itself*'. This 'itself' must not be understood too strictly, as if there must be some percept bringing the object itself to actual phenomenal presence. It is possible that, in the progress of knowledge, in the gradual ascent from acts of poorer, to acts of ever richer epistemic fulness, we must at length always reach fulfilling percepts: this does not mean that each step, each individual identification that we call a fulfilment, need contain a percept as its fulfilling act. The relative manner in which we speak of 'more or less direct' and of 'self', indicates the main point: that the synthesis of fulfilment involves an *inequality in worth* among its related members. The fulfilling act has a *superiority* which the mere intention lacks: *it imparts to the synthesis the fulness of 'self', at least leads it more directly to the thing itself.* The relativity of this 'directness', this 'self', points further to the fact that the relation of fulfilment is of a sort that admits of degrees. A concatenation of such relations seems accordingly possible where the epistemic superiority steadily increases. Each such ascending series points, however, to an *ideal limit*, or includes it as a final member, a limit setting an unsurpassable goal to all advances: *the goal of absolute knowledge, of the adequate self-presentation of the object of knowledge.*

We have thereby achieved, at least in preliminary fashion,[1] the *characteristic differentiating mark of fulfilments* within the wider class of identifications. For not every identification represents such an approach to a goal of knowledge: there can well be a purpose-less infinity of ever further identifications. There are, e.g., indefinitely many arithmetical expressions having the same numerical value 2, which permit us to add identification to identification *in infinitum*. Just so there may be infinitely many images of one and the same thing, determining again the possibility of endless

[1] Cf. the deeper analyses of §24.

chains of identifications tending to no goal of knowledge. The same holds for the endlessly many percepts of one and the same thing.

If we pay heed to the constitutive elementary intentions in these intuitive examples, we shall of course find moments of true fulfilment entering into the total act of identification. This happens when we set image-presentations side by side which are not of completely equal intuitive content, so that the new image brings out many things much more clearly, and perhaps sets something before us 'just as it is', while a former image merely 'projects' it or denotes it symbolically. If we imaginatively envisage an object turning itself to every side, our sequence of images is constantly linked by syntheses of fulfilment in respect of its partial intentions, but each new image-presentation does not, as a whole, fulfil its predecessor, nor does the whole series progressively approach any goal. Just so in the case of the manifold percepts belonging to the same external thing. Gain and loss are balanced at every step: a new act has richer fulness in regard to certain properties, for whose sake it has lost fulness in regard to others. But against this we may hold that the *whole synthesis* of the series of imaginations or percepts represents an increase in fulness in comparison with an act singled out from the series: the imperfection of the one-sided representation is, relatively speaking, overcome in the all-sided one. We say 'relatively speaking', since the all-sided representation is not achieved in such a synthetic manifold in the single flash which the ideal of adequation requires, as a pure self-presentation without added analogizing or symbolization: it is achieved piecemeal and always blurred by such additions. Another example of an intuitive fulfilment-series is the transition from a rough drawing to a more exact pencil-sketch, then from the latter to the completed picture, and from this to the living finish of the painting, all of which present the same, visibly the same, object.

Such examples from the sphere of mere imagination show that the character of fulfilment does not require that assertive quality in the intending and fulfilling acts which is part of the logical concept of knowledge. We prefer to speak of 'knowledge' where an opinion, in the normal sense of a *belief*, has been confirmed or attested.

§17 *The question of the relation between fulfilment and intuitive illustration*

We must now enquire into the part played in knowledge by the various kinds of objectifying acts – signitive and intuitive acts – and, under the latter rubric, acts of perception and imagination. Here intuitive acts plainly seem to be preferred, so much so, in fact, as to incline one to call all fulfilment *intuitive illustration* (*Veranschaulichung*) – as we did above in passing – or to describe the work of fulfilment, wherever one deals with intuitive intentions, as a mere increase in intuitive fulness. The relation between intention and fulfilment plainly underlies the formation of the conceptual couple: *thought* (more narrowly, *concept*), on the one hand, and *corresponding intuition*, on the other. But we must not forget that a notion of intuition oriented towards this relation does not at all coincide with that of an *intuitive act*, although, through the inherent tendency towards intuition which enters into the sense of all fulfilment, it closely depends on the latter and even presupposes it. To make a thought clear to oneself means, primarily, to give epistemic fulness to the content of one's thought. This can, however, be achieved, *in a certain fashion*, even by a signitive presentation. Of course, if we ask for a clearness which will make matters self-evident, which will make 'the thing itself' clear, render its possibility and its truth knowable, we are referred to intuition in the sense of our intuitive acts. For this reason talk of 'clearness' in epistemological contexts plainly has this narrower sense, it indicates recourse to fulfilling intuition, to the 'originative source' of concepts and propositions in their subject-matters themselves.

Carefully analysed examples are now needed if we are to confirm and develop what has just been suggested. These will help us to clear up the relation between fulfilment and intuitive illustration, and to render quite precise the part played by intuition in *every* fulfilment. Differences between authentic and inauthentic illustration (or fulfilment) will distinguish themselves clearly, and the difference between mere identification and fulfilment will also therewith reach final clarity. The work of intuition will be shown to be that of contributing to the intended act, when authentically fulfilled, a genuinely novel element, to which the name 'fulness' may be given. We are thereby made aware of a hitherto unstressed side of the phenomenological content of acts, which is fundamental for knowledge. 'Fulness' must take its place as a new 'moment' in an intuitive act alongside of its quality and its matter, a moment specially belonging to the matter which it in some manner completes.

§ 18 *The gradations of mediate fulfilments. Mediate presentations*

The formation of every mathematical concept which unfolds itself in a chain of definitions reveals the possibility of *fulfilment-chains built member upon member out of signitive intentions*. We clarify the concept $(5^3)^4$ by having recourse to the definitory presentation: Number which arises when one forms the product $5^3 . 5^3 . 5^3 . 5^3$. If we wish to clarify this latter concept, we must go back to the sense of 5^3, i.e. to the formation $5.5.5$. Going back further, we should have to clarify 5 through the definitory chain $5 = 4 + 1$, $4 = 3 + 1$, $3 = 2 + 1$, $2 = 1 + 1$. After each step we should have to make a substitution in the preceding complex expression or thought, and, were this proceeding indefinitely repeatable – it is certainly so *in itself*, just as it is certainly not so *for us* – we should at last come to the completely explicated sum of ones of which we should say: 'This is the number $(5^3)^4$ "itself"'. It is plain that an act of fulfilment not only corresponded to this final result, but to each individual step leading from one expression of this number, to the expression next in order, which clarified it and enriched its content. In this manner each ordinary decimal number points to a possible chain of fulfilments, whose links are one less in number than the number of their component units, so that chains of indefinitely many numbers are possible *a priori*.

We usually talk as if, in the sphere of mathematics, the straightforward meaning of a word were identical with the content of its complex defining expression. In this case there could be no talk of fulfilment-chains: we should be moving among pure identities wholly tautological in character. But if one considers the complexity of the thought-formations which arise through substitution, and compares them, in those very simple cases where such substitution can be fully carried out, with the significative intentions that one at first experienced, one can hardly seriously think that in these last intentions all this complication was present from the start. It is plain that there are real differences in intention which, whatever their more precise description, are knit together through relationships of fulfilment which identify them as wholes.

A remarkable property of the cases just discussed, and of the class of significative presentations which they illustrate, lies in the fact that in them the *content* of the presentations – or, more clearly their 'matter' – *dictates a determinate order of fulfilment a priori*. The fulfilment which here results mediately, can never also result immediately. To each signitive intention of this class there is a *definite*, proximate fulfilment or group of fulfilments, which in its turn has a definite, proximate fulfilment, etc. This property is also characteristic of certain intuitive intentions, as when we *represent a matter to ourselves through images (pictures) of images (pictures)*. The matter of the presentation here also prescribes a prime fulfilment, which puts the primary image 'itself' before our eyes, but to this intention a new intention pertains, whose fulfilment leads on to the thing itself. What is common to all mediate presentations, whether intuitive or signitive, may be put by saying that they are presentations which do not present their objects straightforwardly, but by way of presentations built upon other presentations to a higher or lower degree. To put it more pointedly, they are presentations which present their objects *as objects of other presentations, or as related to objects so presented*. As objects can be presented in relation to any other objects, so they can be presented in relation to presentations. These presentations are *presented presentations* in the relational presentation: they belong among its intentional *objects*, not among its constituents.

In connection with the class of cases just mentioned, we speak of *mediate* (or superordinate) intentions or fulfilments. The rule holds that *every mediate intention requires a mediate fulfilment*, which naturally, after a finite number of steps, ends up in an immediate intuition.

§ 19 *Distinction between mediate presentations and presentations of presentations*

From these mediate presentations we must, however, distinguish *presentations of presentations*, i.e. presentations simply directed upon other presentations as their objects. Although such presented presentations are, generally speaking, themselves intentions, and so capable of fulfilment, the nature of the presenting presentations which are in question requires no mediate fulfilment through fulfilment of the presented presentation. The intention of $P1$ $(P2)$, a presentation of a presentation, is directed to $P2$: it is fulfilled, and completely fulfilled, when $P2$ 'itself' is present. It is not enriched when the intention of $P2$ is fulfilled in its turn, when its object appears in an image or in a richer image, or even in a percept. For $P1$ refers, not to this object, but only to its presentation $P2$. Nothing obviously alters if the *emboîtement* becomes more complex, e.g. in the case expressed by the symbol $P1(P2(P3))$ etc.

The thought 'signitive presentation', for instance, is fulfilled in the intuition of a signitive presentation, e.g. of the presentation 'integral', or of the presentation 'signitive presentation' itself. These examples must not be misunderstood as meaning that the signitive presentation 'integral' itself claimed an intuitive status, as if the concepts of *intuition* and *signitive act* (meaning-intention) were here confounded. It is not the signitive presentation 'integral' but the *inner percept* of this presentation that serves as the fulfilling intuition to the thought 'signitive presentation'. This presentation is not the fulfilling intuition, but the *object* of the fulfilling intuition. As the thought of a colour has its fulfilment in the act of intuiting this colour, so the thought of a thought has its fulfilment in an act of intuiting this thought, and its final intuitive fulfilment in an adequate percept of the same. Here as elsewhere, the mere being of an experience involves neither its intuition, nor, more particularly, its perception. It must be noted that, in our general opposition between thought or intention, and fulfilling intuition, intuition is not to be understood as mere outward intuition, the perceiving or imagining of external physical objects. As our just discussed example shows, and as the nature of presentation makes obvious, 'inner' perception or 'inner' imagination can function as a fulfilling intuition.

§ 20 *Genuine intuitive illustration in every fulfilment. Authentic and inauthentic intuitive illustration*

Now that we have sufficiently stressed and clarified the distinction between mediate presentations and presentations of presentations, it will be proper to turn to what they have in common. Each mediate presentation includes, on the above analysis, presentations of presentations, inasmuch as it refers to its object as the object of certain presentations, which it itself presents. Thus if we think of 1000 as 10^3, we think of it as the number characterized as the *object* of the *presentation* which would arise were we to carry out the exponentiation in question. From this it is clear that *genuinely intuitive illustrations play the essential part in all fulfilment of mediate intentions, and at each step in such fulfilment.* The characterization of an object as object of a presented presentation (or as one related in a certain manner to objects so defined) presupposes in its fulfilment the fulfilment of these presentations of presentations, and these 'inwoven' *intuitive* fulfilments are the first to give the whole identification its character of a fulfilment. Its gradual increase in 'fulness' consists solely in the fact that, one by one, all its presentations of presentations have been fulfilled, whether such presentations were 'inwoven' in it from the beginning, or have emerged in the process of fulfilment through realizing 'construction' of these *presented presentations*, and through *intuition* of them when realized, so that in the end the dominant, total intention, with its structure of conjoined and subordinate intentions, appears as identified with an immediate intention. This last identification thereby has as a whole the *character of a fulfilment.* This kind of fulfilment is, however, a case of *inauthentic* intuitive illustration, since we are only entitled to predicate *authentic intuitive illustration* if fulness is not added *anywhere*, but only imparts an increase to the object presented by the presentation *as a whole*, which accordingly becomes more fully presented. This means no more, ultimately, than that a purely signitive presentation is without any fulness, and that all fulness rather resides in the actual 'making present' (*Vergegenwärtigung*) of properties that pertain to the object itself.

We shall presently pursue this last thought. Here we shall add that the difference we called one of 'authentic' and 'inauthentic intuitive illustration' could also be called one of *authentic and inauthentic fulfilment*, since an intention aims at its object, is as it were desirous of it, and since *fulfilment, in the pregnant sense of the word* only registers the fact that some part of the fulness of the object is imparted to the intention. We must, however, still hold that inauthentic and authentic fulfilments are alike marked out among syntheses of identification by a common phenomenological character (that of fulfilment in the wider sense), and that there is a peculiar principle to the effect that *all inauthentic fulfilment implies authentic fulfilments*, and indeed borrows its character of fulfilment from these authentic cases.

To demarcate the difference between authentic and inauthentic intuitive illustrations somewhat more precisely, and at the same time deal with a class of cases where inauthentic intuitive illustrations have every appearance of authenticity, we add the following remarks:

It is not always the case that, when the fulfilment of a signitive intention is consummated on an intuitive basis, the 'matters' of the acts concerned, as presupposed above, are in a *relationship of coincidence*, so that the object which appears intuitively also comes before us as *itself* meant in our act of meaning. Only *when this happens*, however, *may one talk of intuitive illustration in the true sense*: only then is a thought realized perceptually, or illustrated imaginatively. The case is different when the fulfilling intuition presents an *indirectly* represented object, as when the use of a geographical name calls up the imaginative presentation of a map, which blends with the meaning-intention of this name, or as when a statement about certain street-connections, courses of rivers, features of mountains, is confirmed by what stands inscribed on a map before us. Here intuition should not be said to fulfil in the true sense of the word: its own matter does not enter into action. The real basis of fulfilment does not lie in it at all, but in a plainly *signitive* intention intertwined with it. That the apparent object here functions as *indirectly* representing the object meant and named, means, phenomenologically speaking, that its constitutive intuition is now the bearer of a novel intention, an intention pointing beyond the apparent object, and thereby characterizing it as a sign. The analogy of what appears and what is meant, which may be present here, does not lead to a straightforward presentation by way of an image, but to a sign-presentation resting upon the latter. The outline of England as drawn in the map, may indeed represent the form of the land itself, but the pictorial image of the map which comes up when England is mentioned, does not *mean* England itself in pictorial fashion, not even mediately, as the country pictured on the map. It means England after the manner of a mere sign, through external relations of association, which have tied all our knowledge of land and people to the map-picture. When, therefore, our naming intention is fulfilled through this mental picture, it is not the object imagined in the latter (the map), which counts as the very thing meant by the name, but the original object which the name represents.

§21 The 'fulness' of a presentation

It will, however, now be necessary to view the achievement of intuitive intentions more closely. Since the fulfilment of mediate intentions refers back to the fulfilment, the intuitive fulfilment of immediate intentions, and since it has transpired that the final outcome of the whole mediate process is an immediate intention, we now concern ourselves with the question of the intuitive fulfilment of immediate intentions and of the relationships and laws governing their sphere. This question we therefore attack. But we may observe from the start that, in the following investigations, only the 'matter'-side of an act's intentional essence will have relevance for the relationships to be established. The qualities of our intention (whether assertive or merely presentative) can be varied indifferently.

We begin with the following proposition:

To every intuitive intention there pertains, in the sense of an ideal possibility, a signitive intention precisely accommodated to its material. This unity of identification necessarily has the character of a unity of fulfilment, in which the intuitive, not the signitive member, has the character of being the fulfiller, and so also, in the most authentic sense, the *giver* of fulness.

We only express the sense of this last statement in a different way if we say that signitive intentions are in themselves '*empty*', and that they 'are in *need* of fulness'. In the transition from a signitive intention to the corresponding intuition, we experience no mere increase, as in the change from a pale image or a mere sketch to a fully alive painting. The signitive intention is rather lacking in every sort of fulness: the intuitive presentation first brings fulness to it, and, through identification, into it. A signitive intention merely points to its object, an intuitive intention gives it 'presence', in the pregnant sense of the word, it imports something of the fulness of the object itself. However far an imaginative presentation may lag behind its object, it has many features in common with it, more than that, it is like this object, depicts it, makes it really present to us. A signitive presentation, however, does not present analogically, it is 'in reality' no 'presentation', in it nothing of the object comes to life. The ideal of complete fulness is, accordingly, the fulness of the object itself, as the sum total of its constitutive properties. The *fulness of the presentation* is, however, the sum total of properties pertaining to the presentation itself, through which it analogically gives presence to its object, or apprehends it as itself given. *Fulness is, accordingly, a characteristic moment of presentations alongside of quality and matter,* a positive constituent only in the case of intuitive presentations, a privation of the case of signitive. The 'clearer' a presentation is, the higher its *pictorial level,* the richer it is in fulness. The ideal of *fulness* would, accordingly, be reached in a presentation which would embrace its object, entire and whole, in its phenomenological content. If we include individualizing features in the fulness of the object, such features can be embraced by no imagination, only by a percept. But, if we ignore these features, a definite ideal exists for imagination as well.

We must accordingly return to the features of the presented object: *The more of these features enter into the analogical representation,* and, as regards each separate feature, the greater the similarity with which the presentation represents it in its content, the greater is the fulness of the presentation. Somehow, no doubt, *every* feature of an object is included in the scope of every presentation, and so in that of the pictorial presentation, but not every property is analogically represented, *the phenomenological content of the presentation does not contain a peculiar, so-to-say analogizing or depicting moment for each. The sum total of the intimately fused moments* which are thought to underlie *purely* intuitive (in this case imaginative) ways of regarding things, which first gives them the character of being representative of corresponding objective moments, constitutes the *fulness* of the imaginative presentation. Hence in addition to imaginative representations, there are also perceptual ones, graspings of the thing itself, self-exhibitions of objective moments. If we assemble the sum total of the imaginatively or perceptively functioning moments of the perceptual presentation, we have marked off the fulness of the latter.

§22 *Fulness and intuitive substance (Gehalt)*

Closely regarded, the concept of fulness is still fraught with an ambiguity. The above mentioned moments can be looked at in respect of their own existential content, without regard to the functions of pure imagination or perception, which first confer on them the value of being a picture or a perspectivally slanted self-revelation, and so a value for the function of fulfilment. On the other hand, one can consider these moments *in* their interpretation, i.e. not these moments alone, but the full pictures or slanted self-revelations in question. Ignoring only intentional qualities, one can deal with purely intuitive acts as wholes, which include these moments in themselves, since they give them an objective significance. These 'purely intuitive' acts we conceive as mere constituents of the intuitions just mentioned, being the element in them which gives to the moments previously mentioned, a relation to corresponding objective properties which are represented through them. We ignore therewith (in addition to the qualities) the yet further attached *signitive* relations to further parts or sides of the object *which are not, properly speaking, (intuitively) represented*.

It is plainly these purely intuitive constituents which impart to total acts the character of percepts or imaginings, i.e. their intuitive character, and which function in the system of serially ordered fulfilments as the element which confers 'fulness', or which enriches or increases the same when already present. To deal with this ambiguity in our talk of 'fulness' we shall introduce the following distinguishing terms:

By *intuitively presentative or intuitively representative contents (Inhalten)* we understand those contents of intuitive acts which, owing to the purely imaginative or perceptual interpretations that they sustain, point unambiguously to definitely corresponding contents in the object, represent these in imagined or perceived perspectival slantings. The act-aspects which characterize them in this manner, we ignore. Since the character of imagination lies in analogical picturing, in 'representation' in a narrower sense, while the character of perception can be called strictly presentative, the following distinctive names suggest themselves: For the intuitively presentative contents in either case – *analogizing* or *picturing* contents, on the one hand, and *strictly presentative* or *self-presentative* contents, on the other. The expressions 'imaginatively slanted contents' and 'perceptively slanted contents' are also very apt. The intuitively presentative contents of outer perception define the concept of *sensation* in the ordinary, narrow sense. The intuitively presentative contents of external fantasy are *sensory phantasms* or images.

The intuitively presentative or intuitively representative contents in and with the interpretation put upon them, we call the *intuitive substance (Gehalt) of the act*: in this we still ignore the quality of the act (whether assertive or not), as being indifferent to the distinctions in question. On the above, all signitive components of an act are excluded from its intuitive 'substance'.[1]

§ 23 *Relationships of weight between the intuitive and signitive 'substance' (Gehalt) of one and the same act. Pure intuition and pure signification. Perceptual and imaginal content, pure perception and pure imagination. Gradations of fulness*

To increase the clearness of the concepts just marked off, and to aid in the marking off of a new set of concepts, rooted in the same soil, we embark on the following discussion:

In an intuitive presentation (*Vorstellung*) an object is meant in the manner of perception or imagination: in this manner it is more or less perfectly made apparent. To each part and each property of the object, including its reference to a *here* and a *now*, there must necessarily be a corresponding part or moment of the conscious act. What we do not mean, is simply not there for our presentation (*Vorstellung*). We now find in general that it is possible to draw the following phenomenological distinction between

(1) *The purely intuitive 'substance' (Gehalt)* of the act, i.e. all that corresponds in the act to the sum total of the object's properties that 'become apparent',

(2) *The signitive 'substance'* of the act, which corresponds to the sum total of the remaining, subsidiarily given properties of the object, which do not themselves become apparent.

We all draw such a distinction, in purely phenomenological

---

[1] In the above paragraph, the German terms '*darstellen*', '*Darstellung*' etc. are translated by 'intuitively present', 'intuitive presentation' etc. The terms 'strictly present' etc. are used to translate '*präsentieren*' etc. 'Presentation' *simpliciter* still translates '*Vorstellung*'.

fashion, in the intuition involved in the percept or image of a thing, between whatever in the object is truly made apparent, the mere 'side' from which the object is shown to us, and whatever lacks intuitive presentation (*Darstellung*), is hidden by other phenomenal objects etc. Such talk plainly implies, what phenomenological analysis within certain limits definitely proves, that even what is *not* presented (*Nicht-Dargestelltes*) in an intuitive presentation (*Vorstellung*) is subsidiarily meant, and that an array of signitive components must accordingly be ascribed to the latter, from which we have to abstract, if we wish to keep our *intuitive* content pure. This last gives the intuitively presenting (*darstellende*) content its direct relation to corresponding objective moments: other novel, and, to that extent, mediate, signitive intentions, are attached to these by contiguity.

If we now define the *weight* of the intuitive (or signitive) content as the sum total of the intuitively (or signitively) presented (*vorgestellte*) moments of the object, both 'weights' in each presentation (*Vorstellung*) will add up to a single total weight, i.e. the sum total of the object's properties. Always therefore the symbolic equation holds: $i+s = 1$. The weights i and s can plainly vary in many regards: the same, intentionally same, object can be intuitively given with more or less numerous, ever varying properties. The signitive content also alters correspondingly, it is increased or diminished.

Ideally we now have the possibility of two limiting cases:

$$i = 0 \quad s = 1$$
$$i = 1 \quad s = 0.$$

In the former, the presentation (*Vorstellung*) would have only signitive content: no property of its intentional object would remain over which was brought to intuitive presentation (*Darstellung*) in its content. The special case of purely signitive presentations, well-known to us as pure meaning-intentions, therefore appears here as a limiting case of intuition.

In the second case the presentation (*Vorstellung*) has *no* signitive content whatever. In it all is fulness: no part, no side, no property of its object fails to be intuitively presented (*dargestellt*), none is merely indirectly and subsidiarily meant. Not only is everything that is intuitively presented also meant – so much is analytically true – but whatever is meant is also intuitively presented. This new class of presentations may be defined as *pure intuitions*, the term here used with innocuous ambiguity, at times to cover complete acts, at times such acts in abstraction from their quality. We may speak distinguishingly of *qualified* and *unqualified* pure intuitions.

In each presentation (*Vorstellung*) we can therefore surely abstract from all signitive components, and limit ourselves to what is really represented in its representative content. By so doing we form a *reduced* presentation, with a reduced object in regard to which it is purely intuitive. We can accordingly say that the *intuitive substance* (*Gehalt*) of a presentation comprises *all that is pure intuition in it*, just as we may also speak of *the object's* purely intuitive content, of all that is rendered intuitive in this presentation. The like applies to the signitive substance of the presentation: this can be said to be all that is *pure signification* in it.

Each total act of intuition has either the character of a percept or an imagination: its intuitive substance is then either *perceptual* or *imaginative* substance or content. This must not be confused with the perceptually or imaginatively presenting content in the sense defined in §22.

Perceptual content comprises (though not in general exclusively) strictly presentative contents: imaginative contents comprise only analogizing contents. It is not to the point that these latter contents permit of *another* interpretation (as in the case of physical images), in which they function strictly presentatively.

On account of the mixture of perceptual and imaginative components which the intuitive substance of a percept permits and usually exhibits, we can again consider adopting a division of perceptual content into *pure perceptual content*, on the one hand, and *supplementary image-content*, on the other.

If then, in each pure intuition we take P_p and I_p to be the weights of its *purely* perceptual and *purely* imaginative components, we can write down the symbolic equation

$$P_p + I_p = 1$$

where 1 symbolizes the weight of the total intuitive content of the pure intuition, and thus the total content of its object. If $I_p = 0$, i.e. if the pure intuition is free from all imaginal content, it should be called a *pure perception*: we shall here ignore the qualitatively assertive character usually embraced in the sense of the term 'perception'. But if $P_p = 0$, the intuition is called *pure imagination*. The 'purity' of pure perception relates, therefore, not merely to signitive, but also to imaginative supplements. The narrowing of an impure percept which throws out symbolic components yields the pure intuition which is immanent in it: a further reductive step then throws out everything imagined, and yields the substance of pure perception.

Can the intuitively presentative content in the case of pure perception be identified with the object itself? The essence of pure presentation (in the strict sense) surely consists in being a pure self-presentation of the object, one which means the intuitively presentative content *directly* (in the manner of 'self') as its object. This would, however, be a paralogism. The percept, as presentation in the strict sense, so interprets the intuitively presentative content, that the object appears as itself given with and in this content. Presentation (in the strict sense) is *pure*, when each part of the object is actually and intuitively presented in the content, and none is merely imagined or symbolized. As there is nothing in the object not strictly presented, so there is nothing in the content not strictly presentative. Despite such exact correspondence, self-presentation may still have the character of the mere, even if all-sided perspectivity (of a completed perceptual picture): it need not attain the ideal of adequation, where the intuitively presenting content is also the intuitively presented content. The pure picture-presentation, which completely depicts its object through its freedom from all signitive additions, holds in its intuitively presentative content a complete likeness of the object. This likeness can approach the object more or less closely, to a limit of complete resemblance. The same may be true in the case of pure perception, with the sole difference, that imagination treats the content as a likeness or image, whereas perception looks on it as a self-revelation of the object. Pure perception no less than pure imagination admits, accordingly, of differing degrees of fulness, without thereby altering its intentional object. Regarding the *degrees of fulness of intuitive content*, to which degrees of fulness of representative content run *eo ipso* parallel, we may distinguish:

1. The *extent* or *richness* of the fulness, according as the content of the object achieves intuitive presentation with greater or less completeness.

2. The *liveliness* of this fulness, i.e. the degree of approximation of the primitive resemblances of the intuitive presentation to the corresponding moments of content in the object.

3. The reality-level (*Realitätsgehalt*) of the fulness, the greater or less number of its strictly presentative contents.

In all these regards, adequate perception represents an ideal: it has a maximum of extent, liveliness and reality: it is the self-apprehension of the whole, full object.

§ 24 *Graded series of fulfilments*

We framed our talk of 'fulness' with an eye to relationships of 'fulfilment', that peculiar form of the synthesis of identification. But in our last results we not only threw light on the concept of fulness, but also on its differences of greater or lesser complete-ness, liveliness and reality, as well as on the gradations in pictor-ialization and perspectival projection, and all by way of relation-ships among the inner 'moments' of our presentations, or among these and the objective moments that they intend. But it is plain that to these relationships there correspond *possible gradients of increase, founded on syntheses of fulfilment.*

Fulfilment arises out of the first application of fulness as such, in the identifying accommodation of 'corresponding' intuition to a signitive intention. In the context of coincidence the intuitive act 'gives' its fulness to the signitive act. The consciousness of in-crease is here founded on the partial coincidence of the fulness with correlative parts of the signitive intention, while to the correspond-ing empty parts of both intentions, which alike enter this identify-ing coincidence, no part of this sense of increase can be ascribed.

A continuous increase in fulfilment is further achieved in the con-tinuity of intuitive acts or serial fulfilments which present the object with ever more extended and intense illustrativeness. That B_2 is a 'more perfect' image than B_1, means that fulfilment obtains in the synthetic context of the pictorial presentation in question, and increased fulfilment in the direction of B_2. Here as elsewhere distances pertain to increases, and transitivity to concatenated relationships. If B_2 is at once $> B_1$, and $B_3 > B_2$, then $B_3 > B_1$ and this last distance exceeds those which mediate it. This is so at least if we take separate account of the three moments of fulness, i.e. extent, liveliness and reality, which were distinguished above.

These increases and gradients of increase correspond, as analysis shows, to resemblances and gradients of resemblance among the *intuitively presentative* contents of the fulnesses. Likeness of presentative contents, or concatenations of such likenesses, are not, however, to be taken to be the same as simple or concatenated increases: they are not so when these 'fulnesses' are considered in their own being as contents, in abstraction from their representative function in the relevant acts. Only through this latter function, i.e. through the fact that, in the order of graded fulfilments, and of the increases obtaining among its acts, each later act of fulness appears richer, do the representative contents of the acts achieve their ascending order. They appear one after the other as not only themselves furnishing fulness, but as furnishing it ever more abundantly. To call such components 'fulnesses' is to talk relatively and functionally: it is to express a characteristic accruing to the contents through the acts, and through the part played by these acts in possible syntheses of fulfilment. Our term here resembles the term 'object'. To be an object represents no positive mark, no possible species of content: it refers to the content only as intentionally correlated with a presentation. For the rest, relationships of fulfilment and increase plainly have their foundation in the phenomenological 'substance' (*Gehalt*) of our acts, *considered purely in their specificity*. We are concerned throughout only with ideal relationships determined by the ideal Species in question.

In the synthesis of intuitive acts there is, however, not always an increase in fulness: partial fulfilment can go hand in hand with partial emptying, as we mentioned above. *The distinction between mere identification and fulfilment* points back to the fact, we may say, that in the case of the former there may be either no genuine fulfilment, since we have to do only with asserted identities among acts alike lacking in fulness, or because the fulfilment or enriched fulfilment which obtains goes together with a simultaneous emptying or surrender of previous fulness, so that no emphatic unmixed consciousness of increase arises. In any case the primitive relations among our elementary intentions are either fulfilments of empty (i.e. purely signitive) intentions, or supplementary fulfilment of intentions already to some extent filled, i.e. increase and realization of an imaginative intention.

§25 *Fulness and intentional 'matter'*

We now wish to discuss the relation between the new concept of presentational content covered by the name 'fulness', with content in the sense of 'matter', which last has played such a large part in our investigation up to this point. 'Matter' was classed as that moment in an objectifying act which makes the act present *just this object in just this manner*, i.e. in just these articulations and forms, and with special relation to just these properties or relationships. Presentations which agree in their matter do not merely present the same object in some general fashion: they mean it in the most complete fashion *as* the same, as having exactly the same properties. The one presentation confers nothing on the object in its intention which the other presentation does not likewise confer. To each objectifying articulation and form on one side there is a corresponding articulation and form on the other, in such a manner that the agreeing elements of the presentations have an identical objective reference. In this sense we said in our Fifth Investigation, in elucidating the concepts of 'matter' and 'semantic essence': 'Two judgements are in essence the same judgement (i.e. judgements with the same 'matter'), if everything that would hold of the state of affairs judged according to one, would likewise hold of it according to the other, and nothing different would hold of it in either case. The truth-value of the judgements is the same'. They *mean* the same in regard to the object, even if they are otherwise quite different, if the one, e.g., is achieved signitively, while the other is more or less illustrated by intuition.

I was led to form this notion through a consideration of what is identical in the assertive and understanding use of the same expression, where one may 'believe' the content of some statement, while another leaves it undecided, without disturbing this content's identity, in which case it also makes no difference whether expression occurs in connection with correspondent intuition, and whether it can so occur or not. One might therefore be tempted – I myself hesitated long on this point – to define meaning as this very 'matter', which would, however, have the inconvenience that the moment of *assertion* in, e.g., a predicative statement, would fall outside of that statement's meaning. (One could no doubt limit the concept of meaning in this fashion, and then distinguish between qualified and unqualified meanings.) Our comparison of meaning-intentions with their correlative intuitions, in the static and dynamic unity of identifying coincidence, showed us, however, that the very thing that we marked off as the 'matter' of meaning, reappeared once more in the corresponding intuition, and furnished the means for an identification. Our freedom, therefore, to add to or take away intuitive elements, and even all correspondent intuitions, wherever we limited our concern to the abiding meaningfulness of a given expression, was based on the fact that the whole act attaching to the sound of our words had the same 'matters' on the intuitive as on the meaning side, in respect, that is, of such elements of meaning as receive intuitive illustration at all.

It is clear, therefore, that the concept of 'matter' must be defined by way of the unity of total identification as *the element in our acts which serves as a basis for identification*, and that all differences of fulness which go beyond mere identification, and which variously determine peculiarities of fulfilment and increase of fulfilment, have no relevance in the formation of this conception. However the fulness of a presentation may vary within its possible gradients of fulfilment, its intentional object, intended as it is intended, remains the same: its 'matter', in other words, stays the same. Matter and fulness are, however, by no means unrelated, and, when we range an intuitive act alongside a signitive act to which it brings fulness, the former act does not differ from the latter merely by the joining on of a third distinct moment of fulness to the quality and matter common to the two acts. This at least is not the case where we mean by 'fulness' the intuitive content of intuition. For intuitive content itself already includes a complete 'matter', the matter of an act *reduced* to a pure intuition. If the intuitive act in question was already *purely* intuitive, its matter also would be a constituent of its intuitive content.

The relations which obtain here will be best set forth by establishing the following parallelism between signitive and intuitive acts.

A purely *signitive* act would be a mere complex of quality and matter, if indeed it could exist by itself at all, i.e. be a concrete experiential unity 'on its own'. This it cannot be: we always find it clinging to some intuitive basis. This intuition of a sign may have 'nothing at all to do' with the object of the significative act, it may stand to it in no relation of fulfilment, but it realizes its possibility *in concreto* of being an altogether unfulfilled act. The following proposition therefore seems to hold: An act of signification is only possible in so far as an intuition becomes endued with a new intentional essence, whereby its intuitive object points beyond itself in the manner of a sign (whether as a sign regularly or fleetingly used). More closely considered, this proposition does not, however, seem to express the necessities of connection which obtain here with the needed analytic clearness, and perhaps says more than is justified. For we can, it seems, say that *it is not our founding intuition as a whole, but only its representational content,* which really assists the signitive act. For what goes beyond this content, what pins down the sign as a natural object, *can be varied at will* without disturbing the sign's signitive function. Whether the letters of a verbal sign are of wood, iron or printer's ink etc., or seem to be such objectively, makes no difference. Only their repeatedly recognizable shape is relevant, not as the objective shape of the thing of wood etc., but as the shape actually present in the intuitively presentative sensuous content of intuition. If there is only a connection between the signitive act and the intuitively presentative content of our intuition, and if the quality and matter of this intuition mean nothing to this signitive function, then we ought not to say that each signitive act requires a founding intuition, but only that it requires a founding content. It would seem that *any* content can function in this fashion, just as any content can function as the intuitively presentative content of an intuition.

If we now turn our regard to the parallel case of the *purely intuitive act,* its quality and matter (its intentional essence) are not capable of separate existence on their own: here too a supplement is required. This is furnished by the representative content, i.e. the content – sensuous in the case of a sensuous intuition – which in its present fusion with an intentional essence has acquired the character of being an intuitive representative. If we bear in mind the fact that the same (e.g. sensuous) content can at one time carry a meaning, and at another time an intuition – denoting in one case and picturing in the other – we are led to widen the notion of a representative content, and to distinguish between *contents which represent signitively* (signitive representatives) and *contents which represent intuitively* (intuitive representatives).

Our division is, however, incomplete. We have so far considered only the purely intuitive or purely signitive acts. If we bring in the *mixed* acts as well, those we ordinarily class as intuitive, we find them peculiar in the fact that their representative content is pictorial or self-presentative in respect of one part of what it objectively presents, while being merely denotative as to the remaining part. We must accordingly range *mixed* representatives beside purely signitive and purely intuitive representatives: *these represent signitively and intuitively at the same time, and in regard to the same intentional essence.* We may now say:

Each concretely complete objectifying act has three components: its quality, its matter and its representative content. To the extent that this content functions as a purely signitive or purely intuitive representative, or as both together, the act is a purely signitive, a purely intuitive or a mixed act.

§ 26 *Continuation. Representation or interpretation (Auffassung). Matter as the interpretative sense, the interpretative form and the interpreted content. Differentiating characterization of intuitive and signitive interpretation*

We may now ask *what this 'functioning' really stands for*, since we have it as an *a priori* possibility that the same content, bound up with the same quality and matter, should function in this threefold manner. It is plain that it can only be *the phenomenological peculiarity of the relevant form of unity* that can give a phenomenologically discoverable content to our distinction. This form specially unites the *matter* to the representative content, since the representative function is unaffected by change in the quality. Whether, e.g., an imaginative picturing claims to be the calling up of a real object or to be merely imaginative, makes no difference to its pictorially presentative character, that its content bears the function of an image-content. We therefore call *the phenomenological union of matter with representative content*, in so far as it lends the latter its representative character, the *form of representation*, and the *whole* engendered by these two moments the representation *pure and simple*. This designation expresses the relation between representing and represented content (latter = the object or part of the object represented) by going back to its phenomenological foundation. Leaving aside the object as something not phenomenologically given, and endeavouring merely to express the fact that,

when a content functions representatively, we are always differently 'minded', we may speak of a change in *interpretation*
(*Auffassung*). We may also call the form of representation the
interpretative form. Since the matter after a manner fixes the *sense*
in which the representative content is interpreted, we may also
speak of the *interpretative sense*. If we wish to recall the older term,
and at the same time indicate an opposition to form, we may also
speak of the *interpretative matter*. In each interpretation we must
therefore distinguish phenomenologically between: *interpretative
matter* or *sense*, *interpretative form* and *interpreted content*; this last is
to be distinguished from *the object of the interpretation*. The term
'apperception' is unsuitable despite its historical provenance,
on account of its misleading terminological opposition to 'perception'; 'apprehension' would be more usable.

Our next question concerns the distinguishing marks of the
various modes of representation or interpretation, which, as we
saw, can be different even when the interpretative matter – the
'as what' of interpretation – is constant. In the previous chapter
we characterized differences of representations through differences
in forms of fulfilment, in the present context we have regard to an
internal characterization limited to the proper descriptive stuff
of intentions. If we may make use of the beginnings of an analytical clarification which our previous treatment suggested, as well
as of our subsequent advances in the general grasp of 'representation', the following train of ideas suggests itself:

We begin with the observation that *signitive representation* institutes a *contingent, external* relation between matter and representative content, whereas intuitive representation institutes one that
is *essential, internal*. The contingency of the former consists in the
fact that an identical signification can be thought of as attached
to every content whatsoever. *Significative matter has a general need
for supporting content, but between the specific nature of the former and
the specific being of the latter no bond of necessity can be found.* Meaning
cannot, as it were, hang in the air, but for what it means, the sign,
whose meaning we call it, is entirely indifferent.

The case of *purely intuitive representation* is quite different. Here
*there is an internal, necessary connection between matter and representing
content*, fixed by the specific stuff of both. Only those contents can
be intuitively representative of an object that resemble it or are
like it. Phenomenologically put: we are not wholly free to inter-

pret a content *as* this or *as* that (or in this or that interpretative sense) and this has more than an empirical foundation – *every* interpretation including a significative one is empirically necessary – since the content to be interpreted sets limits to us through a certain sphere of similarity and exact likeness, i.e. through its specific substance. The internality of the relation does not merely forge a link between *the interpretative matter as a whole* and *the whole content*: it links their parts on each side *piece by piece*. This occurs in the presupposed case of pure intuition. In the case of *impure intuition* the specific union is partial: a part of the matter – the matter of the reduced, and therefore, of course, pure, intuition – provides the intuitive sense in which the content is interpreted, while the remainder of the matter undergoes no representation through similarity or exact likeness, but merely through contiguity, i.e. in mixed intuition the representative content functions as intuitive representative for one part of the matter, but as signitive representative for the remaining part.

If one finally asks how one and the same content (in the sense of 'same matter') can at times be 'taken up' in the manner of an intuitive, and at times in the manner of a signitive representative, in what the differing nature of these interpretative forms consists, I can give them no further answer. We are facing a difference that cannot be phenomenologically reduced.

In these discussions we have treated representation independently as a union of matter and representative content. If we go back again to the complete acts, these reveal themselves as combinations of act-quality with either intuitive or signitive representation. The whole acts are called intuitive or signitive, a difference determined by these inwrought representations. The study of relations of fulfilment led us above to the concept of intuitive substance or fulness. If we compare that case of concept-formation with the present one, it sets bounds to the purely intuitive representation (i.e. pure intuition) that belongs to an act of impure intuition. 'Fulness' was a notion specially framed for the comparative treatment of acts in their fulfilling function. The limiting case opposed to pure intuition, pure signification, is of course the same as purely signitive representation.

§ 27 *Representations as the necessary bases of presentation in all acts. Final clarification of talk about the different modes of the relation of consciousness to its object*

Each objectifying act includes a representation in itself. Every act whatever, following the conclusions of the Fifth Investigation (see particularly the penultimate chapter, §41) is either itself an objectifying act, or has such an act as its basis. The ultimate bases of all acts are therefore 'presentations' in the sense of representations.

Talk of *the differing mode of relation of an act to its objects* has been shown, in the above discussions, to cover the following essential ambiguities:

1. The quality of acts, the modes of believing, entertaining, wishing, doubting etc.

2. The underlying *representation*, and

(a) *the interpretative form*, i.e. whether the object is presented in purely signitive, or intuitive, or mixed fashion. Here also belong the differences between a perceptual and an imaginative presentation etc.;

(b) *the interpretative matter*: whether the object is presented in this or that 'sense', e.g. significatively through differing meanings, presenting the same object but qualifying it differently;

(c) *the interpreted contents*: whether the object is presented by way of this or that sign, or by way of this or that representative content. In the latter case, if we consider the matter more closely, the laws connecting intuitive representatives with matter and form, entail that we are also concerned with differences that affect form even where matter remains constant.

§ 28 *Intentional essence and fulfilling sense. Epistemic essence. Intuitions in specie*

In our First Investigation (§ 14) we opposed 'fulfilling sense' to meaning (or fulfilling meaning to intending meaning) by pointing to the fact that, in fulfilment, the object is 'given' intuitively in the same way in which the mere meaning means it. We then took the ideally conceived element which thus coincides with the meaning, to be the *fulfilling sense*, and said that, through this coincidence, the merely significant intention (or expression) achieved relation to the intuitive object (expressed this and just this object).

This entails, to employ conceptual formations later introduced, that the fulfilling sense is interpreted as the intentional essence of the completely and adequately fulfilling act.

This conceptual formation is entirely correct and suffices for the purpose of pinning down the entirely general aspects of the situation where a signitive intention achieves relation to its intuitively presented object: it expresses the important insight that the semantic essence of the signitive (or expressive) act reappears *identically* in corresponding intuitive acts, despite phenomenological differences on either side, and that the living unity of identification realizes this coincidence itself, and so realizes the relation of the expression to what it expresses. On the other hand it is clear, in virtue precisely of this identity, that the 'fulfilling sense' carries no implication of fulness, that *it does not accordingly include the total content of the intuitive act, to the extent that this is relevant for the theory of knowledge.* It might be thought objectionable that we have conceived the intentional essence so narrowly as to exclude such an important constituent of the act, and one so decisive for knowledge. We were guided by the thought that the essence of an objectifying intention must be something which no intention of this sort could lack, or which could not be freely varied in it, without having an ideally necessary effect on its relation to its object. Purely signitive acts are, however, 'empty' acts, acts lacking in the moment of fulness, and so only the unity of quality and matter can count as the essence of an objectifying act. It might now be objected that signitive intentions without sensuous support are impossible, that they also have intuitive fulness in their fashion. But, in the sense of our treatment of signitive representation, and our earlier treatments of authentic and inauthentic illustration, this is really not fulness. Or rather it is fulness, but not fulness of the signitive act, but of the act on which it is founded, the act in which the sign is set up as an intuitive object. This fulness may, we saw, vary without limit, without affecting the signitive intention, and what concerns *its* object. Taking into account this circumstance, as well as the fact that, even in intuitive acts, fulness may vary, albeit within bounds, while the same object is constantly meant, with the same properties and with the same act-quality, we plainly need a term to stand for the mere unity of quality with matter.

But it is now also useful, on the other hand, to frame a more embracing concept. We accordingly define as *the epistemic essence of an objectifying act* (in opposition to its merely *semantic* essence) *all the content which has relevance for its knowledge-function*. The three components of quality, matter and fulness (or intuitive content) all belong to it. If we wish to avoid the overlap of the last two components, and have wholly exclusive components, we may make it consist of quality, matter and *intuitively representative content*, the last of which falls away in empty intentions, together with all 'fulness'.

All objectifying acts having the same epistemic essence are the 'same' act for the ideal purposes of the theory of knowledge. When we speak of objectifying acts *in specie*, we have a corresponding idea in mind. The same holds of (deliberately) restrictive talk of *intuitions in specie* etc.

§29 *Complete and mutilated intuitions. Adequate and objectively complete intuitive illustrations. Essentia*

In an intuitive presentation a *varying amount of intuitive fulness* is possible. This talk of a varying amount points, as we argued, to possible gradients of fulfilment: proceeding along these, we come to know the object better and better, by way of a presentative content that resembles it ever more and more closely, and grasps it more and more vividly and fully. We know also that intuition can occur where whole sides and parts of the object meant are not apparent at all, i.e. the presentation has an intuitive content not containing pictorial representatives of these sides and parts, so that they are only presented 'inauthentically', through inwrought signitive intentions. In connection with these differences, which result in very different modes of presentation for one and the same object, with meaning governed by the same matter, we spoke above of differences in the *extent* of fulness. Here two important possibilities must be distinguished.

1. The intuitive presentation presents its object *adequately*, i.e. with an intuitive substance (*Gehalt*) of such fulness, that to each constituent of the object, as it is meant in this presentation, a representative constituent of the intuitive content corresponds.

2. Or this is *not* the case. The presentation contains no more than an incomplete projection of the object: it presents it *inadequately*.

Here we are talking of the adequacy or inadequacy of a presentation *to its object*. Since, however, we speak more widely of adequacy in contexts of fulfilment, we introduce yet another set of terms. We shall speak of *complete* and *mutilated intuitions* (more particularly of complete and mutilated percepts or imaginations). All pure intuitions are complete. The following considerations will at once show that the converse does not hold, and that our proposed division does not simply coincide with that of *pure* and *impure* intuitions.

Whether presentations are simple or complex is a matter regarding which nothing is presupposed in the distinction just drawn. Intuitive presentations may, however, be complex in two ways:

(*a*) The relation to the object may be simple in so far as the act (more specifically, its matter) has no constituent acts (or no separate matters) that *independently present the same total object*. This does not preclude the possibility that an act should be made up of partial intentions homogeneously fused, which relate to the individual parts or sides of its object. One can scarcely avoid assuming such complexity in the case of 'external' percepts and imaginations, and we have proceeded on this assumption. But, on the other hand we have

(*b*) the kind of complexity in which the total act is built out of constituent acts, *each of which independently is a full intuitive presentation of the same object*. This we have in those extremely remarkable *continuous syntheses* which bind together a multitude of percepts which pertain to the same object, into a single 'many-sided' or 'all-sided' percept, which deals with the object continuously in 'varying positions'. There are the corresponding syntheses of imagination. In the continuity of a prolonged fusion-into-sameness not broken up into isolated acts, the same single object appears singly, not as often as individual acts can be distinguished. It appears, however, with *altering* fulness of content, though the matters, and likewise *the qualities remain steadfastly the same*, at least when the object is known from all angles, and repeatedly comes to light in its unenriched familiarity.

The distinction between adequacy and inadequacy relates also to these continuous syntheses. An adequate presentation of, e.g., an external thing is possible in synthetic form in respect of its all-sided surface-contours: in the form of an objectively simple presentation, it is impossible.

Of complete intuitions it is plain that objectively simple ones, but by no means always objectively complex ones, are *pure* intuitions. The pure intuition which corresponds to an empirical thing is denied to us, it lies hidden after a fashion in the complete synthetic intuition itself, but as it were dispersedly, with a perpetual admixture of signitive representation. If we reduce this synthetic intuition to its pure form, we do not have the pure intuition possible in an objectively simple presentation, but a continuum of intuitive contents, in which each aspect of the object quite often achieves intuitive representation, achieves ever varied perspectival projection, and in which only the continuous fusion of identity constitutes the phenomenon of objective unity.

When an intuitive fact serves to give fulness in connection with a signitive intention, perhaps in connection with a meaning-intention expressed in words, similar possibilities arise. The object as it is meant can receive an adequate or an inadequate intuitive illustration. The former possibility covers two separable possibilities in the case of complex meanings:

First, that to all parts (members, moments, forms) of the meaning, which themselves have a meaning-character, fulfilment should accrue through corresponding parts of the fulfilling intuition.

Secondly, that the fulfilling intuition, to the extent that its object is meant in any articulations and forms which have been drawn into the function of fulfilment, is intrinsically adequate to its object.

The first determines the completeness of the adaptation of signitive acts to *corresponding intuitions*; the second the completeness of the adaptation of signitive acts – through *complete* intuitions – *to the object itself.*

The expression 'a green house' can thus be intuitively illustrated if a house is really present to our intuition as green. This is a case of the first perfection. The second requires an adequate presentation of a green house. We generally only have the former in mind when we speak of an adequate illustration of expressions. To find distinct terms for this *double* perfection we shall speak of an *objectively perfect* intuitive illustration of our signitive presentation as opposed to its adequate, but *objectively mutilated*, intuitive illustration.

Similar relationships obtain in the case of an intuitive illustration which *conflicts with, rather than fulfilling a meaning*. When a signitive intention encounters frustration from an intuition, because perhaps it refers to a *green A*, though the same *A*, perhaps any *A* at all, is red, and is now intuited as red, the *objective completeness* of the intuitive realization of conflict requires that *all* constituents of the meaning-intention should find an objectively complete intuitive illustration. It is therefore necessary, not merely that the *A*-intention should receive complete objective fulfilment in the intuition in question, but also that the green-intuition should be fulfilled, though naturally in another intuition which cannot be united to the intuition of the *red A*. It is not then merely the signitive green-intention, but the same intention in its objectively complete fulfilment, which is at odds with the red-intuition: these two intuitive moments are in total 'rivalry', while the correlative intuitive wholes are in partial rivalry. This rivalry especially touches, as one might say, the *intuitive* or *intuitively presentative* contents of these fulfilling acts.

If nothing special is prefaced we shall in future speak of 'intuitive illustrations' only in the case of fulfilments (not frustrations).

Distinctions of fulness in cases where quality and matter are identical, prompt us to frame one further important concept:

We shall say that two intuitive acts have the same *essentia* (*Essenz*), *if their pure intuitions have the same matter*. A percept, and the whole possibly existent infinity of imaginative presentations, which all present the same object with the same breadth of fulness, have one and the same *essentia*. All objectively complete intuitions with one and the same matter have the same *essentia*.

A signitive presentation has no *essentia* in its own right. But a certain *essentia* may, in an inauthentic sense, be ascribed to it, if it permits of complete fulfilment through one of the possible manifold of intuitions pertaining to this *essentia*, or, what is the same, if it has a 'fulfilling sense'.

This probably clarifies the true meaning of the scholastic term *essentia*, which certainly hinges on the possibility of a 'concept'.

CHAPTER FOUR

Consistency and Inconsistency

§30 *The ideal distinction of meanings into the possible or real (reale) and the impossible or imaginary*

IT is *not* possible to fit intuitive acts to every signitive intention in the manner of an 'objectively complete intuitive illustration'.[1] Meaning-intentions may accordingly be divided into the *possible* (internally consistent) and the *impossible* (internally inconsistent, imaginary). This division, and the law underlying it, does not concern *acts in isolation* – this applies also to all other propositions propounded here – but *their epistemic essence in general*, and therein their 'matters' taken generally. For it is not possible that a signitive intention with matter M should find a possibility of fulfilment in some intuition, while another signitive intention with the same matter M, should lack this possibility. These possibilities and impossibilities do not refer to intuitions actually found in certain empirical interweavings of consciousness: they are not real (*reale*), but ideal possibilities, with their sole ground in specific character. In the sphere of the verbally expressed, to which we may without essential loss limit ourselves, the axiom runs: *Meanings* (*i.e. concepts and propositions in specie*) *divide into the possible and the impossible* (*the real and the imaginary*).

Drawing on our just made notional constructions, we may define the *possibility* (reality) of a meaning by saying *that there is an adequate essentia which corresponds to it in specie in the sphere of objectifying acts, an essentia whose matter is identical with its own*, or what is the same, that it *has a fulfilling sense*, or that there *exists in specie a complete intuition whose matter is identical with its own*. This 'exists' has here the same ideal sense as in mathematics; to reduce it to the

---

[1] Understanding of the analytical clarifications attempted in this chapter and the next, and assessment of their possible achievements, depends entirely on keeping the strict concepts hitherto elaborated firmly in mind, and not letting the vague ideas of popular speech take their place.

possibility of corresponding particulars is not to reduce it to the possibility of anything different, but merely to employ an equivalent turn of phrase. (This is true, at least, when 'possibility' is given its 'pure', and therefore non-empirical, sense, and is 'real' only in this 'pure' fashion.)

The idea of the possibility of a meaning really expresses, to look at the matter more exactly, a *generalization of the relation of fulfilment in the case of objectively complete intuitive illustration*, and the above definitions are to be regarded, not as classifications of words, but as the *ideal*, necessary and sufficient *criteria* of possibility. They really state the specific *law* that where such a relationship obtains between the matter of a meaning and the matter of an *essentia*, possibility also *obtains*, and conversely also that in every case of possibility such a relationship obtains.

Further: that such an ideal relationship obtains at all, i.e. that this generalization holds objectively, and is therefore in its own turn 'possible' – this itself amounts to a law which may be simply expressed in the words: *There are possible meanings* (it must be noted that 'meaning' does not stand for the act of meaning). Not every empirical relationship permits such a generalization. If we find this intuited paper rough, we cannot pronounce generally 'Paper is rough', as we can pronounce generally, on the basis of a certain actual act of meaning: 'This meaning is possible (real)'. Just for this reason the proposition 'Every meaning is either possible or impossible', is no mere case of the law of excluded middle, in the familiar sense which excludes contradictory predicates from *individual subjects*, and can only pronounce such an exclusion for such subjects. The exclusion of contradictory predicates in an *ideal* sphere (e.g. the sphere of numbers, of meanings etc.) is by no means obvious, but must be demonstrated afresh in each such sphere, or set up as an axiom. We may recall that we cannot, for instance, say that every kind of paper is either rough or not rough, for this would entail that every individual paper of a particular sort was rough, or that every individual paper of that particular sort was not rough: such assertions are obviously not valid for every possible species. There accordingly really lies, behind the division of *meanings* into possible and impossible, a peculiar general law rich in content, a law that governs phenomenological moments in ideal fashion by binding their species in the manner of general propositions.

To be able to utter such an axiom, one must *see* its truth, and that we possess self-evidence in our case is certain. If we realize, e.g., the meaning of the expression 'white surface' on an intuitive basis, we experience the reality of the concept; the intuitive appearance really presents something white and a surface, and precisely as a white surface. This implies that the fulfilling intuition does not merely present a white surface, but brings it to intuitive givenness through its content as completely as its meaning-intention demands.

Impossibility is ranged beside possibility as an Idea of equal title, which should not merely be defined as a negation of possibility, but should be realized by way of a peculiar phenomenological fact. This is, moreover, presupposed by the fact that the concept of impossibility can find application, and that it can appear in an axiom: *There are impossible meanings*. The equivalence of talk about impossibility and *inconsistency* shows us that this phenomenological fact is to be sought in the realm of conflict.

§31 *Compatibility or consistency as an ideal relationship in the widest sphere of contents in general. Compatibility of 'concepts' as meanings*

We start with the concept of consistency or compatibility, which governs the widest sphere of contents in general (objects in the widest sense of the word).

Two *contents*, which are parts of any whole, are united in it, and are accordingly *compatible, consistent* within the unity of the whole. This seems emptily obvious, but the same contents will still be compatible when they chance not to come together. There is good sense in speaking of a compatibility of contents, whose actual union always has been, and always will be, excluded. But if two contents are unified, their union proves not only their own compatibility, but that of an ideal infinity of other cases, namely of all pairs of contents exactly like them and belonging to similar kinds. It is clear what this points to, and that the following axiom is by no means an empty assertion: *Compatibility does not pertain to dispersed individual specimens, but to the Species of contents*. If, e.g., the moments of redness and roundness have once been found unified, a complex Species is at once reached by *ideative abstraction, and can forthwith be given*, which embraces both the Species of redness and roundness in its specifically grasped form of combination. It is the ideal 'existence' of this complex Species in which the compatibility of redness and roundness, in each thinkable instance, has its *a priori* foundation, a compatibility which is an ideally valid relationship whether empirical union occurs anywhere in the world or not. If the valuable sense of talk of compatibility is pinned down as the ideal being of the corresponding complex Species, a yet weightier point must be made: that *talk of compatibility always relates to some sort of whole*, which is the decisive point for our logical interest. Such talk is applied when we are considering whether or not certain given contents can be fitted together on a pattern set by certain forms, a question decided in the affirmative if we can exhibit a whole of the sort in question. The correlate of this compatibility of contents is the 'possibility' of the complex *meanings*: this follows from our above criteria of possibility. The appropriate *essentia*, the complete intuitive illustration of the corresponding complex content, proves the compatibility of its parts, and conversely furnishes an *essentia* and a corresponding meaning to such incompatibility. The reality of a meaning is therefore equivalent to: the meaning is an *objectively complete 'expression'* of an intuitive compatibility of content. In the limiting case of a simple content one can define the validity of the simple species as a 'compatibility with self'. Obviously the combination of expression and expressed (meaning and *corresponding*, i.e. objectively quite adequate, intuition) is itself again a combination of compatibles, whose specific content we determined above. In talk of *compatibility as regards meanings* ('concepts'), we are not merely concerned with their compatibility in a whole – this would rather be a *purely logico-grammatical* compatibility in the sense of our Fourth Investigation – but are rather concerned with a compatibility of meanings in a 'possible' meaning, i.e. a meaning compatible with corresponding intuition in the unity of objectively adequate knowledge. We have here accordingly a *derived*, secondary form of speech. The same is true of the term 'possibility'. The original possibility (or reality) is the validity, the ideal existence of a Species: it is at least fully guaranteed by this. Next the intuition of an individual case which corresponds to this possibility, and the intuitable individual itself, are possible. Finally the meaning realized with objective completeness in such an intuition is said to be possible. The difference between talk about compatibility and talk about possibility consists solely in the fact that, while the latter denotes the simple validity of a Species, the former (prior to the widening of the notion to cover the limiting case) connotes the *relationship of the component Species* in a Species which counts as one, and in connection therewith also the relationship of the partial intuitions in a total intuition, of the partial contents to be intuited within a total content to be intuited as one, of partial meanings to be fulfilled within a total meaning to be fulfilled as one.

Finally we remark that the concept of *essentia*, like the concepts of possibility and compatibility, imparts its original sense derivatively to the realm of meaning. *The original concept of essentia* is expressed in the proposition: *Every valid species is an essentia.*

§32 *Incompatibility (conflict) of contents in general*

Contents are *incompatible*, to pursue the opposed case down to its general grounds, if they cannot suffer each other in the unity of a whole. Put phenomenologically: no unified intuition must be possible which presents such a whole with complete adequacy. But how shall we know this? In empirical instances we attempt to unite contents, sometimes successfully, sometimes without success – we experience an absolute resistance. But the *factual failure* does not establish a *necessary failure*. Possibly greater power could ultimately overcome the resistance. Nonetheless, in our empirical concern with the contents in question, and our attempted removal of their 'rivalry', we experience a peculiar relationship of the contents, again grounded in their specific being, and with an ideality quite independent of the empirical effort, and all the other features of the individual case. *It is the relationship of conflict.*

This relationship puts quite definite *sorts* of content into relation, within *quite definite associations of contents*. Colours conflict with one another, not in general, but only in specific contexts: several moments of colour, of varying specific difference, are incompatible as simultaneous overlays of one and the same bodily extension, while they are quite compatible if set side by side within a single extension. This is universally the case. A content of the sort q is never *simply incompatible* with a content of the sort p: talk of their incompatibility always relates to a definite sort of combination of contents $W(a, b...p)$ which includes p, and should now include q as well. The word 'should' certainly indicates an intention, a presentative and generally also a voluntary intention, which thinks of the q, given in any intuition $I(q)$, as brought into the present intuition of W, which presents q signitively in W. This intention we shall, however, ignore, just as, in the case of compatibility, we ignored the intention towards unification, as well as the process of transference and union. We only maintain the presence of a descriptively peculiar relationship between q – the remainder of A is variable at will and plays no further part – and p, within the whole of contents W, and that this whole is independent of the individual element in the case. In other words, it is grounded purely in the Species W, p and q. What is specific in the consciousness of conflict pertains to these Species, i.e. the generalization of the situation is actual, is realizable in an intuitively unified consciousness of universality, it yields a unified, valid ('possible') Species which *unites* p and Q, through *conflict*, on the basis of W.

§33 *How conflict can also be a foundation for unity. Relativity of the talk of compatibility and conflict*

To this last expression and sentence there attach a series of disquieting doubts and questions. Does conflict unify? Is the unity of conflict a unity of possibility? Unity in general certainly underlies possibility, but does not the latter absolutely exclude conflict, inconsistency?

These difficulties are resolved when we remember that not only talk of an incompatibility, but also talk of a compatibility, necessarily relates to a certain whole W which, subjectively speaking, governs our intention. Looking out from the specific make-up of this whole, we call its parts compatible. We should call the same contents p, q...(which here function as parts) incompatible, if in our symbolic intention towards their unity within such a whole, we experienced intuitive conflict instead of intuitive unity. The correlation of the two possible cases in relation to the two definite sorts of wholes, or combinations of compatible or incompatible contents, is clear. This relation also determines the sense of these terms. We do not call p, q...simply *compatible*, merely considering *that* they are unified and not at all *how* they are so, but in the light of *their union after the manner of W*, and that this union of p, q...excludes the conflict of the same p, q...*in relation to the same W.* Contents *p, q*. . .are similarly not said to be simply *incompatible,* but in the light of the fact that they will not 'suffer' one another within the framework of a unity of the sort *W* which just happens to interest us. The intention to such a unity brings out a conflict *instead* of such a unity: the exclusion of unity by correlated conflict once more also plays its part.

The consciousness of conflict entails 'disunity', since it excludes the *W*-type unity which is in question here. With this direction of interest, conflict does not itself count as unity, but as separation, not as a combination but a sundering. But if we change the relations, an incompatibility can also function as a unity, e.g. between the character 'conflict' and the contents separated by it. This character is compatible with these contents, and perhaps incompatible with others. If our dominant intention is upon the whole-shaped-by-conflict which is the whole for the parts just mentioned, then, when we find such a whole, when conflict accordingly obtains, there is compatibility among these parts, *p, q*. . .in this context, and in the *conflict* which separates them. *This* conflict is not a conflict among the members of the intended conflict, whose absence it in fact indicates, but a conflict attaching to the contents *p, q*. . .united without conflict in one intuition, and the moment of *conflict* which is made intuitive in *another* intuition.

The paradox of talking of a unification-through-conflict is cleared up by noting the relativity of these concepts. One can no longer object: 'Conflict absolutely excludes unity. In the manner of conflict anything and everything could ultimately be unified. Where unity fails, there conflict obtains, and to allow this conflict once more to count as a unity, is to obliterate the absolute, stark distinction between unity and conflict, and corrupt its true sense'. No, we may now presume to reply, conflict and unity do not 'absolutely' exclude one another, but only in a variously determined correlation which changes from case to case. In *this* correlation, they exclude each other as stark opposites, and only if we limit our 'absolutely' to some such tacitly presupposed correlation can we be satisfied with our polemical assertion. Not everything, moreover, can be unified in the form of a conflict, but only such things as serve to base a conflict, and none of the things that are or could be unified. For in the meaning of this talk of union-in-the-form-of-conflict it is implied that the form of conflict of a

p, q...thought of as in a certain combination W_0, shall count as a *unity*, which as a unity re-establishes union and compatibility, and so corresponds to the W we mentioned above. But if unity obtains among p, q...in respect of the combination W_0, then these p, q...will not permit themselves to be brought into a relationship of conflict in respect of *this* combination, since combination as such means unity.

So not everything can really be united in the form of conflict, at least not for the stated reason that failure of unity would be manifest in a conflict, which would therefore restore unity through conflict. We understand the confusion here fallen into, the confounding of underlying relations. The failure of the unity W_0, fixes the character of the conflict attaching to p, q...within the context determined by the notion W_0. This conflict does not, however, yield the unity W_0, but *another* unity. As regards the former it has the character of a separation, as regards the new unity that of a combination. All this is in order, as an example will make clear. In relation to a peculiar phenomenal context, *red* and *green* are called incompatible, *red* and *round* compatible. The character of conflict determines incompatibility in the first case, it produces separation between *red* and *green*. Despite this, in regard to another kind of combination, it helps to establish a unity, i.e. in regard to the type of combination *conflict among the sensuous qualities of a phenomenal object*. Conflict is now a unity between *red* and *green*, a unity in respect of the elements *conflict, red, green*. As opposed to this 'conflict of *red* and *round*' is now disunity in respect of these elements *conflict, red, round*.

§34 *Some axioms*

After this elucidation, very important for our basic analysis, of the sense of relations of compatibility, we can lay down primitive axioms and complete their phenomenological clarification. The first would be the *axiom of the convertibility of relations of compatibility* (or incompatibility), which our analysis of the underlying phenomenological relationships makes immediately clear.

The next axiom to be set up requires more consideration: *that unity and conflict* (or *compatibility and incompatibility*) – *each pair related to the same basis of correlation* – *exclude each other reciprocally* (or *are incompatible* with one another). We need no longer emphasize that incompatibility is not the mere privation of compatibility, not the mere fact that a certain unity does not objectively obtain. Union and conflict are notions with different phenomenological foundations, and we are therefore really uttering a statement with content if we say that if a p conflicts with a q as regards the form of unity $W(p, q . . .)$ – such conflict is a phenomenologically positive character – the union of a p with a q in the sense of the same W is 'impossible'. The phenomenological ground of this fact has been laid bare in the previous discussion: when we try to unite actual conflict between $p, q . . .$ with the *corresponding unity* of $p, q . . .$ – actually to impose the form of unity W which has been somewhere really intuited in the case of items $m, n . . .$ in the pertinent case of conflict on the same items $p, q . . .$ – a *new conflict* emerges, which has its roots in the first conflict and the elsewhere intuited form of unity. Analogous things are plain in the converse case, which may for the rest be regarded as an application of the first axiom.

The propositions that there is a *conflict*, and the proposition that there is *no* unity among any given $p, q . . .$ (the same in both cases), say exactly the same thing. *Every 'not' expresses a conflict.*

When a conflict attaches to the circumstance that p, q shall be in conflict, that $p, q . . .$ shall be one in the form of conflict, $p, q . . .$ *are* one. In other words:

If p, q are not in conflict, are not not unified, they are unified (axiom of double negation) which entails that:

Either unity or conflict obtains – one or other is the case – there is no third possibility.

Four possibilities must here be distinguished, expressed in the following terms:

$$\left.\begin{array}{l}\text{Unity}\\\text{Conflict}\end{array}\right\}\quad\left\{\begin{array}{l}\text{obtains}\\\text{does not obtain.}\end{array}\right.$$

Non-unity is, however, another name for conflict, and non-conflict (according to the previous axiom) an equivalent of unity.

The final elucidation of these axioms, and their relation to purely logical axioms, goes beyond the boundaries of the present Investigation. What we have here adduced is only intended to point to the internal relations that we desire to track down later: they make us aware, very vividly, that we are here already working to lay down the phenomenological foundations of pure logic.

§35 *Incompatibility of concepts as meanings*

Incompatibility, like compatibility, appears in thought in connection with signitive intentions directed to certain combinations, in connection, accordingly, with signitive and intuitive identifications. The concept of incompatibility does not relate to intentions, but the identically styled concept which relates to intentions is *derivative*, is a special case of the original notion, very definite in scope, and with limited openings for relations of frustration. Here we have an analogue of the matters set forth above (§31) in regard to compatibility or consistency. Talk of incompatibility in regard to meanings ('concepts') may again be said to express, not any and every ideal incompatibility of the same, not, e.g., a purely grammatical incompatibility. It has to do only with the relationship of the partial meanings within a complex meaning, which does not fulfil itself in an objectively complete illustration, but is, or *may* be frustrated. Plainly conflict of the intuitively illustrated contents underlies such frustration, although (be it noted) this conflict is not itself meant and expressed. Otherwise conflict would pertain to the fulfilling 'intuition', and the expression would express adequately, and in an entirely 'possible' manner, an objective impossibility.

The connection between the meaning and *each* of the unified intuitions which cancel each other in the process of intuitive conflict, is likewise one of conflict (of course with partial coincidence).

The ideal laws to be set up for the possibility of meanings are based on the original, more general concepts, and on the axioms set up for such concepts above (which have, however, to be carried further). Here we have such propositions as:

Incompatibility and compatibility among the same meanings, in relation to identical context, are mutually exclusive.

Of a pair of contradictory meanings – of meanings such that what the one means as incompatible the other means as compatible – one is possible and the other impossible.

The negative of a negative – i.e. a meaning which presents incompatibility in a given matter M as itself involving incompatibility – is equivalent to the corresponding positive meaning. This positive meaning is defined as the meaning which presents the inner consistency of the same M through the same presentative matter (the matter left over after the negations have been cancelled).

Quite obviously a real theory of meanings according to their logical relations would demand that all such propositions should be enunciated and proved in a systematically ordered fashion.

We break off our fragmentary discussions, leaving their completion to later investigations. We need, in the interests of logic, a much more extensive, completely executed phenomenology and theory of identifications and differentiations, particularly of such as are partial, as well as of their obviously close relations to the doctrine of unity and conflict.

CHAPTER FIVE

The Ideal of Adequation. Self-Evidence and Truth

§36 *Introduction*

IN our discussions up to this point we have said nothing of the *qualities* of acts, nor presumed anything in regard to them. Possibility and impossibility have indeed no special relation to these qualities. It makes no difference, e.g., to the possibility of a proposition, whether we realize the propositional matter as matter for an act of *assertion* (not of an act that assents to something in the accepting or recognizing manner of approval, but in the manner of a simple act of belief or taking for true), or whether we use it, in qualitatively modified fashion, as the matter of a pure presentation. A proposition is always 'possible', when the concrete act of propositional meaning permits of a fulfilling identification with an objectively complete intuition of matching material. It is likewise irrelevant if this fulfilling intuition is a percept, or a pure construction of fantasy, etc. Since the summoning up of imaginative pictures is more subject, in varying degrees, to our will, than that of percepts and assertions, we incline to relate possibility specially to the picture-life of fantasy. A thing counts as possible, if it allows itself, objectively speaking, to be realized in the form of an adequate imaginative picture, whether we ourselves, as particular empirical individuals, succeed in thus realizing it or not. But through the ideal linkage between perception and imagination, which assures us *a priori* that to each percept a possible image corresponds, this proposition is equivalent to our own, and the limitation of the concept to imagination not essential.

What we have now to do, quite briefly, is to discuss the effect of these just indicated differences upon relationships of fulfilment, so that our treatments may at least reach a provisional term, as well as a view over further researches.

§37 *The fulfilling function of perception. The ideal of ultimate fulfilment*

We have seen that differences in the completeness of 'fulness' have an important bearing on the manner in which objects are made present in presentations. Signitive acts constitute the lowest step: they possess no fulness whatever. Intuitive acts have fulness, in graded differences of more and less, and this is already the case within the sphere of imagination. The perfection of an imagination, however great, still leaves it different from a perception: it does not present the object itself, not even in part, it offers only its image, which, as long as it is an image at all, never is the thing itself. The latter we owe to perception. Even this, however, 'gives' us the object in varied gradations of perfection, in differing degrees of 'projection'. The intentional character of perception, as opposed to the mere representation of imagination, is that of direct presentation. This is, as we know, an *internal* difference of acts, more precisely of their interpretative form. But 'direct' presentation does not in general amount to a true being-present, but only to an appearance of presence, in which objective presence, and with it the perfection of veridicity (*Wahr-nehmung*, perception) exhibits degrees. This is shown by a glance at the corresponding scale of fulfilment, to which all exemplification of perfection in presentation is here, as elsewhere, referred. We thereby become clear that a difference extends over the fulness of perception that we sought to cover by our talk of perceptual *projection*, a difference that does not concern fulness in respect of its sensuous stuff, its internal character, but means a graded extension of its character *as* fulness, i.e. of the interpretative character of the act. From this point of view many elements of fulness count for us – quite apart from anything genetic, for we know full well that these, like all similar differences, have an associative origin – as *final presentations* of the corresponding objective elements. They offer themselves as identical with these last, not as their mere representatives: they are *the thing itself* in an absolute sense. Other cases again count as mere adumbrations of colour, perspectival foreshortenings etc., in which case it is clear that to such locutions something corresponds in the phenomenological content of the act prior to all reflection. We have already dealt with these 'projective' differences, and found them, pictorially transferred, in the case of imagination. Every projection is representative in character, and represents by way of similarity, but the manner of this representation by similarity differs according as the representation takes the projected content as picture or self-presentation (self-projection) of the object.[1] The ideal limit, which an increase of fulness of projection permits, is, in the case of perception, the absolute self of the thing (as in imagination it is its absolutely resembling image), and that for every side and for every presented element of the object.

The discussion of possible relationships of fulfilment therefore points to *a goal in which increase of fulfilment terminates, in which the complete and entire intention has reached its fulfilment*, and that not intermediately and partially, but ultimately and finally. The intuitive substance of this last fulfilment is the absolute sum of possible fulness; the intuitive representative is the object itself, as it is in itself. Where a presentative intention has achieved its last fulfilment, the genuine *adaequatio rei et intellectus* has been brought about. *The object is actually 'present' or 'given', and present as just what we have intended it*; no partial intention remains implicit and still lacking fulfilment.

And so also, *eo ipso*, the ideal of every fulfilment, and therefore of a *significative* fulfilment, is sketched for us; the *intellectus* is in this case the thought-intention, the intention of meaning. And the *adaequatio* is realized when the object meant is in the strict sense *given* in our intuition, and given as just what we think and call it. No thought-intention could fail of its fulfilment, of its last fulfilment, in fact, in so far as the fulfilling medium of intuition has itself lost all implication of unsatisfied intentions.

One sees that the perfection of the adequation of thought to thing is twofold: on the one hand there is a perfect adaptation to intuition, since the thought means nothing that the fulfilling intuition does not completely present as belonging to the thought. In this the two previously (p. 747) distinguished 'perfections' are plainly comprehended: they yield what we called the 'objective completeness' of the fulfilment. On the other hand the complete intuition itself involves a perfection. The intuition fulfils the intention which terminates in it as not itself again being an intention which has need of further fulfilment, but as offering us the *last* fulfilment of our intention. We must therefore draw a distinc-

[1] Cf. §23.

tion between the perfection of the *adaptation to intuition*, which is 'adequation' in the natural, wider sense, and the perfection of final fulfilment which presupposes this fulfilment, and which is an adequation with the 'thing itself'. Each faithful, unalloyed description of an intuitive object or event provides an example of the former perfection. If the object is something in interior experience, and is grasped as it is in reflex perception, then the second perfection may be added, as when, for instance, looking back on a categorical judgement just made, we speak of the subject-presentation in this judgement. The first perfection is, however, lacking, when we call the tree standing before us a 'cultivated' variety of apple-tree, or when we speak of the 'vibratory frequency' of the note just dying away, or, in general, when we speak of such properties of perceptual objects as, however much they may be marginally meant in our perceiving intention, are not even more or less projectively present in what actually appears.

The following observation is also in place. Since an ultimate fulfilment may contain absolutely no unfulfilled intentions, it must issue out of a *pure* percept. An objectively complete percept, but one achieved by the continuous synthesis of impure percepts, will not fill the bill.

Against our mode of treatment, which places the final fulfilment of all intentions in perception, it may be objected that the realized consciousness of the universal, the consciousness which gives fulness to conceptually general presentations, and which sets the 'universal object itself' before our eyes, rests on a ground of mere imagination, or is at least indifferent to the difference between perception and imagination. The same is obviously true, as a consequence of what has just been said, of all self-evident general assertions, which make themselves plain to us, in axiomatic fashion, 'from our very notions alone'.

This objection points to a gap in our investigation that has already been touched on from time to time. We first took perception, with immediate obviousness, as being the same as *sense*-perception, intuition as being the same as sensuous intuition. Tacitly, without any clear consciousness, we have frequently gone beyond the bounds of these notions, e.g. in connection with our discussions of compatibility. We regularly did this, when, e.g., we spoke of intuiting a conflict or a union, or some other synthesis as such. In our next chapter, which deals generally with categorial forms we shall show the need to widen the concepts of perception and other sorts of intuition. To remove our objection, we shall now only say that the imagination, which serves as basis for generalizing abstraction, does not therefore exercise an actual, authentic function of fulfilment, and so does not play the part of a 'corresponding' intuition. What is individually singular in phenomena, is not itself, as we have several times stressed, the universal, nor does it contain the universal as a real (*reell*) 'piece' of itself.

§38 *Assertive acts in the function of fulfilment. Self-evidence in the loose and strict sense*

Under the rubric of 'intentions', assertive and non-assertive acts have so far been indiscriminately ranged. Nonetheless, though the general character of fulfilment essentially depends on the 'matter' of acts, which alone is relevant to an array of most important relationships, the quality of acts shares in the determination of others, and to such a degree that talk of intention, of directed aiming, really only seems to suit assertive acts. Our *thought* (*Meinung*) aims at a thing, and it hits its mark, or does not hit it, according as it agrees or does not agree in a certain way with perception (which is here an assertive act). Assertion then agrees with assertion: the intending and fulfilling act are alike in this quality. Mere presentation, however, is passive: it leaves matters 'in suspense'. Where by chance an adequate percept accompanies a mere presentation, a fulfilling coincidence certainly issues from the mutually fitting 'matters' of the acts: in the transition, however, the presentation acquires an assertive note, and the unity of coincidence itself certainly has this note quite homogeneously. *Each actual identification or differentiation is an assertive act*, whether itself founded on assertions or not. This last briefly-worded proposition adds an all-important characterization to the results of our last chapter, a characterization determining all relationships of compatibility: the theory of identifications and differentiations thereby reveals itself, with more clearness than before, as a chapter in the theory of judgement. For according as assertive or non-assertive acts function in our intentions or their fulfilments, they illuminate distinctions like that between *illustration*, perhaps *exemplification*, on the one hand, and *verification or confirmation* and its opposite *refutation*, on the other. The concept of verification relates exclusively to *assertive acts in relation to their assertive fulfilment*, and ultimately to their *fulfilment through percepts*.

To this last pre-eminent case we now give closer consideration. It is a case in which the ideal of adequation yields us *self-evidence* (*Evidenz*). We speak somewhat loosely of self-evidence wherever an assertive intention (a statement in particular) finds verification in a corresponding, fully accommodated percept, even if this be no more than a well-fitting synthesis of coherent single percepts. To speak of *degrees and levels of self-evidence* then has a good sense. Here are relevant all approximations of percepts to the objective completeness of their presentation of their object, all further steps towards the final ideal of perfection, the ideal of adequate perception, of the complete self-manifestation of the object, however it was referred to in the intention to be fulfilled. But the *epistemologically pregnant sense* of self-evidence is exclusively concerned with this last unsurpassable goal, *the act of this most perfect synthesis of fulfilment*, which gives to an intention, e.g. the intention of judgement, the absolute fulness of content, the fulness of the object itself. The object is not merely meant, but in the strictest sense *given*, and given as it is meant, and made one with our meaning-reference. It does not matter, for the rest, whether one is dealing with an individual or a universal object, with an object in the narrower sense or with a state of affairs, the correlate of an identifying or distinguishing synthesis.

Self-evidence itself, we said, is the act of this most perfect synthesis of fulfilment. Like every identification, it is an objectifying act, its objective correlate being called *being in the sense of truth*, or simply *truth* – if one does not prefer to award this term to another concept of the many that are rooted in the said phenomenological situation. Here, however, a closer discussion is needed.

§39 *Self-evidence and truth*

1. If we at first keep to the notion of truth just suggested, *truth* as the correlate of an identifying act is a *state of affairs (Sachverhalt)*, as the correlate of a coincident identity it is an *identity*: *the full agreement* of what is meant with what is *given as such*. This agreement we *experience* in self-evidence, in so far as self-evidence means the actual carrying out of an adequate identification. The

proposition that self-evidence is the 'experience' of truth cannot, however, be simply interpreted as telling us that the self-evidence is the perception (in a sufficiently wide sense) of truth, and, in the case of strict self-evidence, the *adequate perception of truth*. For, to recur to a previously voiced doubt (see the addendum to §8 and chapter 7), we must allow that the carrying out of an identifying coincidence is not as yet an actual perception of objective agreement, but becomes so only through its own act of objectifying interpretation, its own looking towards present truth. Truth is indeed 'present'. Here we have always the *a priori* possibility of looking towards this agreement, and of laying it before our intentional consciousness in an adequate percept.

2. A second concept of truth concerns the *ideal relationship* which obtains in the unity of coincidence which we defined as self-evidence, *among the epistemic essences of the coinciding acts*. While truth in sense 1 was the *objective* item corresponding to the act of self-evidence, truth in *this* sense is the Idea which belongs to the act-form: *the epistemic essence interpreted as the ideal essence of the empirically contingent act of self-evidence, the Idea of absolute adequation as such.*

3. We also experience in self-evidence, from the side of the act which furnishes 'fulness', *the object given in the manner of the object meant*: so given, the object is fulness itself. This object can also be called being, truth, the 'truth' in so far as it is here not experienced as in the merely adequate percept, but as the ideal fulness for an intention, as that which makes an intention true (or as the ideal fulness for the intention's *specific* epistemic essence).

4. Lastly, considered from the standpoint of the intention, the notion of the relationship of self-evidence yields us truth as the *rightness of our intention* (and especially that of our judgement), its adequacy to its true object, or *the rightness of the intention's epistemic essence in specie*. We have, in the latter regard, the rightness, e.g., of the judgement in the logical sense of the proposition: the proposition 'directs' itself to the thing itself, it says that it is so, and it really is so. In this we have the expression of the ideal, and therefore general, possibility that a proposition of such and such a 'matter' admits of fulfilment in the sense of the most rigorous adequation.

We must further particularly note that the 'being' here in question in our first objective sense of truth, is not to be confused with the 'being' covered by the *copula* in the affirmative categorical judgement. Self-evidence is a matter of *total coincidence*, whereas the 'being' of the copula corresponds generally, if not invariably to partial identifications (i.e. judgements of quality).

But even where total identification is predicated, the two 'beings' will not coincide. For we must observe that in the case of a self-evident judgement, i.e. of a self-evident predicative assertion, *being in the sense of truth is experienced but not expressed*, and so never coincides with the being meant and experienced in the 'is' of the assertion. This second 'being' is the synthetic moment in what *is* in the sense of *is true* – how could it express the fact that the latter is true? There are in fact *several agreements* which are here brought to synthesis: *one* of these, the partial, predicative one, is meant assertively and perceived adequately, and so self-presented. (What this means will become clearer in the next chapter by way of the more general doctrine of categorial objectification.) This is the *agreement of subject with predicate*, the suiting of predicate to subject. We have, in the second place, *the agreement which constitutes the synthetic form of the act of self-evidence*, and therefore of the total coincidence of the meaning-intention of our assertion with the percept of the state of affairs itself, a coincidence naturally achieved in stages, which do not here concern us further. *This* agreement is plainly not asserted, it is not objective like the first agreement, which belongs to the state of affairs judged. No doubt it *can* always be asserted and asserted with self-evidence. It then becomes the verifying state of affairs for a new self-evidence, of which the like is true, and so on. At each step, however, one must distinguish the verifying state of affairs from the state of affairs constitutive of the self-evidence itself, we must distinguish the objectified from the not-objectified state of affairs.

The distinctions just drawn lead to the following general discussion.

In our exposition of the relationships of the concepts of self-evidence and truth, we have not drawn a distinction which touches the *objective* side of the acts which, whether functioning as intentions or fulfilments, find their absolute adequation in self-evidence: we have not, that is, distinguished between states of affairs, on the one hand, and other objects, on the other. We have paid no heed, correspondingly, to the phenomenological difference between acts which relate, on the one hand – acts of agreement and disagreement, predicative acts – and acts which do not relate, on the other. We have paid no need, therefore, to the difference between relational and non-relational meanings, or to the rela-tional-non-relational distinction among ideally apprehended essences in general. Strict adequation can bring non-relating as much as relating intentions into union with their complete ful-filments. If we now particularly consider the field of expressions, we need not concern ourselves with judgements as assertive intentions or assertive fulfilments; acts of naming can also achieve their adequation. The concepts of truth, rightness, the true, are generally interpreted more narrowly than we have done: they are connected with judgements and propositions, or with the states of affairs which are their objective correlates. 'Being' is meanwhile mainly spoken of in relation to absolute objects (not states of affairs), though no definite lines are drawn. Our right to our more general interpretation of these concepts is unassailable. The very nature of the case demands that the concepts of truth and falsehood, should, in the first instance at least, be fixed so widely as to span the whole sphere of objectifying acts. It seems therefore most suitable that the concepts of truth and being should be so distinguished, that our concepts of truth – a certain range of equivocation remaining inevitable but hardly dangerous once our concepts are clarified – are applied *from the side of the acts themselves* and their ideally graspable moments, whereas the concepts of *being* (genuine being) are applied to the corresponding *objective correlates*. Truth would then have to be defined in the manner of (2) and (4) as the Idea of adequation, or as the rightness of objectifying assertion and meaning. Being would then have to be pinned down according to (1) and (3) as the identity of the object at once meant and given in adequation, or (in conformity with the natural sense of words) as the adequately perceivable thing as such, in an indefinite relation to an intention that it is to make true or fulfil adequately.

After our concepts have been thus widely fixed and assured phenomenologically, we may pass on, having regard to the dis-tinction between relational and non-relational acts (predications versus absolute assertions) to define *narrower concepts of truth and being*. The narrower concept of truth would be limited to the ideal adequation of a *relational* act to the corresponding adequate percept of a state of affairs: just so the narrower concept of being would concern the being of absolute objects, and would separate this off from the 'subsistence' of the state of affairs.

The following is accordingly clear: if one defines a judgement as an assertive act in general, then the sphere of judgement, subjectively speaking, coincides with the joint spheres of the concepts *true* and *false* in the widest sense of these words. But if one defines it by way of the statement and its possible fulfilment, and ranges under judgements only the sphere of relational assertions, then the same coincidence obtains again, provided that the *narrower* concepts of truth and falsehood are again used as a basis.

In one-sided fashion we have hitherto favoured the case of self-evidence, the act described as one of total coincidence. But, turning to the correlated case of conflict, we encounter *absurdity*, the experience of the total conflict between intention and quasi-fulfilment. To the concepts of truth and being the correlated concepts of *falsehood* and *non-being* then correspond. The phenomenological clarification of these concepts can be carried out without particular difficulty, once all foundations have been prepared. The negative ideal of an *ultimate frustration* would first have to be exactly circumscribed.

When self-evidence is conceived strictly, in the manner made basic here, it is plain that such doubts as have from time to time been expressed in modern times are absurd, doubts as to whether the experience of self-evidence might not be associated with the matter A for one man, while absurdity is associated with it for another. Such doubts are only possible as long as self-evidence and absurdity are interpreted as peculiar (positive or negative) *feelings* which, contingently attaching to the act of judgement, impart to the latter the specific features which we assess logically as truth and falsehood. If someone experiences the self-evidence of A, it is *self-evident* that no second person can experience the absurdity of this same A, for, that A is self-evident, means that A is not merely meant, but also genuinely given, and given as precisely what it is thought to be. In the strict sense it is itself present. But how could a second person refer in thought to this same thing A, while the thought that it is A is genuinely excluded by a genuinely given non-A? One is, it is plain, dealing with a matter of essence, the same matter, in fact, that the law of contradiction (into whose ambiguities the correlations discussed on p. 766 naturally enter) successfully expresses.

It is reliably clear, as a result of our analyses, that being and non-being are not concepts which in their origin express opposition among the *qualities* of our judgements. Following our interpretation of the phenomenological relationships involved, every judgement is assertive: this assertion does not characterize the 'is' of which the 'is not' is the *qualitative* contrary. The qualitative contrary of a judgement is a mere presentation having the same 'matter'. Differences between 'is' and 'is not' are differences in intentional 'matter'. Just as an 'is' expresses predicative agreement after the manner of a meaning-intention, so an 'is not' expresses a predicative conflict.

Second Section

SENSE AND UNDERSTANDING

CHAPTER SIX

Sensuous and Categorial Intuitions

---

§40 *The problem of the fulfilment of categorial meaning-forms,*
with a thought leading towards its solution

IN our discussions up to this point we have repeatedly and strongly
felt a large gap. It had to do with the categorial objective forms,
or with the synthetic functions in the sphere of objectifying acts
through which these objective forms come to be constituted,
through which they may come to 'intuition' and thereby also to
'knowledge'. We shall now attempt to some extent to fill in this
gap, taking our point of departure from the investigation of our
first chapter; this was concerned with one limited aim of epistemological clarification: the relation of a meaning-intention as the
thing to be expressed, with an expressed sensuous intuition. We
shall for the time being again build on the simplest cases of perceptual and other intuitive statements, and shall use them to shed
light on the theme of our next treatments, in the following manner:

In the case of a perceptual statement, not only the inwrought
nominal presentations are fulfilled: the whole sense of the statement finds fulfilment through our underlying percept. We say
likewise that the whole statement gives utterance to our percept:
we do not merely say 'I see this paper, an inkpot, several books',
and so on, but also 'I see that the paper has been written on, that
there is a bronze inkpot standing here, that several books are
lying open', and so on. If a man thinks the fulfilment of nominal
meanings clear enough, we shall ask him how we are to understand the fulfilment of total statements, especially as regards that
side of them that stretches beyond their 'matter', in this case
beyond their nominal terms. What may and can furnish fulfilment for those aspects of meaning which make up propositional
form as such, the aspects of '*categorial form*' to which, e.g., the
copula belongs?

Looked at more narrowly, this question also applies to nominal meanings, in so far as these are not totally formless like the meanings for individuals. The name, like the statement, even in its grammatical appearance, possesses both 'matter' and 'form'. If it comprises words, the form lies partly in the way these words are strung together, partly in its own form-words, partly in the mode of construction of the individual words, which allows us to draw a distinction between its moments of 'matter' and its moments of 'form'. Such grammatical distinctions refer us back to distinctions of meaning. There is at least a rough expression of the articulations and forms which are rooted in our meaning's essence and the articulations and forms of grammar. In our meanings, therefore, parts of very different kinds are to be found, and among these we may here pay special attention to those expressed by formal words such as 'the', 'a', 'some', 'many', 'few', 'two', 'is', 'not', 'which', 'and', 'or' etc., and further expressed by the substantival and adjectival, singular and plural inflection of our words etc.

How does all this stand as regards fulfilment? Can the ideal of completely adequate fulfilment formulated by us in our third chapter still be maintained? *Are there parts and forms of perception corresponding to all parts and forms of meaning?* In that case we should have the *parallelism* between meaningful reference and fulfilling intuition that talk of 'expression' suggests. The expression would be an image-like counterpart of the percept (i.e. in all its parts and forms to be expressed) but reconstituted in a new stuff – an *ex-pression* in the *stuff of meaning*.

The prototype for interpreting the relation between meaning and intuiting would then be the relation of the 'proper' individual meaning to corresponding percepts. The man who knows Cologne itself, and therefore possesses the genuine 'proper meaning' of the word 'Cologne', has in his contemporary actual experience something exactly corresponding to the future confirming percept. It is not, properly speaking, a representation of the percept, as, e.g., the corresponding imagination would be. But just as the city is thought to be itself present to us in the percept, so the proper name 'Cologne', in its 'proper meaning', refers, as previously argued, to the same city 'directly': it means that city itself, and as it is. The straightforward percept here renders the object apparent without the help of further, superordinate acts, the object *which* the meaning-intention means, and *just as* the latter means it. The meaning-intention therefore finds in the mere percept the act which fulfils it with complete adequacy.

If instead of considering directly naming, unstructured expressions, we rather consider structured, articulated expressions, the matter seems quite the same. I *see* white paper and *say* 'white paper', thereby expressing, with precise adequacy, only what I see. The same holds of complete judgements. I *see* that this paper is white, and express just this by saying: 'This paper is white'.

We are not to let ourselves be led astray by such ways of speaking; they are in a certain manner correct, yet are readily misunderstood. One might try to use them to show that meaning here has its seat in perception, which, as we have shown, is not so. The word 'white' certainly means something attaching to the white paper itself; this 'meaning' therefore coincides, in the state of fulfilment, with the partial percept which relates to the 'white-aspect' of the object. But the assumption of a mere coincidence with this part-percept is not enough: we are wont to say here that the *white* thus apparent is known *as white* and is called so. In our normal talk of 'knowledge', we are, however, more inclined to call the object which is our (logical) subject the thing 'known'. In *such* knowledge another act plainly is present, which perhaps includes the former one, but is nonetheless different from it: the *paper* is known as white, or rather as a white thing, whenever we express our percept in the words 'white paper'. The intention of the word 'white' only partially coincides with the colour-aspect of the apparent object; a surplus of meaning remains over, a form which finds nothing in the appearance itself to confirm it. White paper is paper which *is* white. Is this form not also repeated, even if it remains hidden, in the case of the noun 'paper'? Only the quality-meanings contained in its 'concept' terminate in perception. Here also the whole object is known as paper, and here also a supplementary form is known which includes being, though not as its sole form, in itself. The fulfilment effected by a straight percept obviously does not extend to such forms.

We have but to ask, further, what corresponds in perception to the difference between the two expressions 'this white paper' and 'this paper is white', which are both realized on the same perceptual basis, we have but to ask what side of perception is really brought out by this difference – the difference, that is, of the attributive and the predicative mode of statement – and what, in the case of adequate adaptation, this difference brings out with peculiar exactness, and we experience the same difficulty. Briefly we see that the case of structured meanings is not so simple as the case of a 'proper' individual meaning, with its straightforward relation of coincidence with perception. Certainly one can tell one's auditors, intelligibly and unambiguously that 'I see that this paper is white', but the thought behind such talk need not be that the meaning of this spoken sentence expresses *a mere act of seeing*. It may also be the case that the epistemic essence of our seeing, in which the apparent object announces itself as self-given, serves to base certain connective or relational or otherwise formative acts, and that it is to *these* that our expression in its changing forms is adjusted, and that it is in such acts, per-formed on a basis of actual perception, that our expression, in respect of such changing forms, finds fulfilment. If we now combine these founded acts or rather act-forms with the acts which serve as their foundation, and give the comprehensive name 'founded act' to the whole act-complexes that result from such formal 'founding', we may say: Granted the possibility just sketched, our parallelism may be re-established, but it is no longer a parallelism between the meaning-intentions of expres-sions and the mere percepts which correspond to them: it is a parallelism between meaning-intentions and the above mentioned *perceptually founded acts*.

§41 *Continuation. Extension of our sphere of examples*

If we suppose our range of examples widened so as to cover the whole field of predicative thinking, we shall encounter similar difficulties and similar possibilities of resolving them. Judgements in particular will come up which have no definite relation to anything individual which ought to be given through any intui-tion: they will give *general* expression to relations among ideal unities. The general meanings embodied in such judgements can also be realized on a basis of corresponding intuition, since they have their origin, mediately or immediately, in intuition. The intuited individual is not, however, what we mean here; it serves at best only as an individual case, an example, or only as the rough analogue of an example, for the universal which alone interests us. So, for instance, when we speak generically of 'colour' or specifically of 'red', the appearance of a single red thing may furnish us with a documenting intuition.

It also at times happens, that one calls such a general statement an expression of intuition. We say, e.g., that an arithmetical axiom expresses what we find in intuition, or we raise objection to a geometrician that he merely expresses what he sees in his figure without deducing it formally, that he borrows from his drawing and omits steps in his proof. Such talk has its good sense (as when the objection scores no mean hit against the formal validity of Euclidean geometry) but 'expression' here means something different from the previous cases. Even in *their* case expression was not a mere counterpart of intuition: this is even less the case here, where our thought's intention is not aimed at intuitively given phenomena nor at their intuitive properties or relationships, and *can* in our case not be aimed at them. For a figure understood geometrically is known to be an ideal limit incapable in principle of intuitive exhibition in the concrete. Even in our case, nonetheless, and in the generic field as such, intuition has an essential relation to expression and to its meaning: these, therefore, constitute an experience of general knowledge related to intuition, no mere togetherness of them all, but a unity of felt belongingness among them. Even in our case, concept and proposition are oriented towards intuition, through which alone, after corresponding adjustment, self-evidence, the crown of knowledge, emerges. It requires little reflection, on the other hand, to see that the meaning of the expressions in question is not found in intuition at all, that such intuition only gives them a filling of clarity and in the favourable case of self-evidence. We in fact know only too well that the overwhelming majority of general statements, and in particular those of science, behave meaningfully without any elucidation from intuition, and that only a vanishing section, even of the true and the proven, are and remain open to complete intuitive illumination.

Even in the general realm, as in the realm of individuals, our natural talk has a relation to intuitively founded acts of thought. Should intuition fall wholly away, our judgement would cease to know anything. It means, in all cases, in cogitative style, just what could be known by the aid of intuition, if such judgement is indeed true at all. Knowledge always has the character of a fulfilment and an identification: this may be observed in every case where we confirm a general judgement through subsequent intuition, as in every other case of knowledge.

Our difficulty then is how identification can arise where the form of the general proposition, and in particular its form of universality, would vainly seek sympathetic elements in individual intuition. To remove this difficulty, as in the previous case, the possibility of 'founded acts' suggests itself. This possibility, carried out more fully, would run more or less as follows:

Where general thoughts find fulfilment in intuition, certain new acts are built on our percepts and other appearances of like order, acts related quite differently to our appearing object from the intuitions which constitute it. This difference in mode of relation is expressed by the perspicuous turn of phrase employed above: that the intuited object is not here itself the thing meant, but serves only as an elucidatory example of our true general meaning. But if *expressive* acts conform to these differences, their significative intention will not move towards what is to be intuitively presented, but towards what is universal, what is merely documented in intuition. Where this new intention is adequately fulfilled by an underlying intuition, it reveals its own objective possibility (or the possibility or 'reality' of the universal).

§42 *The distinction between sensuous stuff and categorial form throughout the whole realm of objectifying acts*

After these provisional treatments have shown us our difficulty, and have provided us with a thought leading to its possible removal, we shall embark upon our actual discussion.

We started by assuming that, in the case of structured expressions, the notion of a more or less mirror-like mode of expression was quite unavailing in describing the relation which obtains between meanings to be expressed, on the one hand, and expressed intuitions, on the other. This is doubtless correct and need now only be made more precise. We need only earnestly ponder what things can be possible matter for perception, and what things possible matter for meaning, to become aware that, *in the mere form of a judgement, only certain antecedently specifiable parts of our statement can have something which corresponds to them in intuition, while to other parts of the statement nothing intuitive possibly can correspond.*

Let us consider this situation a little more closely.

Perceptual statements are, completely and normally expressed, articulate utterances of varying pattern. We have no difficulty in distinguishing such types as '*A* is *P*' (where '*A*' serves as index for a proper name), 'An *S* is *P*', 'This *S* is P', 'All *S* are *P*' etc. Many complications arise through the modifying influence of negation, through the introduction of distinctions between absolute and relative predicates (attributes), through conjunctive, disjunctive and determinative connectives etc. In the diversity of these types certain sharp distinctions of meaning make themselves clear. To the various letters (variables) and words in these types correspond sometimes *members*, sometimes *connective forms*, in the meanings of the actual statements which belong to these types. Now it is easy to see that *only at the places indicated by letters (variables)* in such 'forms of judgement', *can* meanings be put that are themselves fulfilled in perception, whereas it is hopeless, even quite misguided, to look directly in perception for what could give fulfilment to our supplementary formal meanings. The letters (variables) on account of their merely functional meaning, can doubtless take complex thoughts as their values: statements of high complexity can be seen from the standpoint of very simple judgement-types. The same difference between 'matter' and 'form' therefore repeats itself in what is looked upon, in unified fashion, as a 'term'. But eventually, in the case of each perceptual statement, and likewise, of course, in the case of every other statement that in a certain primary sense, gives expression to intuition, we shall come down to certain final elements of our terms – we may call them elements of stuff – which find direct fulfilment in intuition (perception, imagination etc.), while the supplementary *forms*, which as forms of meaning likewise crave fulfilment, can find nothing that ever could fit them in perception or acts of like order.

This fundamental difference we call, in a natural extension of its application over the whole sphere of objectifying presentation, the *categorial* and *absolute* distinction between the *form* and *matter* of *presentation*, and at the same time separate it off from the *relative* or *functional* difference which is closely bound up with it, and which has just been subsidiarily touched on above.

We have just spoken of a natural extension of our distinction over the whole sphere of objectifying presentation. We take the constituents of the *fulfilment* which correspond to the material or formal constituents of our *meaning-intentions* as being material or formal constituents respectively, so making clear what is to count as 'material' or 'formal' in the general sphere of objectifying acts.

Of matter (stuff) and form we often talk in many other senses. We must expressly point out that our present talk of 'matter', which has its contrast in categorial form, has nothing whatever to do with the 'matter' which contrasts with the quality of acts, as when, e.g., we distinguish the 'matter' in our meanings from their assertive or merely presentative quality, this 'matter' being what tells us *as what*, or as *now* determined and interpreted, an object is meant in our meanings. To make the distinction easier, we shall not speak of 'matter' in our categorial contrast, but of 'stuff', while wherever 'matter' is meant in our previous sense, we shall talk pointedly of '*intentional* matter' or of 'interpretative sense'.

§43 *The objective correlates of categorial forms are not 'real'*
(realen) moments

It is now time to illuminate the distinction to which we have just given a name. We shall link on, for this purpose, to our previous examples.

The form-giving flexion *Being*, whether in its attributive or predicative function, is not fulfilled, as we said, in any percept. We here remember Kant's dictum: *Being is no real predicate*. This dictum refers to being *qua* existence, or to what Herbart called the being of 'absolute position', but it can be taken to be no less applicable to predicative and attributive being. In any case it precisely refers to what we are here trying to make clear. I can see colour, but not *being*-coloured. I can feel smoothness, but not *being*-smooth. I can hear a sound, but not that something *is* sounding. Being is nothing *in* the object, no part of it, no moment tenanting it, no quality or intensity of it, no figure of it or no internal form whatsoever, no constitutive feature of it however conceived. But being is also nothing attaching *to* an object: as it is no real (*reales*) internal feature, so also it is no real external feature, and therefore not, in the *real* sense, a 'feature' at all. For it has nothing to do with the *real* forms of unity which bind objects into more comprehensive objects, tones into harmonies, things into more comprehensive things or arrangements of things (gardens, streets, the phenomenal external world). On these real forms of unity the external features of objects, the right and the left, the high and the low, the loud and the soft etc., are founded. Among these anything like an 'is' is naturally not to be found.

We have just been speaking of *objects*, their constitutive features, their factual connection with other objects, through which more comprehensive objects are created, and also, at the same time, external features in the partial objects. We said that something corresponding to *being* was not to be sought among them. For all these are perceptible, and they exhaust the range of possible percepts, so that we are at once saying and maintaining *that being is absolutely imperceptible*.

Here, however a clarifying supplement is necessary. *Perception* and *object* are concepts that cohere most intimately together, which mutually assign sense to one another, and which widen or narrow this sense conjointly. But we must emphasize that we have here made use of a certain naturally delimited, natural, but also *very narrow concept of perception (or of object)*. It is well-known that one also speaks of 'perceiving', and in particular of 'seeing', in a greatly widened sense, which covers the grasping of whole states of affairs, and even ultimately the *a priori* self-evidence of laws (in the case of 'insight'). In the *narrower* sense of perception (to talk roughly and popularly) we perceive everything objective that we see with our eyes, hear with our ears or can grasp with any 'outer' or even 'inner sense'. In ordinary speech, no doubt, only *external* things and connective forms of things (together with their immediate qualities) can count as 'perceived by the senses'. But once talk of an 'inner sense' had been introduced, one should in consistency have widened the notion of sense-perception suitably, so as to include 'inner perception', and so as to include under the name 'sense-object' the correlated sphere of 'inner objects', the ego and its internal experiences.

In the sphere of sense-perception thus understood, and in the sphere, likewise, of sensuous intuition in general – we adhere to our much widened talk of the 'sensuous' – a meaning like that of the word 'being' can find no possible *objective correlate*, and so no possible fulfilment in the acts of such perception. What holds of 'being' is plainly true of the remaining categorial forms in our statements, whether these bind the constituents of terms together, or bind terms themselves together in the unity of the proposition. The 'a' and the 'the', the 'and' and the 'or', the 'if' and the 'then', the 'all' and the 'none', the 'something' and the 'nothing', the forms of quantity and the determinations of number etc. – all these are meaningful propositional elements, but we should look in vain for their objective correlates (if such may be ascribed to them at all) in the sphere of *real* objects, which is in fact no other than the sphere of *objects of possible sense-perception*.

§44 *The origin of the concept of being and of the remaining categories does not lie in the realm of sense-perception*

This holds – we stress it expressly – both of the sphere of outer sense, and of that of 'inner sense'. It is a natural but quite misguided doctrine, universally put about since the time of Locke, that the meanings in question (or the corresponding substantivally hypostatized meanings) – the *logical categories* such as being and non-being, unity, plurality, totality, number, ground, consequence etc. – arise through *reflection upon certain mental acts, and so fall in the sphere of 'inner sense', of 'inner perception'*. In this manner, indeed, concepts like Perception, Judgement, Affirmation, Denial, Collecting, Counting, Presupposing and Inferring arise, which are all, therefore, 'sensuous' concepts, belonging, that is, to the sphere of 'inner sense'. The previous series of concepts do not arise in this manner, since they cannot at all be regarded as concepts of mental acts, or of their real constituents. The thought of a Judgement fulfils itself in the inner intuition of an actual judgement, but the thought of an 'is' does not fulfil itself in this manner. Being is not a judgement nor a constituent of a judgement. Being is as little a real constituent of some inner object as it is of some outer object, and so not of a judgement. In a judgement, a predicative statement, 'is' functions as a side of our meaning, just as perhaps, although otherwise placed and functioning, 'gold' and 'yellow' do. The *is* itself does not enter into the judgement, it is merely meant, signitively referred to, by the little word 'is'. It is, however, *self-given*, or at least putatively given, in the *fulfilment* which at times invests the judgement, the *becoming aware* of the state of affairs supposed. Not only what is meant in the partial meaning *gold*, nor only what is meant in the partial meaning *yellow*, itself appears before us, but also *gold-being-yellow* thus appears. Judgement and judgemental intuition are therefore at one in the self-evident judgement, and pre-eminently so if the judgement is self-evident in the ideally limiting sense.

If one now understands by 'judging', not merely meaning-intentions connected with actual assertions, but the fulfilments that in the end fit them completely, it is indeed correct that *being can only be apprehended through judging*, but this does not *at all mean* that the concept of being must be arrived at 'through reflection' on certain judgements, or that it can ever be arrived at in this fashion. 'Reflection' is in other respects a fairly vague word. In epistemology it has at least the relatively fixed sense that Locke gave it, that of internal perception: we can only adhere to this sense in interpreting a doctrine which imagines it can find the origin of the concept of *Being* through reflecting on judgements. The relational being expressed in predication, e.g. through 'is', 'are' etc., lacks independence: if we round it out to something fully concrete, we get the *state of affairs* in question, the objective correlate of the complete judgement. We can then say: *As the sensible object stands to sense-perception so the state of affairs stands to the 'becoming aware' in which it is* (more or less adequately) *given* – we should like to say simply: so the state of affairs stands to the *perception* of it. As the concept *Sensuous Object (Real Object)* cannot arise through reflection upon perception, since this could only yield us the concept *Perception* (or a concept of certain real constituents of Perception), so the concept of State of Affairs cannot arise out of reflection on judgements, since this could only yield us concepts of judgements or of real constituents of judgements.

That percepts in the one case, and judgements (judgemental intuitions, percepts of states of affairs) in the other, must be *experienced*, in order that each such act of abstraction should get started, goes without saying, but to be experienced is not to be made objective. 'Reflection', however, implies that what we reflect upon, the phenomenological experience, is rendered objective to us (is inwardly perceived by us), and that the properties to be generalized are really given in this objective content.

Not in reflection upon judgements, nor even upon fulfilments of judgements, but in the fulfilments of judgements themselves lies the true source of the concepts State of Affairs and Being (in the copulative sense). Not in these *acts as objects*, but in *the objects of these acts*, do we have the abstractive basis which enables us to realize the concepts in question. And naturally the appropriate modifications of these acts yield just as good a basis.

It is in fact obvious from the start that, just as any other concept (or Idea, Specific Unity) can only 'arise', i.e. become *self-given* to us, if based on an act which at least sets some individual instance of it imaginatively before our eyes, so the concept of Being can arise only when *some being, actual or imaginary, is set before our eyes.* If 'being' is taken to mean predicative being, some *state of affairs* must be given to us, and this by way of an *act which gives it, an analogue of common sensuous intuition.*

The like holds of all *categorial forms* (or of all *categories*). An aggregate, e.g., is given, and can only be given, in an actual act of assembly, in an act, that is, expressed in the conjunctive form of connection *A and B and C*...But the concept of *Aggregate* does not arise through reflection on this act: instead of paying heed to the act which presents an aggregate, we have rather to pay heed to what it presents, to the *aggregate* it renders apparent *in concreto*, and then to lift the universal form of our aggregate to conceptually universal consciousness.

§45 *Widening of the concept of Intuition, and in particular of the concepts Perception and Imagination. Sensible and categorial intuition*

If we now ask: 'Where do the categorial forms of our meanings find their fulfilment, if not in the "perception" or "intuition" which we tried provisionally to delimit in talking of "sensibility"'', our answer is plainly prefigured in the discussions just completed.

We have taken it for granted that forms, too, can be genuinely fulfilled, or that the same applies to variously structured total meanings, and not merely to the 'material' elements of such meanings, and our assumption is put beyond doubt by looking at each case of faithful perceptual assertion. This will explain also why we call the whole perceptual assertion an expression of perception, and, in a derivative sense, of whatever is intuited or itself presented in perception. But if the 'categorial forms' of the expression, present together with its material aspects, have no terminus in perception, if by the latter we understand merely *sense*-perception, then talk of expressing a percept must here rest on a different meaning: there must at least be an act which renders identical services to the categorial elements of meaning that merely sensuous perception renders to the material elements. The essential homogeneity of the function of fulfilment, as of all the ideal relationships necessarily bound up with it, obliges us to give the name 'perception' to each fulfilling act of confirmatory self-presentation, to each fulfilling act whatever the name of an 'intuition', and to its intentional correlate the name of '*object*'. If we are asked what it means to say that *categorially structured meanings* find fulfilment, confirm themselves in perception, we can but reply: it means only that they relate to the object itself *in its categorial structure*. The object with these categorial forms is not merely referred to, as in the case where meanings function purely symbolically, but it is set before our very eyes in just these forms. In other words: it is not merely thought of, but intuited or perceived. When we wish, accordingly, to set forth what this talk of 'fulfilment' is getting at, what structured meanings and their structural elements express, what unitary or unifying factor corresponds to them objectively, we unavoidably come on 'intuition' (or on 'perception' and 'object'). We cannot manage without these words, whose widened sense is of course evident. What shall we call the correlate of a non-sensuous subject-presentation, one involving non-sensuous structure, if the word 'object' is not available to us? How shall we speak of its actual givenness, or apparent givenness, when the word 'perception' is denied us? In common parlance, therefore, *aggregates, indefinite pluralities, totalities, numbers, disjunctions, predicates* (right-ness), *states of affairs*, all count as 'objects', while the acts through which they seem to be given count as 'percepts'.

Plainly the connection between the wider and narrower, the *supersensuous* (i.e. raised above sense, or categorial) and *sensuous concept of perception*, is no external or contingent matter, but one rooted in the whole business on hand. It falls within the great class of acts whose peculiarity it is that in them something appears as 'actual', as 'self-given'. Plainly this appearance of actuality and self-givenness (which may very well be delusive) is throughout characterized by its difference from essentially related acts through which alone it achieves full clarity – its difference from an imaginative 'making present', or from a merely significative 'thinking of', which both exclude 'presence' (so to say appearance 'in person'), though not excluding the belief in being. As regards the latter, imaginal or symbolic representation is possible in two manners: in an assertive manner, asserting something's being in imaginal or symbolic fashion, and in a non-assertive manner, as 'mere' imagination or thinking without taking something to be. We need not enter more closely into the discussion of these differences after the analyses of the previous section, which permit of a sufficiently general interpretation. It is clear, in any case, that the concept of imagination must be *widened in correspondence with* the concept of perception. We could not speak of something super-sensuously or categorially *perceived*, if we could not *imagine* this thing 'in the same manner' (i.e. not merely sensuously). We must therefore draw a quite general distinction between *sensuous* and *categorial* intuition (or show the possibility of such a distinction).

Our extended concept of Perception permits, further, of a narrower and a wider interpretation. In the widest sense even universal states of affairs can be said to be perceived ('seen', 'beheld with evidence'). In the narrower sense, perception terminates upon individual, and so upon temporal being.

§46 *Phenomenological analysis of the distinction between sensuous and categorial perception*

In our next treatments we shall first only discuss individual percepts, then widen our treatment to take in individual intuitions of the same order.

The division between 'sensuous' and 'supersensuous' percepts was only very superficially indicated and quite roughly characterized above. Antiquated talk of external and internal senses, plainly stemming from the naïve metaphysic and anthropology of daily life, may be useful in pointing out the sphere to be excluded, but a true determination and circumscription of the sensory sphere is not thereby reached, so depriving the concept of categorial perception of its descriptive underpinning. To ascertain and clarify the said distinction is all the more important, since such fundamental distinctions as that between categorial form and sensuously founded matter, and the similar distinction between categories and all other concepts, depends wholly on it. Our concern is therefore to seek more profound descriptive characterizations, which will give us some insight into the essentially different constitution of sensuous and categorial percepts (or intuitions in general).

For our immediate purposes it is, however, unnecessary to carry out an exhaustive analysis of the phenomena involved. That would be a task that would require extraordinarily comprehensive treatments. Here it is sufficient to concentrate on some weightier points, which may help to mark off both sorts of acts in their mutual relation.

It is said of every percept that it grasps its object *directly*, or grasps this object *itself*. But this direct grasping has a different sense and character according as we are concerned with a percept in the narrower or the wider sense, or according as the directly grasped object is *sensuous* or *categorial*. Or otherwise put, according as it is a *real* or an *ideal* object. Sensuous or real objects can in fact be characterized as *objects of the lowest level of possible intuition*, categorial or ideal objects as *objects of higher levels*.

In the sense of the *narrower, 'sensuous' perception*, an object is directly apprehended or is itself present, if it is set up in an act of perception *in a straightforward (schlichter) manner*. What this means is this: that the object is also an *immediately given object* in the sense that, as *this object perceived with this definite objective content*, it is not *constituted* in relational, connective, or otherwise articulated acts, *acts founded on other acts which bring other objects to perception*. Sensuous objects are present in perception *at a single act-level*: they do not need to be constituted in many-rayed fashion in acts of higher level, whose objects are set up for them by way of other objects, already constituted in other acts.

Each straightforward act of perception, by itself or together with other acts, can serve as basic act for new acts which at times include it, at times merely presuppose it, acts which in their new mode of consciousness likewise bring to maturity *a new awareness of objects which essentially presupposes the old*. When the new acts of conjunction, of disjunction, of definite and indefinite individual apprehension (that – something), of generalization, of straightforward, relational and connective knowledge, arise, we do not then have *any* sort of subjective experiences, nor just acts connected with the original ones. What we have are acts which, as we said, *set up new objects*, acts in which something *appears as actual and self-given*, which was not given, and could not have been given, as what it now appears to be, in these foundational acts alone. *On the other hand, the new objects are based on the older ones, they are related to what appears in the basic acts.* Their manner of appearance is essentially determined by this relation. We are here dealing with a sphere of objects, *which can only show themselves 'in person' in such founded acts.* In such founded acts we have the categorial element in intuition and knowledge, in them assertive thought, functioning expressively, finds fulfilment; the possibility of complete accord with such acts determines the truth, the rightness, of an assertion. So far we have of course only considered the sphere of perception, and only its most elementary cases. But one sees at once that the distinction of straightforward and founded acts can be extended from percepts to all intuitions. We clearly envisage the possibility of complex acts which in mixed fashion have a part-basis in straightforward percepts and a part-basis in straightforward imaginations, and the further possibility of setting up new foundations on intuitions which themselves have foundations, and so building up whole series of foundings upon foundings. We further see that signitive intentions have structures patterned on such foundings whether of lower or higher order, and that again mixtures of signitive and intuitive acts emerge out of such 'founding', founded acts, in short, that are built on acts of one or the other sort. Our first task, however, is to deal with the elementary cases and elucidate them completely.

§47 *Continuation. Characterization of sense-perception as 'straightforward' perception*

We shall now scrutinize the acts in which sensuous concreta and their sensuous constituents are presented as given; as opposed to these we shall later consider the quite different acts in which concretely determinate States of Affairs, Collections and Disjunctions are given as complex thought-objects, or as objects of higher order, *which include their foundational objects as real parts (reell) in themselves.* We shall then deal with acts of the type of generalizing or indefinitely individual apprehension, whose objects certainly are of higher level, but which do *not* include their foundational objects in themselves.

In *sense*-perception, the 'external' thing appears 'in one blow', as soon as our glance falls upon it. The manner in which it makes the thing appear present is *straightforward*: it requires no apparatus of founding or founded acts. To what complex mental processes it may trace back its origin, and in what manner, is of course irrelevant here.

We are not ignoring the obvious complexity that can be shown to exist in the phenomenological content of the straightforward perceptual act, and particularly in its unitary intention.

Many constitutive properties certainly pertain to the thing when it appears with a given content, some of them themselves 'falling under perception', others merely intended. But we certainly do not live through all the articulated acts of perception which *would* arise were we to attend to all the details of the thing, or, more precisely, to the properties of the 'side turned to us', were we to make them objects in their own right. No doubt ideas of such supplementary properties, not given in perception, are 'dispositionally excited', no doubt intentions which relate to them contribute to perception, and determine its total character. But, just as the thing does not appear before us as the mere sum of its countless individual features, which a later preoccupation with detail may distinguish, and as even the latter does not dirempt the thing into such details, but takes note of them only in the ever complete, unified thing, so the act of perception also is always a homogeneous unity, which gives the object 'presence' in a simple, immediate way. The unity of perception does *not* therefore arise through *our own synthetic activity*, as if only a form of synthesis, operating by way of founded acts, could give unity of objective reference to part-intentions. It requires no articulation and hence no actual linkage. The unity of perception comes into being as a *straightforward* unity, *as an immediate fusion of part-intentions, without the addition of new act-intentions*.

We may also be unsatisfied with a single glance, we may handle the thing from all sides in a *continuous perceptual series*, feeling it over as it were with our senses. But each single percept in this series is already a percept of the thing. Whether I look at this book from above or below, from inside or outside, I always see *this book*. It is always one and the same thing, and that not merely in some purely physical sense, but in the view of our percepts themselves. If individual properties dominate variably at each step, the thing itself, as a perceived unity, is not in essence set up by some overreaching act, founded upon these separate percepts.

Considering things more closely, we should not present the

matter as if the one sensible object *could* be presented in a founded act (in a continuously developing act of perceiving), while it merely does not *need* to be presented in such an act. Closer analysis shows that even a continuous perceptual flux involves a *fusion* of part-acts in one act, *rather than a peculiar act founded upon such part-acts*.

To prove this we embark on the following discussion.

The individual percepts of our series have a continuous unity. Such continuity does not amount to the mere fact of temporal adjunction: the series of individual acts rather has the character of a phenomenological unity, in which the individual acts are fused. In this unity, our manifold acts are not merely fused into a phenomenological whole, but into *one act*, more precisely, into *one concept*. In the continuous running on of individual percepts we continuously perceive the single, selfsame object. Can we now call this continuous percept, since it is built out of individual percepts, a percept *founded* upon them? It is of course founded upon them in the sense in which a whole is founded on its parts, not however in the sense here relevant, according to which a founded act manifests a new act-character, grounded in the act-characters that underlie it and unthinkable apart from these. In the case before us perception is merely, as it were, extended: it allows parts to be broken off from itself which can function as complete, independent percepts. But the unification of these percepts into a continuous percept is not the performance of some peculiar act, through which a new consciousness of something objective is set up. We find, instead, that absolutely nothing new is objectively meant in the extended act, but that the same object is continuously meant in it, the very object that the part-percepts, *taken singly*, were already meaning.

One might lay stress on this sameness, and say that our unity is plainly a *unity of identification*, that the intention of the serially arranged acts coincides continuously, and that so the unity arises. This is certainly right. But *unity of identification* is unavoidably distinct, *does not say the same as the unity of an act of identification*. An act *means* something, an act of identification means identity, presents it. In our case an identification is performed, but no identity is meant. The object meant in the differing acts of the continuous perceptual series is indeed always the same, and the acts are one through coincidence, but what is perceived in the series, what is rendered objective in it, is solely the sensible object, never its identity with self. Only when we use the perceptual series to found a novel act, only when we articulate our individual percepts, and relate their objects to each other, does the unity of continuity holding among these individual percepts – the unity of fusion through their coinciding intentions – provide a *point d'appui* for a consciousness of identity. Identity itself is now made objective, the moment of coincidence linking our act-characters with one another, serves as *representative content for a new percept, founded upon* our articulated individual percepts. This brings to intentional awareness that what we now see and what we saw before are one and the same. Naturally we have then to do with a regular act of our second group. Our act of identification is in sober fact a new awareness of objectivity, which causes a new 'object' to appear to us, an object that can only be apprehended or given in its very selfhood in a founded act of this sort.

Before we penetrate further into our new class of acts and objects, we must, however, first round off our treatment of straightforward percepts. If we may presume to have cleared up the sense of the concept of a *straightforward* percept, or, what we take for the same, of sense-perception, then we have also cleared up the concept of a *sensible* or *real object* (in the most basic sense of 'real'). We define a real object as the possible object of a straightforward percept. There is a necessary parallelism between perception and *imagination*, which guarantees that a possible imagination (or more precisely a whole series of imaginations) having the same essence, corresponds to each possible percept, a *straightforward* imagination is correlated with each straightforward percept, thereby giving certainty to the wider concept of *sensible intuition*. We can then define *sensible* objects as the possible objects of sensible imagination and sensible intuition in general: this of course involves no essential generalization of our previous definition. The parallelism just stressed makes both definitions equivalent.

Through the concept of a real object, the concept of a *real* part, or more particularly, the concepts of a *real piece*, and a *real* moment (real feature), and a *real form*, are determined. Each part of a real object is a real part.

In straightforward perception we say that the whole object is explicitly given, while each of its parts (in the widest sense of 'parts') is implicitly given. The sum total of objects that can be *explicitly or implicitly given* in straightforward percepts constitutes *the most widely conceived sphere of sensible objects.*

Each concrete sensible object is perceptible in explicit fashion, and so also every piece of such an object. How does the matter stand in regard to abstract moments? Their nature makes them incapable of separate being: their representative content, even where there is merely representation by way of analogy, cannot be experienced alone, but only in a more comprehensive concrete setting. But this does not mean that their intuition need be a founded act. It would be one, if the apprehension of an abstract moment was necessarily preceded by the *apprehension* of the concrete whole or of its complementary moments, such an apprehension being an act of intuitive turning towards its object. This I do not find obvious. It is clear, *per contra*, that the apprehension of a moment and of a part generally *as* a part of the whole in question, and, in particular, the apprehension of a sensuous feature *as* a feature, or of a sensuous form *as* a form, point to acts which are all founded: these acts are in our case of a relational kind. This means that the sphere of 'sensibility' has been left, and that of 'understanding' entered. We shall now subject the just mentioned group of founded acts to a closer consideration.

§48 *Characterization of categorial acts as founded acts*

A sensible object can be apprehended by us in a variety of ways. It can, first of all, of course, be apprehended in 'straightforward' fashion. It is this possibility, which like all the other possibilities here in question must be throughout interpreted as 'ideal', which characterizes the sensible object as a sensible object. Understood in this manner, it stands as it were simply before us: the parts which constitute it are indeed in it, but are not made our explicit objects in the straightforward act. The same object can, however, be grasped by us in explicating fashion: acts of articulation can put its parts 'into relief', relational acts bring the relieved parts into relation, whether to one another or to the whole. Only through such new modes of interpretation will the connected and related members assume the character of 'parts' (or of 'wholes'). The articulating acts, and, taken in retrospect, the act we call 'straightforward', are not merely experienced one after the other: *overreaching unities of act* are rather always present, in which, *as new objects*, the *relationships of the parts* become constituted.

Let us first look at the relationships of parts and wholes: limiting ourselves to the simplest cases, let us consider the relationships *A is or has* α and α *is in A*. To point to the founded acts in which these typical states of affairs become constituted as data, and to clear up the just employed forms of categorical statement (to lead them back to their intuitive origin and adequate fulfilment) are one and the same. We are not, however, here concerned with the qualities of acts, but only with the constitution of their interpretative forms: to that extent our analysis, if regarded as an analysis of judgement, will be defective.

An act of perception grasps *A* as a whole, at one 'blow' and in straightforward fashion. A second act of perception is trained upon α, the part or dependent moment, that belongs constitutively to *A*. These two acts are not merely performed together, or after one another, in the manner of disjoined experiences; rather are they bound together in a single act in whose synthesis *A* is first given as containing α in itself. Just so, α can, with a reversal of the direction of relational perception, achieve self-givenness as pertaining to *A*.

Let us now try to penetrate a little deeper.

The total intuitive reference to our object implicitly contains an intention to α. For perception purports to grasp the object itself: its 'grasping' must therefore reach to all its constituents in and with the whole object. (Naturally we are here only concerned with what constitutes the object *as* it appears in perception, and *as what* it appears in perception, and not with such constituents as may pertain to it in 'objective reality', and which only later experience, knowledge and science will bring out.)

In the narrowing down of our total percept to one specific percept, the part-intention to α will not be torn out of the total appearance of *A*, so as to break up the latter's unity, but an *independent* act will have α as its own perceptual object. At the same time one's continuously operative total percept will coincide with this specific percept in respect of one implicit part-intention. The 'content' which represents α, will be functioning as the same content in a twofold fashion, and, in so far as it does this, it will effect a coincidence, a peculiar unity of the two representative

functions; we shall, in other words, have two coincident interpretations, both sustained by the representative content in question. But this unity of these two representative functions will
now itself take on a representative role. It will not itself count in
its own right as an experienced bond among acts: it will not set
itself up as our object, but will help to set up another object. It
will act representatively, and to such effect, that A will now appear
to contain α in itself (or, with a reversed direction, α will appear
as contained in A).

According, therefore, to our 'interpretative standpoint', or to
the 'sense of our passage' from part to whole or contrariwise –
which are both *novel phenomenological characters* making their contribution to the total intentional matter of the relating act – there
will be two possibilities, marked off in *a priori* fashion, in which
the 'same relation' can achieve actual givenness. To these correspond two *a priori* possibilities of relation, objectively different,
yet tied together by an ideal law, possibilities *which can only be
directly constituted in founded acts of the sort in question*, which can
achieve 'self-givenness to perception' only in acts built up in this
manner.

Our exposition obviously applies to all specific forms of the
relation between a *whole* and its *parts*. All such relationships are
of categorial, ideal nature. It would be a mistake to try to locate
them in the straightforwardly given whole, to discover them in
this whole by analysis. The part certainly lies hidden in the whole
before all division into members, and is subsidiarily apprehended
in our perceptual grasp of this whole. But this fact, that it thus
lies hidden in the whole, is at first merely the ideal possibility
of bringing the part, and the fact that it is a part, to perception in
correspondingly articulated and founded acts.

The matter is plainly similar in the case of *external* relations,
from which predications such as 'A is to the right of B', 'A is
larger, brighter, louder than B etc.', take their rise. Wherever
sensible objects – directly and independently perceptible – are
brought together, despite their mutual exclusion, into more or
less intimate unities, into what fundamentally are more comprehensive objects, then a possibility of such external relations
arises. They all fall under the general type of the relation of *part
to parts within a whole. Founded acts* are once more the media *in which
the primary appearance of the states of affairs in question*, of such

external relationships, is achieved. It is clear, in fact, that neither the straightforward percept of the complex whole, nor the specific percepts pertaining to its members, are in themselves the relational percepts which alone are possible in such a complex. Only when one member is picked out as principal member, and is dwelt on while the other members are still kept in mind, does a determination of members by members make its appearance, a determination which varies with the kind of unity that is present and plainly also with the particular members set in relief. In such cases also the choice of a principal member, or of a direction of relational apprehension, leads to phenomenologically distinct forms of relationship, correlatively characterized, which forms are not genuinely present in the unarticulated percept of the connection as a straightforward phenomenon, but which are in it only as *ideal possibilities*, the possibilities, that is, of fulfilling relevant founded acts.

A real (*reelle*) location of these relations of parts in the whole would be a confusion of distinct things: of *sensuous* or *real* (*realen*) forms of combination, with *categorial* or *ideal* ones. Sensible combinations are aspects of the real (*realen*) object, its actual moments, present in it, if only implicitly, and capable of being 'lifted out of it' by an abstractive percept. As against this, forms of categorial combination go with the manner in which acts are synthesized: they are constituted as objects in the synthetic acts built upon our sensibility. In the formation of external relations sensuous forms may serve as foundations for the categorial forms which correspond to them, as when, in the face of the sensuously intuited contact of the contents A and B within a comprehensive whole W, we, observe, and perhaps verbally express our observation, in the synthetic forms 'A is in contact with B', or 'B is in contact with A'. But, in constituting the latter forms, we bring new objects into being, objects belonging to the class of 'states of affairs', which includes none but 'objects of higher order'. In the sensible whole, the parts A and B are made one by the sensuously combinatory form of contact. The abstraction of these parts and moments, the formation of intuitions of A, B and *contact*, will not yet yield the presentation A *in contact with* B. This demands a novel act which, taking charge of such presentations, shapes and combines them suitably.

§49 *Added note on nominal formations*

We shall now make an important addition to our analysis up to this point: this concerns the *shaping* which synthetically combined presentations, each on their own account, may undergo. We have already studied this important point in a special class of cases: we observed, in our Fifth Investigation that an assertion can never be made, in unmodified form, the basis of a synthetic act built upon it, the subject- or object-member of a new assertion. An assertion, we said, must first of all take on nominal form, whereby its state of affairs becomes objective in a new, nominal fashion. In this fact the intuitive distinction we have in view is brought out, a distinction which does not merely hold of the relata of the hitherto discussed syntheses of lowest grade, immediately based on sensibility, but of all presentations presided over by 'many-rayed' syntheses of whatever kind or level.

We may at first then hazard the general statement: *Objectifying acts which exist purely 'on their own', and 'the same' objectifying acts serving to constitute the terms of some relation or other,* are not really the same acts: they *differ phenomenologically, and differ in respect of what we have called their intentional matter.* Their *interpretative sense* has changed, and hence the *changed meaning* of their adequate expression. It is not as if something had merely been shoved in between unchanged presentations, a bond which combined them in merely external fashion. The working of synthetic thought, of intellection, has done something to them, has shaped them anew, although, being a categorial function, it has done this in categorial fashion, so that the sensuous content of the apparent object has not been altered. The object does not appear before us with new real (*realen*) properties; it stands before us as this same object, but in a *new manner.* Its fitting into its categorial context gives it a definite place and role in this context, the role of a *relatum,* and in particular of a subject- or object-member. These are differences that are phenomenologically evident.

It is no doubt easier to pay heed to changes of meaning in our expressive symbols than to modifications of our direct presentations themselves: the situation, e.g., in the field of straightforward intuitions, when we compare such intuitions within and without some relational function, is far from clear, and I have not therefore touched on it in my last Investigation. There isolated sense-percepts were put on a level with nominally functioning acts (see Inv. v, §33). Just as the object in a straightforward percept directly confronts us, so too does the state of affairs in the act which names it, and so too does any categorially formed object. The gradual constitution of the object has been completed, as a finished object it becomes a term in a relation: it keeps, it seems, its constitutive sense quite unaltered. One can certainly say that the phenomenological change in sense made by entry into a relational act is at first masked by the very fact that the new form includes the whole previous interpretative sense in itself, to which it only imparts the new sense of a 'role'. Perception remains perception, the object is given as it was before given, 'only' it is 'put into relation'. Such shapings due to our synthetic function do not alter the object itself, we count them only as pertaining to our subjective activity, and we therefore overlook them in phenomenological reflections aiming at a clarification of knowledge. We should in consistency therefore say: A state of affairs also is the same state of affairs when it functions as logical subject (or generally when it functions nominally), and it *has its ultimate constitution in the same act of originative intuition as when it functioned in isolation.* When, however, it functions as a relatum in an act of higher level, it is constituted with a new form (and with, so to say, the characterizing costume of its *role*) of which the nominal form is the adequate expression. Further researches will however be necessary for a last clearing-up of the phenomenological situation just tackled.

§50 *Sensuous forms categorially grasped but not functioning nominally*

We have so far only spoken of the re-shapings of terms put into such relations as that of whole and part. External relations, however, show us how sensuous forms enter into the unity of a relation (in its predicate) *without undergoing nominal reification*, e.g. '*A* brighter than *B*', '*A* to the right of *B*' etc. There are undeniable phenomenological differences – differences in interpretative sense – between cases where we, so to say, pay direct attention to the form of brightness, and make this our *nominal* object, as when we say 'This relation of brightness (between *A* and *B*) is more readily noticeable than that one (between *M* and *N*)', and the quite different cases, where this form of brightness is meant as in the above expression '*A* is brighter than *B*'. In the latter class of cases we once more have a categorial form pointing to a peculiar function in the total relational situation. Concepts such as Terms of Relations, Form of Relation, Subject, Object etc., concepts not always clearly expressed and certainly insufficiently clarified, plainly lead back to differences in such categorial forms with which in this and previous paragraphs we have become familiar.

§51 *Collectiva and Disjunctiva*

We have so far discussed, as instances of categorial and synthetic object-forms, only certain very simple forms of states of affairs, those of total and partial relations of identity, and of simple external relations. We now turn our regard to two further examples, to synthetic forms, i.e. which, though not themselves states of affairs, nevertheless play a large part in connection with states of affairs: Collectiva and Disjunctiva. The acts in which these are constituted as data are those which furnish a fulfilling intuition for the meanings of the conjunctions 'and' and 'or'.

What intuitively corresponds to the words 'and' and 'or', to 'both' or 'either', is not anything, as we rather roughly put it above, that can be grasped with one's hands, or apprehended with some sense, as it can also not really be represented in an image, e.g. in a painting. I can paint *A* and I can paint *B*, and I can paint them both on the same canvas: I cannot, however, paint the *both*, nor paint the *A and* the *B*. Here we have only the one possibility which is always open to us: to perform a new act of conjunction or collection on the basis of our two single acts of intuition, and so *mean* the *aggregate* of the objects *A* and *B*. In the situation just viewed as an example this act is constituted as an *imaginative* presentation of *A and B*, while this aggregate is only given as 'itself', in the manner of perception, and can only be so given, in just such an act, an act merely modified in a conformable manner, and which is founded on the *percepts* of *A* and *B*.

That we speak of an act which unites these percepts, and not of any connection or mere coexistence of these percepts in consciousness, depends on the fact that a *unitary intentional* relation is here given, and a unitary object which corresponds to it; this object can only be constituted in such a connection of acts, just as a State of Affairs can only be constituted in a *relational* act-connection. We at once see the essential mistake made by those eminent modern logicians who have tried to explain the conjunctive association of names or statements through a mere conscious coexistence of nominal or propositional acts, and have so surrendered *and* as an objective form in Logic.[1]

We must also guard against confusing the *straightforward percepts of sensuously unified manifolds, series, swarms* etc., with the *conjunctive percepts* in which alone the consciousness of plurality is itself properly constituted. I have tried to show in my *Philosophy of Arithmetic* how the sensuously unifying characters – I there called them 'figural' or 'quasi-qualitative' moments of sensuous intuitions – serve as signs of plurality. This means that they serve as sensuous *points d'appui* for the signitively mediated cognition of plurality as such, and of plurality of the kind in question – which cognition now has no need of an articulated grasp and knowledge of individual items, but does not therefore as yet possess the character of a genuine intuition of the collection as such.[2]

§ 52 *Universal objects and their self-constitution in universal intuitions*

The simple synthetic acts with which we have so far concerned ourselves were so founded upon straightforward percepts that the *synthetic intention was subsidiarily directed to the objects of these founding percepts*, inasmuch as it held them together in ideal 'contents' or brought them to a relational unity. This is a *universal* character of synthetic acts as such. We now turn to examples from *another set of categorial acts*, in which the objects of the founding

---

[1] Thus we read in Sigwart (*Logic*, 1 (ed. 2), p. 206): 'The verbal conjoining of sentences through "and"...expresses only the subjective fact of their coexistence in one conciousness, and it therefore has no objective meaning.' Cf. also p. 278.

[2] It was precisely this question: how estimates of plurality and number are possible at a glance, and may therefore be achieved in straightforward, and not in founded intuition, while true collection and counting presuppose articulated acts of higher order – it was this question that independently led me to take note of those intuitively unifying characters which v. Ehrenfels called 'Gestalt-qualities', and which he dealt with in a penetrating manner in a work which appeared before mine, and which was dominated by quite different points of view. ('Über Gestaltqualitäten', *Viertelj. f. wiss. Philosophie*, 1890. Cf. my *Philosophie der Arithmetik*, ch. xi.)

acts do not *enter into* the intention of the founded one, and would only reveal their close relation to it in relational acts. Here we have the field of the *universal intuition* – an expression which no doubt will not seem better to many than 'wooden iron'.

Abstraction gets to work on a basis of primary intuitions, and with it a new categorial act-character emerges, in which a new style of objectivity becomes apparent, an objectivity which can *only* become apparent – whether given as 'real' or as 'merely imagined' – in just such a founded act. Naturally I do not here mean 'abstraction' merely in the sense of a setting-in-relief of some non-independent moment in a sensible object, but Ideational Abstraction, where no such non-independent moment, but its Idea, its Universal, is brought to consciousness, and achieves *actual givenness*. We must presuppose such an act in order that the Very Sort, to which the manifold single moments 'of one and the same sort' stand opposed, may *itself* come before us, and may come before us *as one and the same*. For we become aware of the identity of the universal through the repeated performance of such acts upon a basis of several individual intuitions, and we plainly do so in an overreaching act of identification which brings all such single acts of abstraction into one synthesis. Through such acts of abstraction, woven into new act-forms, there arise, further, acts of universal determination, acts, that is, which determine objects *generally* as subsumed under certain species *A*, or acts in which *unspecified* objects *of a sort A* become present to us.

In an act of abstraction, which need not necessarily involve the use of an abstract name, the universal *itself is given to us*; we do not think of it merely in significative fashion as when we merely understand general names, but we apprehend it, *behold* it. Talk of an *intuition*, and, more precisely, of a *perception of the universal* is in this case, therefore, well-justified.

Difficulties arise, however, from another quarter. Talk of 'perception' presupposes the possibility of correspondent imagination: a distinction between them, we held, is part of the natural sense of our ordinary talk about 'intuition'. But it is just this distinction that we cannot here draw. This seems to stem from the fact that abstractive acts do not differ in consonance with the character of the straightforward intuitions which underlie them; they are quite unaffected by the assertive or non-assertive character of such underlying acts, or by their perceptual or imaginative character. The *Red*, the *Triangle* exemplified in mere phantasy is specifically the same as the *Red*, the *Triangle* exemplified in our percepts. Our consciousness of the universal has as satisfactory a basis in perception as it has in parallel imagination, and, wherever it arises, the Idea *Red*, the Idea *Triangle*, is *itself* apprehended, is intuited in the one unique way which permits no distinction between image and original.

We must, however, note that the examples adduced were all cases of the *adequate* perception of the universal. The universal was here truly grasped and given on the basis of truly correspondent instances. Where this is the case, there seems in fact to be no parallel imagination having the same intuitive content, and this is so in *every* case of adequate perception. For how, we may ask, even in the realm of individuals, could a content pattern itself on itself, since, taken as itself, it cannot also be meant as its own analogon? And how can the note of *assertion* be wanting, where the meant content is the one experienced and given? It is quite different in, e.g., the case where mathematical analysis has given us an indirectly conceived Idea of a certain class of curves of the third order, though we have never *seen* any curve of this sort. In such a case an intuitive figure, e.g. of a familiar third-order curve, perhaps actually drawn, perhaps merely pictured, may very well serve as an intuitive image, an analogon, of the universal we are intending: our consciousness of the universal is here intuitive, but analogically intuitive, in its use of an individual intuition. And does not an ordinary rough drawing function analogically in comparison with an ideal figure, thereby helping to condition the *imaginative character of the universal presentation*? This is how we contemplate the Idea of a steam-engine, basing ourselves on a model of a steam-engine, in which case there can naturally be no talk of an adequate abstraction or conception. In such cases we are not concerned with significations, but with universal representations by way of analogy, with universal imaginations, in short. If, however, the consciousness of mere analogy lapses, as may happen, e.g., in the intuition of a model, we have a case of the *perception of the universal*, even if it is one of *inadequate* perception.

In the same way we may now discover the previously missing differences between *an assertive, and a merely contemplative, consciousness of the universal*. Where we contemplate a universal object in a merely analogizing, imaginative fashion, we may also mean it assertively, and this act, like any assertive reference, may be confirmed or refuted by adequate future perception. The former happens wherever the universal meaning is fulfilled by an adequate percept, i.e. by a new consciousness of the universal which constitutes itself on the basis of a 'true' abstraction from the corresponding individual percept. The universal object is then not merely presented and posited, but is itself given to us. Again we can have an analogizing presentation of the universal, without actually positing it. We conceive it, but leave it in suspense. The intention to the universal which here rests on an intuitive basis makes no decision regarding 'being' or 'non-being', only one regarding the *possibility* or impossibility of the universal, and of its presentation through adequate abstraction.

CHAPTER SEVEN

A Study in Categorial Representation

§53 Backward reference to the researches of our first section

THE founded acts analysed by us in select examples were considered by us to be intuitions, and intuitions of the new types of object that they brought to light, objects which can only be given in founded acts of a sort and form which corresponds to each of them. The explanatory value of this extended use of the concept Intuition can only lie in the fact that we are not here dealing with some inessential, merely disjunctive widening of a concept, which permits us to extend the sphere of that concept over the spheres of any heterogeneous concepts whatsoever,[1] but with an authentic generalization, which rests on a community of essential features. We call the new acts 'intuitions' in that, with a mere surrender of a 'straightforward' relation to their object – the peculiar sort of immediacy defined by us as 'straightforwardness' – they yet have all the essential peculiarities of intuitions: we find in their case the same essential divisions, and they show themselves capable of achieving the same fully performed *fulfilments*. This last mentioned capacity is particularly important for our purposes, for it was with a view to such performances that this whole investigation has been conducted. Knowledge as the unity of fulfilment is not achieved on a mere basis of straightforward acts, but in general, on a basis of categorial acts: when, accordingly, we oppose *intuition* to *thought* (as meaning), we cannot mean by 'intuition' merely sensuous intuition.

---

[1] If α represents the constitutive features in a concept and β those of any other concept *whatever*, one can always construct the form: Something that is *either* α or β. This external sort of conceptual extension which I call 'disjunctive', can at times prove very useful. It plays, e.g., an important role in the development of artificial mathematical techniques not sufficiently appreciated by logicians. The logic of mathematics is in fact in its infancy: few logicians have even seen that here is a field of great problems, fundamental for the understanding of mathematics and of mathematicizing natural science, and admitting of strict solution despite all their difficulty

24-2

The conception of categorial acts as intuitions, first brings true perspicuity into the relation of thought to intuition – a relation that no previous critique of knowledge has made tolerably clear: it is the first to render knowledge itself intelligible, in its essence and its achievement. Through such a conceptual extension the theses of our first section first gain adequate confirmation. To all intuitions, in our present widest sense, however near or far they may stand from sensibility, expressive meanings correspond – as their possible ideal counterparts. The divisions drawn by us within 'epistemic essence', and the concepts framed in close connection therewith, retain their validity in this wider sphere, though marked off by us in relation to a narrower one.

Each categorial act of intuition has therefore:

1. its quality;
2. its (intentional) material, or interpretative sense;
3. its representing contents.

These distinctions do not reduce to distinctions among *underlying* acts. The quality of a total act may differ from that of a basic act, just as basic acts, when many, may be differently qualified, as, e.g., in an idea of a relation between a fictitious object and one taken to be real.

Not only has each of the underlying acts its own material, but the founded act imports its own material: it is true to say that this *novel material*, or, where this includes the materials of basic acts, the *newly added part* of it, is *founded on the materials of the basic act*.

Finally, also, the new act has *representing contents* in regard to which there are serious difficulties. *Must new representing contents be assumed for this new material*, and *what* can these be?

§54 *The question of the representing contents of categorial forms*

When one begins to analyse categorial acts, one is struck by the apparently irrefutable observation, that all differences of categorial acts reduce to corresponding differences of the acts on which they are founded, i.e. that the new element imported by the categorial function represents an increase of content that cannot be further differentiated. How else could an imaginative presentation of a collection differ from the percept of the same collection, than in respect of the intentional manner in which its members are given? As regards the *form of connection*, one would say, no further intelligible distinction can be drawn in the two cases. Or should one say that the form of a collection – what we express by the word 'and' – is specifically different according as it is perceptually or imaginatively apparent? In that case we ought to think that the appearances of phantasy might be bound together by the collective form of perception, while perceptual phenomena might be bound together by the collective form of phantasy, and each differently. But this is plainly unthinkable, nay, unintelligible.

Nothing, it might be objected, is easier than just what has been said. Why should we not assemble certain perceptual objects in thought in order to refer imaginatively to some other aggregate? And why should we not assemble imaginative phenomena in thought in order to refer only to this imaginative aggregate, and so to perceive the latter? We may certainly do exactly this. But the perceptual objects will then be functioning as images, and the act of collection will not be directly founded on percepts, but on the imaginations built upon them. Just so, in the other case, we shall not be collecting the objects of our fancyings, but those fancyings themselves, i.e. the act of collection will not be directly founded on fancyings, but upon 'inner percepts' directed upon these latter. This establishes no difference between 'real' collections on a basis of perceived objects, and 'imaginary' collections on a basis of imagined objects: such a difference does not exist, except as a difference in underlying acts.

The same seems to hold for all other modifications that the collective consciousness can show us. The universality or specificity, definiteness or indefiniteness, or whatever other categorial forms may come into play for our underlying objects, will also determine the character of our collective presentation, but not so that we shall be able to find phenomenological differences in the connective character itself: it is always the same *and*. According as our underlying presentations differ in type, we have a collection of universal objects before us (e.g. Species of colour, *Red and Blue and Yellow*), or a collection of individual objects (*Aristotle and Plato*), a collection of definite objects (as in the previous example) or of indefinite ones (*a person and another person, a colour and a tone*). One cannot conceive how differences in acts of collection should be possible except in respect of differences in the acts which underlie them.

The same also seems immediately clear in regard to relational intuitions. Relating always displays an identity of form, all variation depending on the underlying acts.

In this situation can we still hope for ascertainable differences between *representing contents* and *interpretative sense* in respect to the newly added part of a founded act, the *form of connection* in the case of synthetic acts? In the case of *straightforward* intuitions, interpretative sense (*material*) and representing content were intimately united: they were mutually related, and far from independent in their variations. Nonetheless they underwent abundant shifts as against one another. The representing sensum could stay the same while the interpretative sense altered, and could vary while the latter remained constant. An imaginative presentation, e.g., can remain identical in respect, not only of material, but also of extent of fulness, and can nonetheless notably change in respect of vivacity. In the sphere of sense, the distinction between material and representing content can be readily pointed out and unhesitatingly acknowledged. How is it, however, in the case of *categorial* acts, where, if we ignore their act-foundation, variability seems entirely absent? Are we to say that they lack the distinction in question as regards their form, that they have no representing contents which extend beyond the representing contents of their underlying acts? When these underlying acts are themselves categorial, e.g. acts of ideation, these too will lack representation, which will be found only in their ultimate foundation of straightforward intuitions.

§55 *Arguments for the assumption of peculiar categorial representing contents*

In default of an attitude to this question we must emphatically observe that, in the previous exposition, the complete absence of differentiation among forms, as against the multifarious changes in the total act and its foundation, has perhaps been exaggerated, even misinterpreted. For when the whole act is a perceptual presentation, its form, *qua* form of a perceptual presentation, certainly differs in character from that of an imaginative presentation. If the form is what is really new and essential in the categorial presentation, it must share in the import of each essential character that penetrates the whole and that belongs to it as a whole. If reflection fails to show us differences of interpretative sense in the form, or at least in the form of the *synthetic* act – the matter has already been treated sufficiently as regards the abstractive act in the discussions of §52 – this can be explained by the fact that we involuntarily abstract from these interpretative characters, since they do not distinguish and mark off the moment of synthesis, but rather pervade the complete, founded act equally. Instead we attend exclusively to the common element that confronts us in, e.g., all forms of collective synthesis. But just this common element could be the representing content that we are looking for. As, in straightforward sense-perception, the homogeneous unity of the perceptual sense pervades the total representation, having definite relations to each separate part of the representing content, without seeming to inner reflection to be made up of separate partial conceptions, so, in the case of categorial intuitions, the interpretative sense pervades the total act and its representing content, without being clearly divided to match the representing contents that can be distinguished by reflection. The above exposition contains, if we allow the interpretation, the important truth that *in all change of underlying acts and interpretative forms, there is a unique representing content for each sort of founded act.* The abundant multiplicity of sense-qualities, of sensible forms etc., is at the disposal of straightforward sensuous intuition for purposes of representation. In the sphere of collective intuitions or intuitions of identity etc., we were always limited to *one* sort: the form of *and* is everywhere the same, and so is the *is*-form etc. These forms were here to be understood as analogues of the sense-kernel, of what is sensuous in sensuous intuition: there was to be abstraction from quality and from interpretative sense.

One might here suspect that the wish was being father to the thought, and might direct attention to a fact issuing from our former treatment: that representing contents are by no means essential constituents of acts. For it is the peculiarity of all signitive acts that they lack representing contents, i.e. *authentic* representing contents which themselves relate to the internal being of the object. For signitive acts, too, have their *non*-authentic representing contents, which do not stand for the object meant in the act, but for some other object, the object of an underlying act. If non-authentic representing contents suffice, then we of course have no more difficulty, for such contents are present in our case, since underlying acts always provide them. The authentic representing contents of these underlying acts can be seen as non-authentically representative in relation to the acts founded on them.

But the comparison with merely signitive acts makes us vividly aware that founded acts cannot do without authentic representation, and representation as regards categorial form. We are made mindful of relations of possible fulfilment, of the 'fulness' which intuitive acts confer on signitive ones, of the ascending scales formed among intuitive acts by variable fulness, of final adequation as an ideal limit. Representing contents constitute the difference between 'empty' signification and 'full' intuition; they are responsible for 'fulness', as is shown by the fact that they determine one sense of 'fulness' (see § 22). Only intuitive acts render their object apparent, seeable, for the reason, namely, that a representing content is there, which the interpretative form sees as a likeness, or as the very self, of the object. This is a fact rooted in the universal essence of the relation of fulfilment, and must therefore be demonstrable in our present sphere too. In this present sphere, too, we find 'signitively' opposed to 'intuitively': the opposition between objectifying acts which mean a categorial object signitively, and the parallel acts which present the same object through the same interpretative sense intuitively, whether 'in likeness' or 'in very self'. Since the intentional material is the same in both cases, we can again only treat the new element in our categorial intuition as being representative, as setting the object before us *in its content*, as treating experienced contents as representing an object meant. Such representation cannot, however, be exclusively carried out in underlying acts, for it is not solely *their* objects that are presented, but the whole state of affairs, the whole aggregate etc.

§ 56 *Continuation. The mental linkage of combined acts and the categorial unity of corresponding objects*

One might for a moment suppose that, in the case, e.g., of a relation, only the relata were presented, and that the new element consisted in a mere mental character connecting the two appearances. A connection of acts is not, however, *pro tanto*, a connection of objects. At best it can help to make such a connection apparent: it is not itself the connection that appears in it. A mental bond can be established among acts, and can cause an objective relation to appear before us, while this relation, though it unites truly existent objects, has no being at all. If we judge significatively, without intuitive representation of the state of affairs judged – as is the case in ordinary arithmetical judgements – the relational unity of the act is articulated, and has a mental form of connection entirely analogous to that of the corresponding intuition. But the state of affairs is not, in the strong sense of the word, 'apparent': it is merely meant. If we contrast with this a case of intuitive representation, as when we identify the colour of two perceived surfaces, or of two surfaces recalled in memory, or a person represented in two imaginative presentations, then identity is likewise meant, but is meant in a perceptual manner, in a manner that *gives* us the object, or, in the case of imagination, that gives us a likeness of it. What makes such differences possible? Ought we to locate the whole difference in the underlying acts? Against this we must object that, e.g., in the signitive identification, the identity of the meant objects is not experientially *lived through* but is merely *thought of*, whereas, in the case of intuited objects, the identity is indeed perceived or imagined, but is only given and lived through where adequation is full and strict. *The mental bond, which establishes the synthesis, is therefore a bond of thought or meaning (Meinung) and is as such more or less fulfilled.* It is merely a non-independent constituent of the total meaning, a significative constituent of a significative meaning, and an intuitive constituent of an intuitive meaning, but at all events a constituent which itself shares the character of this meaning, and with this its differences of fulness. We are therefore not unjustified in interpreting the situation as involving *that this constituent also exercises a representative function.* As we compare different cases in the light of the possibility just raised, we believe that we may reduce the mental bond experienced in *actual* identification, collection etc. ('actual' = authentic, intuitive) to a *universal common feature*, to be thought of separately from quality and interpretative sense, and yielding in such reduction the representative content that pertains specially to the moment of categorial form.

§57 *The representing contents of the underlying intuitions are not immediately connected by the representing content of the synthetic form*

Certain not unimportant observations must here suggest themselves as natural additions.

Objectively considered, a synthesis, e.g. one of identity, of attribution etc., belongs to the underlying *objects*: identity is, e.g., identity of the person, attribution the relation between the subject *tree* and the predicate *fruit-bearing*. The connected objects appear before us by way of their representing contents, and it might be thought that the synthetic bond, in which (or by way of which, perhaps in the manner of a representing content) the connection comes before us as a form, is also the simple and direct phenomenological bond between the representing contents of the underlying objects.

As against this we affirm that *the moment of synthesis establishes no direct connection between the representing contents of the basic acts*, but that, e.g., the phenomenological form of identification has its essential basis *in the underlying acts as such*, i.e. it has its basis in what these acts are and contain, in addition to their representing contents.

If the lived-through moment of identity, its mental character, were an immediate bond between the representing sense-contents – we may confine ourselves to the simplest case where the underlying acts and objects are sensuous – the unity established by this moment would also be a sensuous unity, like, e.g., the spatial or qualitative patterns or other forms of unity which likewise have their foundation in the sense-contents in question. All sensuous (real) unity, as our Third Investigation has set forth, is unity founded in the various kinds of sense-content. The concrete contents are many-sided, they sustain various abstract moments in themselves, they underlie manifold possibilities of alteration and connection. We accordingly refer many kinds of connection to this or that moment in such contents. If particular unions are not always founded in the generic characters of complex wholes, taken in their complete specific content, they are nonetheless founded in the primitive generic characters which correspond to the moments of the whole in question. The real lack of relation between categorial act-forms and the sense-contents of their

bases, shows itself in the limitless variability of the generic characters of these contents; in other words, no genus of content lacks
an *a priori* possibility of functioning in the foundation of categorial
acts of every sort. What is categorial is not bound up with representing sensuous contents, but only and necessarily with their
objects, and yet not with them in their sensuous (real) content. This
means that *the mental character in which the categorial form is constituted is bound up phenomenologically with the acts in which the objects
are constituted*. In these acts, sense-contents are representatively
present, and so certainly contribute to such acts. They do not,
however, make up the characteristic essence of these acts, and
they can also exist without the interpretation which first renders
them representative: in the latter case, they *are there*, but nothing
thereby *appears*, and nothing is consequently there to be connected, or to be treated as subject or predicate etc., in categorial
fashion. The *categorial moment* of the synthetically founded act
does not bind these *unessential* elements of the underlying acts
together, but binds what is *essential* to them both: it connects, in
all circumstances, their *intentional materials*, and is in a real sense
founded upon these last. This is what was said above quite
generally: in all categorial acts, we maintained, the material of
the founded acts was founded *in the materials* of the underlying
acts. Identity, e.g., is no immediate form of unity among sensuous
contents, but is a 'unity of consciousness' based upon one or
another (repeated or inwardly different) consciousness of the same
object. This holds in all cases. It is true, no doubt, that intuitions
of all sorts, whether straightforward or categorial, by their
nature submit to the same categorial formations, but this only
means that categorial formation rests phenomenologically on
what is universal in an objectifying act, or is a function essentially
bound up with the generic element in objectifying acts. Only
experiences of this class permit categorial syntheses, and such
synthesis directly connects their intentional essences.

Particularly in the case of adequate synthetic intuitions, immediately based on individual intuitions, must we guard against the
tempting delusion of an immediate phenomenological connection,
present at least on this lowest level of categorial synthesis,
between the representing sense-contents of the one underlying
act and those of the other. In virtue of the functional dependence
of the adequation (evidence) of the total act on the adequation

of its underlying intuitions, the situation would seem to have the following pattern: since the underlying acts are adequate, the representing contents coincide with the object represented. If on such a basis the intuition of a relation arises, a relation, e.g., between part and whole, the relational act too is evident in character: the relation itself is truly given with the truly given contents. The mental bond of relating, conceived as a relation among sensuous contents and objects, here binds these experienced sense-contents as with a direct bond.

Binds them with nothing, one might object. Not the sense-contents, but the adequate intuitions of such contents, serve to base the unity of the act of relating. Here as elsewhere we must look to the objects, to the sensuous contents at once representing and represented, in order to perform the act of relating, to relate this content as whole to that content as part. Relations can only be given on a basis of *given* objects: objects are, however, not given in mere lived experience, in itself blind, but only and solely in percepts, and in our case in the perception of lived through contents which no longer represent something beyond themselves.

All this confirms our original introduction of categorial acts as founded acts. It is *essential* to these acts, in which all that is intellectual is constituted, that they should be achieved in stages. Objectivations arise on a basis of objectivations, and constitute objects which, as objects of higher order, objects in a wider, intellectual sense, can only come to light in such founded acts. This excludes from synthetic acts that immediate unity of representation which unites all representative contents of straightforward intuitions. The complete synthetic intuition therefore arises (if we are right in our above attempted interpretation which requires a most careful pondering) in so far as the mental content which binds the underlying acts itself sustains *interpretation* as the objective unity of the founded objects, as their relation of identity, of part to whole etc.

§58 The relation of our two distinctions: outer and inner sense, also sense for categories

It is now extremely important to bring to complete clearness the relation between the two distinctions introduced by us at the very beginning of this Investigation, the distinction between outer and inner sensibility, on the one hand, and between straightforward and categorial acts, on the other.

A presentation as a mental experience, whether it be straightforward or founded, sensuous or categorial, belongs to the sphere of 'inner sense'. Is there no contradiction in this? Is an inner percept, which reflects on an act, and a founded act to boot, e.g. on an actual insight into the equation $2 + 1 = 1 + 2$, not *eo ipso* a founded percept, and therefore a non-sensuous one? In this act of perception the founded act is given together with the acts that underlie it, and is given in the strongest sense of the word. It belongs to and is part of the real make-up of the (inner) percept. In so far as the latter directs itself to the former act, it is itself related to it, and is therefore itself a founded percept.

We shall here obviously have to reply: to perceive an act, or an act-moment, or an act-complex of any sort, is to perceive sensuously, since it is to perceive *straightforwardly*. This cannot be doubted, since the relation of an act which perceives to an act which is perceived is no relation of foundation, even if we take a founded act to be the act perceived. The foundedness of an act does not mean that it is built on other acts in any manner whatsoever, but that a founded act, by its very nature or kind, is only possible as built upon acts of the sort which underlie it, and that, as a result, the objective correlate of the founded act has a universal element of form which can only be intuitively displayed by an object in a founded act of this kind. The intuitive consciousness of the universal cannot, e.g., exist without underlying individual intuition, nor an identification without underlying acts which relate to the identified objects etc.

The perception, however, which we direct to a founded act could as readily be directed to a non-founded act and to any objects of outer sense, e.g. horses, colours etc. In each case perception consists in a straightforward looking at our object. The material of perception (its interpretative sense) stands in no necessary relation to the material of the perceived act. The whole phenomenological content of this act has rather the sheer character of a representative content, it is objectively interpreted in accordance with the interpretative form of perception, as being this very act of perception itself.

For this reason also, *every* abstraction based on inner sense, e.g. the abstraction which *looks to* a founded act, is a sensuous abstrac-

813

tion. As opposed to this, an abstraction which is itself *built upon a founded act*, is, to the extent that this founded act has the character of an intuition, even that of a categorial intuition, a categorial abstraction. If we look at an intuitive act of identification, i.e. an intuition of identity, and if we abstract from it the moment of *identification*, we have performed a sensuous abstraction. But if, *while living through an identification*, we turn our regard to *objective identity*, and make *this* the basis of our abstraction, we have performed a categorial abstraction (cf. the closer discussion in §60). The objective moment of identity is no act, and no form of an act: it is an objective categorial form. As against this, on the other hand, the moment of identification, that unites the founded acts phenomenologically, is a sensuous and categorial act-form. The same difference essentially divides those concepts framed on a ground of *reflection* on any intuitive acts, from the quite different concepts framed on the ground of these intuitive acts themselves. I perceive a house and, reflecting on my percept, frame the concept of *perception*. But if I look simply at the house, I use my percept itself, rather than the percept of this percept, as the underlying act for an abstraction, and the concept of *house* arises.

There is accordingly nothing remarkable in saying: *The same mental moments which are sensuously given in inner perception* (and which therefore function in it as sensuous representing contents) *may, in a founded act of the character of a categorial perception or imagination set up a categorial form*, and so sustain a totally different *categorial representation*.

The non-independence of categorial forms as forms, is mirrored in the department of inner sense in the fact that the moments in which a categorial form can be constituted – moments[1] narrowly restricted for each form, so that each type of form corresponds to a single type of moment – themselves represent non-independent mental contents, moments founded on characters of acts. Since, however, all characters of acts have their ultimate foundation in the contents of outer sense,[2] we note that there is an essential *phenomenological gulf in the field of sense*.

We have principally to distinguish between:

1. the *contents of reflection*, those contents which are themselves characters of acts or founded upon such characters;

---

[1] See §55.
[2] Naturally not in *particular* kinds of such contents but in the *total* genus of such contents as such.

2. the *primary* contents, those contents in which all contents of reflection are either immediately or mediately founded.

These latter would be the contents of '*external*' *sensibility*, which is here plainly not defined in terms of some metaphysical distinction of outward and inward, but through the nature of its representing contents, as being ultimately foundational, phenomenologically lived-through contents. The primary contents form a unique highest genus, which divides into many species. The manner in which the contents of reflection have their foundation in primary contents is the loosest conceivable: it is such that reflective contents are never bound to a narrower class than the whole class of these primary contents.

Corresponding to the difference between purely sensuous and purely categorial objects of intuition, there is a distinction of representing contents: *only reflective contents can serve as purely categorial representing contents.*

One might now try to pin down the concept of a category by saying that *it comprises all objective forms arising out of the forms, and not out of the matters, of conceptual interpretation.* The following misgiving no doubt might arise. Ought we not also to attribute to sensuous intuition the character of a categorial act, in so far as through it the form of objectivity is constituted? For what we perceive does not merely *exist* in perception, but is given in it as an object. The concept of an object is, however, framed as the correlate of the concept of perception, and so presupposes, not merely an act of abstraction, but also acts of relation. It therefore also qualifies as a categorial concept in our present sense.

CHAPTER EIGHT

The *A Priori* Laws of Authentic and Inauthentic Thinking

§ 59 *The complication into ever new forms. The pure theory of the forms of possible intuitions*

THE varied forms of founded acts where, instead of straight-forward, sensuously-intuitive objects, categorially formed and synthetically connected objects are constituted, permit manifold complications into new forms: in consequence of certain *a priori* categorial laws, categorial unities may again and again become the objects of new connecting, relating or ideating acts. Universal objects, e.g., can be collectively connected, the collections thus formed can in their turn be collectively connected with other collections of similar or different type, and so on *in infinitum*. The possibility of unlimited complication is here self-evident and *a priori*. Just so, within certain law-bound limits, one can unify states of affairs in new states of affairs, pursue an indefinitely extended search for internal and external relations among all such possible unities, use the results of such discovery as terms for novel relations etc. Obviously such complication is achieved in founded acts of ever higher level. The governing legality in this field is the intuitive counterpart of the grammatical legality of pure logic. In this case, also, we are not concerned with laws which seek to assess the real being of the objects presented at different levels. These laws at all events say nothing directly about the ideal conditions of possibilities of adequate fulfilment. To the pure theory of the forms of meanings we here have a corresponding pure theory of the forms of intuitions, in which the possibility of the primitive types of simple and complex intuitions must be established by intuitive generalization, and the laws of their successive complication into ever new and more complex intuitions must be laid down. To the extent that adequate intuition itself represents a type of intuition, the pure theory of intuitive forms embraces all the laws which concern the forms of adequate intuition: these have a peculiar relevance to the laws of the adequate *fulfilment* of significative intentions, or of intentions already intuitive.

§ 60 *The relative or functional difference between matter and form. Acts of pure thought and acts of thought mixed with sense. Sensuous concepts and categories*

The *relative, merely functional* difference of matter and form hangs together with the possibility of making categorial intuitions the foundations for new categorial intuitions, and thereupon of expressing them in corresponding expressions and meanings. This difference was indicated above in passing (§42). In an absolute sense, sensibility underlies, and provides the matter for, all acts of categorial form which are built upon it. In a relative sense, *the objects of underlying acts furnish this matter*, relatively, that is, to the *newly* emergent forms of the founded acts. If we relate two objects already categorial, e.g. two states of affairs, these states of affairs are our matter relatively to the relation which brings them together. To this definite use of the concepts of matter and form the traditional distinction between *the matter and form of statements* corresponds exactly. The terms of a statement express the underlying acts of the whole 'relational presentation', or, what is the same, they are names for its underlying objects, and therefore represent the place in which alone contributions of sense may be sought. But underlying objects may themselves be categorial in type. Plainly *fulfilment is carried out in a chain of acts which take us down a whole ladder of 'foundations'*. Indirect presentations here play an essential part, whose exact investigation is an important task in a clarification of the complex forms of cognitive thought.

Acts of straightforward intuitions we called 'sensuous'; founded acts, whether leading back immediately or mediately to sense, we called 'categorial'. But it is worth our while to draw a distinction, within the sphere of categorial acts, between those acts that are *purely categorial*, acts of 'pure understanding', and *mixed acts of understanding that are blended with sense*. It lies in the nature of the case that everything categorial ultimately rests upon sensuous intuition, that a 'categorial intuition', an intellectual insight, a case of thought in the highest sense, without any foundation of sense, is a piece of nonsense. *The idea of a pure intellect*, interpreted as a faculty of pure thinking (=categorial action), *quite cut off* from a 'faculty of sensibility', could only be conceived *before* there had been an elementary analysis of knowledge in the irrefragable evidence of its being. Nonetheless, the distinctions just indicated, and with them the concept of a purely categorial act, and, if one likes, the further concept of a pure understanding, all have a good sense. If we ponder on the peculiarity of eidetic abstraction, that it necessarily rests on individual intuition, but does not for that reason mean what is individual in such intuition, if we pay heed to the fact that it is really a new way of conceiving, constitutive of generality instead of individuality – *then the possibility of universal intuitions arises, intuitions which not merely exclude all individuality, but also all sensibility from their intentional purview.* In other words, we distinguish between *sensuous abstraction*, which yields *sensuous concepts* – purely sensuous or mixed with categorial forms – and *purely categorial abstraction*, which yields *purely categorial concepts. Colour, house, judgement, wish* are purely sensuous concepts; *colouredness, virtue, the axiom of parallels* etc., have a categorial admixture, while *unity, plurality, relation, concept* are purely categorial. Where we speak absolutely of categorial concepts, purely categorial ones are always meant. Sensuous concepts find their immediate basis in the data of sensuous intuition, categorial concepts in the data of categorial intuition, purely with regard to the categorial form of the whole categorially formed object. If, e.g., the intuition of a relation underlies an abstraction, the abstractive consciousness may direct itself to the relational form *in specie*, so that everything sensuous in what underlies the relation is discounted. So arise *categories*, which rubric, understood pointedly, merely covers the *primitive* concepts in our present context.

We have just identified concept and *Species*: this was implicit in the whole sense of our completed discussion. But, if one understands by 'concepts' *universal presentations* instead of universal objects, whether these be *universal intuitions* or the *universal meanings* which correspond to them, our distinction carries over simply to these. It carries over similarly to presentations of the form *an A*, having regard to the fact that the Species *A* may include or exclude what is sensible. All *logical forms* and *formulae* such as

All S are P, No S is P etc., are purely categorial. Here the letters '*S*', '*P*' etc., merely point indirectly to 'certain', indefinite concepts, variable 'at will'; in the total formula a complex thought, made up of purely categorial elements, corresponds to them. Like all *pure logic*, so all *pure arithmetic*, the *pure theory of manifolds*, *pure mathematics*, in short, in the widest sense, are *pure* in the sense *that they contain no sensuous concept in their whole theoretical fabric.*

§61 *Categorial structuring involves no real reshaping of the object*

Our talk of categorial form, as has been clear from our last set of discussions, is naturally and harmlessly ambiguous, since we have drawn a thoroughgoing distinction between act and object. We mean by categorial form, on the one hand, the *characters of founded acts*, which give form to acts of straightforward or of already founded intuition, and transform them into new presentations of objects. These latter presentations, as opposed to the acts on which they are founded, set up for us a peculiarly modified objectivity: the original *objects* are now seen in certain interpretative and connective forms which are *our categorial forms in the second, objective sense*. The conjunctive connection *A and B*, which as a unified act means a *categorial unity of objects* (the aggregate of them both), will serve as an example.

The expression '*A and B*' illustrates, particularly in relation to the meaning of 'and', a further sense of our talk of categorial form, according to which *significative* forms, forms which find possible fulfilment in founded types of act, are called categorial forms, or, more cautiously, categorial forms in a *loose* sense of the word.

This being premised, we now wish to bring to explicit clearness, for the sake of its importance, a proposition that we have already enunciated and which is really obvious in the light of our whole exposition. This is the proposition that categorial functions, in 'forming' sensible objects, leave their real essence untouched. The object is intellectually grasped by the intelligence, and especially by 'knowledge' (itself a categorial function), but it is not thereby falsified. To clarify this, let us remember the difference mentioned in passing between categorial unities in the objective sense, and real unities such as the unity of the parts of a thing, or of trees in an avenue etc. The unity of the real elements in a mental experience, or the unity of all experiences which coexist in a single individual consciousness, likewise count among such real unities. All such unities, treated as wholes, resemble their parts in being objects in the straightforward, primary sense: they can be intuited in possible straightforward intuitions. They are not merely categorially unified, constituted through a being- considered-together, through collection, disjunction, relation etc. They are intrinsically unified: they have a form of union, perceivable in the whole as a real property, a real moment of unity, and perceivable in the same sense in which any of their connected members and *their* intrinsic properties are perceivable.

It is quite different in the case of categorial forms. The new objects they create are not objects in the primary, original sense. Categorial forms do not glue, tie or put parts together, so that a real, sensuously perceivable whole emerges. They do not form in the sense in which the potter forms. Otherwise the original datum of sense-perception would be modified in its own objectivity: relational and connective thought and knowledge would not be of what is, but would be a falsifying transformation into something else. Categorial forms leave primary objects untouched: they can do nothing to them, cannot change them in their own being, since the result would otherwise be a new object in the primary, real sense. Evidently the outcome of a categorial act, e.g. one of collection or relation, consists in an objective 'view' (*Fassung*) of what is primarily intuited, a 'view' that can only be given in such a founded act, so that the thought of a straightforward percept of the founded object, or of its presentation through some other straightforward intuition, is a piece of nonsense.

§62 Our freedom in the categorial shaping of given material and its limits. Purely categorial laws (laws of authentic thinking)

Real, sensuous forms of unity, whether external or internal, are determined by a law governing the essential nature of the parts to be connected; if the individuation of these parts is taken in its full extent, they are absolutely determined. All unity points to governing legality, as real unity points to real governing legality. What is really one, must also really be made one. Where we speak of *our freedom to unite* or *not to unite*, we are not speaking of contents

in their full reality, which includes their spatio-temporal properties. While in this field the consciousness, and especially the direct
intuition, of real contents, is *eo ipso* the consciousness of their real
connections and forms, the position is quite different in regard to
categorial forms. With real contents none of the categorial forms
which fit them is necessarily given: there is abundant freedom to
connect and relate, to generalize and subsume etc. There are many
arbitrary ways to divide up a sensuously unified group into part-
groups: we may at will arrange these diversely divisible part-
groups, and effect same-level connections among them, we can
also build collections of the second, third...order upon one
another. Many possibilities of categorial shaping therefore arise
on the foundation of the same sensuous stuff. Just so, we can
compare any item from one and the same sense-complex with any
other of its members, or distinguish it from them. We can make
either of them the subject-term, or, by arbitrary conversion, the
object-term of some relation in question. We can put these relations into relation with one another, connect them collectively,
classify them etc.

Great, however, as this *freedom of categorial union and formation*
may be, it still has its *law-governed limits*. The very fact that categorial forms constitute themselves in founded characters of acts,
and in these alone, involves a certain necessity of connection. For
how else could we speak of categorial *perception* and *intuition*, if
any conceivable matter could be put into any conceivable form,
and the underlying straightforward intuitions therefore permitted
themselves to be arbitrarily combined with categorial characters?
Where, e.g., we carry out a whole-part relationship intuitively,
we can normally convert it, but not in such a manner that the part,
with unchanged real content, can be looked on as the whole, and
the whole as the part. It is also not open to us to treat this relation
as one of total identity or of total exclusion etc. We can no doubt
'think' any relation between any set of terms, and any form whatever on the basis of any matter – think them, that is, in the sense
of merely meaning them. But we cannot really carry out 'foundings' on every foundation: we cannot *see* sensuous stuff in any
categorial form we like, let alone *perceive* it thus, and above all not
perceive it *adequately*.

In framing our widened concept of perception, we found, *eo
ipso*, a certain *tied character* in it. This does not mean that the

character of perception is really (*reell*) bound up with sensuous content. This is never the case, for this would mean that nothing existed unperceived, or could exist unperceived. Certainly, however, nothing exists that cannot be perceived. This means that the actual performance of actual acts on the ground of just these straightforward intuitions is in the ideal sense *possible*. And these possibilities, like ideal possibilities in general, are limited by law to the extent that certain impossibilities, ideal incompatibilities, are by law ranged alongside of them.

The *ideal laws* governing the connection of such possibilities and impossibilities, belong among *categorial forms in specie*, i.e. among categories in the objective sense of the word. They determine *what variations in any given categorial forms there can be in relation to the same definite, but arbitrarily chosen, matter*. They circumscribe the ideally closed manifold of the rearrangements and transformations of categorial forms on the basis of constant, selfsame matter. This matter is here only relevant in so far as it must be kept intentionally identical. But, to the extent that the species of this matter are quite freely variable, and are only subject to the obvious ideal condition of capacity to sustain the forementioned forms, the laws in question are of an entirely pure and *analytic* character, and *quite independent of the particularity of their matter*. Their general expression, therefore, contains no reference to material species, but makes exclusive use of algebraical symbols as bearers of indeterminately general presentations of certain matters, variable in all but the identity they must keep with themselves.

To gain insight into these laws, does not therefore require an actual carrying out of a categorial intuition, which makes its matters truly intuitive: any categorial intuition suffices, which puts the *possibility* of the *categorial* formation in question before one's eyes. In the generalizing abstraction of this comprehensive possibility the unitary, intuitive 'insight' into the law is achieved: this insight has, in the sense used in our doctrine, the character of an *adequate general percept*. The general object, which is itself present in it, is the categorial law. We may assert: *The ideal conditions of categorial intuition in general are, correlatively regarded, the conditions of the possibility of the objects of categorial intuition*, and of the possibility of *categorial objects simpliciter*. That an object thus and thus categorially formed is possible, is essentially related to the fact that a categorial intuition – a mere imagination – can set such an object completely before one's eyes, to the fact, in other words, that *the requisite categorial syntheses and other categorial acts can be really performed on the basis of the underlying intuitions concerned* (even if the latter are imaginary).

What categorial formations are in fact permitted by given materials of perception or imagination, what categorial acts can be really carried out on the basis of their constitutive sensuous intuitions: on this point our analytic laws, which are here our ideal conditions, say nothing. That boundless arbitrariness does not here obtain, that 'actual' performability has not here the character of empirical actuality, but of ideal possibility, is shown by our above examples. These also make plain that it is the particularity of the matter which, from case to case, circumscribes possibility, so that we can, e.g., say that W is really a whole as regards w, or that g is really a property of G etc. In such cases, of course, the categorial form (unlike its real counterpart) is not limited to the kinds of content covered by W, w, G, g, so as to have no bearing on contents of other kinds. Contrariwise it is evident that *contents of all kinds can be formed by all categories*. For categorial forms are not founded on material contents, as we have already explained above (cf. §57). These pure laws can therefore not prescribe what forms a *given* matter can assume, but can only tell us that, when it, and any matter in general, assumes a certain form, or is capable of assuming it, a definitely limited circle of further forms remains open to the same matter. There is, i.e., *an ideally closed circle of possible transformation of a functioning form, into ever new forms*. The ideal *possibility* of these new forms in relation to the same matter, has its *a priori* guarantee in the before mentioned analytic laws which embody the presuppositions in question.

These are the pure laws of *authentic thinking*, the laws, that is, of *categorial intuitions in virtue of their purely categorial forms*. For categorial intuitions function in the thought of theory as actual or possible fulfilments (or frustrations) of meanings, and impart to statements (according to their mode of functioning) the logical values of truth and falsehood. On the laws here considered the normative regulation of purely signitive, or admixedly signitive, thought depends.

To expound this matter more precisely, and to clear up the

special sense implied in talk of the laws of *authentic* thinking, we must take a closer look into the sphere of meanings and of meaning-fulfilments.

§63 *The new laws of the validity of signitive and admixedly signitive acts (laws of thought in the loose sense)*

In our discussions up to this point we have thought of categorial acts as free from all significative side-structures, as carried out, but not as underlying acts of knowing or naming. Every unprejudiced analyst will concede that we can, e.g., intuit aggregates, or many primitive states of affairs, without expressing them nominally or propositionally. We now oppose the case of mere signification to the case of mere intuition: we note that to all acts of categorial intuition, with their categorially formed objects, purely significative acts may correspond. This is an obvious *a priori* possibility. There is no act-form relevant here, to which there is not a corresponding possible form of meaning, and each meaning can be thought of as carried out without a correlated intuition. The ideal of a logically adequate language is that of a language which can give unambiguous expression to all possible matters and all possible categorial forms. To its words certain significative intentions unambiguously pertain, which can come alive even in the absence of 'corresponding', i.e. of fulfilling, intuition. There is therefore, running parallel to all possible primary and founded intuitions, a system of primary and founded meanings which could possibly express them.

The realm of meaning is, however, much wider than that of intuition, i.e. than the total realm of possible fulfilment. For, on the meaning-side, an endless host of *complex meanings* arises, which lack 'reality' or 'possibility'. They are patterns of meanings assembled together into *unitary meanings*, to which, however, *no possible unitary correlate of fulfilment* can correspond.

For this reason there is *no complete parallelism between categorial types*, i.e. types of categorial intuition, and *types of meaning*. To each categorial type of lower or higher level a meaning-type corresponds, but to every type formed by free significative welding to complex types, there is not a corresponding type of categorial objectivity. We recall types of analytic contradiction such as 'an *A* which is not an *A*', 'All *A*'s are *B*'s and some *A*'s are not *B*'s' etc. Only in connection with primitive types can and must such parallelism obtain, since all primitive meanings 'originate' in the fulness of correlated intuition, or, to put the matter more plainly, since talk of compatibility and incompatibility applies only in the sphere of what is put together, or is to be put together, simple meanings, as expressions of what is simple, can never be 'imaginary'. This applies also to every simple *form* of meaning. While 'Something that is at once A and not-A' is impossible, 'an A and a B' is possible, since the and-form, being simple, has a 'real' sense.

If we transfer the term 'categorial' to the realm of meaning, a peculiar significative form (and a peculiar meaning-form *in specie*) will correspond to each *authentic* categorial form, whether to one authentic in the objective sense, or to the corresponding categorial form of intuition (in which what is categorially objective is *perceptually or imaginatively* constituted). In this form of signification we achieve significative reference to a collection or a disjunction, an identity or a non-identity etc. Whenever one opposes presentation in the *authentic*, to presentation in an *inauthentic* sense, one normally has the intuitive-significative antithesis in mind (though occasionally, no doubt, one is thinking of the other antithesis of adequate–inadequate). Our present cases would accordingly be cases of collection, disjunction, identification, abstraction etc., *in an inauthentic sense.*

If one includes under the rubric of 'acts of thinking', all the categorial acts through which judgements, as predicative significations, gain fulness and their whole value for knowledge, we must distinguish between *authentic acts of thinking* and *inauthentic* ones. The inauthentic acts of thinking would be the significant intentions behind statements, and, by a natural extension, all significative acts which could possibly function as parts of such predicative intentions: all significative acts can plainly function in this fashion. The *authentic acts of thinking* would lie in the corresponding fulfilments, i.e. the intuitions of states of affairs, and all intuitions which function as possible parts of such intuitions. All intuitions can function in this manner: there is, in particular, no categorial form that could not be a constituent of the form of a state of affairs. The *general doctrine of the form of symbolic judgements* (the meanings of statements) includes that of the forms of meaning in general (the pure logico-grammatical forms). Just so the *general doctrine of the pure forms of the intuitions of states of affairs* (and of the pure forms of states of affairs) includes that of the *categorial forms of intuitions* (and of objective categorial forms) *in general*.

If, as often happens, *thinking* is identified with *judging*, we should have to distinguish between *authentic* and *inauthentic judging*. The concept of judging would then be pinned down by the element common to statement-intention and statement-fulfilment, i.e. by the intentional essence compounded of quality and intentional material. As acts of thinking in the widest sense, not only acts of judging, but also all possible part-acts in judgements, would have to count: we should be brought back to a definition equivalent to our previous definition of the concept Act of Thinking.

In the sphere of inauthentic thinking, of pure signification, we are beyond all bounds of categorial laws. Here anything and everything can be brought together in unity. We spoke of this in our Fourth Investigation: we pointed to the *purely logico-grammatical laws* which, as laws of complication and modification, distinguish the spheres of sense and nonsense. In inauthentic categorial formation and transformation, we are free as long as our meanings are not nonsensically conglomerated. But if we wish to avoid formal and real nonsense, the widest sphere of inauthentic thought, of the significatively combinable, is very much narrowed. We are now concerned with the *objective* possibility of complex meanings, with the possibility of their application to an intuition which fulfils them totally and singly. *The pure laws of the validity of meanings, of the ideal possibility of their adequate intuitive illustration*, obviously runs parallel to the pure laws governing the combination and transformation of *authentic* categorial forms.

In the pure laws of the validity of meanings, we are again not dealing with laws from which the validity of any given meaning can be read off, but with the possibilities, determined in purely categorial fashion, of the combination and transformation of meanings, that can be undertaken, *salva veritate*, in each possible given case, i.e. without prejudicing the possibility of a fulfilment of meaning, to the extent that this previously existed. If, e.g., the statement '*w* is a part of *W*' is valid, then a statement of the form '*W* is a whole relatively to *w*' is also valid. If it is true that there is an *A* which is *B*, then it is also true that a certain *A* is *B*, or that not all A's are not B's etc. In such propositions, what is material is boundlessly variable; hence all material meanings are replaced by algebraical signs of indirect and wholly unfixed significance. For this reason such propositions are characterized as *analytic*. In this situation, it is again irrelevant whether the matter is constituted in percepts or in imaginations. The possibilities and impossibilities concern the setting up of acts giving adequate intuitive illustration to the form of a meaning whatever its material substratum: we are concerned, in short, with the *pure conditions of the possibility of completely adequate signification in general*, which, in their turn, depend on the *pure conditions of the possibility of categorial intuition in general*. These laws of the validity of meanings are not, of course, themselves identical with the authentic categorial laws, but they follow the latter faithfully, in virtue of the law which regulates the connection of significant intentions with fulfilments of meaning.

The whole treatment that we have just completed requires a natural, obvious extension. We have simplified the matter to the extent of confining our discussion to two extremes only: we opposed completely intuitive, i.e. actually executed categorial act-forms, on the one hand, to purely signitive, i.e. not authentically executed act-forms, on the other, forms only to be realized in processes of possible fulfilment. The ordinary cases are, however, mixtures: thought proceeds intuitively in many stretches, in many stretches signitively, here a categorial synthesis, a predication, a generalization is really carried out, there a merely signitive intention directed to such a categorial synthesis attaches to the intuitively, or to the only verbally presented members. The complex acts arising in this manner have, taken as a whole, the character of inauthentic categorial intuitions: their total objective correlate is not actually, only inauthentically, presented. Its 'possibility', i.e. the objective possibility of its correlate, is not guaranteed. The sphere of inauthentic thinking must accordingly be made wide enough for it to take in these mixed act-forms also. Everything we have said then holds, *mutatis mutandis*, for such an extension. Instead of talking of the laws of the validity of mere meanings, merely symbolic judgements etc., we shall also have to speak of the laws of the validity of signitively admixed presentations or judgements. Where there is talk of merely symbolic thinking, it is generally these mixed cases that one has in mind.

*§ 64 The pure logico-grammatical laws are laws for any
understanding whatever, and not merely for any human
understanding. Their psychological meaning and normative
function in relation to inadequate thought*

Both sorts of laws are, of course, of an *ideal* nature. That a piece of
sensory stuff can only be apprehended in certain forms, and bound
together according to certain forms, that the possible transformation of these forms is subject to pure laws, in which the material
element varies freely, that the meanings to be expressed are likewise limited to certain forms, which they can change only in
prescribed manners, if they are not to lose their true expressibility – all this does not depend on the empirical contingencies of
the course of consciousness, not even on the contingencies of our
intellectual or common-human organization. It depends on the
specific nature of the acts in question, on their intentional and epistemic
essence; it belongs not to the nature of just our (individual or
common-human) sensibility, nor just our understanding, but
rather to the *Ideas of Sensibility and Understanding in general*. An
understanding governed by other than the purely logical laws
would be an understanding without understanding. If we define
understanding, as opposed to sensibility, as the capacity for
categorial acts, also, perhaps, as a capacity for expression and
meaning directed upon such acts, and made 'right' by them, then
the general laws rooted in the specific nature of these acts belong
to the definitory essence of understanding. Other beings may
gaze upon other 'worlds', they may also be endowed with
'faculties' other than ours, but, if they are minded creatures at
all, possessing some sort of intentional experiences, with the
relevant differences between perception and imagination, straightforward and categorial intuition, meaning and intuition, adequate
and inadequate knowledge – then such creatures have both
sensibility and understanding, and are 'subject' to the pertinent
laws.

The laws of authentic thinking naturally, therefore, belong
also to the nature of human consciousness, to our common human
'psychic organization'. But they are not characteristic of this
organization in respect of its *peculiar* character. The laws are
rooted, we said, in the purely specific character of certain acts:
this means that they concern these acts not just in so far as they

occur together in a human organization. They pertain rather to all possible organizations which can be made up of acts of this sort. The differentiating peculiarities of each type of mental organization, all that distinguishes, e.g., the *human* consciousness as such, in the manner of a natural historical species, is not at all affected by such *pure* laws as are the laws of thought.

A relation to 'our' mental organization, or to 'consciousness in general' (understood as the aspects of consciousness *common to men in general*), does not define the pure and genuine, but a grossly distorted *a priori*. The notion of a common mental organization, like that of a physical organization, clearly has a merely 'empirical' meaning, the meaning of a mere 'matter of fact'. But pure laws are precisely pure of matter of fact, they tell us not what is generally wont to be in this or that province of the real, but what absolutely goes beyond all wont and all divisions into spheres of reality, and that for the reason that what is in question belongs to the *essential* make-up of what is. The *true logical a priori*, therefore concerns all that pertains to the ideal essence of understanding as such, to the essence of its act-species and act-forms, to that, accordingly, which cannot be eliminated, as long as the understanding, and the acts definitory of it, are what they are, i.e. thus and thus natured, maintaining their selfsame conceptual essence.

The extent, accordingly, to which the logical laws, and, in the first instance, the ideal laws of authentic thinking, also claim a *psychological* meaning, and the extent to which they govern the course of actual mental happenings, is at once clear. Each genuine 'pure' law, expressing a compatibility or an incompatibility grounded in the nature of a given species, will, in relation to species of mentally realizable contents, limit the empirical possibilities of psychological (phenomenological) coexistence and succession. What is seen to be incompatible *in specie*, cannot be brought together, be rendered compatible, in empirical instances. In so far as the logical thought of experience is, to an incomparably major extent, conducted inadequately and signitively, we can think, believe, many things which in *truth*, in the manner of authentic thought, the actual carrying out of merely intended syntheses, cannot be brought together at all. Just for this reason *the a priori laws of authentic thinking and authentic expression become norms for merely opinion-forming, inauthentic thought and expression.* Put somewhat differently: on the laws of authentic thinking other laws are founded, formulable too as practical norms, which express in a manner suited to the sphere of signitive or admixedly signitive presentation, the ideal conditions of a possible truth (or *right*ness in general), the ideal conditions, that is, of 'logical' compatibility (logical, since related to possible adequation) within this sphere of admixedly signitive thinking. The laws of inauthentic thinking do not hold *psychologically* like empirical laws governing the origin and change of such thought, but as the possibilities or impossibilities of adequation founded in their ideal purity in the variously formed acts of inauthentic thinking in relation to corresponding acts of authentic thinking.

§65 *The senseless problem of the real meaning of the logical*

We now also completely understand why the notion of a course of the world violating the laws of logic – the analytic laws of authentic thinking and the consequent norms of inauthentic thinking – or of the need or possibility of first grounding these laws in experience, the 'matter of fact' of sense, and fixing for them their limits of validity – is a piece of pure nonsense. We ignore the fact that even a probabilistic grounding on facts is a grounding which, as such, obeys ideal principles, principles which by anticipation we see to rest upon 'authentic' experiences of probability, both as regards their specific content and their status as laws. Here we must rather stress that the so-to-say facticity of a fact belongs to sensibility, and that to call in sensibility to help provide a basis for purely categorial laws – laws whose very meaning excludes all sensibility and facticity, which make pure assertions of essence about categorial *forms*, as forms of possible correctness and truth as such – represents a most obvious μετάβασις εἰς ἄλλο γένος. Laws which refer to no fact cannot be confirmed or refuted by a fact. The problem, earnestly and profoundly treated by great philosophers, as to the 'real or formal meaning of the logical', is therefore a nonsensical problem. *One requires no metaphysical or other theories to explain the agreement of the course of nature and the 'native' regularities of the understanding.* Instead of an explanation, one needs only a phenomenological clarification of meaning, thinking and knowing, and of the ideas and laws which spring from these.

The world is set up for us as a sensuous unity: its very meaning is to be the unity of actual and possible straightforward percepts. Its true being, however, precludes its being adequately given, or given without qualification, in any closed process of perception. It is for us always a quite inadequately meant unity for theoretical research, in part intended through straightforward and categorial intuition, in part through signification. The further our knowledge progresses, the better and more richly will the idea of the world be determined, the more, too, will inconsistencies be excluded from it. To doubt whether the world really is as it appears to us to be, or as it is thought of in contemporary theoretical science, and as it counts for the well-grounded belief of the latter, has a good sense, since inductive science can never construct an adequate world-picture, however far it may carry us. But it is also nonsensical to doubt whether the true course of the world, the true structure of the world in itself, could conflict with the forms of thinking. For this would mean that a definite, hypothetically assumed sensibility, which would bring the world to adequate representation in an ideally complete set of unending perceptual processes, would be capable of assuming categorial forms, while forcing syntheses upon them that are generically ruled out by the universal nature of such forms. That they are thus ruled out, and that the laws of the categories hold as pure laws in abstraction from all sensuous stuff, and are accordingly unaffected by limitless variation of such stuff, this *we do not merely think, but we see it to be true*. It is given to us in fullest adequacy. This insight is of course achieved subjectively on the basis of any casual empirical intuition, but it is a generic insight relating purely to form. The basis of abstraction contains in this case, as in others, nothing presupposed by the ideal possibility and validity of the Idea abstracted from it.

It would further be possible to demonstrate *ad nauseam* the absurdity involved in considering the *possibility* of an illogical course of the world in signitive thought, thereby making this possibility *hold*, and destroying in one breath, so to say, the laws which make this or any other possibility hold at all. We could also point out that a correlation with perceivability, intuitability, meanability and knowability, is inseparable from the sense of being in general, and that the ideal laws, therefore, which pertain to these possibilities *in specie*, can never be set aside by the contingent content of what itself happens to be at the moment. But enough of such argumentations, which merely ring the changes on one and the same position, and have already given us guidance in the *Prolegomena*.

§66 Distinction between the most important differences mixed up in the current opposition of 'intuiting' and 'thinking'

The above investigations should have imported a satisfactory, general clearness into the much used, but little clarified, relation between *thinking* and *intuiting*. We here list the following oppositions, whose confusion has vexed epistemological research so inordinately, and whose distinctness has become quite clear to ourselves.

1. The opposition between *intuition* and *signification*. Intuition as perception or imagination – it is irrelevant whether categorial or sensuous, adequate or inadequate – is opposed to *mere thinking*, as *merely significative reference*. Our parenthetically noted differences are, of course, generally ignored. We consider them very important, and now specially stress them.

2. The opposition between *sensuous* and *categorial intuition*. We therefore oppose *sensuous intuition* in the ordinary, straightforward sense, to *categorial intuition*, or intuition in the extended sense. The founded acts, characteristic of the latter, now count as the thought which 'intellectualizes' sensuous intuition.

3. The opposition between *inadequate* and *adequate* intuition, or, more generally, between adequate and inadequate presentation (since we are classing intuitive and significative presentation together). In an inadequate representation we merely *think* that something is so (appears so), in adequate presentation we look at the matter itself, and are *for the first time made acquainted with its full selfhood*.

4. The opposition between *individual intuition* (usually conceived, with what is plainly baseless narrowness, as sensuous intuition) and *universal intuition*. A new concept of intuition is fixed by means of this opposition. It is opposed to generalization, and so, further, to the categorial acts implying generalization, and also, in unclear admixture, to the significative counterparts of such acts. 'Intuition', we now say, *merely presents the individual*, while 'thought' points to the *universal*, is carried out by way of 'concepts'. One generally speaks in this context of the opposition between 'intuition and concept'.

How strongly we tend to let these oppositions shade into one another would be shown by a criticism of Kant's theory of knowledge, which throughout bears the impress of the failure to draw any clear distinction among these oppositions. In Kant's thought categorial (logical) functions play a great role, but he fails to achieve our fundamental extension of the concepts of perception and intuition over the categorial realm, and this because he fails to appreciate the deep difference between intuition and signification, their possible separation and their usual commixture. And so he does not complete his analysis of the difference between the inadequate and adequate adaptation of meaning to intuition. He therefore also fails to distinguish between concepts, as the universal meanings of words, and concepts as species of *authentic* universal presentation, and between both, and concepts as universal objects, as the intentional correlates of universal presentations. Kant drops from the outset into the channel of a metaphysical epistemology in that he attempts a critical 'saving' of mathematics, natural science and metaphysics, before he has subjected knowledge as such, the whole sphere of acts in which pre-logical objectivation and logical thought are performed, to a clarifying critique and analysis of essence, and before he has traced back the primitive logical concepts and laws to their phenomenological sources. It was ominous that Kant (to whom we nonetheless feel ourselves quite close) should have thought he had done justice to the domain of pure logic in the narrowest sense, by saying that it fell under the principle of contradiction. Not only did he never see how little the laws of logic are all analytic propositions in the sense laid down by his own definition, but he failed to see how little his dragging in of an evident principle for analytic propositions really helped to clear up the achievements of analytic thinking.

Additional Note

All the main obscurities of the Kantian critique of reason depend ultimately on the fact that Kant never made clear to himself the peculiar character of pure Ideation, the adequate survey of conceptual essences, and of the laws of universal validity rooted in those essences. He accordingly lacked the phenomenologically correct concept of the *a priori*. For this reason he could never rise to adopting the only possible aim of a strictly scientific critique of reason: the investigation of the pure, essential laws which govern acts as *intentional* experiences, in all their modes of sense-giving objectivation, and their fulfilling constitution of 'true being'. Only a perspicuous knowledge of these laws of essence could provide us with an absolutely adequate answer to all the questions regarding our understanding, questions which can be meaningfully raised in regard to the 'possibility of knowledge'.

Third Section

CLARIFICATION OF OUR INTRODUCTORY PROBLEM

Non-Objectifying Acts as Apparent Fulfilments of Meaning

§67 That not every act of meaning includes an act of knowing

HAVING gone far enough in our investigation of the relation between meaning and corresponding intuition in regard to much more general problems, and having thus done enough to lay bare the essence of authentic and inauthentic expression, we have reached clearness on the difficult issues which troubled us at the beginning of this Investigation, and which first prompted us to undertake it.

We have, above all, rid ourselves of the temptation to conceive of the meaning-function of expressions as in some sense a case of knowing, and in fact a case of classification, a temptation which springs from a line of thought touched on above (§1), and which always crops up in important epistemological contexts. One says: An expression must surely give expression to some act of the speaker, but in order that this act should find its appropriate speech-form, it must be suitably apperceived and known, a presentation as a presentation, an attribution as an attribution, a negation as a negation etc.

Our reply is that talk of knowledge refers to a relationship between acts of thought and fulfilling intuitions. Acts of thought are not, however, brought to expression in statements and parts of statements, e.g. names, in such a manner that they in their turn are thought of and known. Otherwise these last acts would be the carriers of meaning, it would be *they* primarily that were expressed, they would accordingly be in need of other new acts of thought, and so on *in infinitum*. If I call this intuited object a 'watch', I complete, in naming it, an act of thought and knowledge, but I know the watch, and not my knowledge. This is naturally so in the case of all acts that confer meaning. Should I utter the word 'or' in a context of expressive speech, I carry out a disjunction, but my thought (of which the disjoining is a part) is not trained upon the disjoining but upon the (objective) *disjunctivum*, in so far as this last enters into the unitary state of affairs. This *disjunctivum* is known and objectively denominated. The word 'or' is accordingly no name, and likewise no non-independent appellation of disjoining; it merely gives voice to this act. Naturally this applies also to complete judgements. If I assert something, I think of *things*, that things stand in this or that manner: this is what I express, and perhaps also know. But I do not think and know my act of judging, as if I were also making it into my object, and were classifying it as a judgement and naming it through this form of expression.

But does not the grammatical adaptation of expression to expressed act point to an act of knowing in which such adaptation is performed? In a certain manner or in certain cases it does, in all those cases, that is, where the sense of 'expression' dealt with by us at the beginning of the present Investigation is relevant. This is not the case where we are dealing with expression as a mere 'voice-giving', in which case all meaning-conferring counts as expressed by our words (as verbal noises), and again not where 'expression' means the same as 'meaning', and what is expressed is one and the same meaning. In the two latter senses, every statement, whether merely significative or intuitively fulfilled, expresses something: it expresses the judgement (our conviction), or that 'judgement's content' (the selfsame propositional meaning). But in the former sense only the intuitively fulfilled statement (or the statement which is *to be* intuitively fulfilled) expresses something, in which case not the verbal noise, but the already sense-enlivened locution represents the 'expression' of the corresponding intuition. It is the function that lends meaning to our words which is primarily and universally responsible for the unitary interweaving of the signitive intentions attaching to those words. The latter merely make up a signitive judgement, in which they lack all fulfilling intuition: the synthesis of agreement or disagreement, which our total signitive intention expresses (or claims to express) is here not authentically carried out, only signitively meant. But if, contrariwise, the indicated synthesis is authentically carried out, the authentic synthesis will coincide with the non-authentic one (the synthesis in signification). Both are one and the same intentional essence, representing one and the same meaning, the simple, selfsame judgement, whether carried out intuitively or merely signitively. Similar things plainly hold for cases where only some of our verbalized intentions enjoy intuitive 'fulness'. The signitive acts involve the same meaning as the intuitive, though without the latter's fulness; they merely 'express' this meaning. The suggestions of this word are the more fitting, since signitive acts likewise preserve the sense of an intuition after the latter has disappeared, like an empty shell without the intuitive kernel. The unity of coincidence is, in the case of the intuitive judgement, a true unity of knowledge (if not a unity of relational cognition): we know, however, that, in the unity of knowledge, it is not the fulfilling act (here the authentic synthesis of judgement) that we know, but the *fact* which is its objective correlate. In intuiting things we carry out a judging synthesis, *an intuitive thus it is* or *thus it is not*. Because our expressive intention, with its associated word-sounds (the grammatical expression) applies itself to this act of fact-envisagement, we achieve knowledge of the intuited fact in question.

§ 68 *The controversy regarding the interpretation of the peculiar grammatical forms which express non-objectifying acts*

We now turn to a final discussion of the seemingly trivial, but, correctly regarded, most important and difficult point at issue (see above, § 1 *ff.*) whether the familiar grammatical forms used in our speech for wishes, questions, voluntary intentions – acts, generally speaking, we do not class as 'objectifying' – are to be regarded as *judgements* concerning our acts, or whether these acts themselves, and not merely such as are 'objectifying', can function as 'expressed', whether in a sense-giving or sense-fulfilling fashion. We are dealing with sentences like 'Is π a transcendental number?' 'May heaven help us!' etc.

The teasing character of the question is shown by the fact that pre-eminent logicians since Aristotle have been unable to agree on its answer. Statements express the fact that something is, or that something is not, they assert, they judge about something. In their case alone can one talk of true and false. A wish or a question asserts nothing. We cannot object to one who utters them: 'What you say is untrue'. He would not even understand our objection.

Bolzano thought this argument invalid. He said: 'A question like "What is the relation of the diameter of a circle to its circumference?" asserts nothing about what it enquires into, but it asserts something nonetheless: our desire, in fact, to be informed concerning the object asked about. It is indeed capable of truth and falsehood, and is false when our desire is mis-stated by it' (Bolzano, *Wissenschaftslehre* I, §22, p. 88).

We may doubt, however, whether Bolzano has not here confused two things: the adequacy or inadequacy of an expression – here a word-sound – to our thought, and the truth or falsehood which relates it to the content of that thought, and its adequacy to the thing. Regarding the adequacy of an expression (as word-sound) to our thought, we can speak in two senses, one which relates to *unsuitability* – as when a speaker chooses to express the thoughts which fill his mind in words whose customary meaning conflicts with the latter – and one relating to *untruthfulness*, i.e. to deliberately deceptive, lying speech – as when the speaker does not wish to express the thoughts actually filling his mind, but others at variance with these, and merely imagined by him: he wishes to express these thoughts *as if* they were filling his mind. A suitable, sincerely employed expression can still state both what is true and what is false, according as *through its sense* it expresses what is or is not, or, what is the same, according as its sense can be adequately fulfilled or frustrated by a possible adequate percept.

One might now counter Bolzano as follows. One can talk of sincerity and insincerity, of suitability and unsuitability, in the case of *every* expression, but one can only talk of truth and falsehood in the case of statements. A speaker can, accordingly, be objected to in different ways. 'What you say is false': this is the *factual objection*. And 'You are not speaking sincerely' or 'You are expressing yourself unsuitably': this is the objection of *insincerity* or *inadequacy* of speech. Objections of the latter sort are the only ones that can be made to a questioner. He is perhaps pretending, or is using his words incorrectly, and saying something different from what he intends to say. But one can raise no factual objection to him, since he is making no factual claim. If one treats the objection concerned with unsuitability of expression as showing that a question expresses a judgement, one, i.e., that would be completely expressed in the form 'I am asking whether...', one would have in consistency to treat each expression in the same manner, and so to treat the true sense of each statement whatever as being what we adequately express in the word-form 'I am asserting that...'. But the same would have to hold of these restatements, which would accordingly land us in an infinite regress. In all this it is easily seen that this abundance of ever new statements is no mere abundance of words, but yields new statements by no means equivalent to the original ones, let alone identical in meaning. Does such nonsensical consistency not compel us to acknowledge an essential difference between one order of sentence-forms and another? (How this difference really must be interpreted is explained in our next section: cf. the final paragraph.)

Here two positions can be taken up. Either one can say: The question of sincerity affects every utterance: a judgement accordingly pertains to each utterance as such, a judgement relating to the experience of the speaker which is to be intimated. A man who speaks, intimates something, and to this the intimating judgement corresponds. But what is intimated or expressed differs from case to case: the interrogative sentence intimates a question, the imperative sentence a command, the indicative sentence a judgement. Each indicative sentence therefore implies a double judgement, a judgement, namely, about this or that fact, and a second judgement, passed by the speaker as such, upon this first judgement as his own experience.

This appears to be Sigwart's position. We read (*Logik*, 1^2, $17f$. Note):

> The imperative undoubtedly includes an assertion, to the effect, namely, that the speaker wills the action he is demanding, the optative that he wishes what he utters. This assertion is involved in *the fact of speech*, not in the content of what he utters; every statement of the form *A* is *B* accordingly involves the assertion, based on the mere fact of speech, that the thinker thinks and believes what he says. *These assertions regarding the subjective state of the speaker, involved in the fact that he speaks*, and valid on the assumption of his sincerity, *accompany all speech in the same fashion*, and can accordingly not serve as a basis for differentiating our various sentence-forms.

Another way of conceiving the matter would be to reject the 'intimating judgement', and to regard the consequent duplication of judgement in the case of indicative sentences as a contingent complication, only exceptionally present, and first brought into the picture, moreover, by descriptive reflection. Against this one might hold that, in each case of adequate, not contextually elliptical speech what was expressed was essentially one, in the interrogative sentence a question, in the optative sentence a wish, in the indicative sentence a judgement. Before I had completed these Investigations, I myself thought this position unavoidable, hard as it was to reconcile with the phenomenological facts. I thought myself compelled by the following arguments, that I now accompany with suitable criticism.

§69 *Arguments for and against the Aristotelian conception*

According to the doctrine which is opposed to that of Aristotle, a man who, e.g., utters a question will be communicating to another his wish to be informed regarding the state of affairs in question. This communication regarding the speaker's actual experience is, it is held, a statement like any communication. In the form of the question itself there is no express saying that one is asking whether...; this form only marks off the question as a question. Our speech, therefore, is a case of contextual ellipticity. The circumstances of utterance make it obvious that it is the speaker himself who asks the question. The complete meaning of the sentence does not, accordingly lie in what its mere word-sounds suggest, but is determined by the occasion, the context, the relation to the person speaking at the moment.

In favour of the Aristotelian conception, many replies could now be given.

(*a*) The argument ought to apply equally to indicative sentences, so that we have to interpret the sentence '*S* is *P*' as a contextual ellipsis for the new expression 'I judge that *S* is *P*', and so on *in infinitum*.

(*b*) The argument is based on the view that the expressed sense of the interrogative sentence differs from its real sense. For, undeniably, in the interrogative or wish-sentence, the relation of the wish to the wisher does not need to be brought out, as little as, in the case of the indicative sentence, the relation of the judgement to the judging person. If this relation is not part of the explicit sense of the sentence, but only of its contextually variable part, this concession gives one all that one could want. The explicit meaning can be altered in certain circumstances, but there will surely also be circumstances where it will be just what we mean. In such cases the mere question (and similarly the mere request or command etc.) will receive wholly adequate expression.

(c) More careful comparison with the indicative sentences of ordinary speech favours the Aristotelian conception. In verbal communication such a sentence intimates that one is judging, and it is the grammatical form of the indicative sentence which brings out the judgement as such. On the utterance of such grammatically framed speech, the effect forthwith attends, that the person addressed takes the speaker to be judging. This effect cannot, however, constitute the meaning of the expression, which surely means the same in soliloquy as in communicative speech. The meaning lies rather in the act of judging as the identical judgement-content.

The same could be the case in regard to interrogative sentences. The meaning of an interrogative sentence is unchanged whether we deal with an internal question or an overt one. The relation of speaker to person addressed belongs here, as in the case compared, to the merely communicative function. And just as in that case the 'content of judgement', i.e. a certain specific character of judgement, determined in this or that manner as regards content, constituted the meaning of the indicative sentence, so here the content of the question constitutes the meaning of the interrogative sentence. In both cases the ordinary meaning can undergo circumstantial modifications. We may utter an indicative sentence with the primary intention, not of communicating the relevant state of affairs, but the fact that we have the conviction in question, and mean to put it forward. This intention, buttressed, perhaps, by non-grammatical aids (stress, gesture), may be understood. Here what underlies our words is a judgement relating to our explicit judgement. Just so, in the case of an interrogative or wish-sentence, our primary intention may lie, not in our mere wish, but in the fact that we wish to express the wish to a hearer. Naturally this interpretation could not hold in all cases. It could not hold, e.g., where a burning wish bursts spontaneously from the heart. The expression then is intimately one with the wish, it clings to it immediately and directly.

Criticism. Regarded more closely, this argument only proves that a thought relating to the communicative function cannot be part of the sense of every sentence. The opposing argument is refuted: it rests on the false assumption that all expression is communicative, and that communication is always a judgement regarding the internal (intimated) experiences of the speaker. But its thesis is unrefuted, at least when suitably modified. For we cannot exclude the possibility that the controversial wish-, request-, and command-sentences etc., are still judgements about the relevant experienced acts of wishing, asking and willing, and that it is only as being so, that they can give these experiences adequate expression. If there is no place for judgements here in the narrower sense of predications – Aristotle certainly had this conception of the controversial sentences – perhaps there is place for them in a wider sense of assertive objectivations in general.

1. As regards (a) we note, further, that the case of statements is not the same as, e.g., that of questions. If we transform the sentence 'S is P' into the sentence 'I judge that S is P', or into any related sentence, which expresses a relation to the judging person, however indefinitely, we obtain not merely altered meanings, but such as are not equivalent to the original ones: for the straightforward sentence may be true, the subjectivized sentence false, and conversely. The situation is wholly different in the case compared. Even if one refuses to speak of true and false in this case, one can surely always find a statement that 'in essence says the same' as the original question or wish-form, e.g. 'Is S P?' = 'I should like to know...' or 'One would like to know whether S is P' etc. May such sentence-forms not imply a relation to the speaker, even if only indefinitely and subsidiarily? Does the preservation of 'essential meaning' in the transformed indicative forms not point to the fact that the meaning-giving acts are at least of the same general sort as judgements? These considerations also deal with (b): not the mere experience of wishing or willing, but the inner intuition of these experiences (and the signification adapted to this intuition) will be relevant to our meaning. This conception is, however, affected by the following argument:

2. There is another way in which one might try to interpret the expressed forms in question as judgements. If we utter a wish, even in soliloquy, we put it, and the wished-for content, into words, we accordingly have a presentation of it, and of what

constitutes it. The wish is, however, not *any* merely presented wish, but the living wish that we have just taken note of. And it is this wish, and this wish as such, that we want to intimate. It is not, accordingly, our mere presentation, but our inner percept, i.e. really a judgement, that achieves expression. It is not, indeed, a judgement of the same sort as our ordinary assertions, that predicate something of something. In the expression of a wish, it is only our concern to grasp the internally noted experience conceptually (significatively) in straightforward affirmation, and to express its simple existence. It is not our concern to make a relational predication about such an experience, connecting it with the experiencing subject.

Against this conception it may be objected that the situation is exactly the same for expressed judgements as for all other expressed experiences. If we state something, we judge, and our words cover not only the presentation underlying our judgement, but also our judgement itself (i.e. in the form of an assertion). We should, therefore, also conclude here that the judgement is internally perceived, and that the meaning of our statement lies in the straightforwardly affirmative judgement about what we perceive, i.e. about our judgement. If no one finds such a conception acceptable in the case of a statement, it cannot be seriously entertained in the case of other independent sentences. We recall what was said in our last section. The expressions which fit themselves to the expressed experiences, are not related to them in the way that names are, nor in any analogous manner. Our experiences are not first *objectively* presented, and then brought under concepts, as if, together with each new word, a subsumption or predication had taken place. A person who judges gold to be yellow, does not judge that the presentation which accompanies his use of the word 'gold' is yellow: he does not judge that the manner of judging he carries out when he utters the word 'is' falls under the concept 'is' etc. The word 'is' does not in fact symbolize judgement, but the being which is found in a state of affairs. 'Gold', likewise, does not name a presentative experience: it names a metal. Expressions name experiences only when such experiences have been made objects of presentation or judgement in reflection. The same holds for all words, even syncategorematic ones, in their relation to what is objective: they mean this in their fashion even when they do not name it.

Expressions are not therefore associated as names with the acts which fill our minds at each moment, acts in which we live without judging about them reflectively: such expressions belong rather to the concrete being of the acts themselves. To judge expressly is to judge, to wish expressly is to wish. To name a judgement or wish is not to judge or wish, but merely to name. A judgement named need never be judged by the man who names it, a wish named never wished by him. And, even when this is not so, the naming expresses no judgement or no wish, but a presentation related to one or the other.

Criticism. This objection also exposes the weakness of our at first attractive preliminary argument. It is clear from it, as from our previous discussions, that not every expression (*qua* the expression it is) presupposes a judgement or other act, which makes the intimated experience its object. This again does not dispose of the thesis: we have not shown, just in the case of the sentence-forms under discussion, that they are not judgements about momentary wishing, questioning or requesting experiences, or that they do not express their straightforward existence in the speaker. True, to name a wish is not *therefore* to wish, but is experiencing a wish and naming it in the same breath, not *also* a case of wishing? So that, even if expressed wishing is necessarily a wishing which involves naming and stating, the proposition still holds, that expressed wishing is wishing and not mere naming.

3. The controversial expressions have the form of sentences, and at times the form of categorical sentences with subjects and predicates. From this it follows that they can also be treated as having predication in their content, and not merely as predications in relation to one, same, unmentioned subject 'I'. E.g. 'May God protect the Kaiser', 'The coachman should harness the horses'. A 'may' or a 'should' is uttered: the subject in question is apprehended as standing under a requisition or an obligation.

One could here rejoin: Where a 'should' counts as an objective predicate and is actually attributed as such, the should-sentence has not merely the force of a wish or a command, or not this alone. An objective obligation can be said to hold, though the man stating it need experience no act of the kind which constitutes an actual consciousness of obligation. If I know that someone's will is bound by a relationship of service or by custom or morality, I can judge that he should and must do something. But this expresses no living wish, desire or obligation. Statements of obligation may indeed serve in appropriate contexts to express acts of this sort, e.g. 'John must harness the horses!' But it is clear that here no mere objective obligation is expressed, but my own will, and this not in my words, but rather in my tone and in the circumstances. In such circumstances the predicative form doubtless does duty for an imperative or optative form, i.e. the thought-predication implied by the words is either not carried out at all, or is merely subsidiary. It is undeniable, lastly, that the predicative interpretation only is plausible in certain cases, and not in the case in question. B. Erdmann, who otherwise leans towards it, does not favour it in this case. (See B. Erdmann, *Logic*, 1^1, §45, pp. 271 *ff*.)

Criticism. It may be questioned whether this refutation suffices. That a should-predicate has an objective sense and value cannot be doubted. But that, where this is not true, nothing is predicated or at least judged, is by no means proved. One might maintain: When we issue a command to someone, e.g. a command to the coachman John to harness the horses, he counts for us as someone subordinate to our will: he is apprehended as such by us and accordingly addressed in this form of expression. We say: 'John, harness the horses!' That he is one who should harness horses is here predicated of him, naturally in the expectation of corresponding practical results, and not merely to attest that he counts as such for me. The expression of the command is relative. We can think of no one commanded, without at the same time thinking, definitely or indefinitely, of someone who commands him. This being wholly obvious requires no explicit expression. Instead of the cumbrous form 'I command etc.', we employ the brief imperative, whose form points to a communicative relation. The speech-forms 'should' and 'must' were not originally used by a commander in face of the commanded to express his actual voluntary intent, but only when a more objective expression of his own or someone else's voluntary intent was needed, e.g. when there was a third person relaying someone else's command or when a legislating will found expression in a law. When communication between commander and commanded lapses, the imperative, which fits the conscious situation of the former, loses application. This conception can be applied generally. One can say: In the optative, what we wish is presented as wished, and stated to be such. Just so, in a requesting form, what we request is presented as requested, in a question what we ask presented as asked etc. These acts are related in our presentation to their intentional objects, and are so themselves made objective as reflexive predicates attaching to the latter.

In the communicative situation, many others of the expressions in question have, like commands, the role of telling the hearer (like essentially occasional expressions) that the speaker is performing certain intimated acts (of request, congratulation, condolence etc.) with an intentional regard to his auditor. To the extent that expressions of all sorts may in full consciousness be informed by the wish to communicate with others, and to acquaint others with one's own convictions, doubts, hopes etc., they are perhaps all accompanied by reflex acts directed upon such inner experiences, and, more precisely, by acts which intuitively relate the latter to the speaker and to the person addressed. This accordingly holds of communicative statements as well. These acts of reflection and reference do not on that account form part of the meaning of a statement and of all other expressions, but this may very well be said of expressions of our controversial class, in virtue of which they are in all cases directed to inner experiences of the speaker.

In solitary mental life – if we disregard exceptional cases of talking to oneself, asking oneself questions, desiring or commanding oneself – relation to an auditor falls away, and the subjective expressions in question, which are still applicable, express the simple being of inner experiences in more or less definite relation to the subject. In a monologue a question is either of the form 'I ask myself whether...', or relation to the subject vanishes entirely: the interrogative expression becomes a mere name, or not really even that. For the normal use of a name is in a context of predicative or attributive relation, of which there is here no question. Since the expression becomes one with the intuited inner experience as a knowing of the latter, an interweaving of factors arises having the character of a self-enclosed phenomenon. To the extent that, in such interweaving, we live principally in an interrogative act, with which our expression merely fits in, and to which it gives articulate voice, the whole interweaving is

called a question. Knowledge is not here a theoretical function –
this is the case only in predication, while here nothing is predicated. The question is known and expressed, without being 'subjectivized', in the sense of being made either the subject or the
object of predicative acts. Plainly this directly expressive sense of
the interrogative sentence helps to constitute the predicative
interrogation – I ask myself whether etc. – or the meaning which
corresponds to such altered circumstances.

§70 *Decision*

If by a 'judgement' one means a predicative act, then our discussions have shown that our disputed sentences *do not invariably
express judgements*. Even in these cases, however, an unbridgeable
gulf separates us from the logicians who side with Aristotle. On
their view, names, statements, optative sentences, interrogations,
commands etc., are *coordinated* expressive forms, and coordinated
in the following manner: names express presentations, statements
express judgements, optative sentences express wishes etc. Presentations, judgements, questions etc., in short, acts of all sorts, can
serve to confer meaning in exactly the same fashion, for to
'express acts' means the same in all cases, i.e. to have one's
meaning in such acts. We, on the other hand, see a *fundamental
difference* between names and statements, on the one hand, and
the expressions of our controversial group, on the other. The acts
of presentation or judging expressed by names or statements may
confer or fulfil meaning, but are not therefore meant; they do not
become objects of naming and predication, but are *constitutive of
such objects*. On the other hand we find, in flat contrast, that the
acts 'expressed' by our controversial expressions, though seeming
to confer meanings, are made into *objects*. This may happen, as
we saw, through inner intuition reflectively directed upon such
acts, and generally also through relational acts based on such
intuitions. It may also happen by way of certain acts of signification, perhaps only partially uttered, which attach as cognitions to
these inner intuitions and acts of relating, thereby making their
objects, the acts, namely, of asking, wishing, commanding etc.,
into objects named and otherwise talked of, and perhaps into
components of predicated states of affairs. In these acts of objectification lie the true meanings of our controversial expressions.

We are not in their case concerned with acts which confer meaning in some fundamentally new manner, but only with contingent specifications of the one, unique class of meaning-intentions. And, just so, the acts which fulfil meaning do not fall into different classes, but belong to the one, unique class of intuitions. It is not the wishes, commands etc., *themselves* that are expressed by these grammatical patterns and their significations; it is rather the intuitions of these acts that serve as fulfilments. When we compare indicative with optative sentences, we must not coordinate judgements with wishes, but *states of affairs* with wishes.

What results accordingly is the fact that:

The ostensible expressions of non-objectifying acts are really contingent specifications of statements and other expressions of objectifying acts which have an immense practical and communicative importance.

The contentious issue here dealt with is of fundamental importance, since on its solution depends, on the one hand, whether we accept a doctrine which makes all meaning, whether in intention or fulfilment, of a single kind – the genus of objectifying acts, with their fundamental division into the significative and the intuitive – or whether, on the other hand, we decide to permit acts of all sorts to confer or fulfil meaning. The issue is, of course, not less important because it is the first to call our attention to the fundamental triplicity of the ambiguity of talk about 'expressed acts', on whose analysis our present Investigation first embarked (cf. §2 above). There it was said that we may mean by 'expressed acts':

1. The *significative acts* which give expressions meaning, and which have, in their significative fashion, a certain objectivity of reference.

2. The *intuitive acts*, which frequently fulfil the significant intent of an expression, and so represent the significantly meant objects intuitively, and in a parallel intuitive 'sense'.

3. The acts which are the *objects* of signification, and likewise of intuition, in all cases where an expression (in sense 2) expresses the speaker's *own experiences of the moment*. If these are not objectifying acts, their nature will not permit them to function under the rubrics 1 and 2.

The root of all our difficulties lies in the fact that, in the direct application of expressions (or acts to be expressed) to intuitively grasped inner experiences, our significative acts are completely fulfilled by the inner intuition which attaches to them, so that both are most intimately blended, while these same intuitions, being internal, exhaust themselves in the straightforward presentation of the acts that they mean.

Finally we must observe that the distinction made above as against Bolzano – between cases where only the *subjective* objection can be raised – the objection to the expression's sincerity or adequacy – and cases where the *factual objection* can be raised – the objection related to objective truth and falsity – that this distinction has, on a closer survey, no true connection with our controversial question. For it has a quite general concern with the difference between expressions relating to intuitively envisaged act-experiences, and experiences not so relating. In the first class there are many quite uncontroversial predications, e.g. all statements of the form 'I ask whether...', 'I command, wish that...' etc. And, be it noted, there can be no factual objections to subjective judgements thus formulated: they are true or false, but *truth here coincides with sincerity*. In the case of other statements which aim at what is 'objective' (i.e. not at the self-expressing subject and his experiences) the factual question concerns our meaning. The question of sincerity depends on the possibility of seeming assertions, from which the genuine, normal act of meaning is absent. Really there is no judgement; the meaning of a statement is presented in the context of an intent to deceive.

External and Internal Perception: Physical and Psychical Phenomena

I

THE concepts of *external perception* and *perception of self*, of *sensuous* and *internal perception*, have for the naïve man the following content. *External perception* is the perception of external things, their qualities and relationships, their changes and interactions. *Perception of self* is the perception that each can have of his own ego and its properties, its states and activities. Asked who this perceived ego may be, the naïve man would reply by pointing to his bodily appearance, or would recount his past and present experiences. To the further question whether all this is included in his percept of self, he would naturally reply that, just as the perceived external thing has many properties, and has had many in the course of its changes, which are not for the moment 'open to perception', so a corresponding fact holds for his perceived ego. In the changing acts of *self*-perception appear, on occasion, such and such presentations, feelings, wishes and bodily activities of the ego, just as the exterior or the interior of a house, or such and such sides and parts of it, enter from time to time into *outer* perception. Naturally, however, the ego remains the perceived object in the one case, as the house is in the other.

For the naïve man our second pair of notions, that of *sensuous* and *internal* perception, does not altogether coincide with the pair just discussed, that of outward perception and perception of self. We perceive sensuously what we perceive by the eye and the ear, by smell and taste, in brief, through the organs of sense. In this field everyone locates, not only external things, but his own body and bodily activities, such as walking, eating, seeing, hearing etc. What we call 'inner perception', on the other hand, concerns mainly such 'spiritual' experiences as thinking, feeling and willing, but also everything that we locate, like these, in the interior of our bodies, do not connect with our outward organs.

In philosophical diction, both pairs of terms – we usually prefer the pair of 'internal and external perception' – express only one pair of concepts. After Descartes had sharply separated *mens* and *corpus*, Locke, using the terms 'sensation' and 'reflection', introduced the two corresponding classes of perception into modern philosophy. This division has remained in force till today. External perception was regarded, following Locke, as our perception of bodies, while inner perception was the perception that our 'spirits' or 'souls' have of their own activities (their *cogitationes* in the Cartesian sense). A *division of perceptions is accordingly mediated by a division among the objects of perception*, though a difference in *origin* is likewise set beside it. In one case perception arises from the effects of physical things operating through the senses on our spirits, in the other case out of a reflection on the activities carried out by the mind on the basis of 'ideas' won through sensation.

2

In quite recent times men have been much concerned to achieve an adequate overhaul and a deepening of Locke's obviously vague and rough positions.

General epistemological interests were, on the one hand, responsible for this move. We recall the traditional estimate of the relative value for knowledge of the two forms of perception: *external perception is deceptive, inner perception evident*. In this evidence lies one of the basic pillars of knowledge, which scepticism cannot shake. Inner perception is also the only case of perception where the object truly corresponds to the act of perception, is, in fact, immanent in it. It is also, to speak pointedly, the one type of perception that deserves the name. In the interest of perceptual theory, we must therefore enter more exactly into the essence of inner, as opposed to outer perception.

Psychological interests were, on the other hand, involved. Men were concerned with the much-debated *fixing of the domain of empirical psychology*, and, particularly, with establishing for it its own justification as against the natural sciences, by marking out for it a peculiar territory of phenomena. Even the prime place in epistemology readily accorded to psychology as basic philosophical discipline, required that its objects be defined with as few epistemological commitments as possible; it should not, therefore, concern itself with transcendent realities of so controversial a type as soul and body as if they were obvious data. Locke's classification of perceptions had just such a presupposition: it was therefore at once unsuited, and not in fact designed, to serve as a basis for a definition of psychology, and to do justice to the interests mentioned. It is clear, further, that if a distinction of perceptions is set up on the basis of an anticipated distinction between bodily and spiritual matters, then the former distinction cannot be used as a basis of distinction between the science of bodily and the science of spiritual phenomena. The matter would be different if one could succeed in finding *purely descriptive marks* for a division of percepts, marks which left our classes unaltered in extent, and which, while lacking all epistemological presuppositions, would serve to demarcate the corresponding bodily phenomena from psychic phenomena.

A possible path seemed here to be opened by the Cartesian approach through doubt, with its emphasis on the epistemological position of inner perception. We have already touched on this above. The line of thought, which develops here, runs as follows:

However widely I may extend my critical doubts regarding knowledge, I cannot doubt that I exist and am doubting, or again, while I experience them, that I am having presentations, am judging, feeling or however else I may designate such inwardly perceived appearances: to doubt in such a case would evidently be irrational. We accordingly have absolute 'evidence' regarding the existence of the objects of inner perception, we have that clearest cognition, that unassailable certainty which distinguishes knowledge in the strictest sense. It is quite different in the case of outer perception. It lacks 'evidence', and the frequent conflicts in statements relying upon it point, in fact, to its capacity to deceive. We have therefore no right to assume from the outset that the objects of outer perception really and truly exist as they seem to us to be. We have, in fact, many reasons to think that they do not really exist at all, but can at best lay claim to a phenomenal or 'intentional' existence. If one makes the reality of a perceived object part of the notion of perception, then outer perception is not, in this strict sense, perception at all. This *evident character*

will in any case give us a *descriptive mark*, free from presuppositions regarding metaphysical realities, which will enable us to
sort out our various classes of perceptions. It is a character given
with, or absent from, the perceptual experience itself, and this
alone determines our division.

If we now consider the *phenomena* presented by these various
classes of perceptions, they unmistakably constitute *essentially
distinct classes*. This is not to assert that the objects in themselves,
i.e. the souls and bodies, that we rightly or wrongly range under
them, differ essentially: a purely *descriptive treatment* that avoids all
transcendence establishes an unbridgeable gulf between these
phenomena. On the one side we have the *sensory qualities*, which
in themselves form a descriptively closed class, whether there are
such things as senses and sense-organs or not. They form a Kind
in the strict Aristotelian sense of the word. To these are added
features necessarily attaching, either to sense-qualities in general,
or to single ranges of such qualities (again strict Aristotelian
species), or, conversely, features themselves necessarily presupposing qualities, and only able to achieve concrete being in
association with them. Here well-known propositions come up
for treatment, e.g. no intuited spatiality without quality. Many
would say that the converse obtained also: No quality without
something spatial. Others would here only approve particular
cases: No colour, no tactile quality without something spatial.
Further propositions of the same class would be: No tone-quality
without intensity, no timbre without tone-qualities etc.[1]

On the other side we have phenomena such as having presentations, judgements, surmises, wishes, hopes etc. We here enter,
as it were, another world. These phenomena have relation to
what is sensible, but are not themselves to be compared with the
latter: they do not belong to one and the same (genuine) kind.
When we have first clearly seen the descriptive unity of this class
through examples, one finds, with a little attention, a positive
mark which characterizes them all: the mark of 'intentional
inexistence'.

One can of course use the above descriptive distinction of inner

[1] It is remarkable that no one has tried to found a positive determination of
'physical phenomena' on these intuitive interconnections. In pointing to them, I
depart from my role as a reporter. To employ them seriously, one must, of course,
have due regard to the ambiguity of talk about 'physical phenomena', an ambiguity
we shall immediately discuss.

and outer perception to arrive at just such a distinction of the two classes of phenomena. It becomes now a good definition to say: Psychic phenomena are the phenomena of inner perception, physical phenomena those of outer perception.[1]

In this manner a closer treatment of the two sorts of perceptions leads, not merely to a descriptive, epistemologically important characterization of these perceptions themselves, but also to a fundamental, descriptive division of phenomena into two classes, the physical and the psychical. And we seem to have achieved, for psychological and scientific purposes, a metaphysically uncommitted definition, not oriented towards supposed data in some transcendent world, but to what is truly given phenomenally.

Physical phenomena are no longer defined as the phenomena which arise out of the operation of bodies on our minds through our sense-organs, psychic phenomena as the phenomena discovered by us in perceiving the activities of our minds. In both cases the descriptive character of the phenomena, as experienced by us, alone furnishes our criterion. Psychology can now be defined as the science of psychic phenomena, as natural science is of physical phenomena.

These definitions require certain limitations in order to correspond truly to our actual sciences, limitations which point to explanatory metaphysical hypotheses, whereas the phenomena, as descriptively differentiated, remain the true starting-points of our treatments, and the objects to be explained.

The definition of natural science is particularly in need of limiting conditions, for it is not concerned with all physical phenomena, not with the phenomena of imagination, but only with those which come before sense-perception. And, even in their case, it only sets up laws to the extent that these depend on the physical stimulation of the sense-organs. One might express the scientific task of natural science, by saying that natural science is the science which seeks to explain the sequence of the physical phenomena of normal, pure sensations – sensations uninfluenced by peculiar physical conditions

[1] Brentano (*Psychologie*, I, pp. 118 f.) says it is a distinguishing mark of all psychic phenomena 'that they are only perceived in an inner consciousness, whereas outer perception alone is possible in the case of physical phenomena'. It is emphatically said on p. 119 that this determination characterizes psychic phenomena adequately. 'Inner consciousness' is here merely another expression for inner perception.

and events – by assuming the action on our sense-organs of a world extended in three space-like dimensions, and taking place in one time-like dimension. Without settling the absolute character of this world, it is satisfied to attribute to it powers provocative of our sensations and influencing each other in their operation, and to set up laws of coexistence and succession for such powers. In stating these, it indirectly states the laws of sequence of the physical phenomena of our sensations, laws conceived in their purity, in scientific abstraction from concomitant mental conditions, as things taking place for an invariant sensibility. The expression 'science of physical phenomena' must be interpreted in this rather complicated way, if it is to be equated with the meaning of 'natural science' (Brentano, *Psychologie*, I, pp. 127–128).

In regard to the conceptual demarcation of psychology, it might appear that the concept of the psychic phenomenon should be widened rather than narrowed, since the physical phenomena of imagination fall as entirely in its field of reference as do psychic phenomena in the previously defined sense, and since even the physical phenomena appearing in sensation cannot be disregarded in the doctrine of sensation. But it is plain that such physical phenomena only enter into descriptions of the peculiarities of psychic phenomena as the content of the latter. The same holds of all psychic phenomena which exist only phenomenally. The true subject-matter of psychology can be regarded as consisting solely of psychic phenomena in the sense of actual states. It is exclusively in regard to the latter that we call psychology the science of psychic phenomena (Ibid. pp. 129 f.).

3

The interesting line of thought that I have just expounded represents, as my longer quotations have made plain, the standpoint of Brentano,[1] and also that of a whole succession of thinkers who are theoretically close to him. There are further respects, as is well known, in which 'inner perception' plays an important role in Brentano's psychology. I am here only concerned with his doctrine of inner consciousness. Every psychic phenomenon is not merely a consciousness, but itself the *content* of a consciousness; we are conscious of it in the narrower sense of perceiving it.

[1] Up to the positive mark of physical phenomena given in 2 above. I hope, further, to have achieved accuracy in restating the main points of view which have been governing factors in the doctrines of the thinkers I value so highly.

The flux of inner experience is therefore also a continuous flux of inner percepts, which are most intimately united with the psychic experiences in question. For inner perception is no second, independent act supervening upon a relevant psychic phenomenon; the latter rather involves, in addition to its relation to a primary object, e.g. an externally perceived content, 'itself in all its completeness as presented and known' (ibid. p. 182). In so far as the act directly intends its primary object, it is also subsidiarily directed upon itself. In this way one avoids the endless complication seemingly threatened by the consciousness which accompanies all psychic phenomena (since their multiple division into three 'ground-classes' itself involves an inner perception). The 'evidence' and infallibility of inner perception will also be rendered possible in this manner (ibid. II, ch. 3, pp. 182 ff.). Brentano is here, in one of his main views, i.e. in his interpretation of consciousness as a continuous stream of internal perception, in harmony with the great thinkers of the past. Even Locke, a true student of experience, defines consciousness as the perception of what goes on in a man's own mind.[1]

Brentano's theories have aroused much opposition. This has not only been directed to the doctrines of inner perception just mentioned, whose subtly constructed complexity still certainly requires a phenomenological foundation, but also against his distinction between perceptions and phenomena, and, in particular, against the laying down of the tasks of psychology and natural science which is based upon this.[2] The relevant questions have repeatedly been made the theme of serious discussion in the past decade, and it is sad that, despite its fundamental importance for psychology and epistemology, agreement has not been reached.

Criticism, it would appear, has not penetrated far enough, to hit upon the decisive points, and to separate what is indubitably

---

[1] Locke's *Essay*, II.i.19. Locke is not perfectly consistent in so far as he expressly makes 'perception' an apprehension of ideas, and yet makes the apprehension of the ideas of mental activities depend on *special* acts of reflection, that only at times supervene on these activities. This is obviously due to the wretched dual concept 'idea' which promiscuously covers the *presentations* of contents that may be experienced, and also the experienced contents themselves. See our Inv. II, §10, p. 355.

[2] Criticism, as it strikes me, generally stops at the first provisional theses of Brentano – psychology as a science of psychic phenomena, natural science of physical phenomena – without thinking of the 'tacit limitations' which Brentano himself expounded with characteristic clarity and acuteness. I have been all the more happy, therefore, to recall them by the full citations given above.

significant in Brentano's thought-motivation from what is erroneous in its elaboration. This is due to the fact that the fundamental psychological and epistemological questions which cause controversy in these dimensions of enquiry, have not been sufficiently clarified, a natural consequence of defective phenomenological analysis. On both sides the conception with which men operated remained ambiguous, on both sides there was a consequent falling into delusive confusions. This will be clear from the following criticism of the illuminating views of Brentano.

4

According to Brentano inner perception distinguishes itself from outer perception:

1. by its evidence and its incorrigibility, and
2. by essential differences in phenomena. In inner perception we experience exclusively psychic phenomena, in outer perception physical phenomena. This exact parallelism makes it possible for the first-named distinction to serve as a characteristic distinguishing mark of the perceivable phenomena as well.

As opposed to this, *inner and outer perception* seem to me, *if the terms are naturally interpreted*, to be of an entirely similar epistemological *character*. More explicitly: there is a well-justified distinction between *evident* and *non-evident*, or between infallible and fallible perception. But, if one understands by *outer* perception (as one naturally does, and as Brentano also does) the perception of physical things, properties, events etc., and classes all other perceptions as *inner* perceptions, then such a division will not coincide at all with the division previously given. For not every perception of the ego, nor every perception of a psychic state referred to the ego, is certainly evident, if by the 'ego' we mean what we all mean by it, and what we all think we perceive in perceiving ourselves, i.e. our own empirical personality. It is clear, too, that most perceptions of psychic states cannot be evident, since these are perceived with a bodily location. That anxiety tightens my throat, that pain bores into my tooth, that grief gnaws at my heart: I perceive these things as I perceive that the wind shakes the trees, or that this box is square and brown in colour, etc. Here, indeed, outer perceptions go with inner perceptions, but this does not affect the fact that the psychic phenomena perceived are, *as they*

859

are perceived, non-existent. Surely it is clear that *psychic* phenomena, also, can be perceived transcendently? Exactly regarded, all psychic phenomena seen in natural or empirical-scientific attitudes are perceived transcendently. The pure presentedness of experience presupposes a purely phenomenological attitude which will inhibit all transcendent assertions.

I know what will here be objected: that we have forgotten the difference between *perception* and *apperception*. Inner perception means the directly-conscious living-through of mental acts, they are here taken as what they *are*, and not as what they are *apprehended* or *apperceived as*. One must, however, reflect that what is true for the case of inner perception must be true also for the case of outer perception. If the essence of perception does not lie in apperception, then all talk of perception in regard to external things, mountains, woods, houses etc., is misguided, and this, the normal sense of the word 'perception', surely illustrated in these cases above all others, must be abandoned. Outer perception is apperception, and the unity of the concept demands that inner perception should be so too. It is of the essence of perception that something should appear in it: *apperception, however, constitutes what we call appearance*, whether veridical or not, and whether it remains faithfully and adequately in the frame of the immediately given, or anticipates future perception in going beyond it. The *house* appears to me – in no other manner than that I apperceive actually experienced sense-contents in a certain fashion. I hear a *barrel organ* – the tones sensed are interpreted *as those of a barrel organ*. In the same way I apperceivingly perceive my own psychic phenomena, the blessedness quivering through 'me', the grief in my heart etc. They are called 'appearances', or rather apparent contents, being contents of apperception.

5

The term 'appearance' is, of course, beset with ambiguities, whose extreme dangers are seen precisely in this case. It will not be useless at this point to list these equivocations explicitly: we have already touched on them in passing in the text of these Investigations. Talk of 'appearance' has a preferred application to acts of intuitive presentation, to acts of *perception*, on the one hand, and to acts of *representation*, on the other, e.g. acts of remembering, imagining, or pictorially representing (in the ordinary sense), on a basis mixed with perception. 'Appearance' accordingly means:

1. The concrete intuitive experience (the intuitive presentedness or representedness of a given object for us); the concrete experience, e.g., when we perceive the lamp standing before us. Since the qualitative character of the act, whether the object is regarded as real or not, is irrelevant, it can also be ignored entirely, and 'appearance' then coincides with what we defined as 'representation' in the last Investigation (cf. VI, §26, p. 740).

2. The intuited (appearing) object, taken as it appears *here* and *now*, e.g. this lamp as it counts for some percept we have just performed.

3. In misleading fashion we also call the *real (reellen) constituents* of appearances in sense 1, i.e. those of the concrete acts of appearing or intuiting, 'appearances'. Such appearances are, above all, the presentative *sensations*, the experienced moments of colour, form etc., which we fail to distinguish from *apparent properties* of the (coloured, formed) *objects* corresponding to them, and apparent in the act which 'interprets' them. That it is important to distinguish between them, that it does not do to confuse a colour-sensation with an apparent bodily colouring, the sensation of form with bodily form etc., we have often stressed. Uncritical theories certainly ignore the distinction. But even those who would refuse to say with Schopenhauer that 'the world is my idea', are accustomed to speak as if apparent things were compounded out of sense-contents. One could certainly say that *apparent* things as such, the mere things of sense, are composed of a stuff analogous to that which as sensation is counted a content of consciousness. This does not affect the fact that the thing's apparent properties are not themselves sensations, but only appear as analogues of sensations. For they are not present, as sensations are, in consciousness, but are merely represented in it, as properties which *appear* in it, which are transcendently referred to. For this reason perceived external things, likewise, are not complexes of sensations: they are rather objects of appearances, objects appearing as complexes of properties, whose types stand in a peculiar *analogy* to types found among sensations. We could put what we have just said somewhat differently. Under the rubric of 'sensations', we range certain sorts of *experiences* of this or that

actual kind belonging to a unity of consciousness. If it now happens that, in a unity of consciousness, real properties of analogous kinds appear as external to, and transcending such sensations, we may then call them after these sensational classes, but they are no longer sensations. We emphasize the word 'external', which must of course not be understood spatially. However we may decide the question of the existence or non-existence of phenomenal external things, we cannot doubt that the reality of each such perceived thing cannot be understood as the reality of a perceived complex of sensations in a perceiving consciousness. For it is plain, and confirmable by phenomenological analysis in each instance, that the thing of perception, this so-called sensational complex, differs in every circumstance, both as a whole and in every distinct moment of property, from the sensational complex actually lived through in the percept in question, whose objective apperception first constitutes the perceptual sense, and thereby the apparent thing, in intentional fashion.

It may indeed be said that the original concept of appearance was the one given in our second place above: the concept of what appears, or of what could appear, of the intuitive as such. Having regard to the fact that all sorts of experiences (including the experiences of outer intuition, whose objects are therefore called *outer* appearances) can be made objects of reflective, inner intuition, we call all experiences in an ego's experiential unity 'phenomena'. *Phenomenology* is accordingly the theory of experiences in general, inclusive of all matters, whether real (*reellen*) or intentional, given in experiences, and evidently discoverable in them. Pure phenomenology is accordingly the theory of the essences of 'pure phenomena', the phenomena of a 'pure consciousness' or of a 'pure ego': it does not build on the ground, given by transcendent apperception, of physical and animal, and so of psycho-physical nature, it makes no empirical assertions, it propounds no judgements which relate to objects transcending consciousness: it establishes no truths concerning natural realities, whether physical or psychic – no psychological truths, therefore, in the historical sense – and borrows no such truths as assumed premisses. It rather takes all apperceptions and judgemental assertions which point beyond what is given in adequate, purely immanent intuition, which point beyond the pure stream of consciousness, and treats them purely as the experiences they are in themselves: it subjects them to a purely immanent, purely descriptive examination into essence. This examination of essence is also pure in a second sense, in the sense of Ideation; it is an *a priori* examination in the true sense. So understood, all the Investigations of the present work have been purely phenomenological, in so far, that is, as they did not have ontological themes, and did not, as in the Third and Sixth Investigation, seek to make *a priori* assertions regarding the *objects* of possible consciousness. They did not speak of psychological facts and laws in an 'objective' nature, only of pure possibilities and necessities, which belong to any form of the pure 'cogito': they spoke of these as regards their real (*reellen*) and their intentional contents, or as regards their *a priori* possibilities of connection with other such patterns in an ideally possible conscious context.

As the term 'appearance' is ambiguous, so also, and consequently, is the term 'perception', and so are all further terms used in connection with perception. These ambiguities fill theories of perception with confused errors. The 'perceived' is, e.g., what appears in perception, i.e. its object (the house), and, further, the sense-content experienced in it, i.e. the sum of the presenting contents, which in their interconnection are 'interpreted' as the house, and singly 'interpreted' as its properties.

5 *a*

Excerpt from the First Edition which was replaced by the first two paragraphs of the third note in the preceding § 5 in Edition II.

3. If we are only clear that we have to draw a distinction in our intuition between sensations as lived experiences, which are accordingly components of the subject, and phenomenal determinations, as components of the intentional object, and that both only coincide in the ideal case of adequate intuition (which does not come into question for us), then we readily see that our inwoven sensations cannot themselves count as appearances, whether in the sense of acts or of apparent objects. Not in the former, since under the rubric of sensations we sum up certain non-acts, which perhaps receive an objectifying interpretation in acts; not in the latter, since acts would have to be part of the phenomenal objectivity of sensations, acts which would have to direct their intention to them. Such acts are indeed possible, but that they are part of the stock-in-trade

of every percept, and this in relation to the percept's presentative sensations, cannot be shown to be necessary either by descriptive analysis or on genetic grounds. All this goes without saying for imaginative intuitions as well, in relation to their imaginatively representative contents.

If one has once got to the point of regarding all components of appearances in sense 1 as themselves appearances, then it is a further, almost unconscious step to regard everything psychic, all lived experiences in the experiential unity of the ego, as phenomena.

6

How misleading such ambiguities show themselves to be appears in Brentano's theory, with its division into inner and outer perception according to evidential character and separate phenomenal class. We are told that:

Outer perception is not evident, and is even delusive. This is undoubtedly the case if we mean by the 'physical phenomena' what such perception perceives, physical things, their properties and changes etc. But when Brentano exchanges this authentic, and alone permissible sense of the word 'perceive', for an improper sense which relates, not to external objects, but to presenting contents, contents, i.e., present as real parts (*reell angehörigen*) in perception, and when he consequently gives the name of 'physical phenomena', not merely to outer objects, but also to these contents, these latter seem infected with the fallibility of outer perception. I believe that stricter divisions are necessary here. If an external object (a house) is perceived, presenting sensations are experienced in *this* perception, but they are not perceived. When we are deluded regarding the existence of the house, we are not deluded regarding the existence of our experienced sense-contents, since we do not pass judgement on them at all, do not perceive them in this perception. If we afterwards take note of these contents – our ability to do this is, within certain limits, undeniable – and if we abstract from all that we recently or usually meant by way of them, and take them simply as they are, then we certainly perceive them, but perceive no external object through them. This new perception has plainly the same claim to inerrancy and evidence as any 'inner' perception. To doubt what is immanent (in consciousness), and is meant precisely as it is, would be quite evidently irrational. I may doubt whether an outer object exists, and so whether a percept relating to such objects is correct, but I cannot doubt the now experienced sensuous content of my experience, whenever, that is, I reflect on the latter, and simply *intuit it as being what it is*. There are, therefore, evident percepts of 'physical' contents, as well as of 'psychical'.

If it were now objected that sensuous contents are invariably and necessarily interpreted objectively, that they are always bearers of outer intuitions, and can only be attended to as contents of such intuitions, the point need not be disputed: it would make no difference to the situation. The evidence of the existence of these contents would be as indisputable as before, and would also not be our evidence for 'psychic phenomena' in the sense of acts. The evidence for the being of the whole psychic phenomenon implies that for each of its parts, but the perception of the part is a new perception with a new evidence, which is by no means that of the whole phenomenon.

An analogous ambiguity to that which affects the notion of a physical phenomenon, will also be found, if our conception is consistent, in the case of the notion of the psychic phenomenon. This is not the case for Brentano. He understands by a psychic phenomenon only an actually present act-experience, and by an inner perception a perception which simply apprehends such an experience, just as it is there. Brentano ignores the fact that he has only done justice to one class of percepts of psychic phenomena under the name of 'inner perception', and that it is not possible to divide all percepts into the two groups of outer and inner. He also ignores the fact that the whole evidential prerogative accorded to his 'inner perception' hangs upon the fact that he has employed an essentially distorted concept of perception in the case of inner perception, and that it does not depend on the peculiarity of inwardly perceived 'phenomena'. Had he treated as genuine percepts of physical phenomena only such objective interpretations and apprehensions as survey their objects adequately, he could have attributed evidence to that perception of sense-experiences which was by him assigned to outer perception, and he could not have said of inner perception (in his sense) that it is 'really the only sort of perception in the true sense of the word' (ibid. p. 119).

It is absolutely clear that the conceptual pairs of inner and outer, and of evident and non-evident perception, need not coincide at all. The first pair is determined by the concepts of physical and psychical, however these may be demarcated; the second expresses the epistemologically fundamental antithesis studied in our Sixth Investigation, the opposition between *adequate* perception (or intuition in the narrowest sense, whose perceptual intention is exclusively directed to a content truly present to it) and the merely supposing, *inadequate* perception, whose intention does not find fulfilment in present content, but rather goes through this to constitute the lively, but always one-sided and presumptive, presentedness of what is transcendent. In the first case the experienced *content* is also the *object* of perception, in the second, content and object fall asunder. The content represents what it does not itself have, what is, however, made manifest in it, and what is, in a certain sense, its analogue (if we confine ourselves to what is immediately intuited), as body-colour is an analogue of sense-colour.

In this separation we have the essence of the *epistemological* difference that men look for between inner and outer perception. It is the operative factor in the Cartesian treatment of doubt. I can doubt the truth of an inadequate, merely projective perception: the intended, or, if one likes, intentional, object is not immanent in the act of appearing. The intention is there, but the object itself, that is destined finally to fulfil it, is not one with it. How could its existence be evident to me? But I cannot doubt an adequate, purely immanent perception, since there are no residual intentions in it that must yet achieve fulfilment. The whole intention, or the intention in all its aspects, is fulfilled. Or, as we also expressed it: the object is not in our percept merely believed to exist, but is also itself truly given, and as what it is believed to be. It is of the essence of adequate perception that the intuited object itself really and truly dwells in it, which is merely another way of saying that *only the perception of one's own actual experiences is indubitable and evident*. Not every such percept is evident. In the percept of toothache, e.g., a real experience is perceived, and yet our perception often deceives: the pain appears to bore a sound tooth. The possibility of our error is plain. The perceived object is not the pain as experienced, but the pain in a transcendent reference as connected with the tooth. Adequate perception involves, however, that in it the perceived is experienced *as* it is perceived (as the perception thinks or conceives it). In this sense

866

we obviously only have an adequate percept of our own experiences, and of these only to the extent that we apprehend them purely, without going apperceptively beyond them.

7

It might now be objected: An experience is surely the same as a psychic phenomenon. What, then, is the dispute all about? I answer: If one means by 'psychic phenomena' the real (*realen*) constituents of our consciousness, the experiences themselves that are there, and if one further means by *inner* percepts, or percepts of psychic phenomena, adequate percepts, whose intention finds immanent fulfilment in the experiences in question, *then* the scope of *inner perception* will of course coincide with that of *adequate* perception. It is important, however, to note:

1. That psychic phenomena in this sense are not the same as psychic phenomena in Brentano's sense, nor as Descartes's *cogitationes*, nor as Locke's *acts or operations of mind*, since in the sphere of experiences as such all sense-contents, all sensations, also belong.

2. That the *non-inner* perceptions (the remainder class) *will not then coincide with outer perceptions* in the ordinary sense of the word, but with the much wider class of *transcendent, inadequate* perceptions. If a sense-content, or sense-complex or sequence of sense-contents is apprehended as a thing out there, as a multitude, an articulated connection of several things, or as a change in things, an external happening etc., we have an outer percept in the ordinary sense. But a non-sensuous content can also belong to the representative stuff of a transcendent percept, particularly in association with sense-contents. Our perceived object can then as readily be an *external* object with perceived *mental* properties (this happens in differing fashion in the apprehension of one's own and other men's bodily being as 'persons') or, as in psychophysical apperception, an *inner* object, a subjective experience, perceived with *physical* properties attaching to it.

3. When in psychology, as the objective science of animal mentality, we mean by perceptions of psychic phenomena the perceptions that a man has of his own experiences, which the perceiver apprehends as belonging to himself, this particular person, all inner perceptions are no less cases of transcendent

apperception than are outer perceptions. Among these there are some which (with some abstraction) count as *adequate*, in so far as they seize the man's own (relevant) experiences in their very selves. But in so far as even such 'adequate' inner perceptions apperceive the experiences they apprehend as those of a percipient, psycho-physical, personal ego, and so as belonging to the presented objective world, they are in this respect infected with an essential inadequacy. There are, further, cases of inner perception, as there are cases of outer perception, where the perceived object, in the sense given to it in our percept, has no existence. *The distinction, fundamental even for psychology, between adequate and inadequate perception – psychological adequateness being understood as the abstraction we mentioned – intersects the distinction between inner and outer perception*, and therefore pervades the sphere of the former.

8

The ambiguities of the word 'phenomenon' allow us first to call apparent objects and their properties 'phenomena', then to apply the term to the experiences which constitute their act of appearing (particularly to the experienced contents in the sense of sensations), and, lastly, to all experiences whatever. These ambiguities explain why we tend to confuse *two essentially different types of psychological division of 'phenomena'*.

1. Divisions of experiences, e.g. the division of experiences into *acts* and *non-acts*. Such divisions naturally fall into the sphere of psychology, which accordingly has to deal with all experiences, which it of course apperceives in transcendent fashion as experiences of animal beings in nature.

2. The division of *phenomenal objects* into, e.g., such as seem to belong to *the consciousness of an ego* and such as *do not seem to do so*, i.e. the division into psychical and physical objects (contents, properties, relations etc.).

In Brentano these two divisions are confused. He simply opposes physical to psychical phenomena, and defines them unmistakably as a division of *experiences* into acts and non-acts. But he at once mixes up, under the rubric of physical phenomena the contents of sense,[1] and apparent external objects (or their

---

[1] Brentano understands by 'sensations' *acts* of sensing, and opposes them to sensed contents. In our mode of speech, as expounded above, no such distinction

phenomenal properties), so that the division now becomes a division of *phenomenal* objects into physical and psychical (in an ordinary or near-ordinary sense), in which the latter division furnishes the names.

Closely connected with this confusion is the erroneous criterion, also used by Brentano, to divide the two classes of phenomena: that physical phenomena only exist 'phenomenally and intentionally, while psychical phenomena also 'have an *actual* existence as well as an intentional one'.[1] If we understand by 'physical phenomena' phenomenal things, it is at least sure that they do not need to exist. The forms of productive fancy, most of the objects of artistic representation in paintings, statues, poems etc., hallucinatory and illusory objects, exist only in a phenomenal and intentional manner, i.e. they do not exist in the *authentic* sense at all; only the relevant *acts of appearing* exist with their real (*reellen*) and intentional contents. The matter is quite different in the case of physical phenomena interpreted as sensed contents. The sensed (experienced) colour-contents, shape-contents etc., which we enjoy when we look at Böcklin's picture of the Elysian Fields, and which, informed by an imaginative act-character, are made into the consciousness of the pictured objects, are real (*reelle*) constituents of this experience. And they do not exist in merely phenomenal, intentional fashion (as apparent, merely intended contents) but in actuality. One must not forget, of course, that 'actual' does not here mean the same as 'external to consciousness', but the same as 'not merely putative'.

obtains. We call 'sensations' the mere fact that a sense-content, and, further, that a non-act in general, is present in the experiential complex. In relation to appearing, talk of 'sensing' only serves to point to the apperceptive function of such contents (that they function as bearers of an interpretation, in which the appearance in question is carried out perceptually or imaginatively).

[1] Cf. Brentano, loc. cit. §7, p. 120. In detailed examples he says: 'Knowledge, joy, desire, exist actually, colour, tone, warmth only phenomenally and intentionally.' On p. 104 he lists as examples of physical phenomena: 'A figure, *landscape* that I *see*...warmth, cold, smell that I *sense*.'

INDEX

International Library of Philosophy & Scientific Method

Editor: Ted Honderich

List of titles, page two

International Library of Psychology Philosophy & Scientific Method

Editor: C K Ogden

List of titles, page six

ROUTLEDGE AND KEGAN PAUL LTD
68 Carter Lane London EC4

International Library of Philosophy and Scientific Method
(Demy 8vo)

Allen, R. E. (Ed.)
Studies in Plato's Metaphysics
Contributors: J. L. Ackrill, R. E. Allen, R. S. Bluck, H. F. Cherniss, F. M.
Cornford, R. C. Cross, P. T. Geach, R. Hackforth, W. F. Hicken, A. C. Lloyd,
G. R. Morrow, G. E. L. Owen, G. Ryle, W. G. Runciman, G. Vlastos
464 pp. 1965. (2nd Impression 1967.) 70s.

Armstrong, D. M.
Perception and the Physical World
208 pp. 1961. (3rd Impression 1966.) 25s.
A Materialist Theory of the Mind
376 pp. 1967. (2nd Impression 1969.) 50s.

Bambrough, Renford (Ed.)
New Essays on Plato and Aristotle
Contributors: J. L. Ackrill, G. E. M. Anscombe, Renford Bambrough,
R. M. Hare, D. M. MacKinnon, G. E. L. Owen, G. Ryle, G. Vlastos
184 pp. 1965. (2nd Impression 1967.) 28s.

Barry, Brian
Political Argument
382 pp. 1965. (3rd Impression 1968.) 50s.

Bird, Graham
Kant's Theory of Knowledge:
An Outline of One Central Argument in the *Critique of Pure Reason*
220 pp. 1962. (2nd Impression 1965.) 28s.

Brentano, Franz
The True and the Evident
Edited and narrated by Professor R. Chisholm
218 pp. 1965. 40s.
The Origin of Our Knowledge of Right and Wrong
Edited by Oskar Kraus. English edition edited by Roderick M. Chisholm.
Translated by Roderick M. Chisholm and Elizabeth H. Schneewind
174 pp. 1969. 40s.

Broad, C. D.
Lectures on Physical Research
Incorporating the Perrott Lectures given in Cambridge University in 1959
and 1960
461 pp. 1962. (2nd Impression 1966.) 56s.

Crombie, I. M.
An Examination of Plato's Doctrine
1. Plato on Man and Society
408 pp. 1962. (3rd Impression 1969.) 42s.
II. Plato on Knowledge and Reality
583 pp. 1963. (2nd Impression 1967.) 63s.

2

International Library of Philosophy and Scientific Method
(Demy 8vo)

Day, John Patrick
Inductive Probability
352 pp. 1961. 40s.

Dretske, Fred I.
Seeing and Knowing
270 pp. 1969. 35s.

Ducasse, C. J.
Truth, Knowledge and Causation
263 pp. 1969. 50s.

Edel, Abraham
Method in Ethical Theory
379 pp. 1963. 32s.

Fann, K. T. (Ed.)
Symposium on J. L. Austin
Contributors: A. J. Ayer, Jonathan Bennett, Max Black, Stanley Cavell,
Walter Cerf, Roderick M. Chisholm, L. Jonathan Cohen, Roderick Firth, L. W.
Forguson, Mats Furberg, Stuart Hampshire, R. J. Hirst, C. G. New, P. H.
Nowell-Smith, David Pears, John Searle, Peter Strawson, Irving Thalberg,
J. O. Urmson, G. J. Warnock, Jon Wheatly, Alan White
512 pp. 1969.

Flew, Anthony
Hume's Philosophy of Belief
A Study of his First "Inquiry"
269 pp. 1961. (2nd Impression 1966.) 30s.

Fogelin, Robert J.
Evidence and Meaning
Studies in Analytical Philosophy
200 pp. 1967. 25s.

Gale, Richard
The Language of Time
256 pp. 1968. 40s.

Goldman, Lucien
The Hidden God
A Study of Tragic Vision in the Pensées of Pascal and the Tragedies of Racine.
Translated from the French by Philip Thody
424 pp. 1964. 70s.

Hamlyn, D. W.
Sensation and Perception
A History of the Philosophy of Perception
222 pp. 1961. (3rd Impression 1967.) 25s.

3

2*

International Library of Philosophy and Scientific Method
(*Demy 8vo*)

Kemp, J.
Reason, Action and Morality
216 pp. 1964. 30s.

Körner, Stephan
Experience and Theory
An Essay in the Philosophy of Science
272 pp. 1966. (2nd Impression 1969.) 45s.

Lazerowitz, Morris
Studies in Metaphilosophy
276 pp. 1964. 35s.

Linsky, Leonard
Referring
152 pp. 1968. 35s.

MacIntosh, J. J., and Coval, S. C. (Ed.)
The Business of Reason
280 pp. 1969. 42s.

Merleau-Ponty, M.
Phenomenology of Perception
Translated from the French by Colin Smith
487 pp. 1962. (4th Impression 1967.) 56s.

Perelman, Chaim
The Idea of Justice and the Problem of Argument
Introduction by H. L. A. Hart. Translated from the French by John Petrie
224 pp. 1963. 28s.

Ross, Alf
Directives, Norms and their Logic
192 pp. 1967. 35s.

Schlesinger, G.
Method in the Physical Sciences
148 pp. 1963. 21s.

Sellars, W. F.
Science, Perception and Reality
374 pp. 1963. (2nd Impression 1966.) 50s.

Shwayder, D. S.
The Stratification of Behaviour
A System of Definitions Propounded and Defended
428 pp. 1965. 56s.

Skolimowski, Henryk
Polish Analytical Philosophy
288 pp. 1967. 40s.

4

International Library of Philosophy and Scientific Method
(*Demy 8vo*)

Smart, J. J. C.
Philosophy and Scientific Realism
168 pp. 1963. (3rd Impression 1967.) 25s.

Smythies, J. R. (Ed.)
Brain and Mind
Contributors: Lord Brain, John Beloff, C. J. Ducasse, Antony Flew, Hartwig
Kuhlenbeck, D. M. MacKay, H. H. Price, Anthony Quinton and J. R. Smythies
288 pp. 1965. 40s.

Science and E.S.P.
Contributors: Gilbert Murray, H. H. Price, Rosalind Heywood, Cyril Burt,
C. D. Broad, Francis Huxley and John Beloff
320 pp. about 40s.

Taylor, Charles
The Explanation of Behaviour
288 pp. 1964. (2nd Impression 1965.) 40s.

Williams, Bernard, and Montefiore, Alan
British Analytical Philosophy
352 pp. 1965. (2nd Impression 1967.) 45s.

Winch, Peter (Ed.)
Studies in the Philosophy of Wittgenstein
Contributors: Hidé Ishiguro, Rush Rhees, D. S. Shwayder, John W. Cook,
L. R. Reinhardt and Anthony Manser
224 pp. 1969.

Wittgenstein, Ludwig
Tractatus Logico-Philosophicus
The German text of the *Logisch-Philosophische Abhandlung* with a new
translation by D. F. Pears and B. F. McGuinness. Introduction by
Bertrand Russell
188 pp. 1961. (3rd Impression 1966.) 21s.

Wright, Georg Henrik Von
Norm and Action
A Logical Enquiry. The Gifford Lectures
232 pp. 1963. (2nd Impression 1964.) 32s.

The Varieties of Goodness
The Gifford Lectures
236 pp. 1963. (3rd Impression 1966.) 28s.

Zinkernagel, Peter
Conditions for Description
Translated from the Danish by Olaf Lindum
272 pp. 1962. 37s. 6d.

International Library of Psychology, Philosophy, and Scientific Method
(*Demy 8vo*)

PHILOSOPHY

Anton, John Peter
Aristotle's Theory of Contrariety
276 pp. 1957. 25s.

Black, Max
The Nature of Mathematics
A Critical Survey
242 pp. 1933. (5th Impression 1965.) 28s.

Bluck, R. S.
Plato's Phaedo
A Translation with Introduction, Notes and Appendices
226 pp. 1955. 21s.

Broad, C. D.
Five Types of Ethical Theory
322 pp. 1930. (9th Impression 1967.) 30s.
The Mind and Its Place in Nature
694 pp. 1925. (7th Impression 1962.) 70s. See also Lean, Martin

Buchler, Justus (Ed.)
The Philosophy of Peirce
Selected Writings
412 pp. 1940. (3rd Impression 1956.) 35s.

Burtt, E. A.
The Metaphysical Foundations of Modern Physical Science
A Historical and Critical Essay
364 pp. 2nd (revised) edition 1932. (5th Impression 1964.) 35s.

Carnap, Rudolf
The Logical Syntax of Language
Translated from the German by Amethe Smeaton
376 pp. 1937. (7th Impression 1967.) 40s.

Chwistek, Leon
The Limits of Science
Outline of Logic and of the Methodology of the Exact Sciences
With Introduction and Appendix by Helen Charlotte Brodie
414 pp. 2nd edition 1949. 32s.

Cornford, F. M.
Plato's Theory of Knowledge
The Theaetetus and Sophist of Plato
Translated with a running commentary
358 pp. 1935. (7th Impression 1967.) 28s.

International Library of Psychology, Philosophy, and Scientific Method
(*Demy 8vo*)

Cornford, F. M. (*continued*)
Plato's Cosmology
The Timaeus of Plato
Translated with a running commentary
402 pp. Frontispiece. 1937. (5th Impression 1966.) 45s.

Plato and Parmenides
Parmenides' *Way of Truth* and Plato's *Parmenides*
Translated with a running commentary
280 pp. 1939. (5th Impression 1964.) 32s.

Crawshay-Williams, Rupert
Methods and Criteria of Reasoning
An Inquiry into the Structure of Controversy
312 pp. 1957. 32s.

Fritz, Charles A.
Bertrand Russell's Construction of the External World
252 pp. 1952. 30s.

Hulme, T. E.
Speculations
Essays on Humanism and the Philosophy of Art
Edited by Herbert Read. Foreword and Frontispiece by Jacob Epstein
296 pp. 2nd edition 1936. (6th Impression 1965.) 40s.

Lazerowitz, Morris
The Structure of Metaphysics
With a Foreword by John Wisdom
262 pp. 1955. (2nd Impression 1963.) 30s.

Lodge, Rupert C.
Plato's Theory of Art
332 pp. 1953. 25s.

Mannheim, Karl
Ideology and Utopia
An Introduction to the Sociology of Knowledge
With a Preface by Louis Wirth. Translated from the German by Louis Wirth
and Edward Shils
360 pp. 1954. (2nd Impression 1966.) 30s.

Moore, G. E.
Philosophical Studies
360 pp. 1922. (6th Impression 1965.) 35s. See also Ramsey, F. P.

International Library of Psychology, Philosophy, and Scientific Method

(*Demy 8vo*)

Ogden, C. K., and Richards, I. A.
The Meaning of Meaning
A Study of the Influence of Language upon Thought and of the Science of Symbolism
With supplementary essays by B. Malinowski and F. G. Crookshank
394 pp. 10th Edition 1949. (6th Impression 1967.) 32s.
See also Bentham, J.

Peirce, Charles, *see* Buchler, J.

Ramsey, Frank Plumpton
The Foundations of Mathematics and other Logical Essays
Edited by R. B. Braithwaite. Preface by G. E. Moore
318 pp. 1931. (4th Impression 1965.) 35s.

Richards, I. A.
Principles of Literary Criticism
312 pp. 2nd Edition. 1926. (17th Impression 1966.) 30s.
Mencius on the Mind. Experiments in Multiple Definition
190 pp. 1932. (2nd Impression 1964.) 28s.

Russell, Bertrand, *see* Fritz, C. A.; Lange, F. A.; Wittgenstein, L.

Smart, Ninian
Reasons and Faiths
An Investigation of Religious Discourse, Christian and Non-Christian
230 pp. 1958. (2nd Impression 1965.) 28s.

Vaihinger, H.
The Philosophy of As If
A System of the Theoretical, Practical and Religious Fictions of Mankind
Translated by C. K. Ogden
428 pp. 2nd edition 1935. (4th Impression 1965.) 45s.

Wittgenstein, Ludwig
Tractatus Logico-Philosophicus
With an Introduction by Bertrand Russell, F.R.S., German text with an English translation en regard
216 pp. 1922. (9th Impression 1962.) 21s.
For the Pears-McGuinness translation—*see page 5*

Wright, Georg Henrik von
Logical Studies
214 pp. 1957. (2nd Impression 1967.) 28s.

International Library of Psychology, Philosophy, and Scientific Method
(*Demy 8vo*)

Zeller, Eduard
Outlines of the History of Greek Philosophy
Revised by Dr. Wilhelm Nestle. Translated from the German by L. R. Palmer
248 pp. 13th (revised) edition 1931. (5th Impression 1963.) 28s.

PSYCHOLOGY

Adler, Alfred
The Practice and Theory of Individual Psychology
Translated by P. Radin
368 pp. 2nd (revised) edition 1929. (8th Impression 1964.) 30s.

Eng, Helga
The Psychology of Children's Drawings
From the First Stroke to the Coloured Drawing
240 pp. 8 colour plates. 139 figures. 2nd edition 1954. (3rd Impression 1966.) 40s.

Koffka, Kurt
The Growth of the Mind
An Introduction to Child-Psychology
Translated from the German by Robert Morris Ogden
456 pp 16 figures. 2nd edition (revised) 1928. (6th Impression 1965.) 45s.

Principles of Gestalt Psychology
740 pp. 112 figures. 39 tables. 1935. (5th Impression 1962.) 60s.

Malinowski, Bronislaw
Crime and Custom in Savage Society
152 pp. 6 plates. 1926. (8th Impression 1966.) 21s.

Sex and Repression in Savage Society
290 pp. 1927. (4th Impression 1953.) 30s.
See also Ogden, C. K.

Murphy, Gardner
An Historical Introduction to Modern Psychology
488 pp. 5th edition (revised) 1949. (6th Impression 1967.) 40s.

Paget, R.
Human Speech
Some Observations, Experiments, and Conclusions as to the Nature, Origin, Purpose and Possible Improvement of Human Speech
374 pp. 5 plates. 1930. (2nd Impression 1963.) 42s.

Petermann, Bruno
The Gestalt Theory and the Problem of Configuration
Translated from the German by Meyer Fortes
364 pp. 20 figures. 1932. (2nd Impression 1950.) 25s.

Piaget, Jean
The Language and Thought of the Child
Preface by E. Claparède. Translated from the French by Marjorie Gabain
220 pp. 3rd edition (revised and enlarged) 1959. (3rd Impression 1966.) 30s.

Judgment and Reasoning in the Child
Translated from the French by Marjorie Warden
276 pp. 1928. (5th Impression 1969.) 30s.

The Child's Conception of the World
Translated from the French by Joan and Andrew Tomlinson
408 pp. 1929. (4th Impression 1964.) 40s.

The Child's Conception of Physical Causality
Translated from the French by Marjorie Gabain
(3rd Impression 1965.) 30s.

The Moral Judgment of the Child
Translated from the French by Marjorie Gabain
438 pp. 1932. (4th Impression 1965.) 35s.

The Psychology of Intelligence
Translated from the French by Malcolm Piercy and D. E. Berlyne
198 pp. 1950. (4th Impression 1964.) 18s.

The Child's Conception of Number
Translated from the French by C. Gattegno and F. M. Hodgson
266 pp. 1952. (3rd Impression 1964.) 25s.

The Origin of Intelligence in the Child
Translated from the French by Margaret Cook
448 pp. 1953. (2nd Impression 1966.) 42s.

The Child's Conception of Geometry
In collaboration with Bärbel Inhelder and Alina Szeminska. Translated from the French by E. A. Lunzer
428 pp. 1960. (2nd Impression 1966.) 45s.

Piaget, Jean, and Inhelder, Bärbel
The Child's Conception of Space
Translated from the French by F. J. Langdon and J. L. Lunzer
512 pp. 29 figures. 1956. (3rd Impression 1967.) 42s.

Roback, A. A.
The Psychology of Character
With a Survey of Personality in General
786 pp. 3rd edition (revised and enlarged 1952.) 50s.

Smythies, J. R.
Analysis of Perception
With a Preface by Sir Russell Brain, Bt.
162 pp. 1956. 21s.

International Library of Psychology, Philosophy, and Scientific Method
(*Demy 8vo*)

van der Hoop, J. H.
Character and the Unconscious
A Critical Exposition of the Psychology of Freud and Jung
Translated from the German by Elizabeth Trevelyan
240 pp. 1923. (2nd Impression 1950.) 20s.

Woodger, J. H.
Biological Principles
508 pp. 1929. (Re-issued with a new Introduction 1966.) 60s.

PRINTED BY HEADLEY BROTHERS LTD 109 KINGSWAY LONDON WC2 AND ASHFORD KENT